SOUL EATER NOT!

2

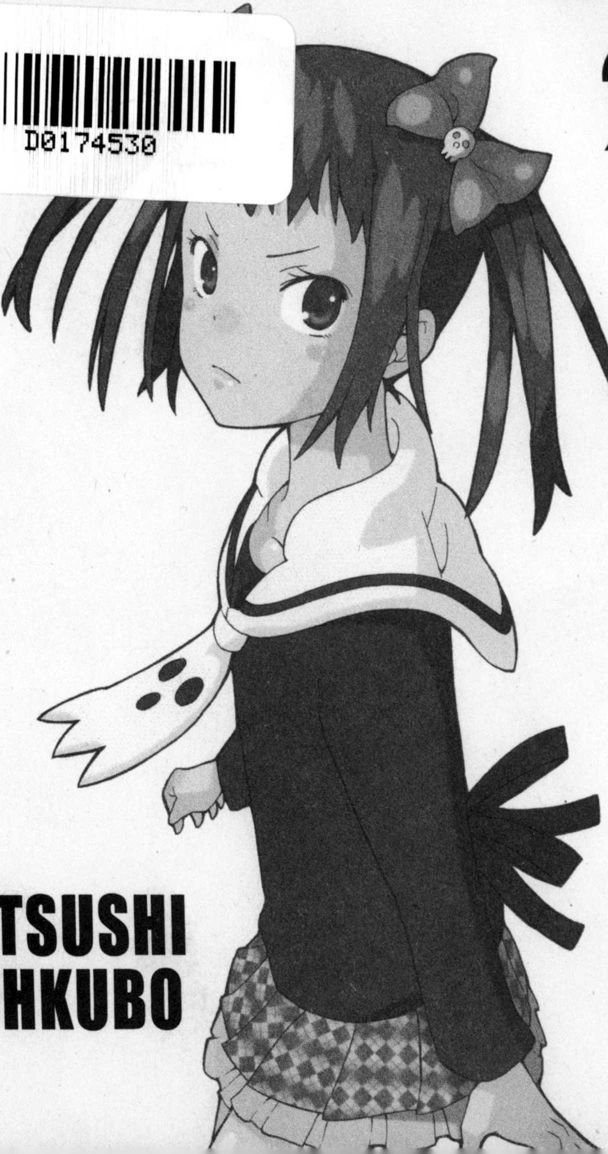

ATSUSHI OHKUBO

EATER

ATSUSHI OHKUBO

SOUL

02

NO

NOT!

SOUL EATER NOT!

02

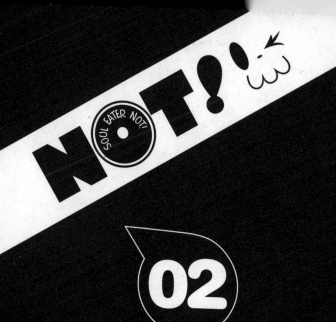

CONTENTS

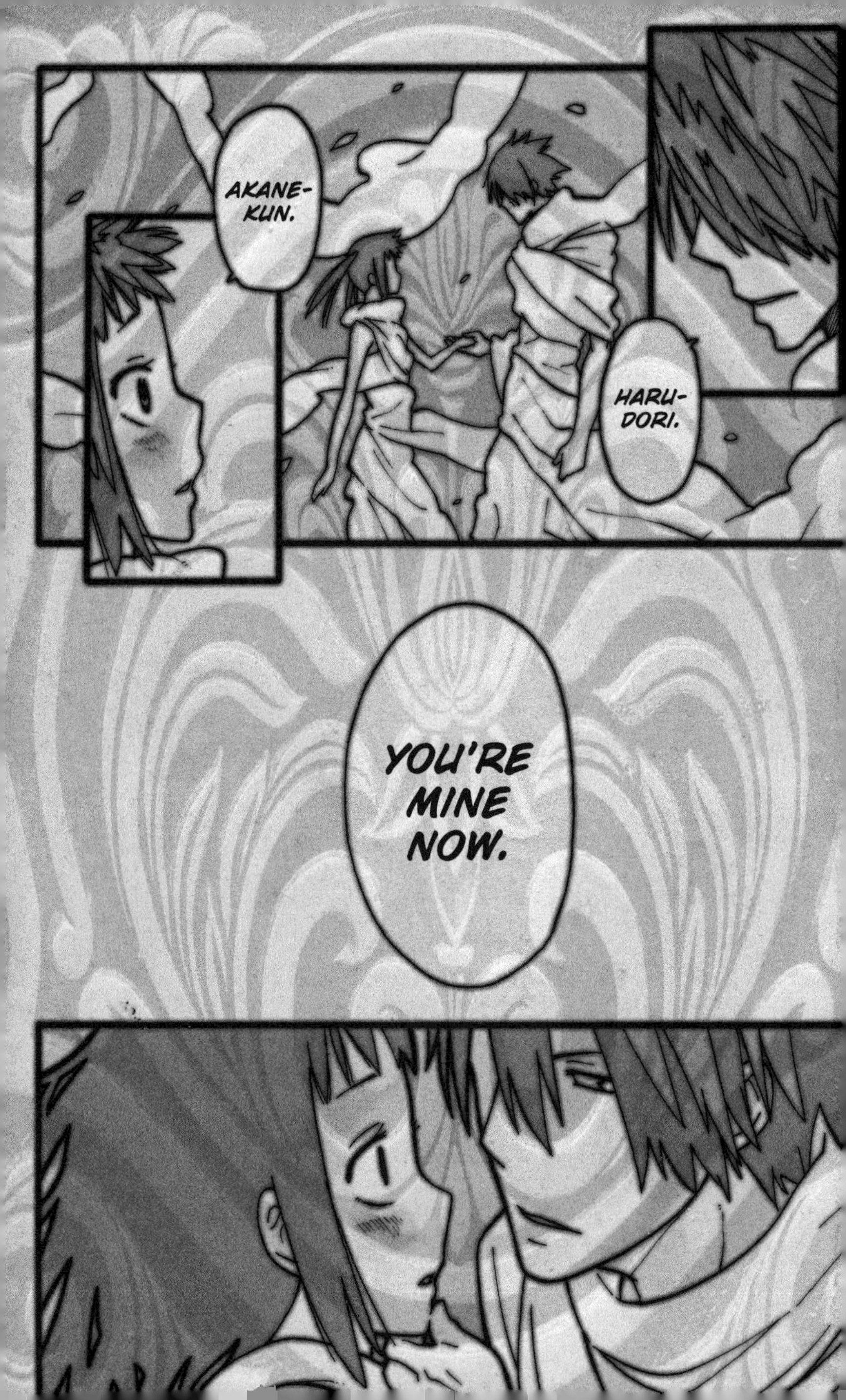
HARU-DORI.
AKANE-KUN.
YOU'RE MINE NOW.

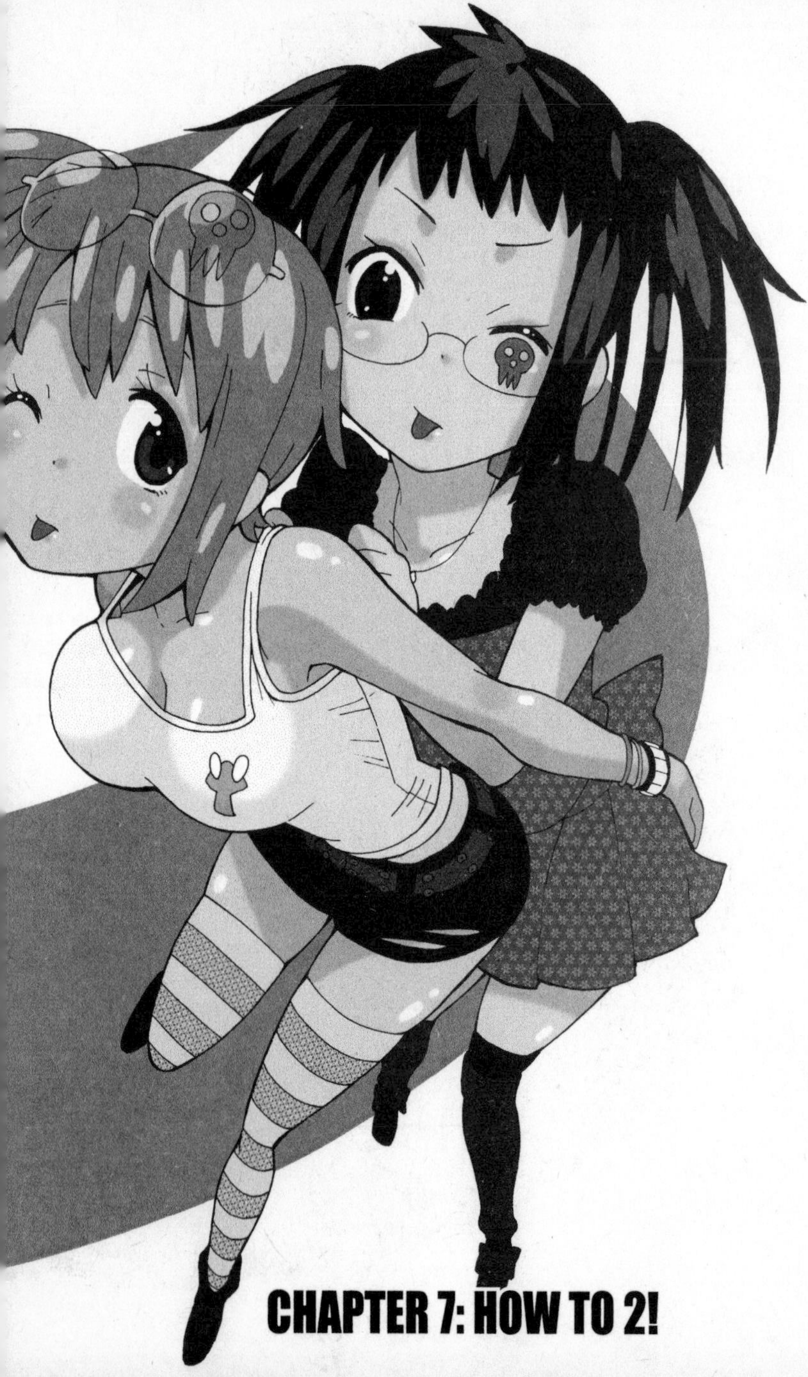

CHAPTER 7: HOW TO 2!

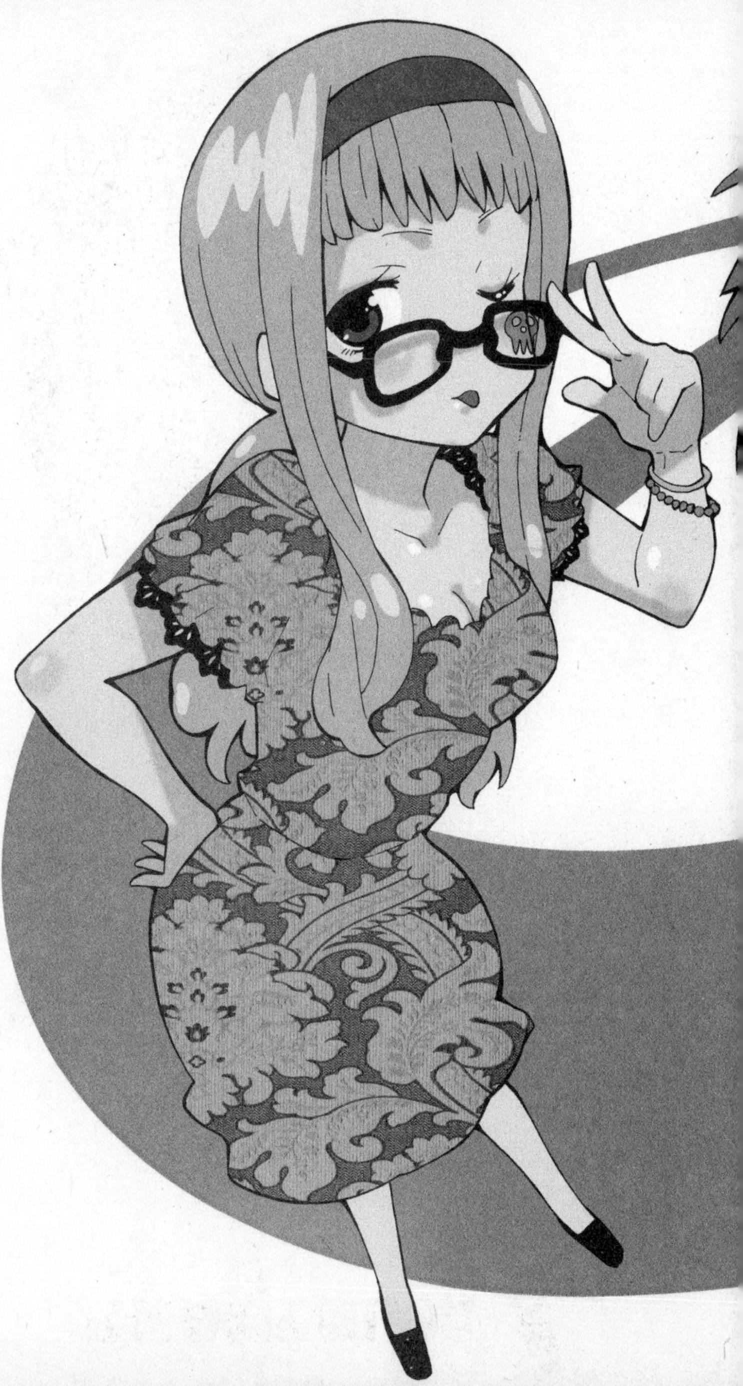

SOUL EATER NOT!

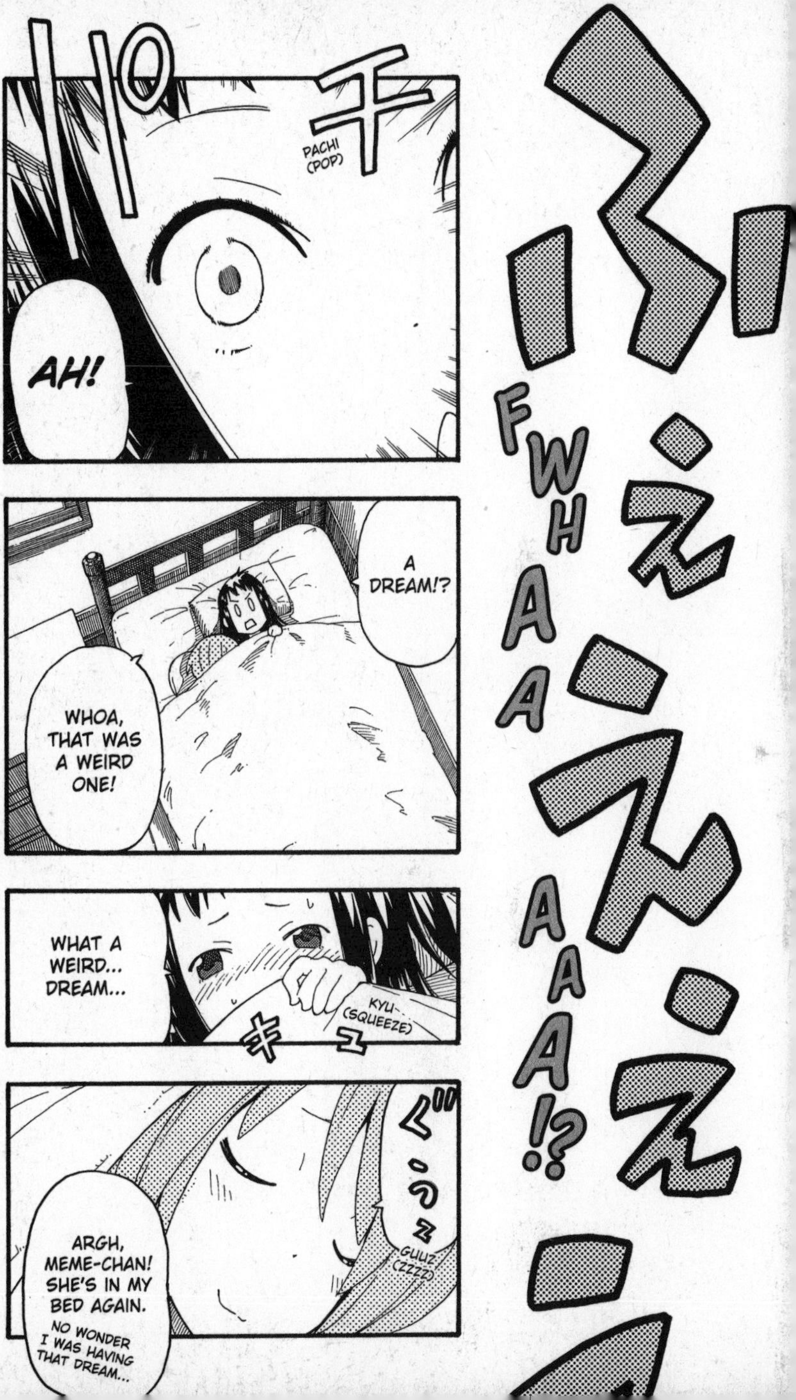
FWHAAAAAAA!?
PACHI (POP)
AH!
A DREAM!?
WHOA, THAT WAS A WEIRD ONE!
WHAT A WEIRD... DREAM...
KYU (SQUEEZE)
GUUZ (ZZZZ)
ARGH, MEME-CHAN! SHE'S IN MY BED AGAIN.
NO WONDER I WAS HAVING THAT DREAM...

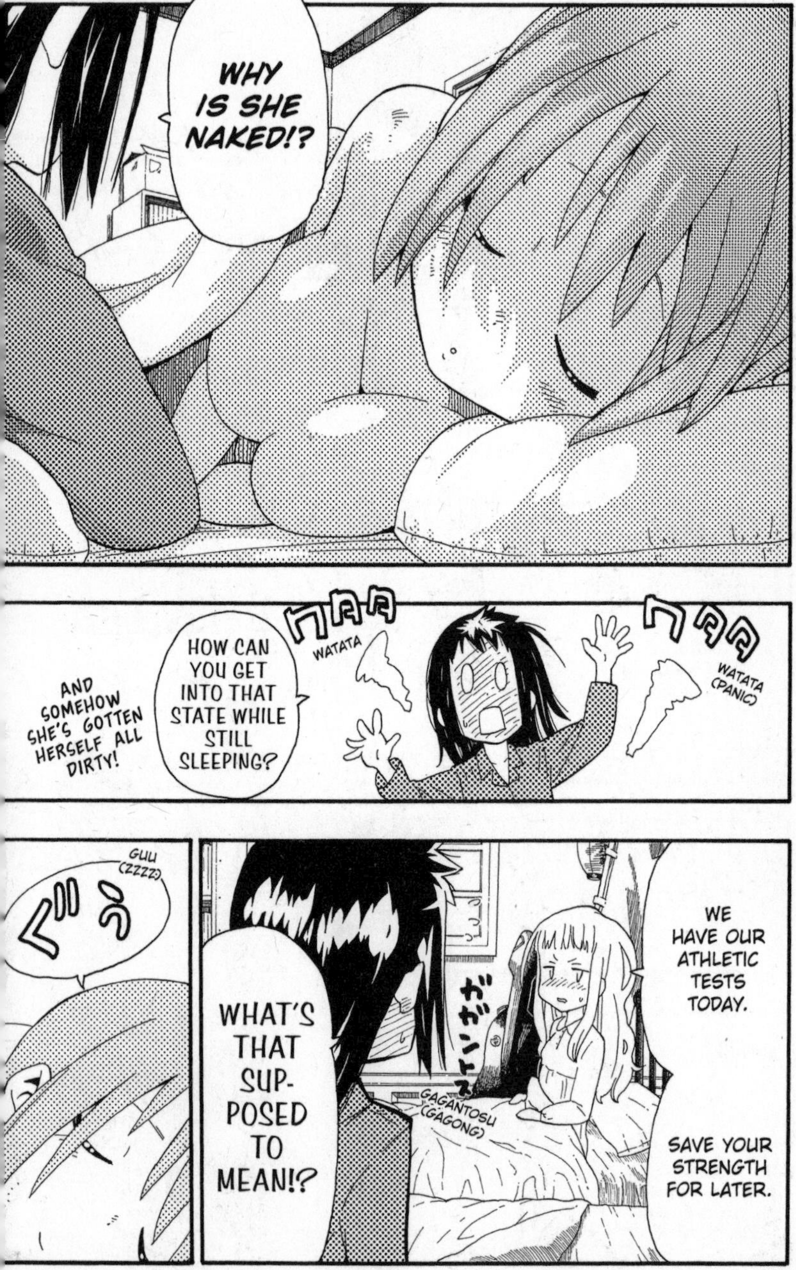
WHY IS SHE NAKED!?
WATATA (PANIC)
WATATA
HOW CAN YOU GET INTO THAT STATE WHILE STILL SLEEPING?
AND SOMEHOW SHE'S GOTTEN HERSELF ALL DIRTY!
WE HAVE OUR ATHLETIC TESTS TODAY.
SAVE YOUR STRENGTH FOR LATER.
GAGANTOSU (GAGONG)
WHAT'S THAT SUP-POSED TO MEAN!?
GUU (ZZZZ)

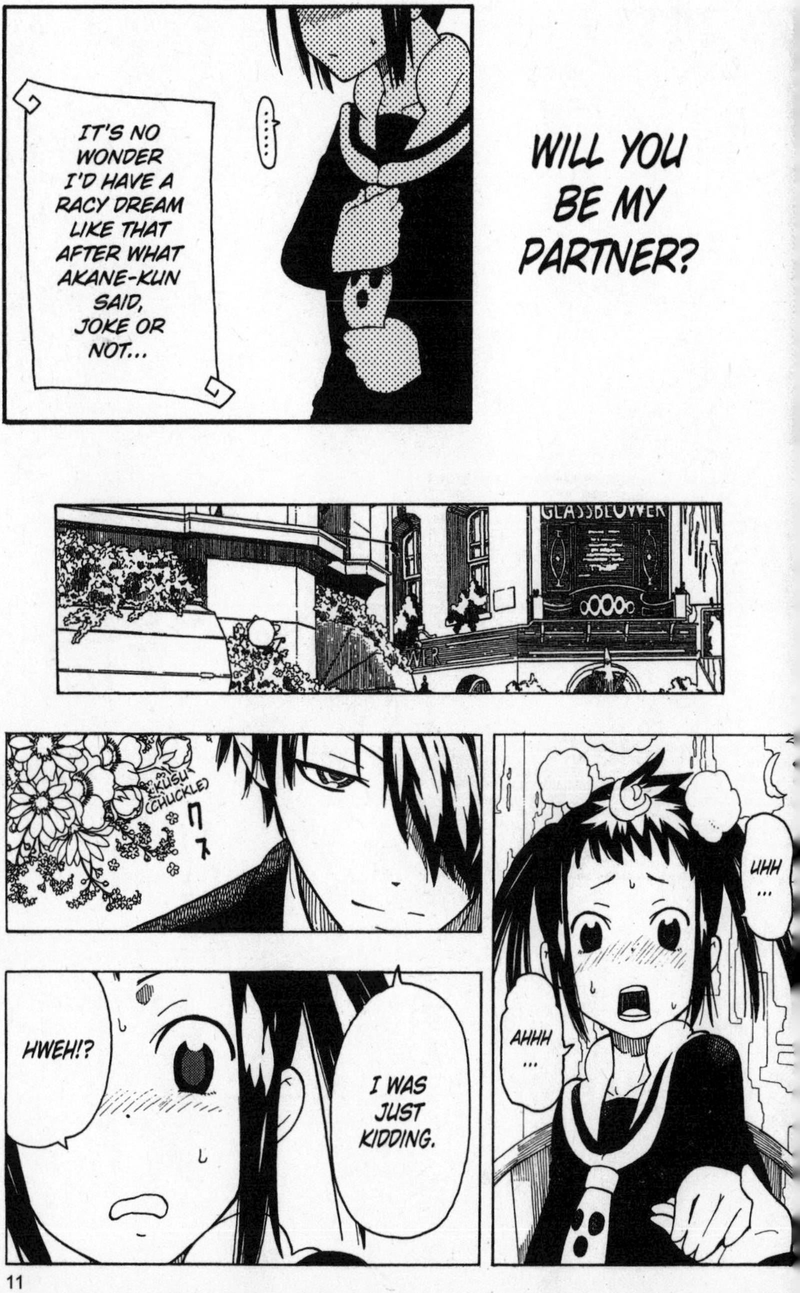
WILL YOU BE MY PARTNER?
......
IT'S NO WONDER I'D HAVE A RACY DREAM LIKE THAT AFTER WHAT AKANE-KUN SAID, JOKE OR NOT...
GLASSBLOWER
UHH ...
AHHH ...
KUSU (CHUCKLE)
I WAS JUST KIDDING.
HWEH!?

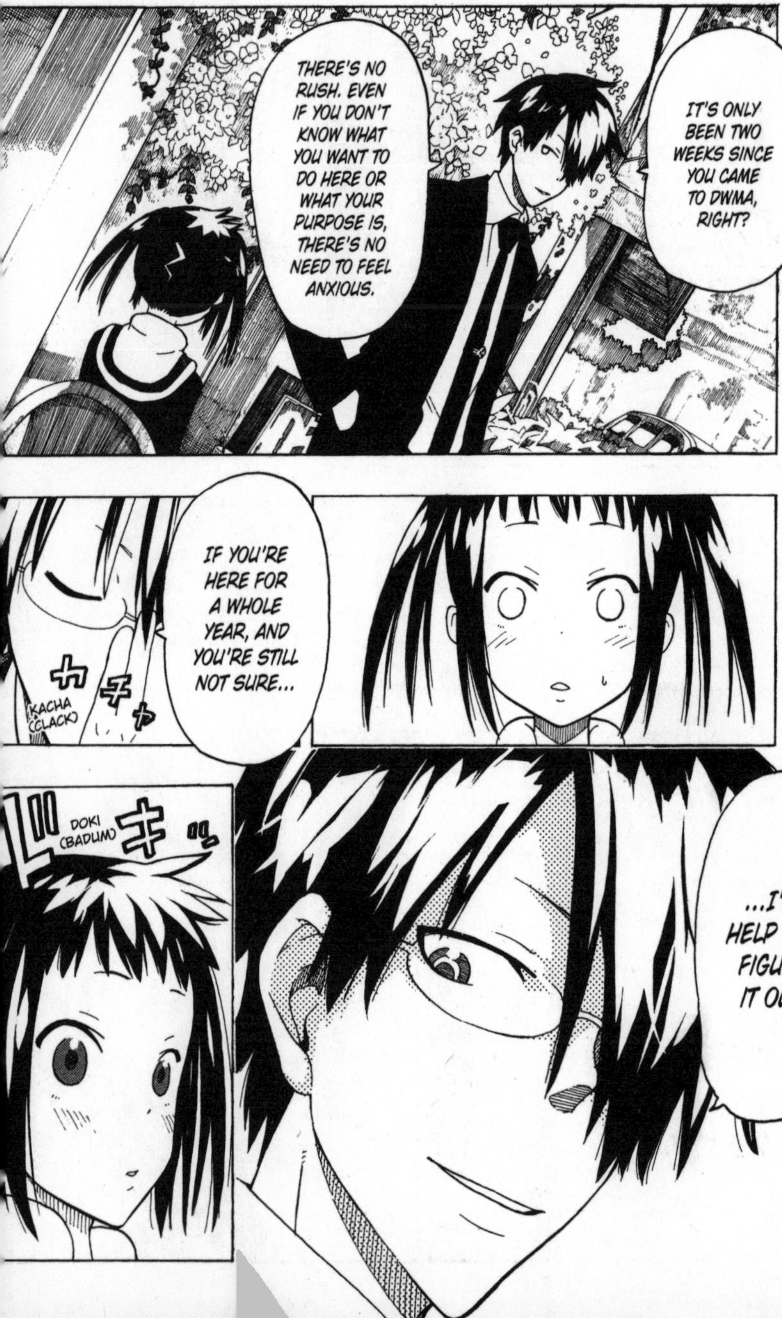
IT'S ONLY BEEN TWO WEEKS SINCE YOU CAME TO DWMA, RIGHT?
THERE'S NO RUSH. EVEN IF YOU DON'T KNOW WHAT YOU WANT TO DO HERE OR WHAT YOUR PURPOSE IS, THERE'S NO NEED TO FEEL ANXIOUS.
IF YOU'RE HERE FOR A WHOLE YEAR, AND YOU'RE STILL NOT SURE...
KACHA (CLACK)
...I'LL HELP YOU FIGURE IT OUT.
DOKI (BADUM)

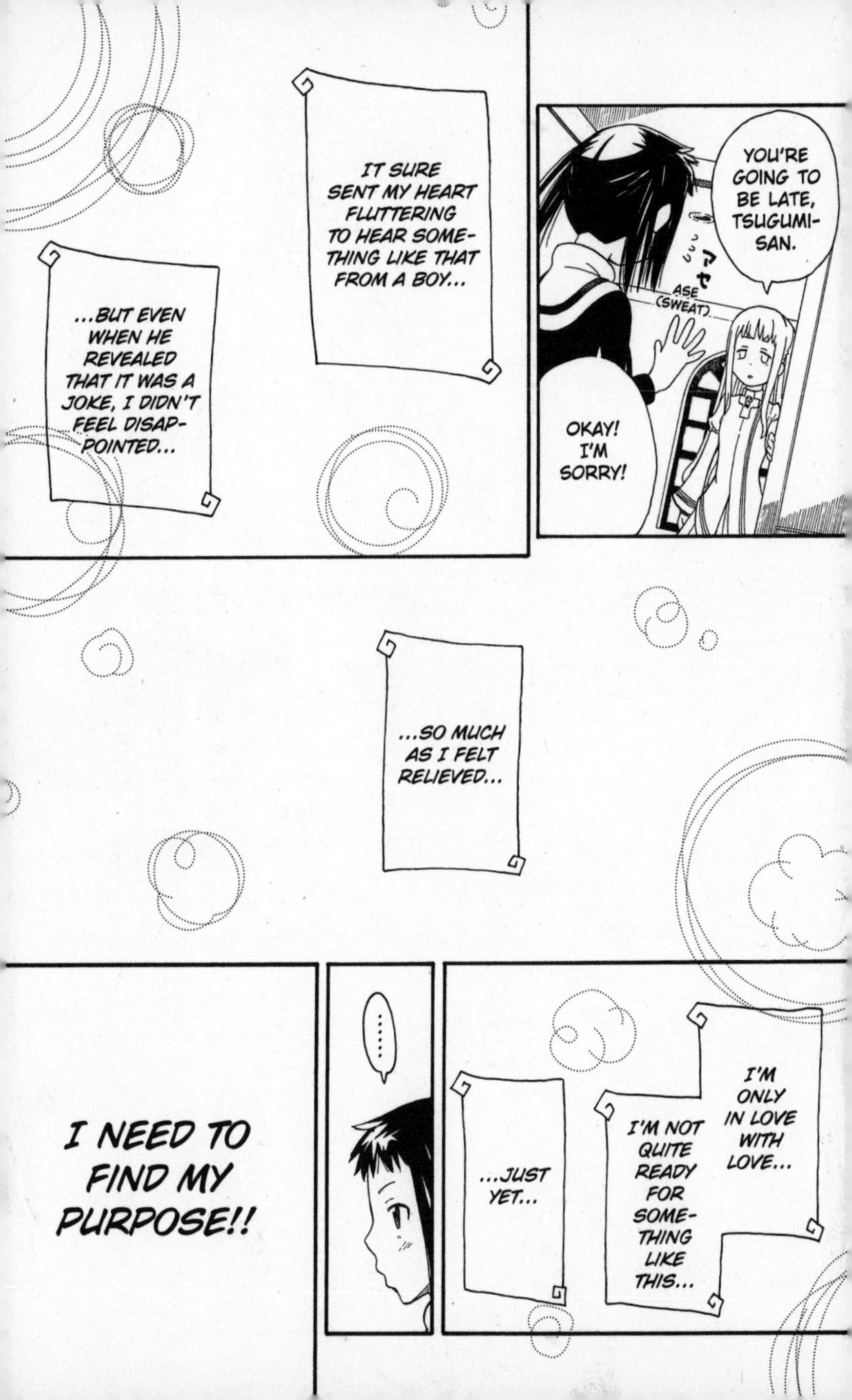
YOU'RE GOING TO BE LATE, TSUGUMI-SAN.
ASE (SWEAT)
OKAY! I'M SORRY!
IT SURE SENT MY HEART FLUTTERING TO HEAR SOMETHING LIKE THAT FROM A BOY...
...BUT EVEN WHEN HE REVEALED THAT IT WAS A JOKE, I DIDN'T FEEL DISAPPOINTED...
...SO MUCH AS I FELT RELIEVED...
I'M ONLY IN LOVE WITH LOVE...
I'M NOT QUITE READY FOR SOMETHING LIKE THIS...
...JUST YET...
......
I NEED TO FIND MY PURPOSE!!

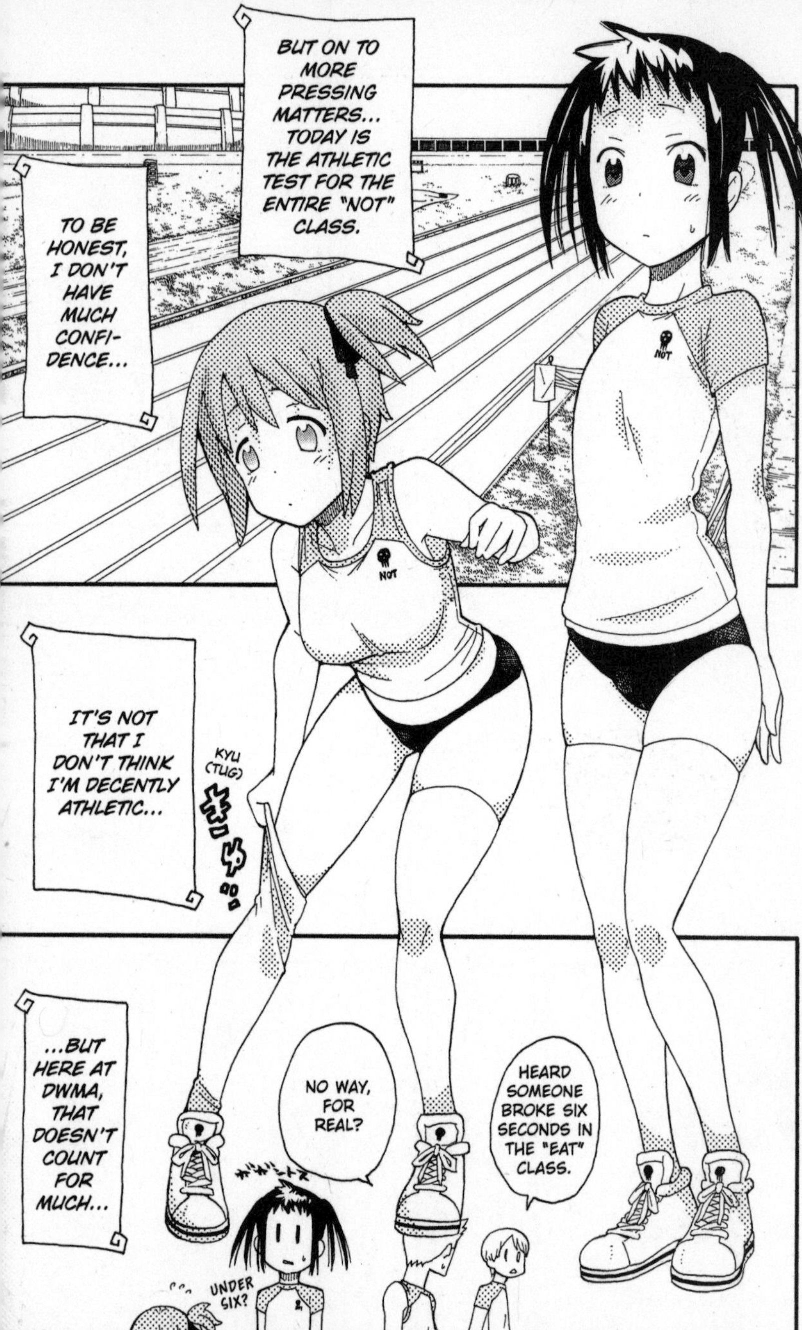
BUT ON TO MORE PRESSING MATTERS... TODAY IS THE ATHLETIC TEST FOR THE ENTIRE "NOT" CLASS.
TO BE HONEST, I DON'T HAVE MUCH CONFI-DENCE...
KYU (TUG)
IT'S NOT THAT I DON'T THINK I'M DECENTLY ATHLETIC...
HEARD SOMEONE BROKE SIX SECONDS IN THE "EAT" CLASS.
NO WAY, FOR REAL?
UNDER SIX?
...BUT HERE AT DWMA, THAT DOESN'T COUNT FOR MUCH...

SFX: GAGANTOSU (GAGONG)

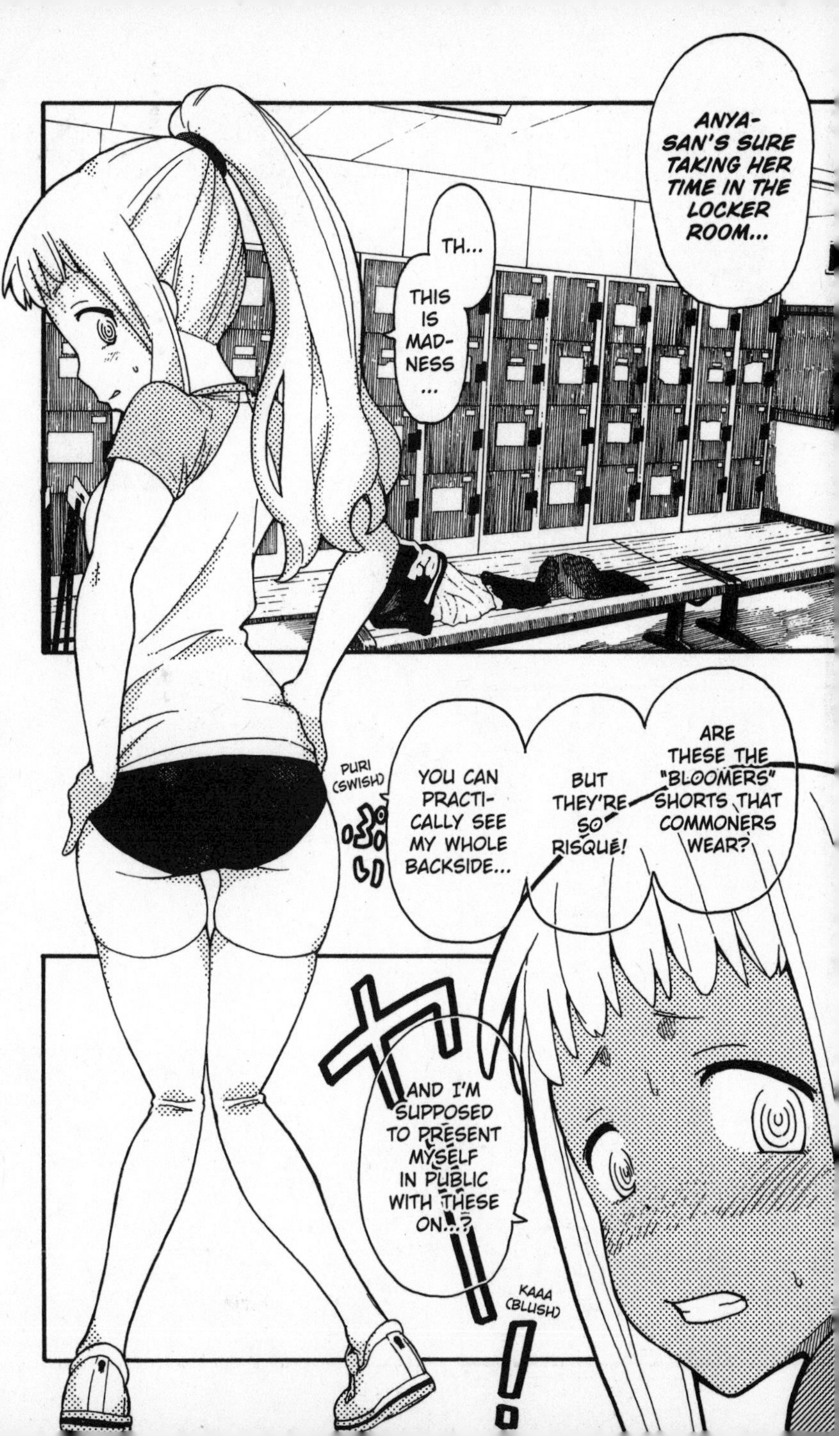
ANYA-SAN'S SURE TAKING HER TIME IN THE LOCKER ROOM...
TH... THIS IS MADNESS...
ARE THESE THE "BLOOMERS" SHORTS THAT COMMONERS WEAR?
BUT THEY'RE SO RISQUÉ!
YOU CAN PRACTICALLY SEE MY WHOLE BACKSIDE...
PURI (SWISH)
KAAA (BLUSH)
AND I'M SUPPOSED TO PRESENT MYSELF IN PUBLIC WITH THESE ON...?

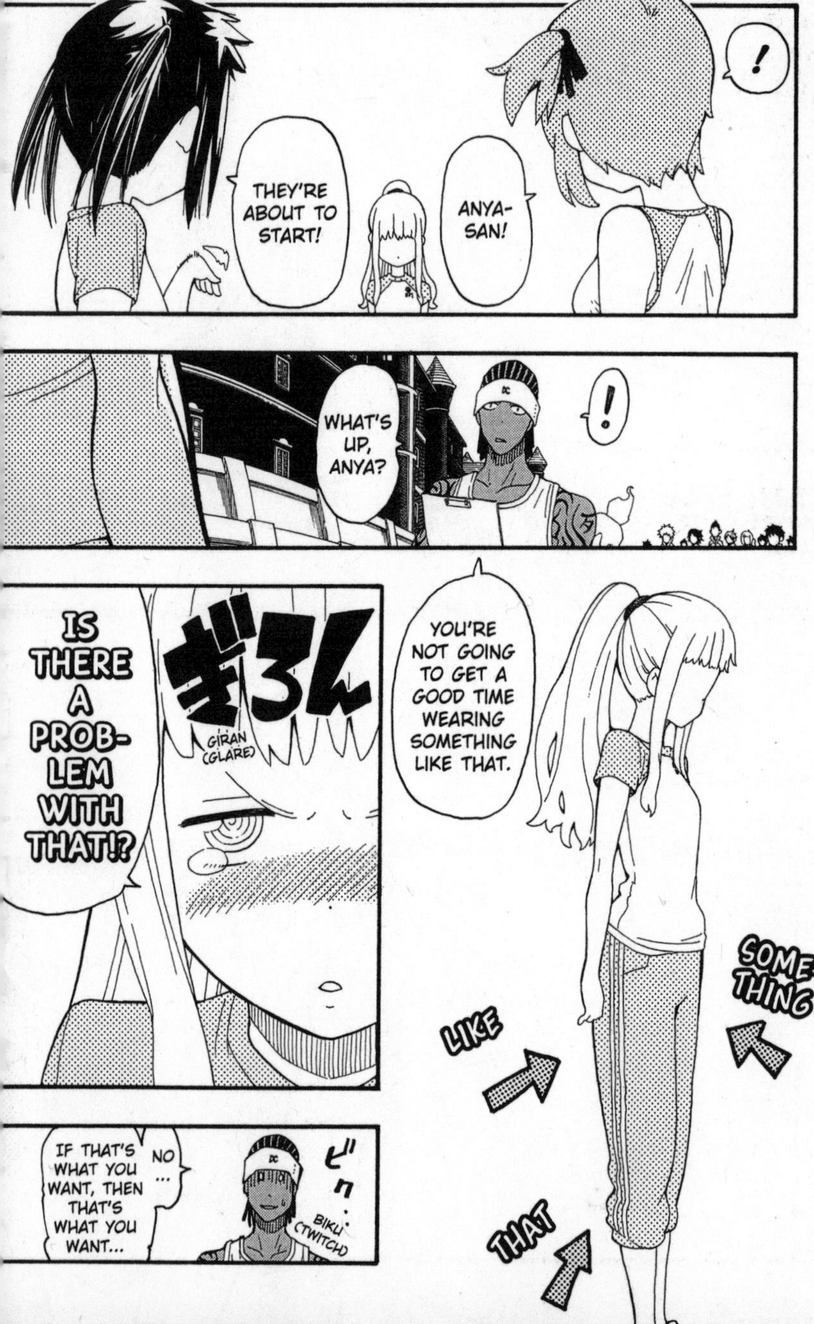
!
ANYA-SAN!
THEY'RE ABOUT TO START!
!
WHAT'S UP, ANYA?
YOU'RE NOT GOING TO GET A GOOD TIME WEARING SOMETHING LIKE THAT.
SOME-THING
LIKE
THAT
ぎろん
GIRAN (GLARE)
IS THERE A PROB-LEM WITH THAT!?
ビク
BIKU (TWITCH)
NO...
IF THAT'S WHAT YOU WANT, THEN THAT'S WHAT YOU WANT...

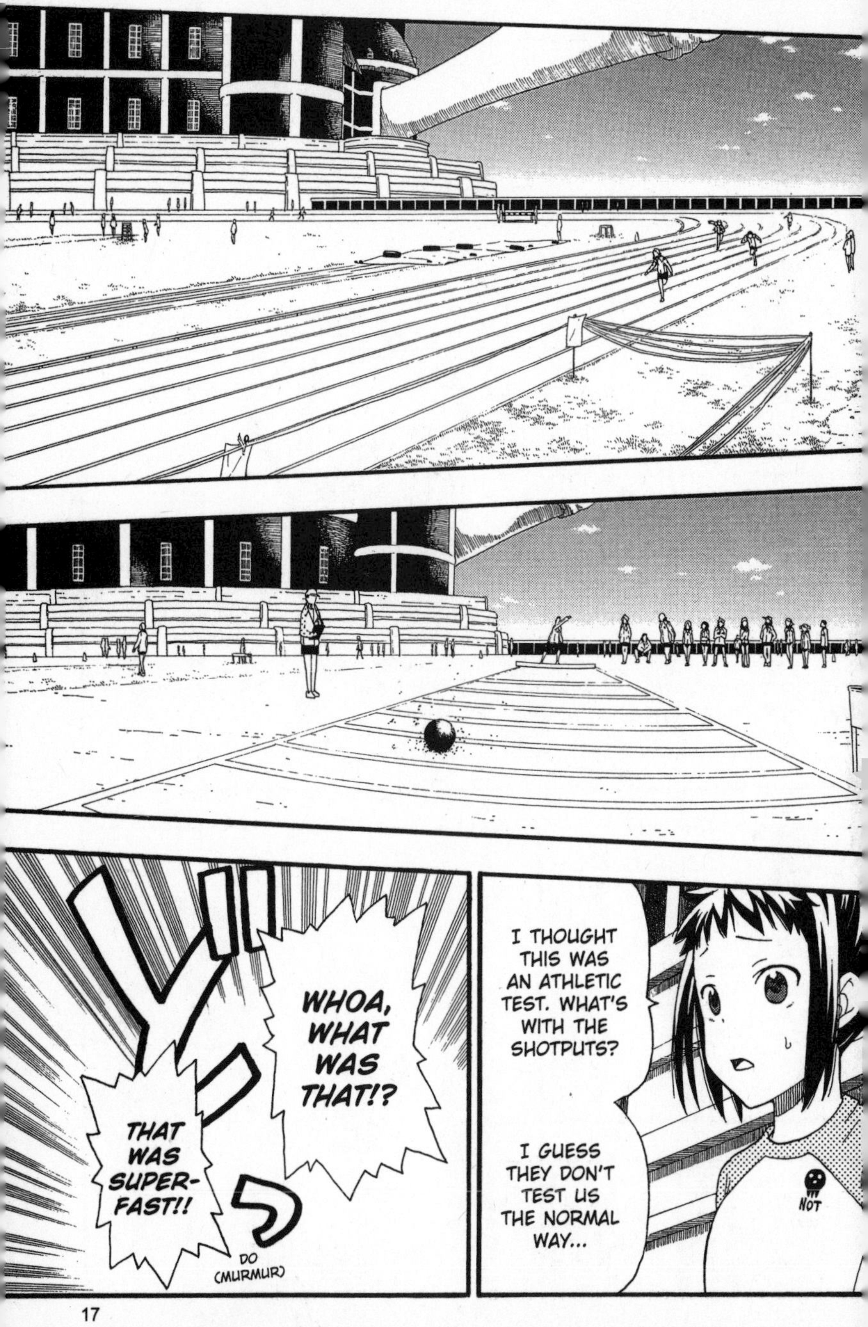

I THOUGHT THIS WAS AN ATHLETIC TEST. WHAT'S WITH THE SHOTPUTS?
I GUESS THEY DON'T TEST US THE NORMAL WAY...
NOT
WHOA, WHAT WAS THAT!?
THAT WAS SUPER-FAST!!
DO (MURMUR)

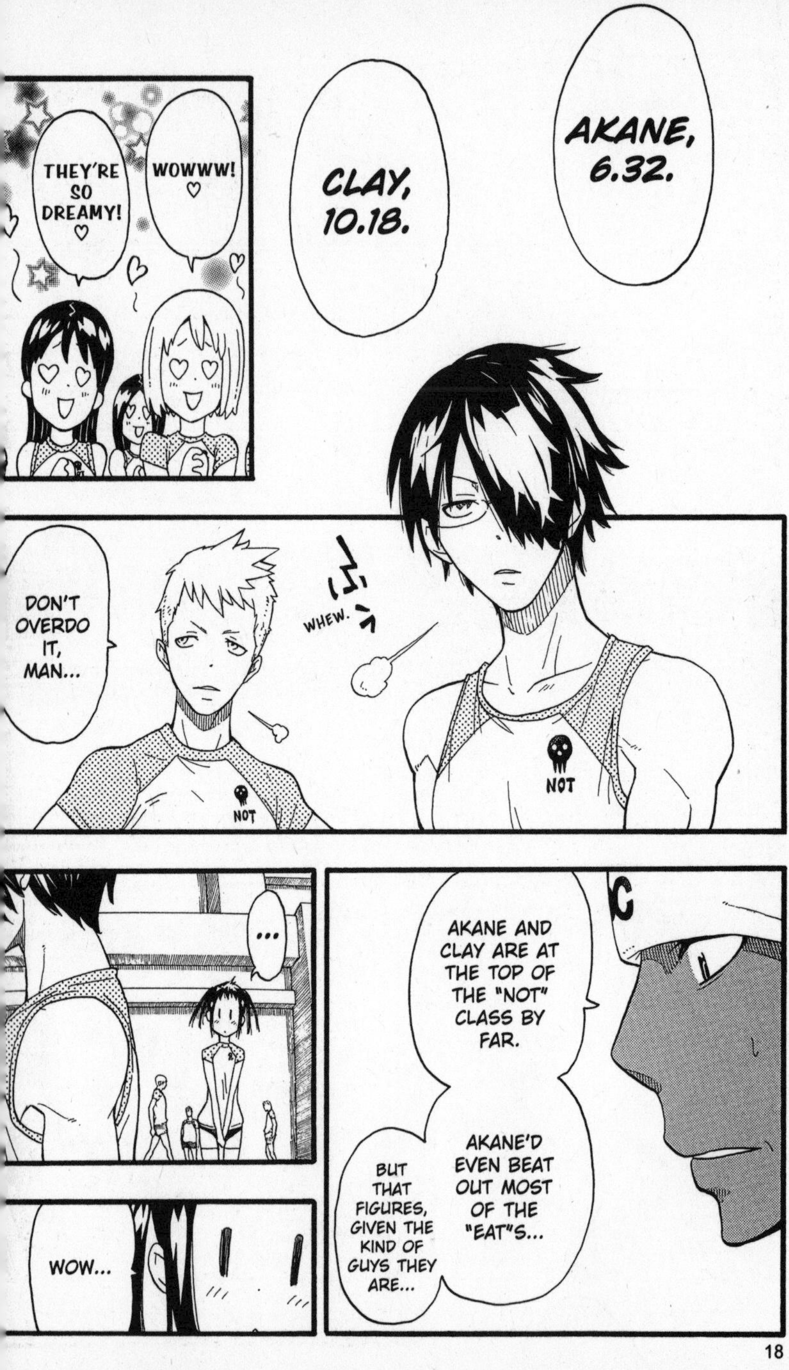
AKANE, 6.32.
CLAY, 10.18.
WOWWW! ♡
THEY'RE SO DREAMY! ♡
WHEW.
DON'T OVERDO IT, MAN...
AKANE AND CLAY ARE AT THE TOP OF THE "NOT" CLASS BY FAR.
AKANE'D EVEN BEAT OUT MOST OF THE "EAT"S...
BUT THAT FIGURES, GIVEN THE KIND OF GUYS THEY ARE...
...
WOW...

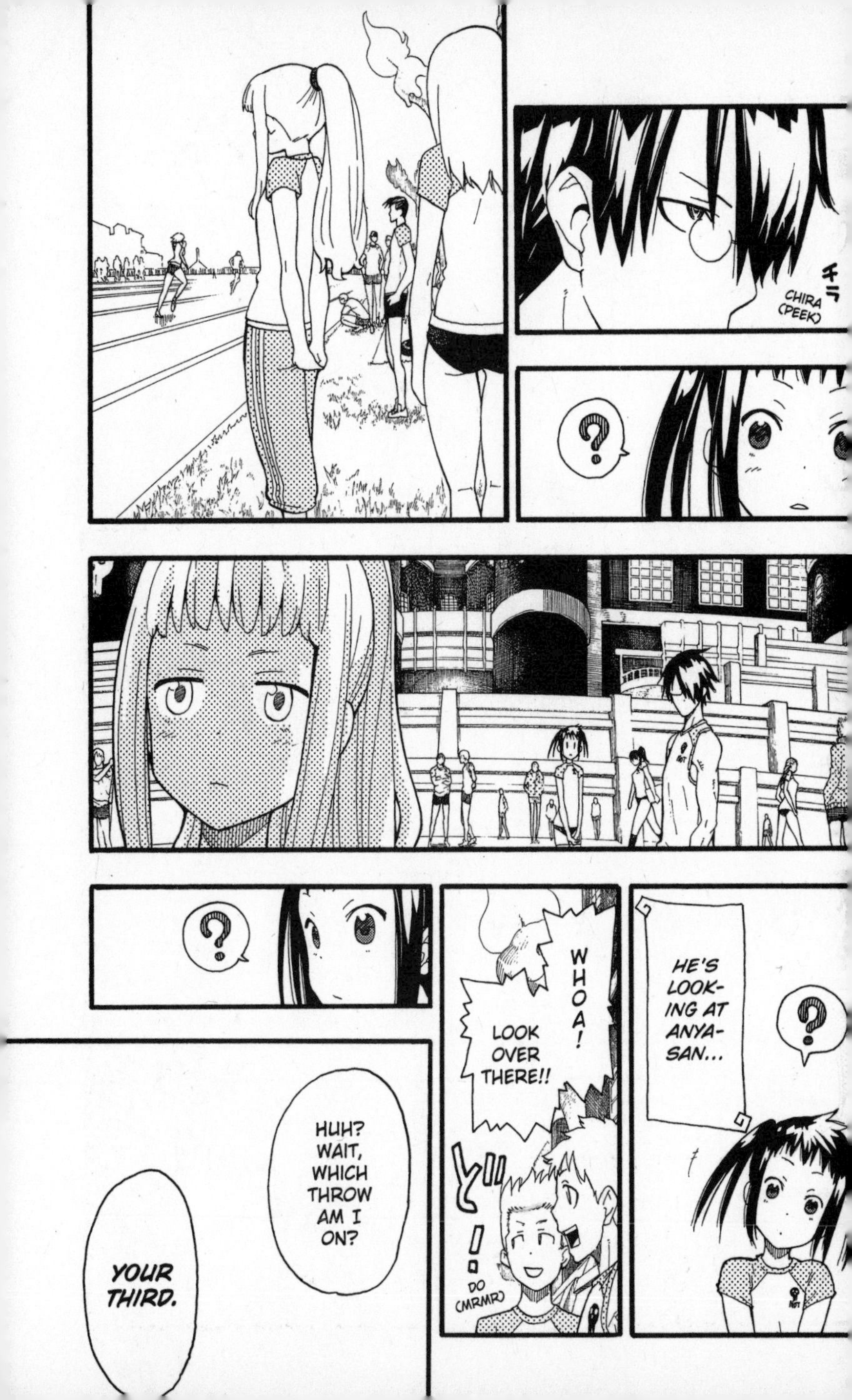
チラ
CHIRA (PEEK)
?
?
HE'S LOOKING AT ANYA-SAN...
?
WHOA!
LOOK OVER THERE!!
DO (MRMR)
?
HUH? WAIT, WHICH THROW AM I ON?
YOUR THIRD.

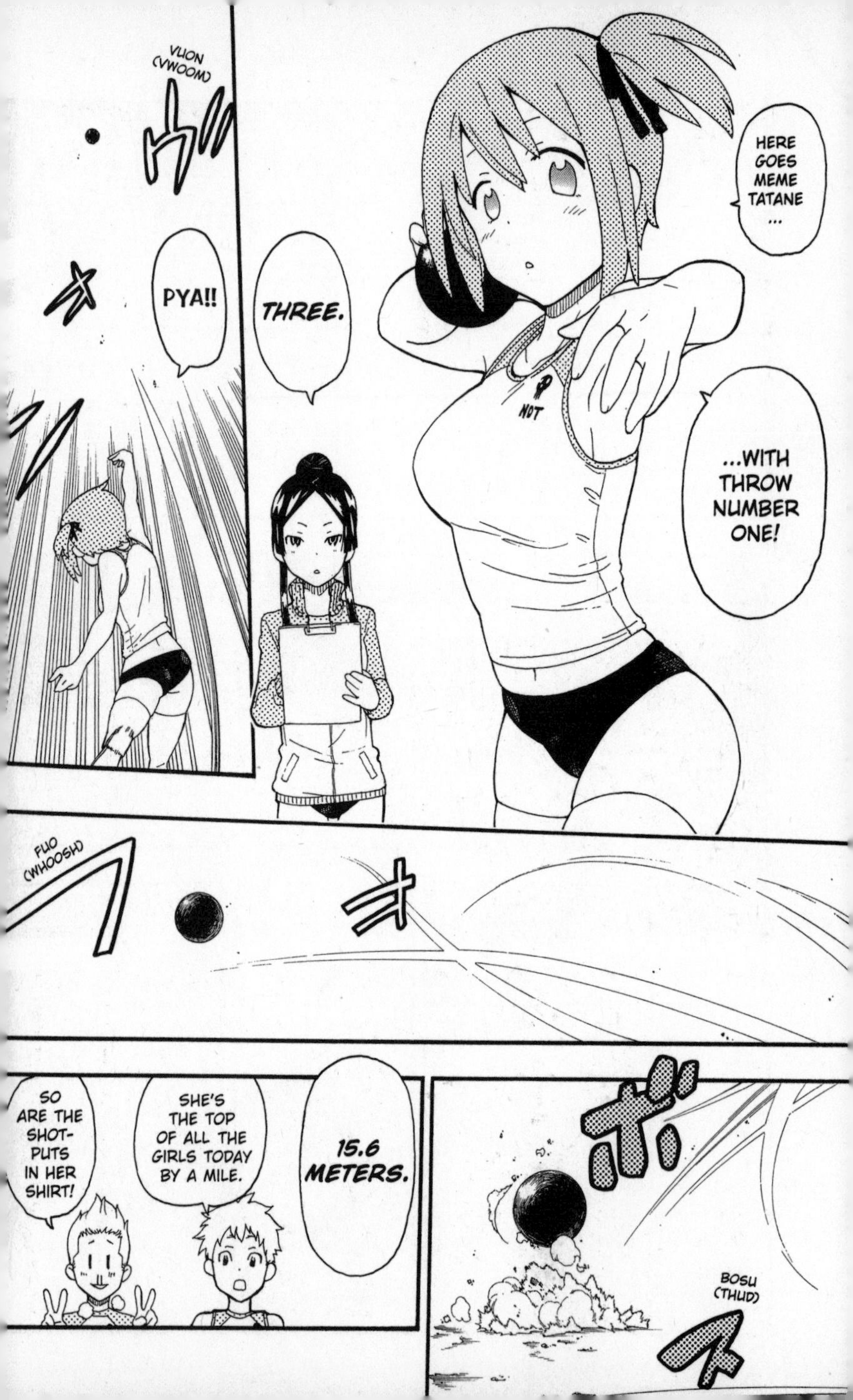
HERE GOES MEME TATANE ...
...WITH THROW NUMBER ONE!
NOT
THREE.
VUON (VWOOM)
PYA!!
FUO (WHOOSH)
BOSU (THUD)
15.6 METERS.
SHE'S THE TOP OF ALL THE GIRLS TODAY BY A MILE.
SO ARE THE SHOT-PUTS IN HER SHIRT!

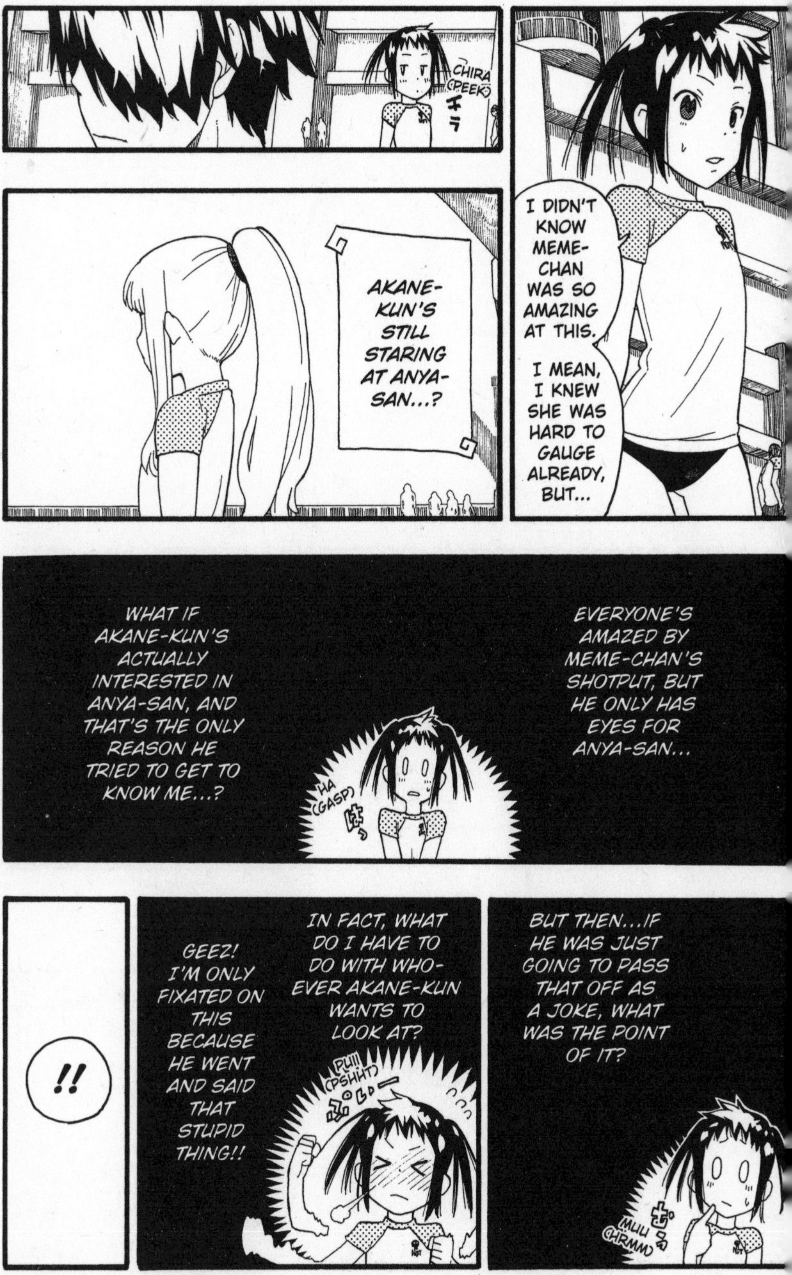
I DIDN'T KNOW MEME-CHAN WAS SO AMAZING AT THIS.
I MEAN, I KNEW SHE WAS HARD TO GAUGE ALREADY, BUT...
CHIRA (PEEK)
AKANE-KUN'S STILL STARING AT ANYA-SAN...?
EVERYONE'S AMAZED BY MEME-CHAN'S SHOTPUT, BUT HE ONLY HAS EYES FOR ANYA-SAN...
WHAT IF AKANE-KUN'S ACTUALLY INTERESTED IN ANYA-SAN, AND THAT'S THE ONLY REASON HE TRIED TO GET TO KNOW ME...?
HA (GASP)
BUT THEN...IF HE WAS JUST GOING TO PASS THAT OFF AS A JOKE, WHAT WAS THE POINT OF IT?
MUU (HRMM)
IN FACT, WHAT DO I HAVE TO DO WITH WHO-EVER AKANE-KUN WANTS TO LOOK AT?
GEEZ! I'M ONLY FIXATED ON THIS BECAUSE HE WENT AND SAID THAT STUPID THING!!
PUI! (PSHHT)
!!

1.87
METERS.

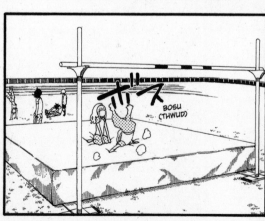

ボス
BOSU
(THWUD)

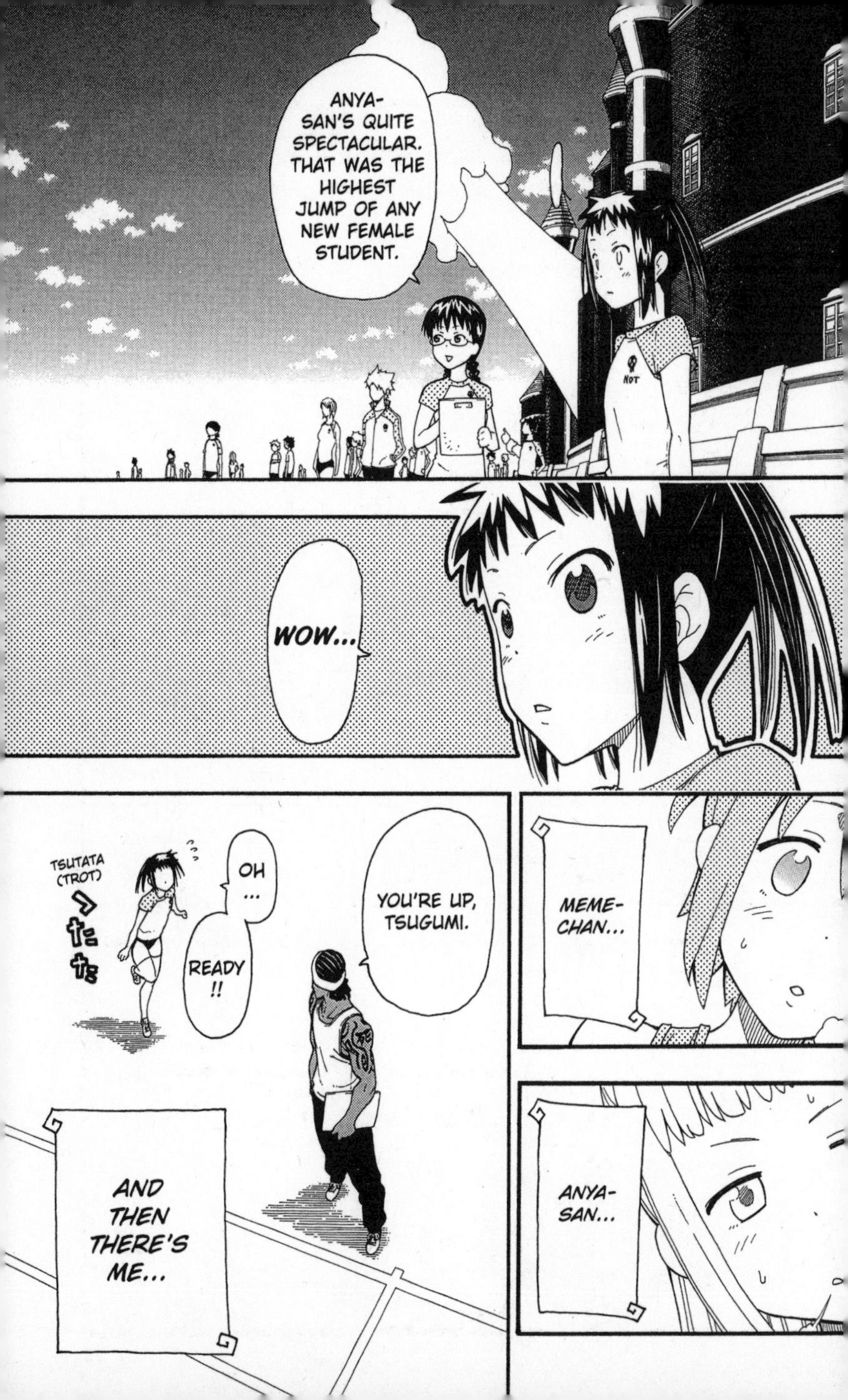
ANYA-SAN'S QUITE SPECTACULAR. THAT WAS THE HIGHEST JUMP OF ANY NEW FEMALE STUDENT.
WOW...
MEME-CHAN...
ANYA-SAN...
YOU'RE UP, TSUGUMI.
OH ...
READY !!
TSUTATA (TROT)
AND THEN THERE'S ME...

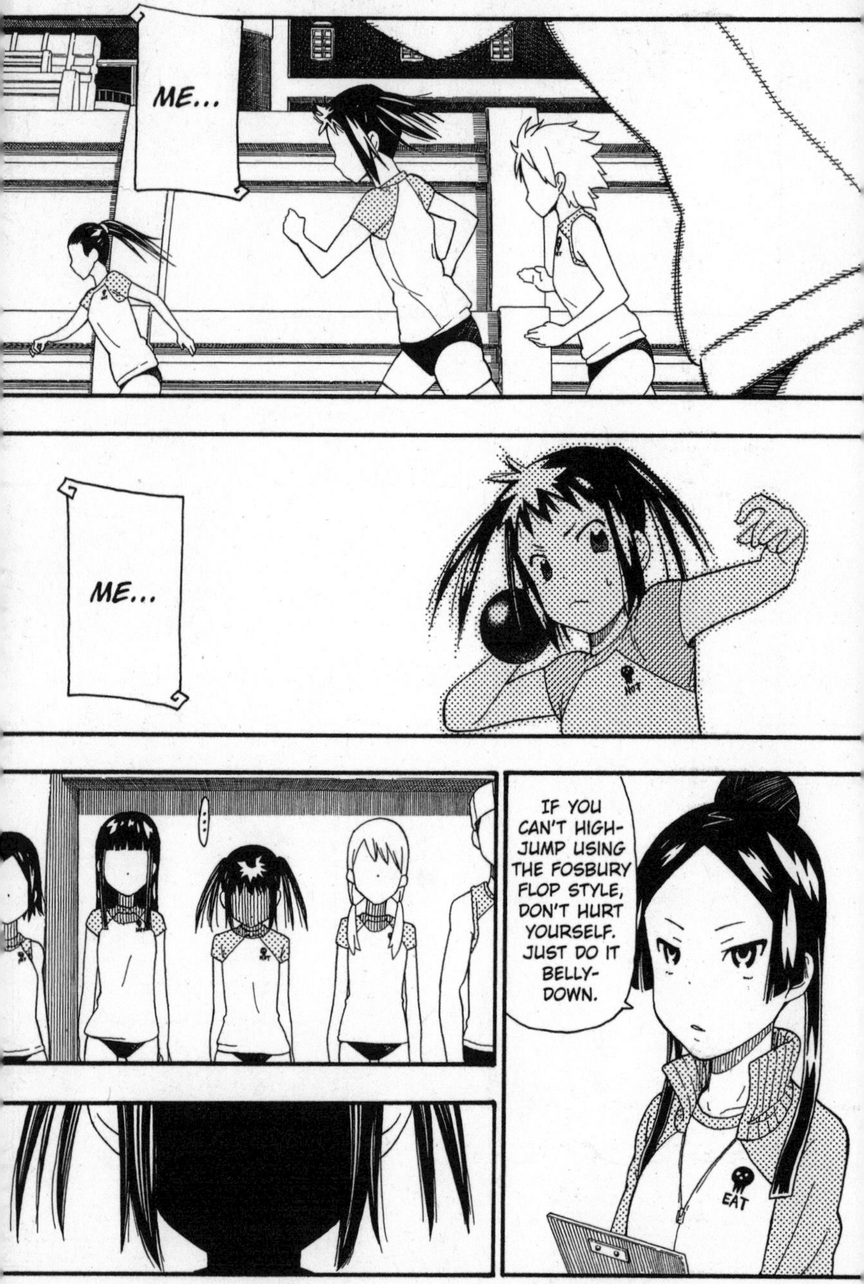
ME...
ME...
IF YOU CAN'T HIGH-JUMP USING THE FOSBURY FLOP STYLE, DON'T HURT YOURSELF. JUST DO IT BELLY-DOWN.
...

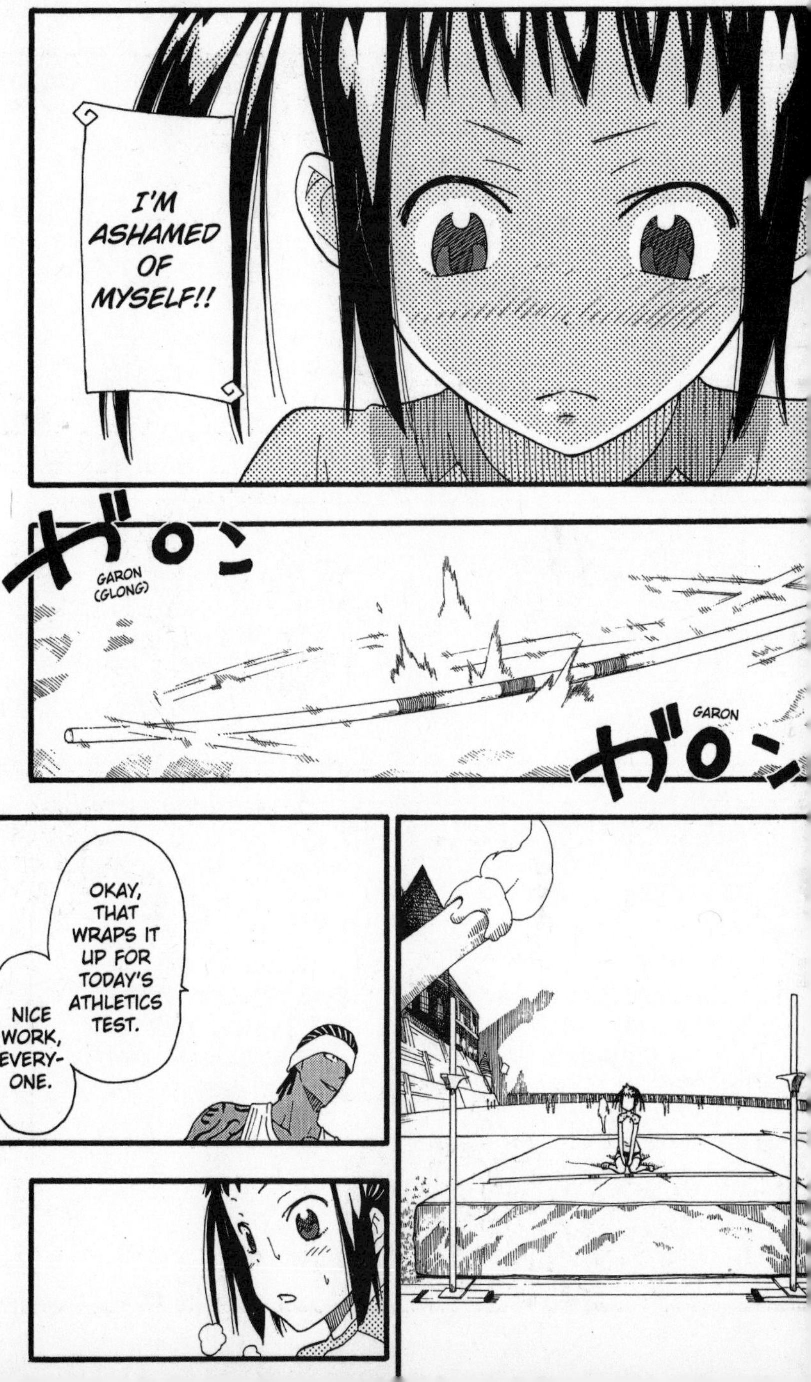
I'M ASHAMED OF MYSELF!!
ガロン
GARON (GLONG)
ガロン
GARON
OKAY, THAT WRAPS IT UP FOR TODAY'S ATHLETICS TEST.
NICE WORK, EVERY-ONE.

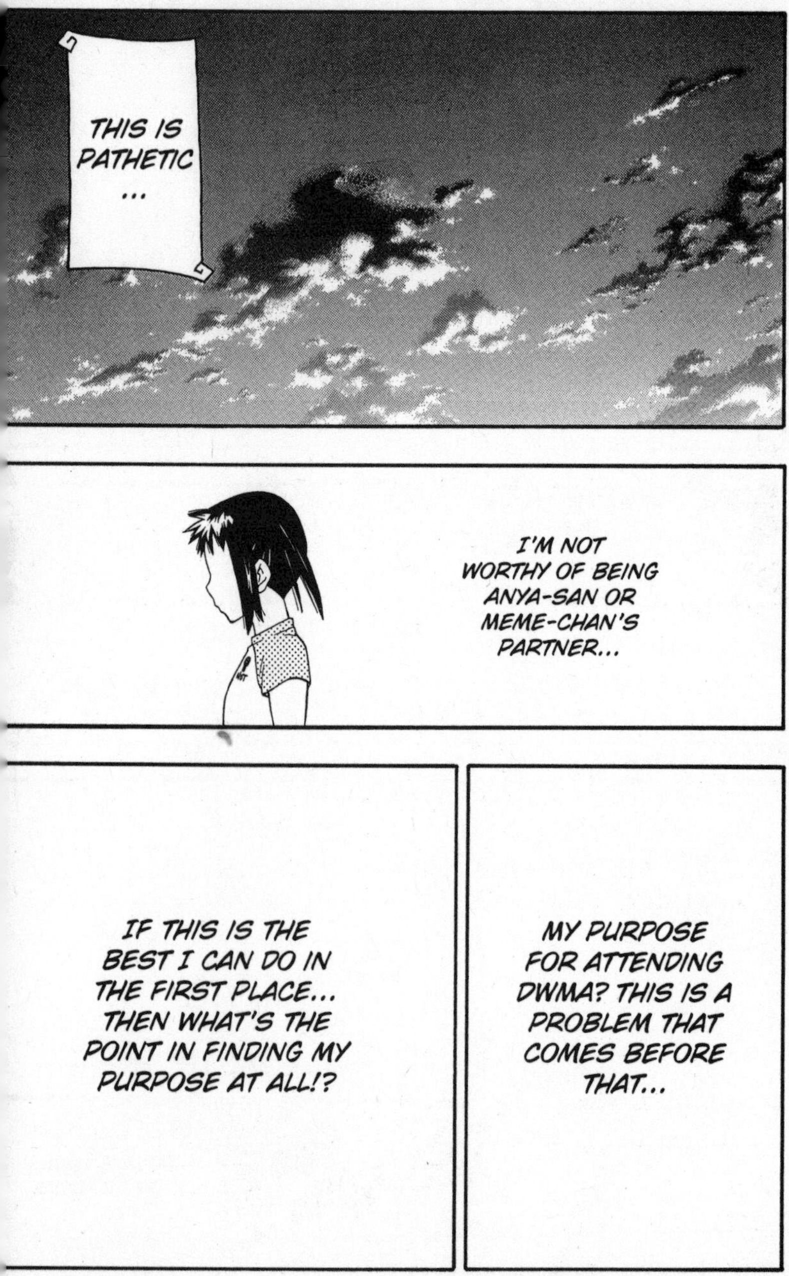
THIS IS PATHETIC ...
I'M NOT WORTHY OF BEING ANYA-SAN OR MEME-CHAN'S PARTNER...
MY PURPOSE FOR ATTENDING DWMA? THIS IS A PROBLEM THAT COMES BEFORE THAT...
IF THIS IS THE BEST I CAN DO IN THE FIRST PLACE... THEN WHAT'S THE POINT IN FINDING MY PURPOSE AT ALL!?

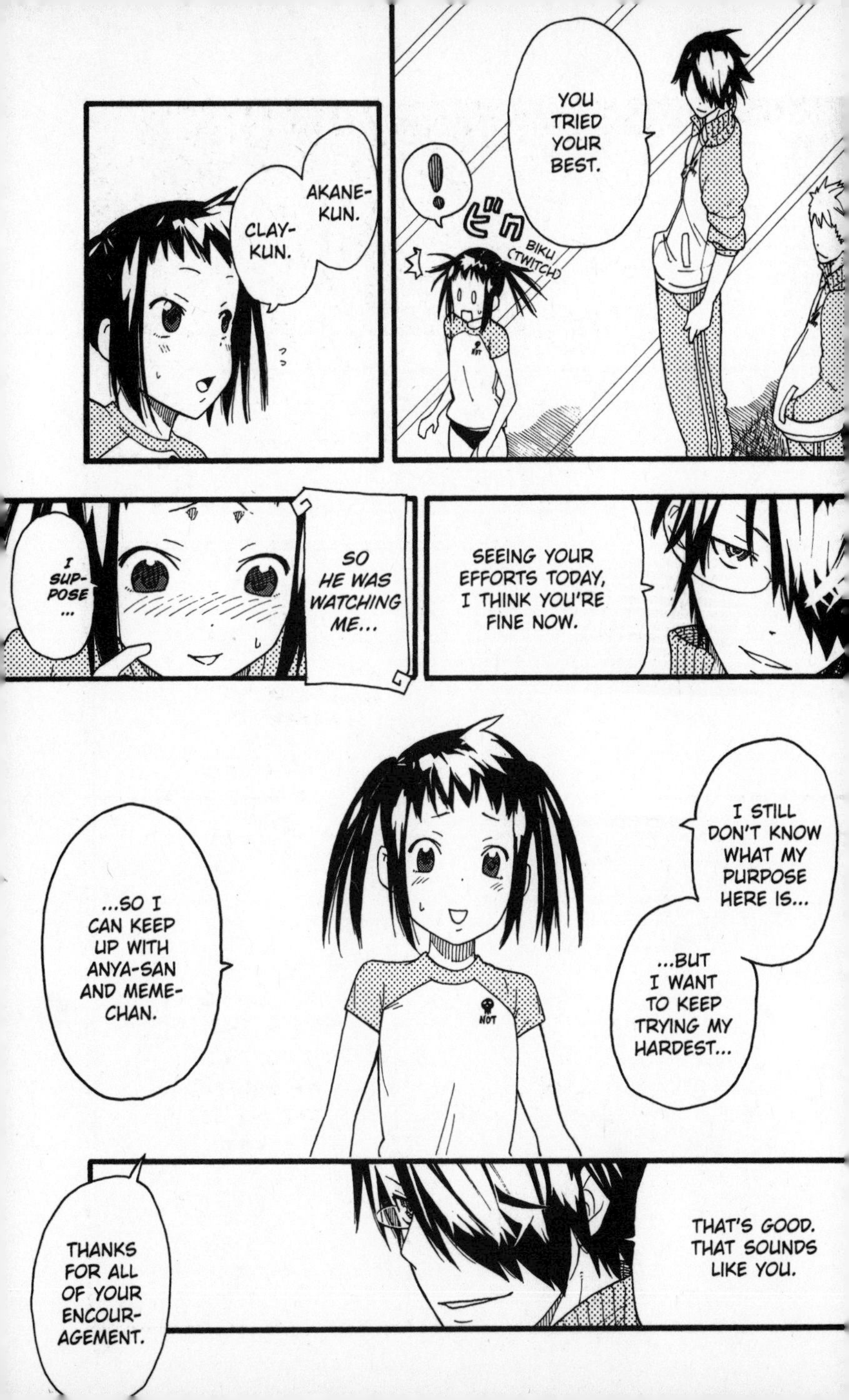

YOU TRIED YOUR BEST.
!
BIKU (TWITCH)
AKANE-KUN.
CLAY-KUN.
SEEING YOUR EFFORTS TODAY, I THINK YOU'RE FINE NOW.
SO HE WAS WATCHING ME...
I SUPPOSE...
I STILL DON'T KNOW WHAT MY PURPOSE HERE IS...
...BUT I WANT TO KEEP TRYING MY HARDEST...
...SO I CAN KEEP UP WITH ANYA-SAN AND MEME-CHAN.
THAT'S GOOD. THAT SOUNDS LIKE YOU.
THANKS FOR ALL OF YOUR ENCOURAGEMENT.

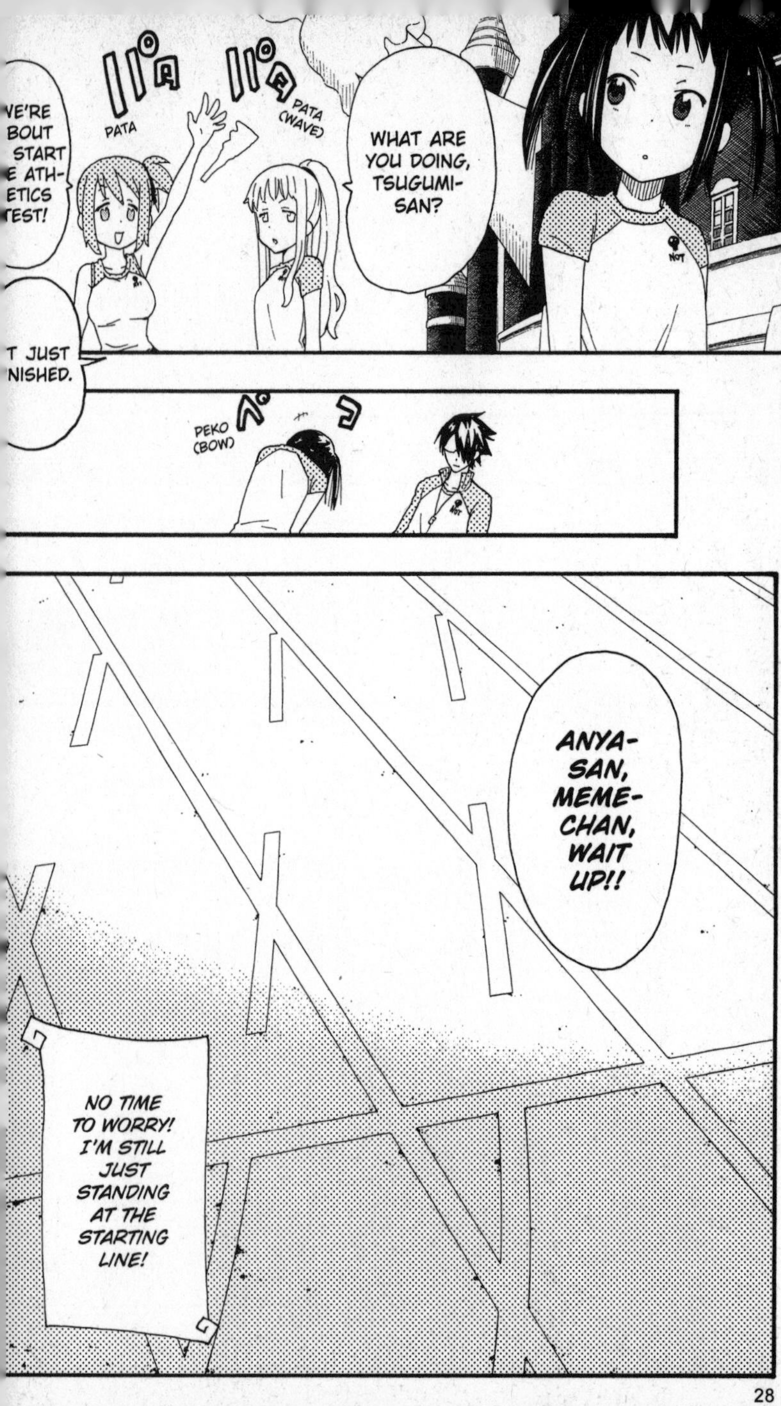
WHAT ARE YOU DOING, TSUGUMI-SAN?
PATA (WAVE)
PATA
VE'RE BOUT START E ATH-ETICS TEST!
T JUST NISHED.
PEKO (BOW)
ANYA-SAN, MEME-CHAN, WAIT UP!!
NO TIME TO WORRY! I'M STILL JUST STANDING AT THE STARTING LINE!

SOUL EATER NOT!

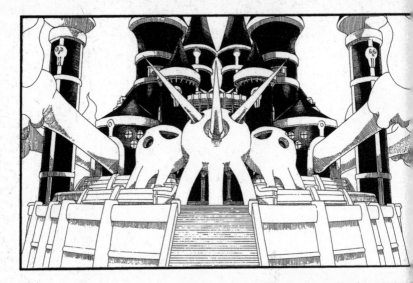

IS THERE A PROBLEM IN THE HOLDING AREA?

YES, WELL...I HAVE SOME MATERIALS I'D LIKE DWMA TO TAKE A LOOK AT...

THESE ARE OUR OLD FRIENDS, THE TRAITORS...

WE SHOULD HAVE THEM IN CUSTODY AS SUS-PECTS— WHAT ABOUT THEM?

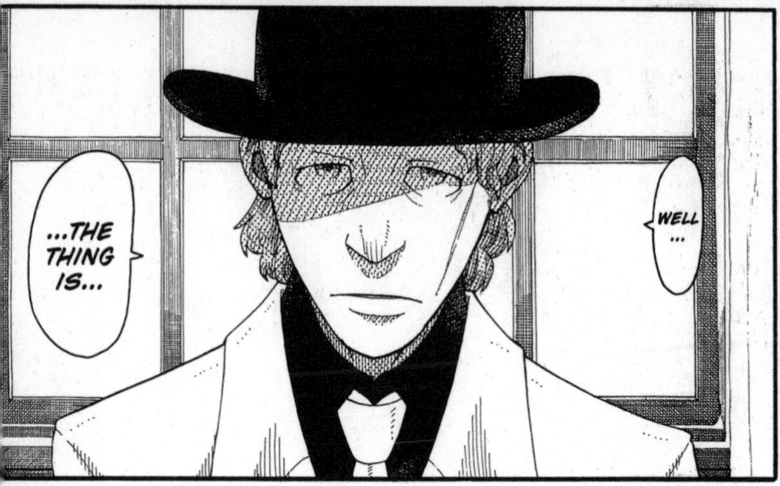
WELL...
...THE THING IS...
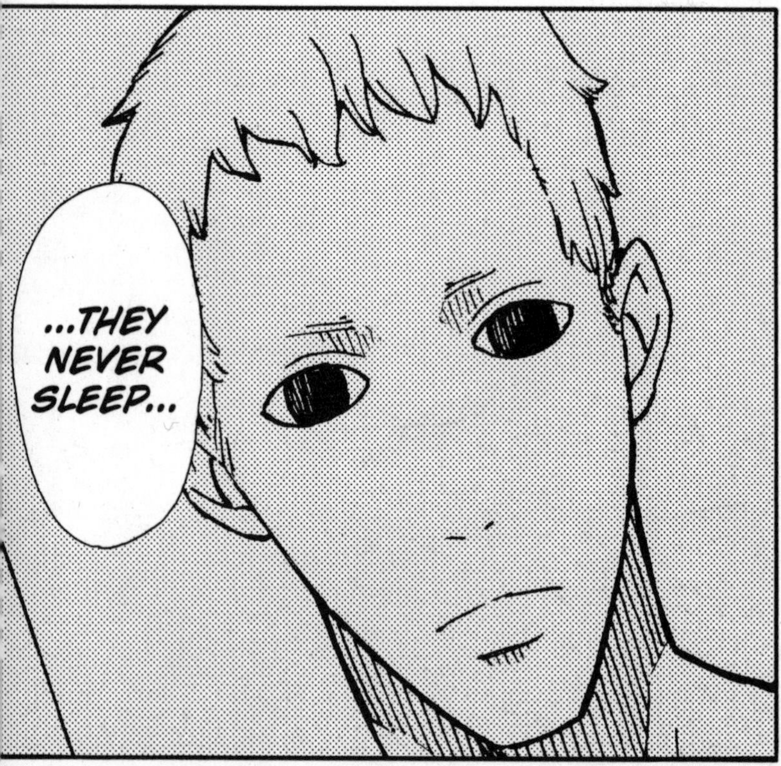
...THEY NEVER SLEEP...

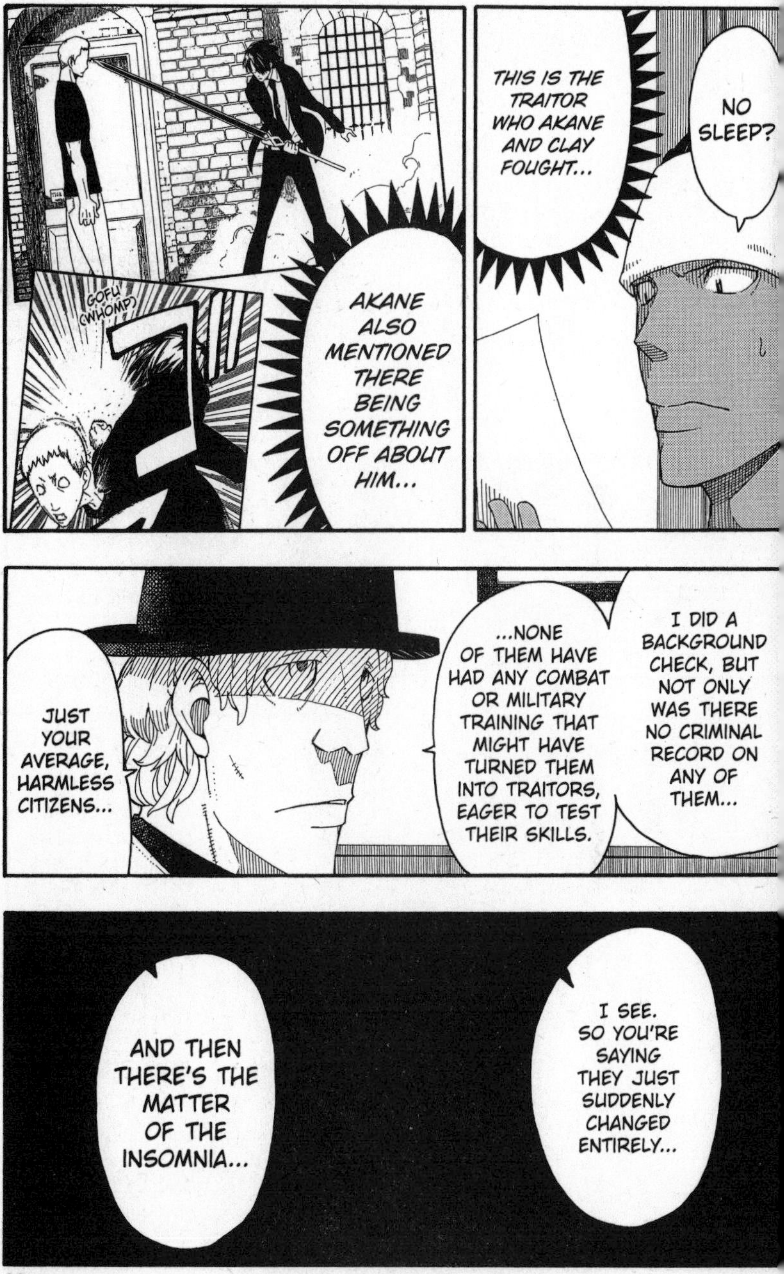
NO SLEEP?
THIS IS THE TRAITOR WHO AKANE AND CLAY FOUGHT...
AKANE ALSO MENTIONED THERE BEING SOMETHING OFF ABOUT HIM...
GOFU (WHOMP)
I DID A BACKGROUND CHECK, BUT NOT ONLY WAS THERE NO CRIMINAL RECORD ON ANY OF THEM...
...NONE OF THEM HAVE HAD ANY COMBAT OR MILITARY TRAINING THAT MIGHT HAVE TURNED THEM INTO TRAITORS, EAGER TO TEST THEIR SKILLS.
JUST YOUR AVERAGE, HARMLESS CITIZENS...
I SEE. SO YOU'RE SAYING THEY JUST SUDDENLY CHANGED ENTIRELY...
AND THEN THERE'S THE MATTER OF THE INSOMNIA...

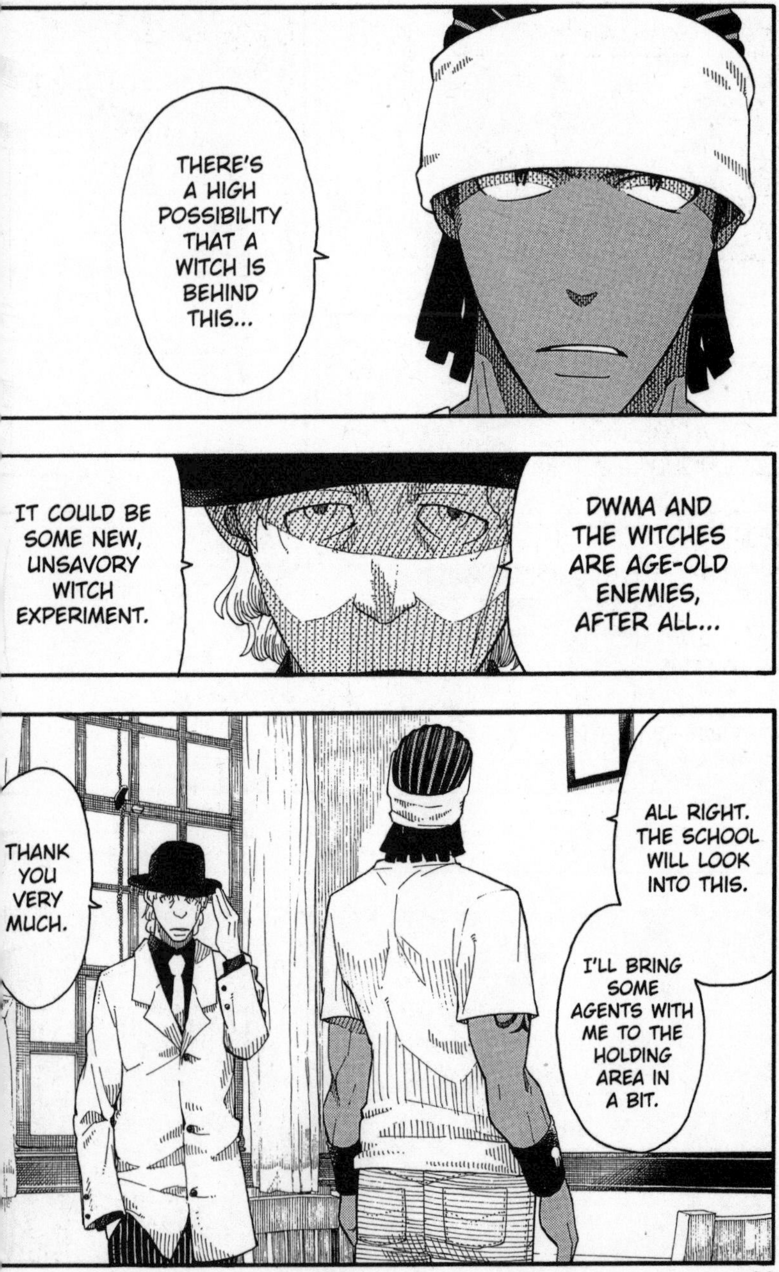
THERE'S A HIGH POSSIBILITY THAT A WITCH IS BEHIND THIS...
DWMA AND THE WITCHES ARE AGE-OLD ENEMIES, AFTER ALL...
IT COULD BE SOME NEW, UNSAVORY WITCH EXPERIMENT.
ALL RIGHT. THE SCHOOL WILL LOOK INTO THIS.
I'LL BRING SOME AGENTS WITH ME TO THE HOLDING AREA IN A BIT.
THANK YOU VERY MUCH.

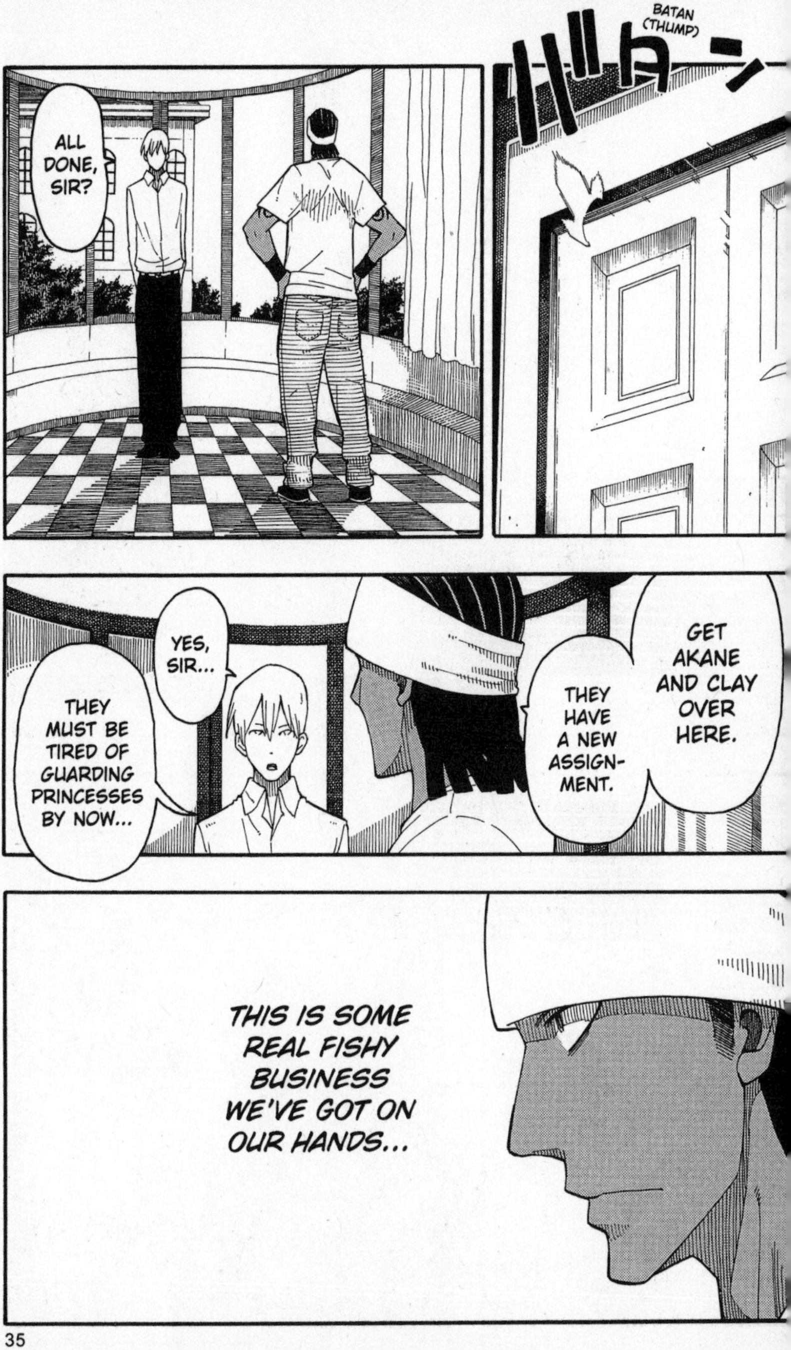
BATAN (THUMP)
ALL DONE, SIR?
GET AKANE AND CLAY OVER HERE.
THEY HAVE A NEW ASSIGNMENT.
YES, SIR...
THEY MUST BE TIRED OF GUARDING PRINCESSES BY NOW...
THIS IS SOME REAL FISHY BUSINESS WE'VE GOT ON OUR HANDS...

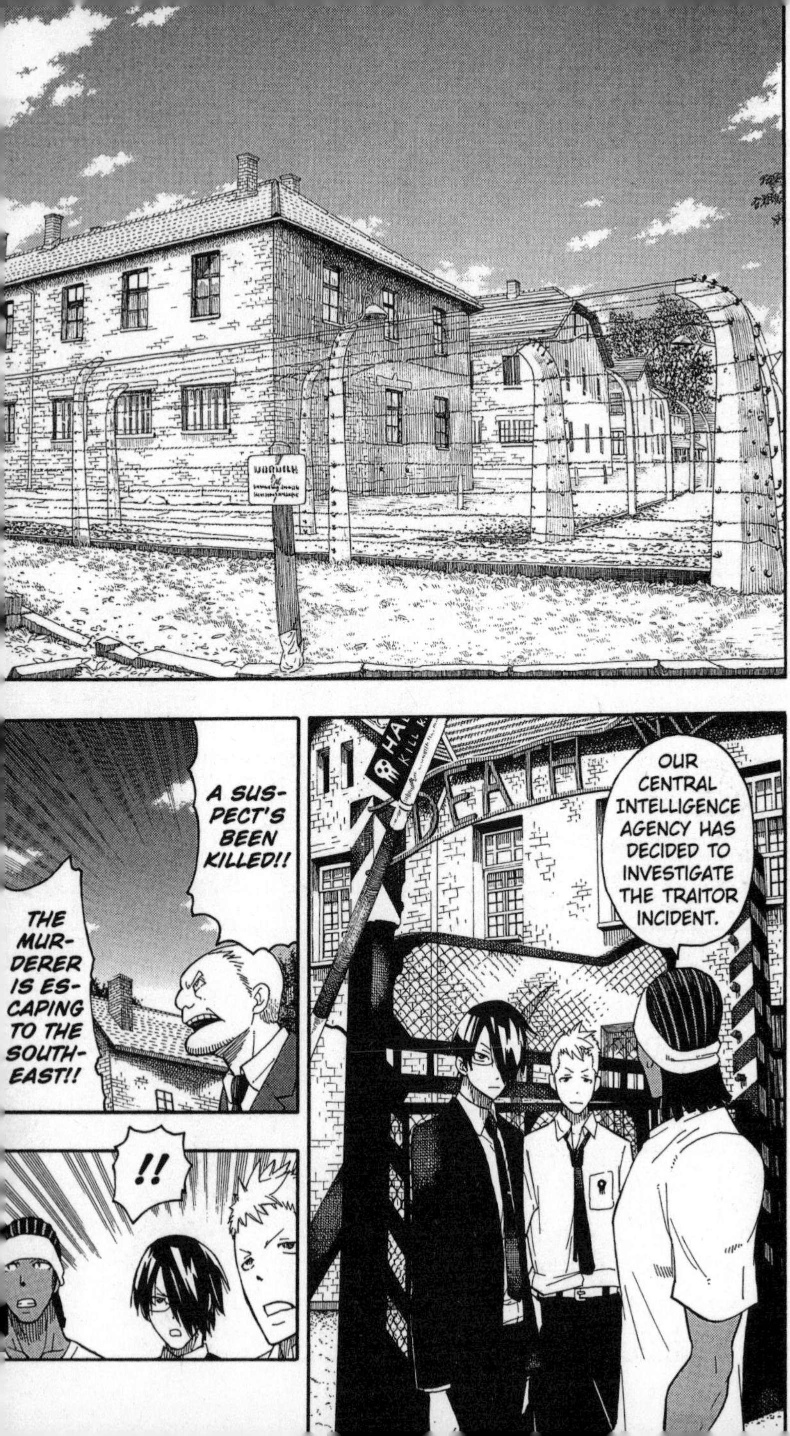
OUR CENTRAL INTELLIGENCE AGENCY HAS DECIDED TO INVESTIGATE THE TRAITOR INCIDENT.
A SUS-PECT'S BEEN KILLED!!
THE MUR-DERER IS ES-CAPING TO THE SOUTH-EAST!!
!!

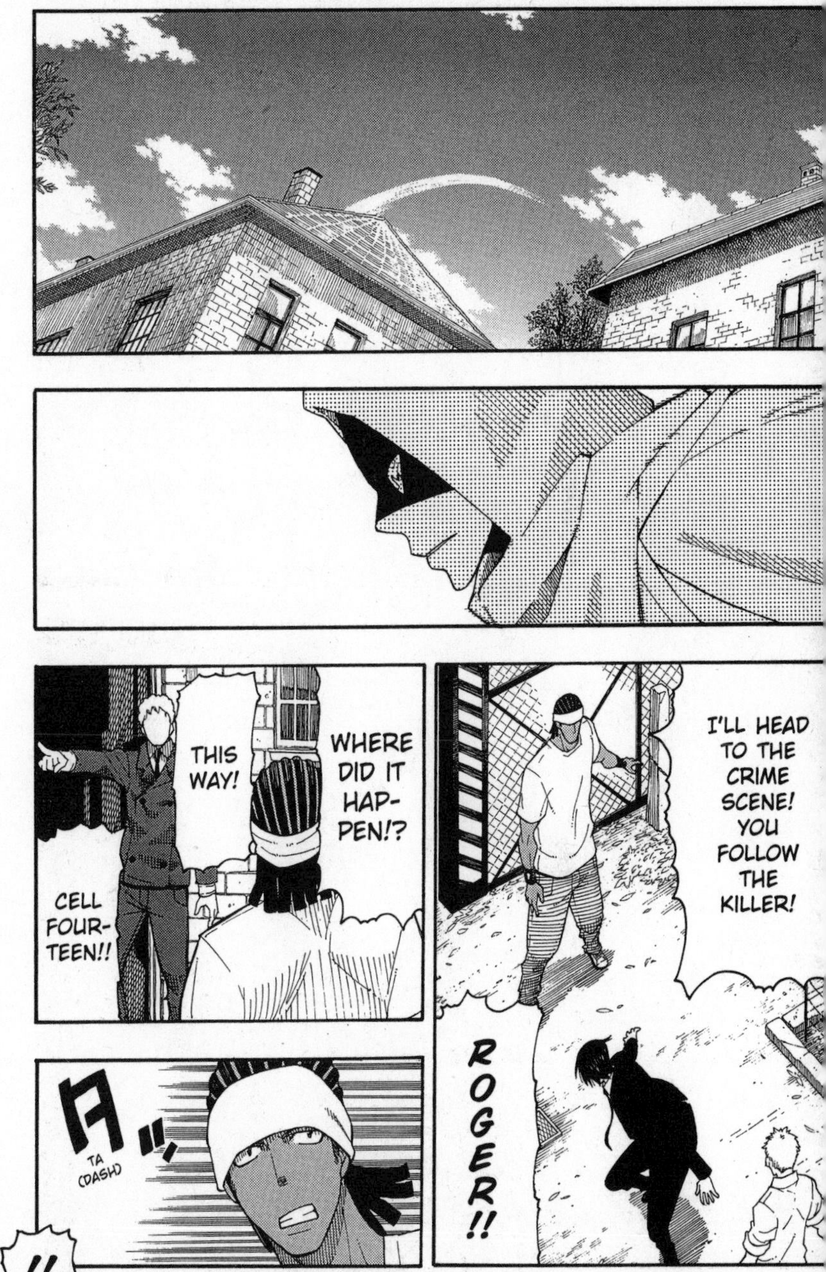
I'LL HEAD TO THE CRIME SCENE! YOU FOLLOW THE KILLER!
ROGER!!
WHERE DID IT HAPPEN!?
THIS WAY!
CELL FOURTEEN!!
TA (DASH)
!!

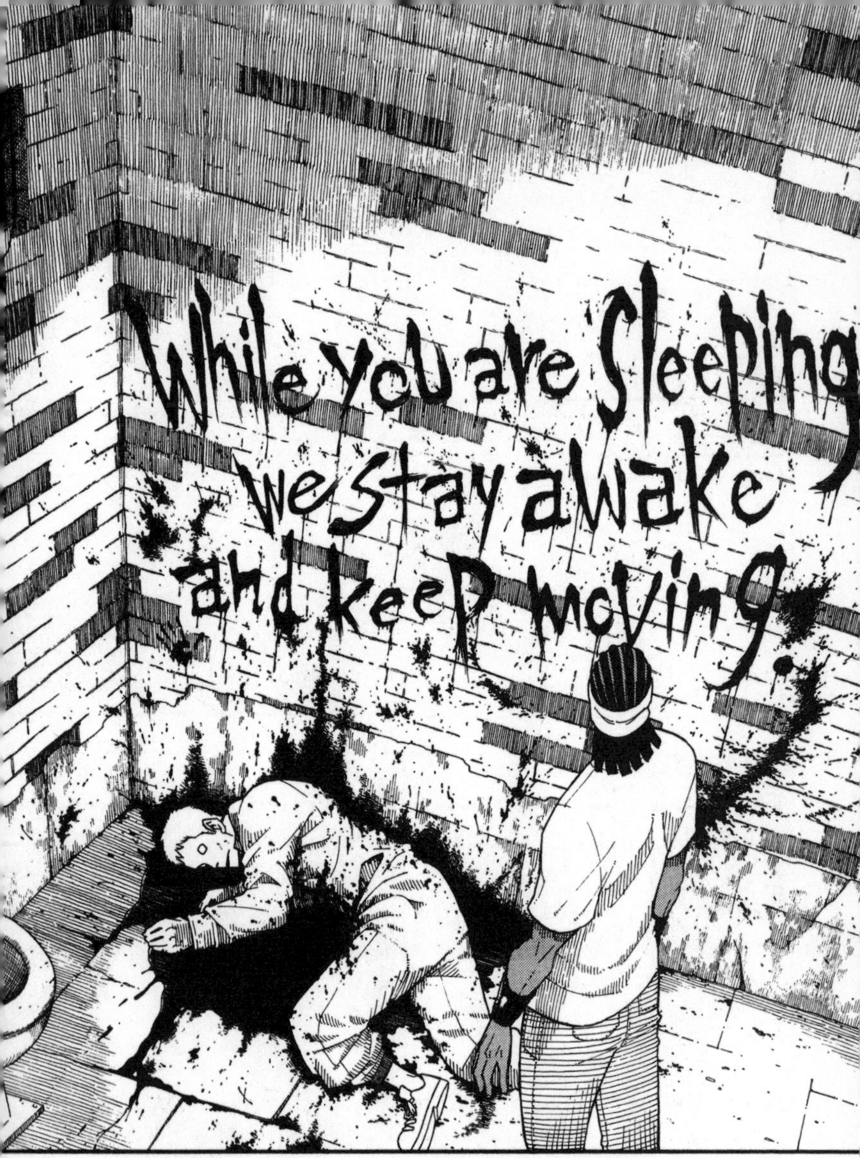
While you are Sleeping
we Stay awake
and keep moving.

WHILE YOU ARE SLEEPING,
WE STAY AWAKE AND KEEP MOVING.

TWO!

ONE!

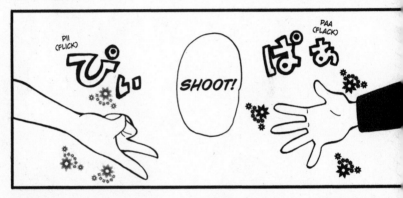

PII (FLICK)

SHOOT!

PAA (FLACK)

HYOI (ZWIP)

...THAT WAY!

!!

HYUI (SWOOSH)

TURN...

SOUL EATER NOT!

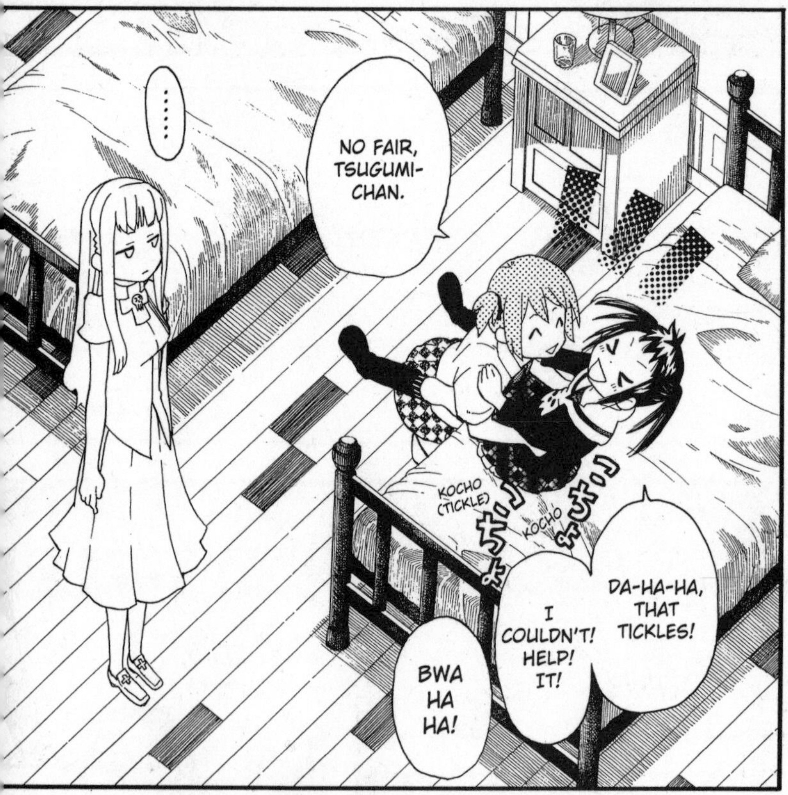
NO FAIR, TSUGUMI-CHAN.
......
KOCHO (TICKLE)
KOCHO
DA-HA-HA, THAT TICKLES!
I COULDN'T! HELP! IT!
BWA HA HA!

CHAPTER 8: INVITATION!

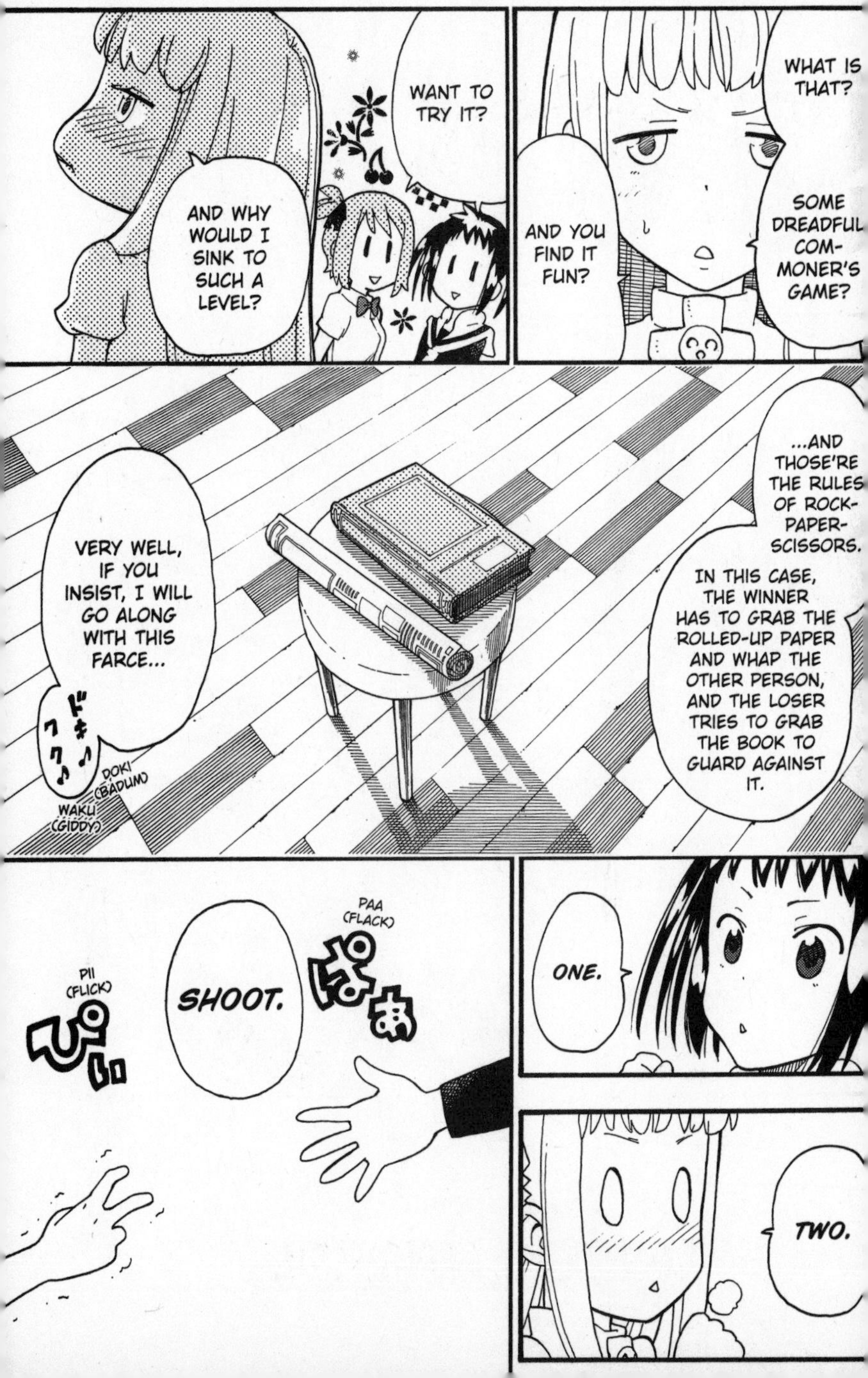
WHAT IS THAT?
SOME DREADFUL COMMONER'S GAME?
AND YOU FIND IT FUN?
WANT TO TRY IT?
AND WHY WOULD I SINK TO SUCH A LEVEL?
...AND THOSE'RE THE RULES OF ROCK-PAPER-SCISSORS.
IN THIS CASE, THE WINNER HAS TO GRAB THE ROLLED-UP PAPER AND WHAP THE OTHER PERSON, AND THE LOSER TRIES TO GRAB THE BOOK TO GUARD AGAINST IT.
VERY WELL, IF YOU INSIST, I WILL GO ALONG WITH THIS FARCE...
DOKI (BADUM)
WAKU (GIDDY)
ONE.
TWO.
PAA (FLACK)
SHOOT.
PII (FLICK)

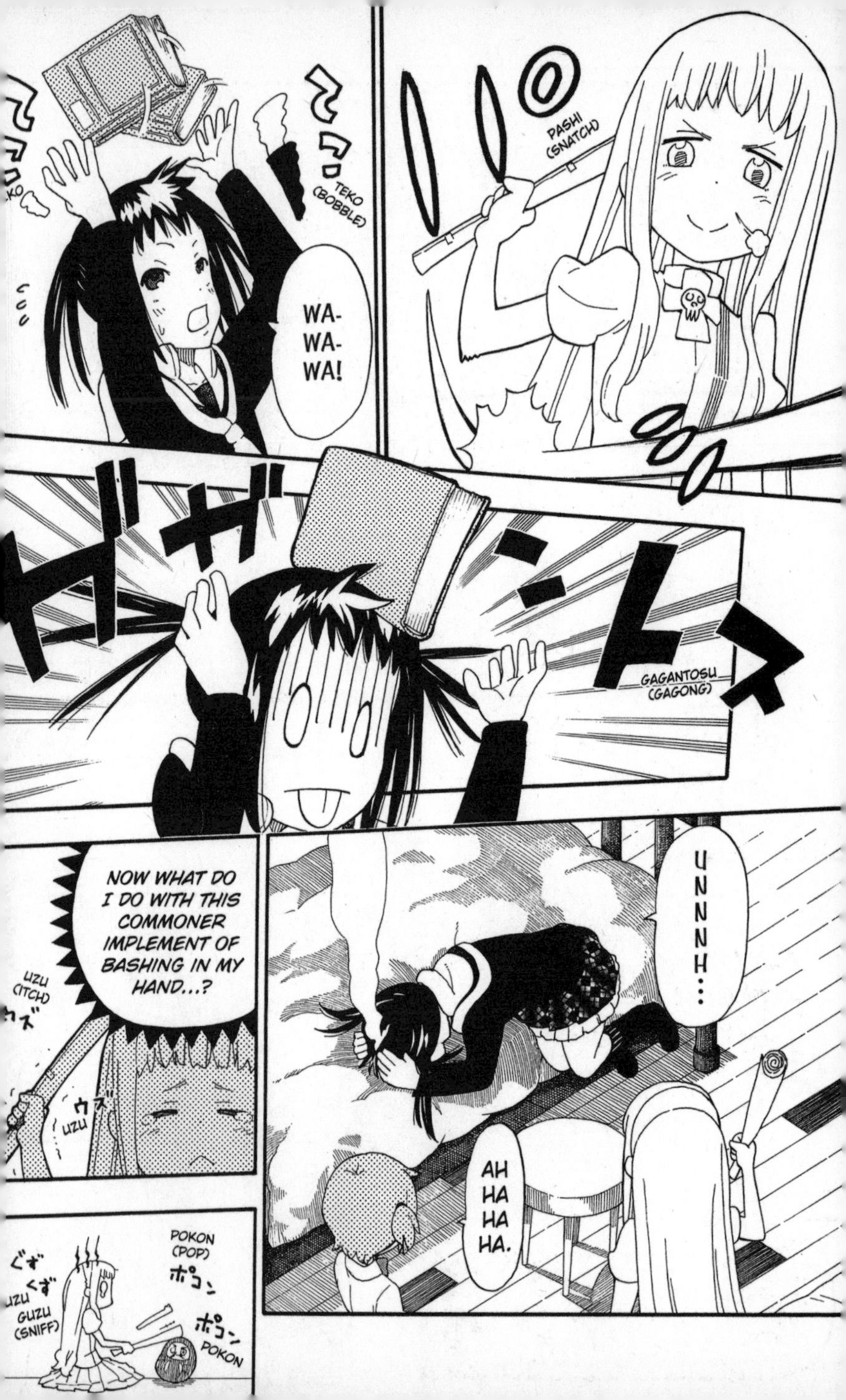
PASHI (SNATCH)
TEKO (BOBBLE)
WA-WA-WA!
GAGANTOSU (GAGONG)
UNNNH...
AH HA HA HA.
NOW WHAT DO I DO WITH THIS COMMONER IMPLEMENT OF BASHING IN MY HAND...?
UZU (ITCH)
UZU
POKON (POP)
ポコン
ポコン
POKON
ぐず ぐず
GUZU (SNIFF)

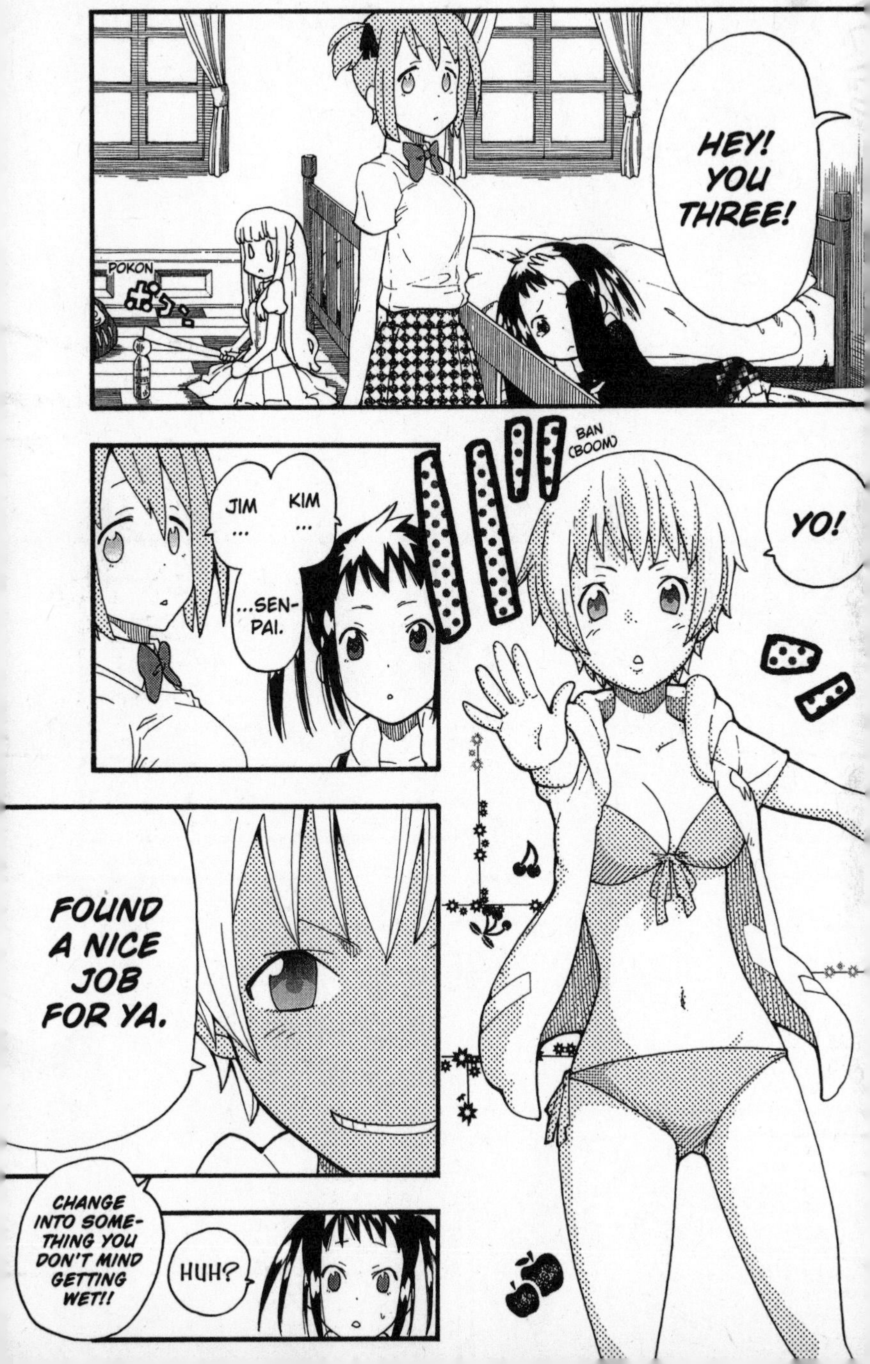
HEY! YOU THREE!
POKON
BAN (BOOM)
YO!
JIM ... KIM ...
...SEN-PAI.
FOUND A NICE JOB FOR YA.
HUH?
CHANGE INTO SOME-THING YOU DON'T MIND GETTING WET!!

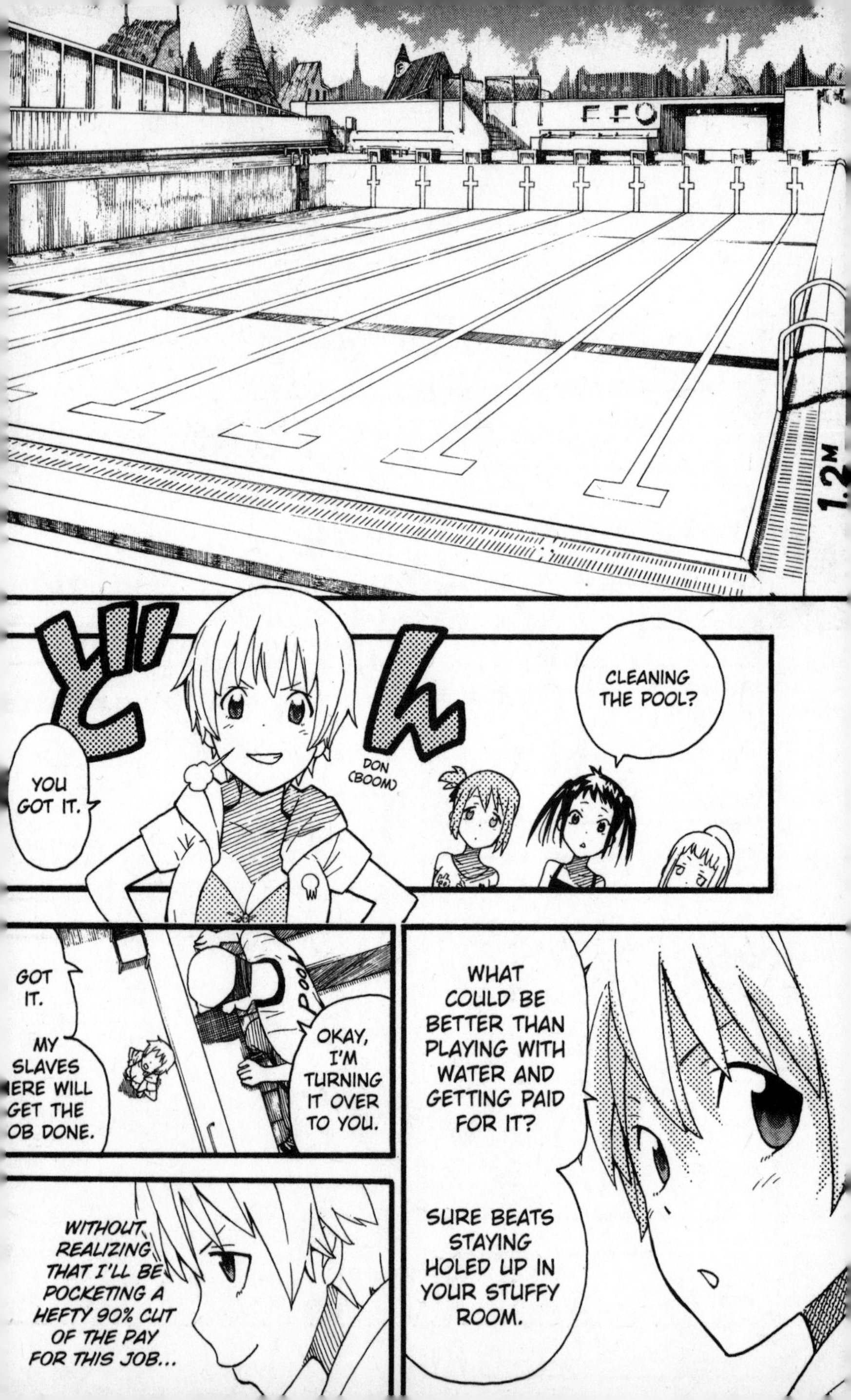
1.2M
CLEANING THE POOL?
DON (BOOM)
YOU GOT IT.
WHAT COULD BE BETTER THAN PLAYING WITH WATER AND GETTING PAID FOR IT?
SURE BEATS STAYING HOLED UP IN YOUR STUFFY ROOM.
OKAY, I'M TURNING IT OVER TO YOU.
Pool
GOT IT.
MY SLAVES IERE WILL GET THE OB DONE.
WITHOUT REALIZING THAT I'LL BE POCKETING A HEFTY 90% CUT OF THE PAY FOR THIS JOB...

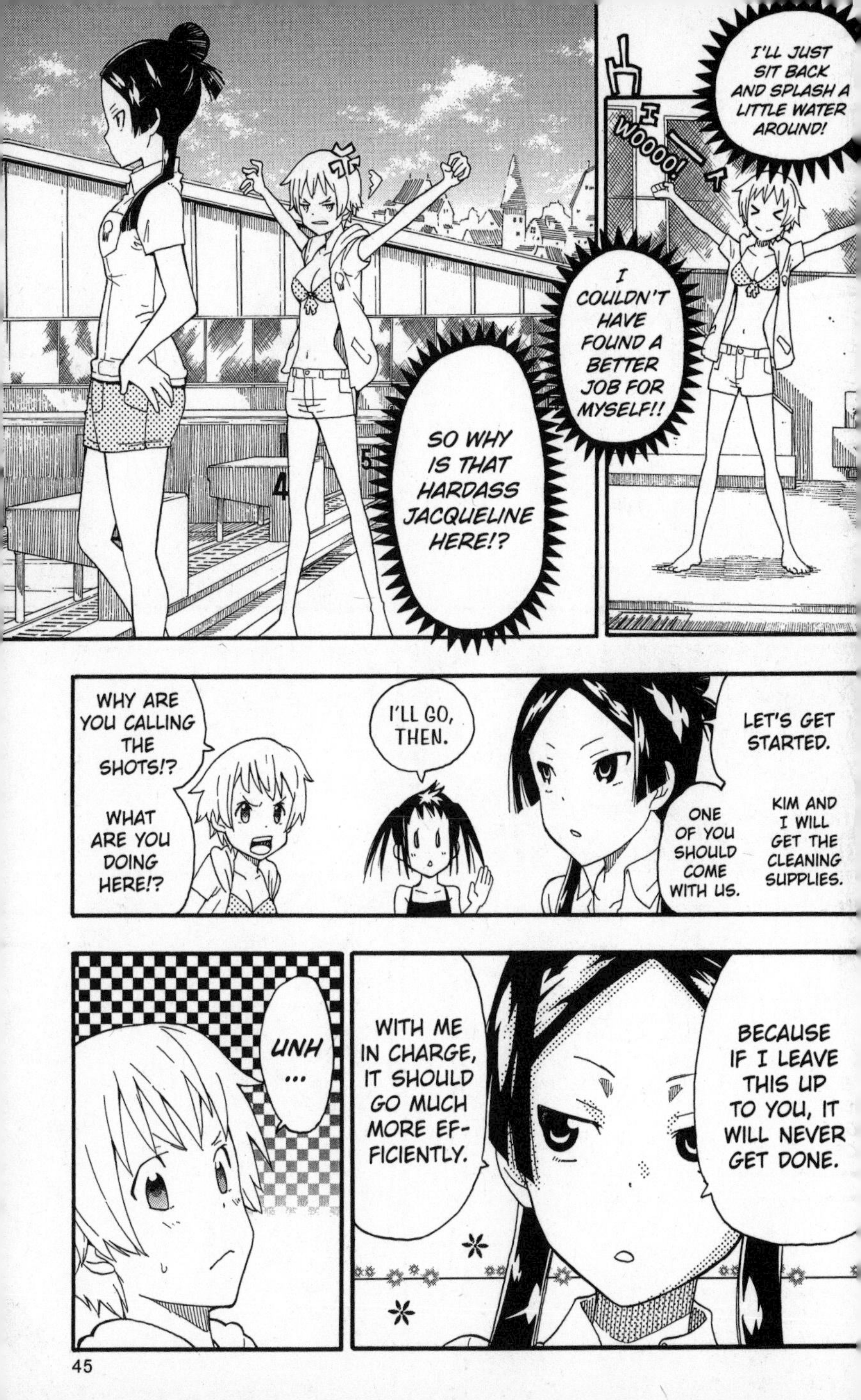
I'LL JUST SIT BACK AND SPLASH A LITTLE WATER AROUND!
WOOOO!
I COULDN'T HAVE FOUND A BETTER JOB FOR MYSELF!!
SO WHY IS THAT HARDASS JACQUELINE HERE!?
LET'S GET STARTED.
KIM AND I WILL GET THE CLEANING SUPPLIES.
ONE OF YOU SHOULD COME WITH US.
I'LL GO, THEN.
WHY ARE YOU CALLING THE SHOTS!?
WHAT ARE YOU DOING HERE!?
BECAUSE IF I LEAVE THIS UP TO YOU, IT WILL NEVER GET DONE.
WITH ME IN CHARGE, IT SHOULD GO MUCH MORE EF-FICIENTLY.
UNH ...

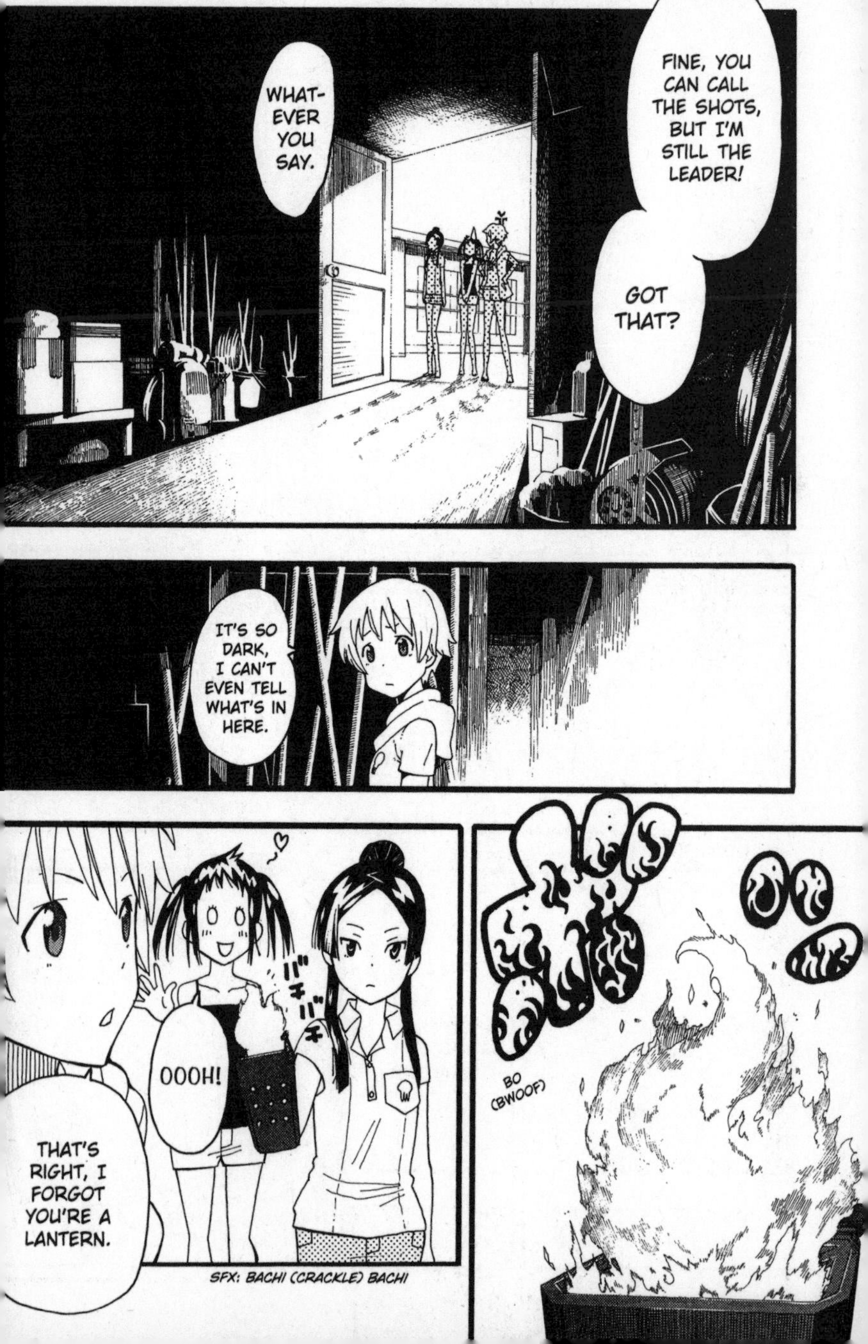
FINE, YOU CAN CALL THE SHOTS, BUT I'M STILL THE LEADER!
GOT THAT?
WHAT-EVER YOU SAY.
IT'S SO DARK, I CAN'T EVEN TELL WHAT'S IN HERE.
BO (BWOOF)
OOOH!
THAT'S RIGHT, I FORGOT YOU'RE A LANTERN.
SFX: BACHI (CRACKLE) BACHI

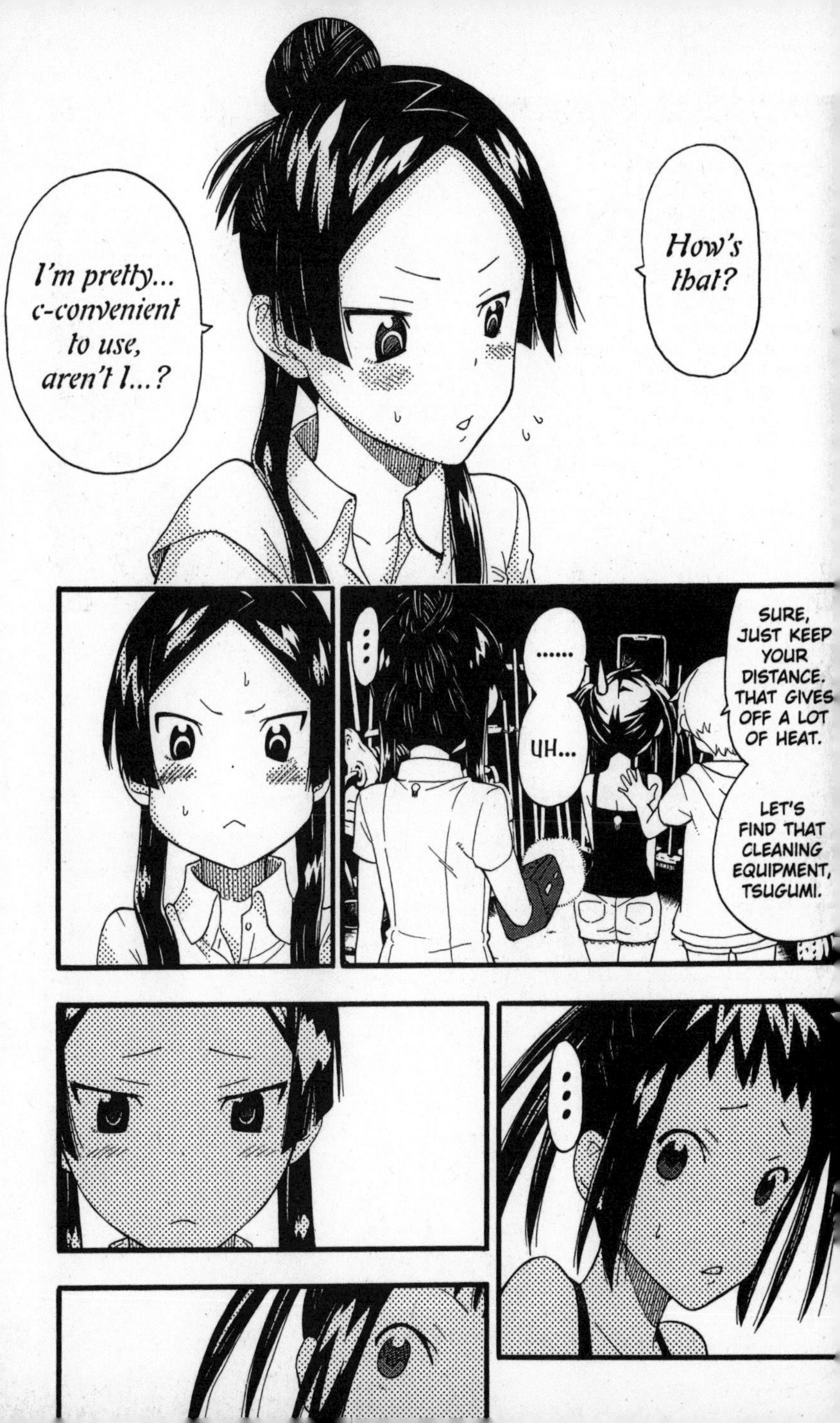
How's that?
I'm pretty... c-convenient to use, aren't I...?
SURE, JUST KEEP YOUR DISTANCE. THAT GIVES OFF A LOT OF HEAT.
......
LET'S FIND THAT CLEANING EQUIPMENT, TSUGUMI.
UH...
...
...

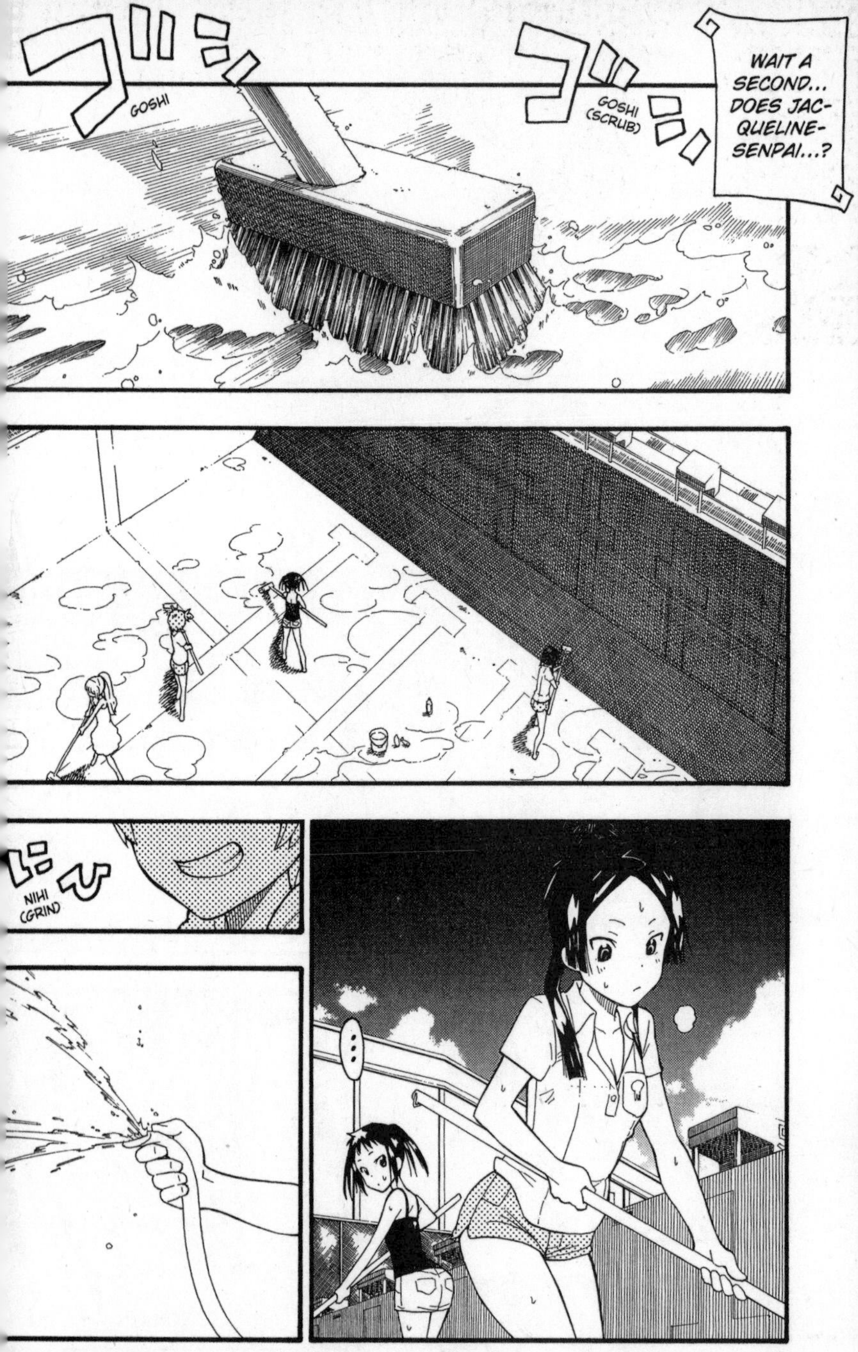
WAIT A SECOND... DOES JACQUELINE-SENPAI...?
GOSHI (SCRUB)
GOSHI
NIHI (GRIN)

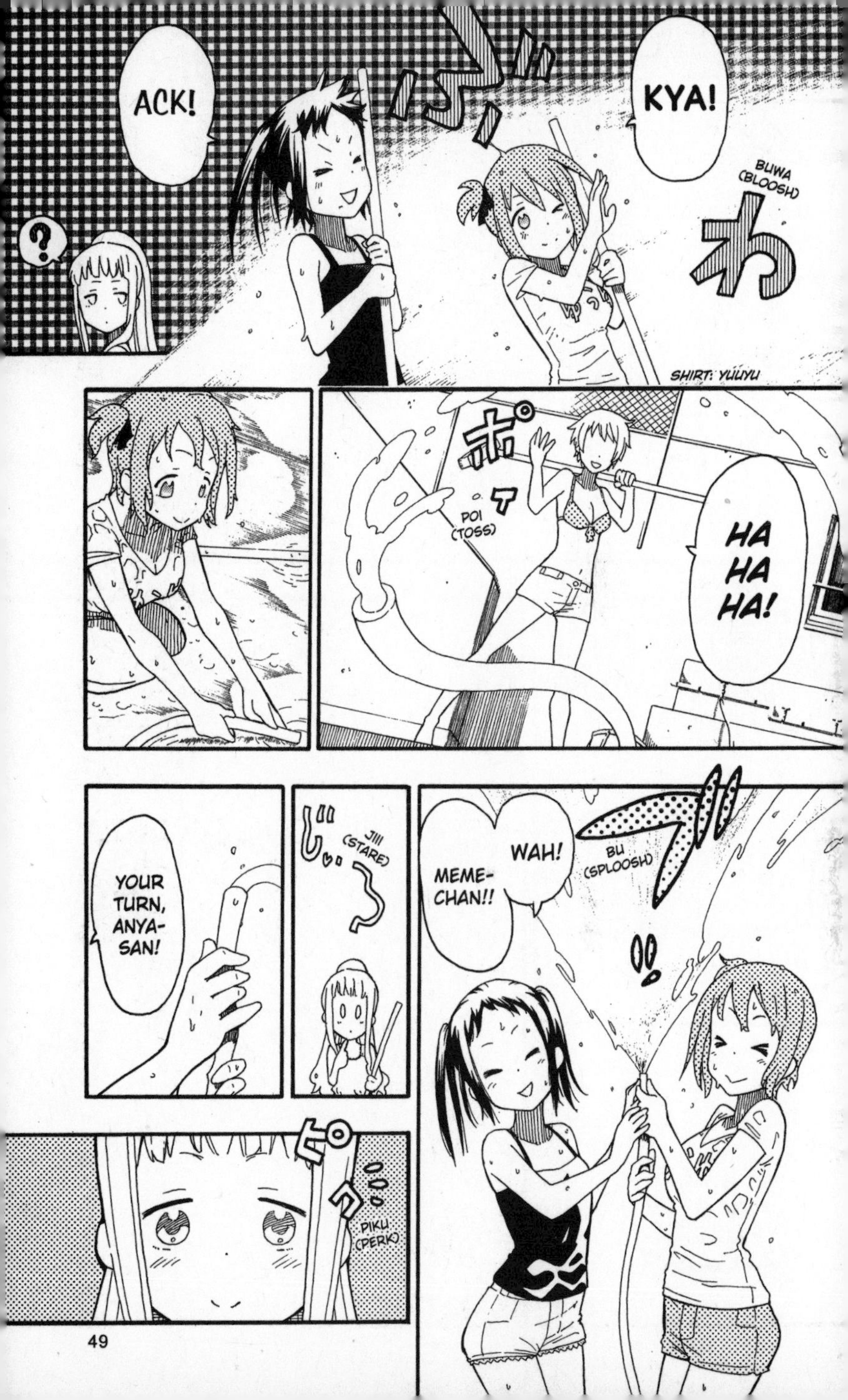
KYA!
BUWA (BLOOSH)
ACK!
?
SHIRT: YUUYU
HA HA HA!
POI (TOSS)
BU (SPLOOSH)
WAH!
MEME-CHAN!!
!!
JIII (STARE)
YOUR TURN, ANYA-SAN!
PIKU (PERK)

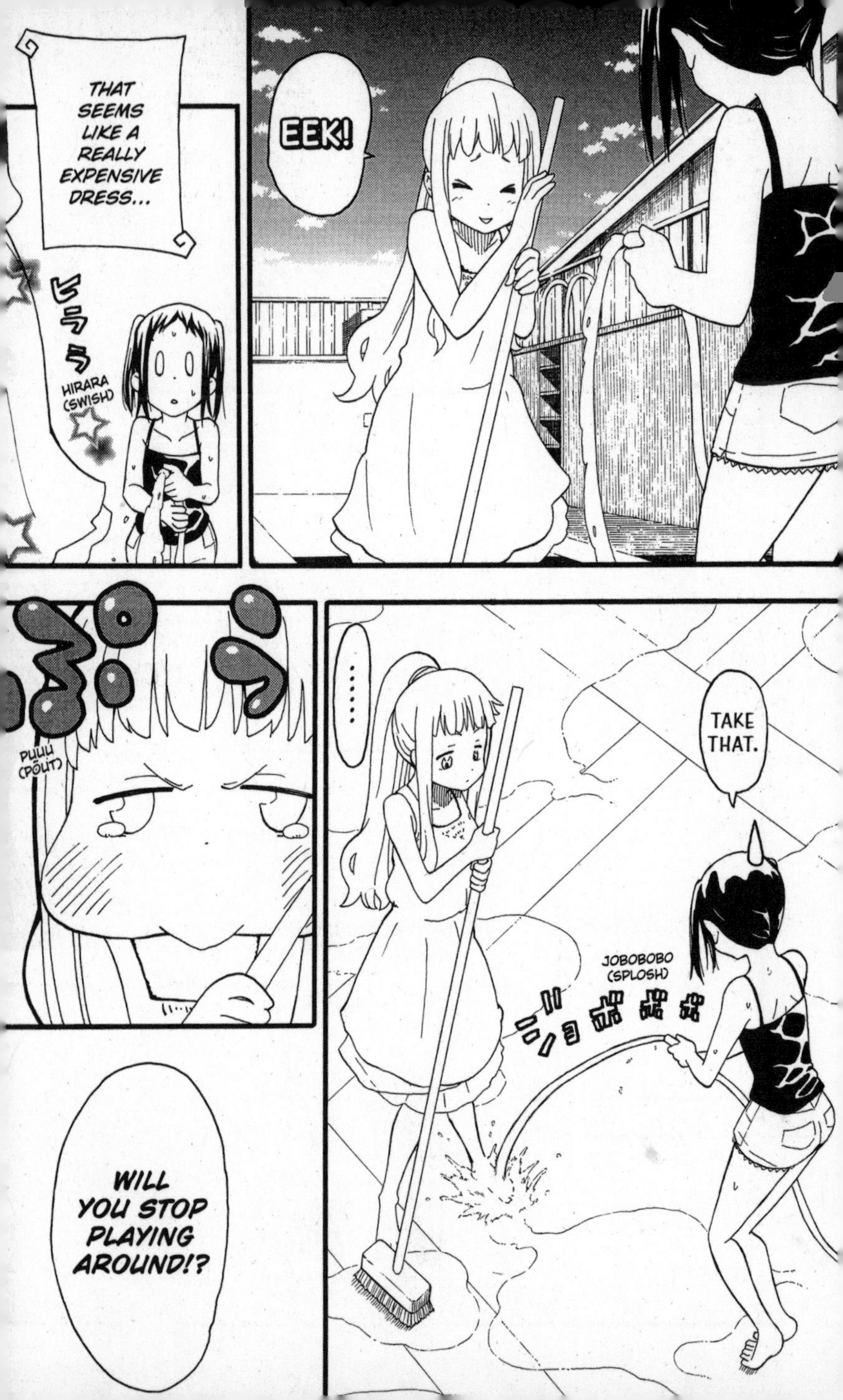
EEK!
THAT SEEMS LIKE A REALLY EXPENSIVE DRESS...
HIRARA (SWISH)
......
TAKE THAT.
JOBOBOBO (SPLOSH)
PUUU (POUT)
WILL YOU STOP PLAYING AROUND!?

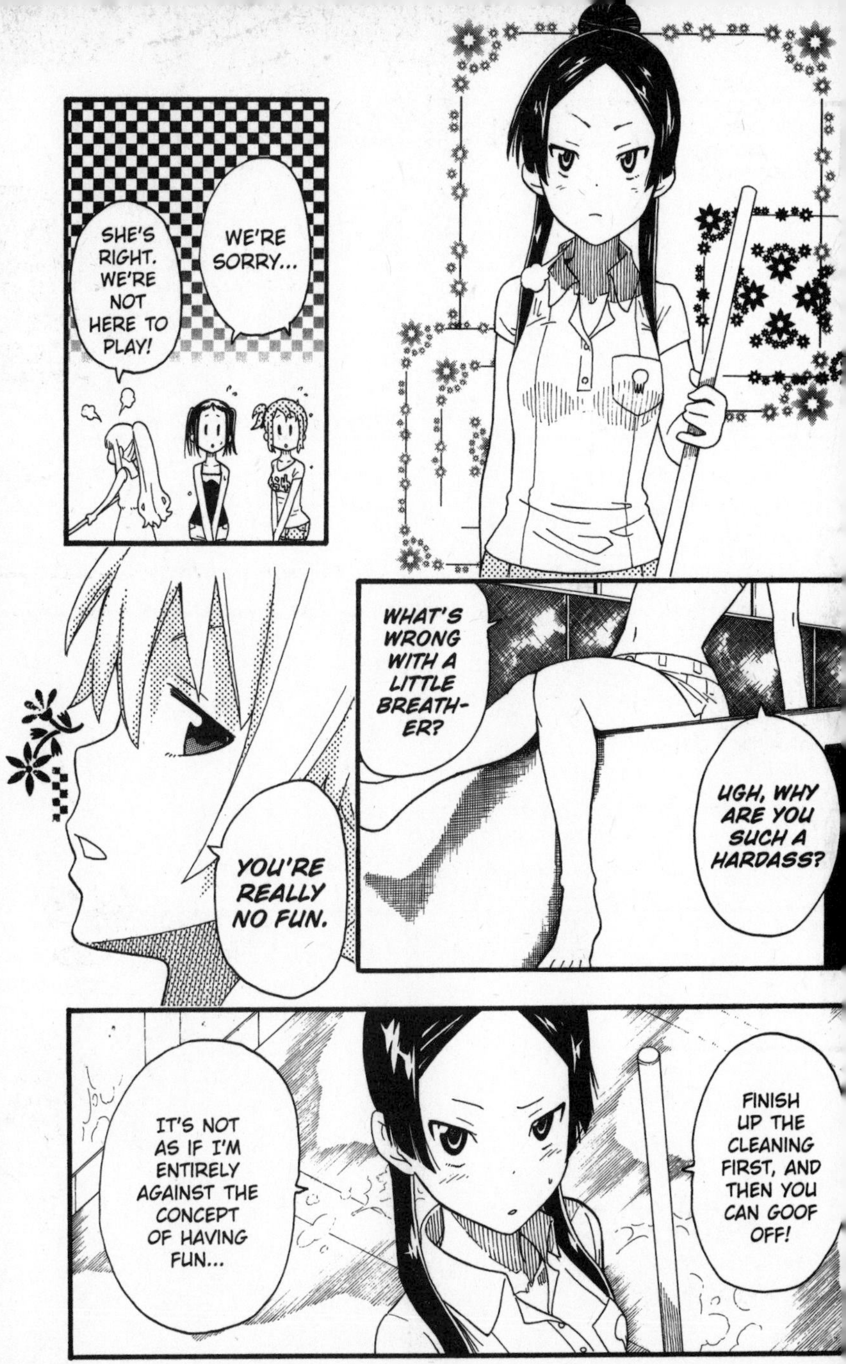

WE'RE SORRY...
SHE'S RIGHT. WE'RE NOT HERE TO PLAY!
WHAT'S WRONG WITH A LITTLE BREATHER?
UGH, WHY ARE YOU SUCH A HARDASS?
YOU'RE REALLY NO FUN.
FINISH UP THE CLEANING FIRST, AND THEN YOU CAN GOOF OFF!
IT'S NOT AS IF I'M ENTIRELY AGAINST THE CONCEPT OF HAVING FUN...

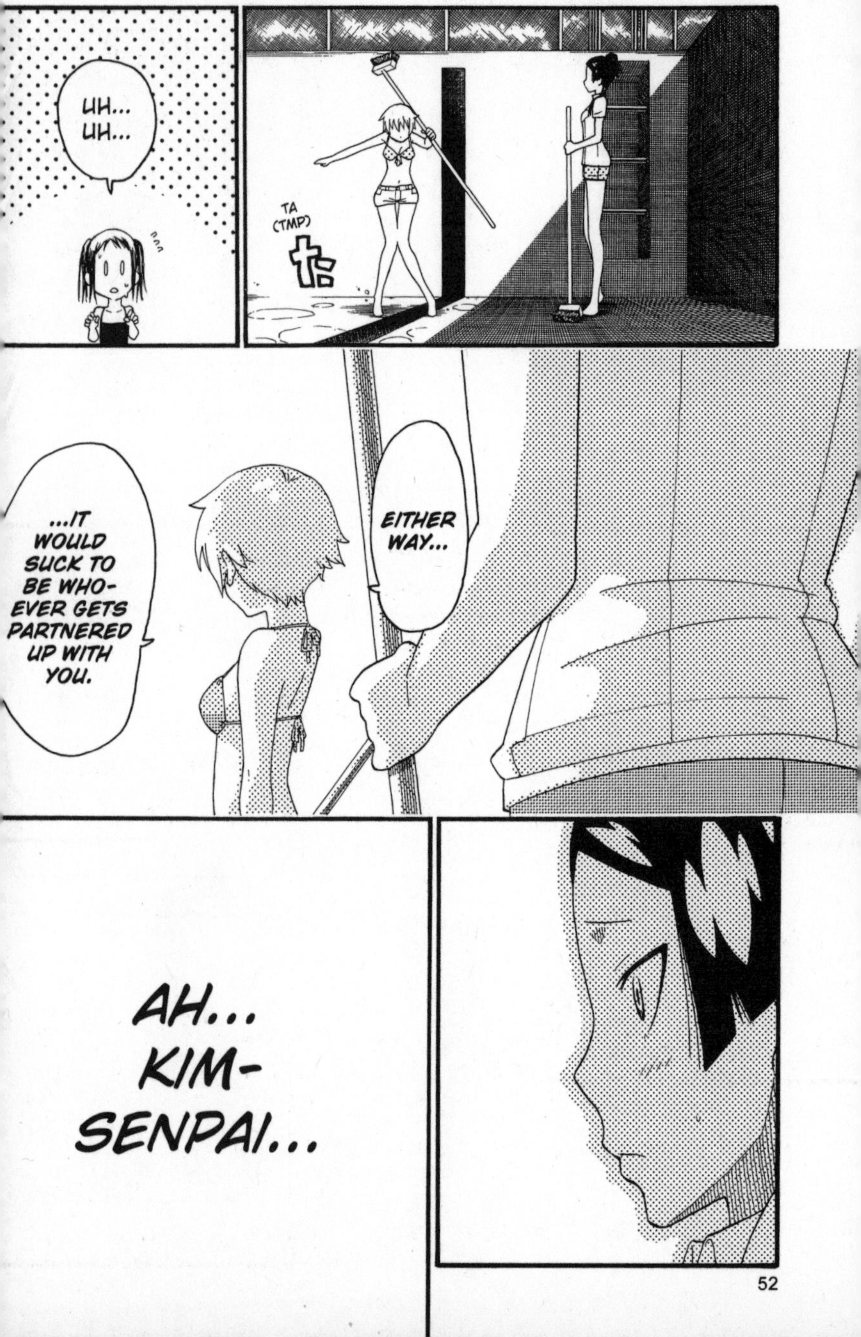
TA (TMP)
UH... UH...
EITHER WAY...
...IT WOULD SUCK TO BE WHO-EVER GETS PARTNERED UP WITH YOU.
AH... KIM-SENPAI...

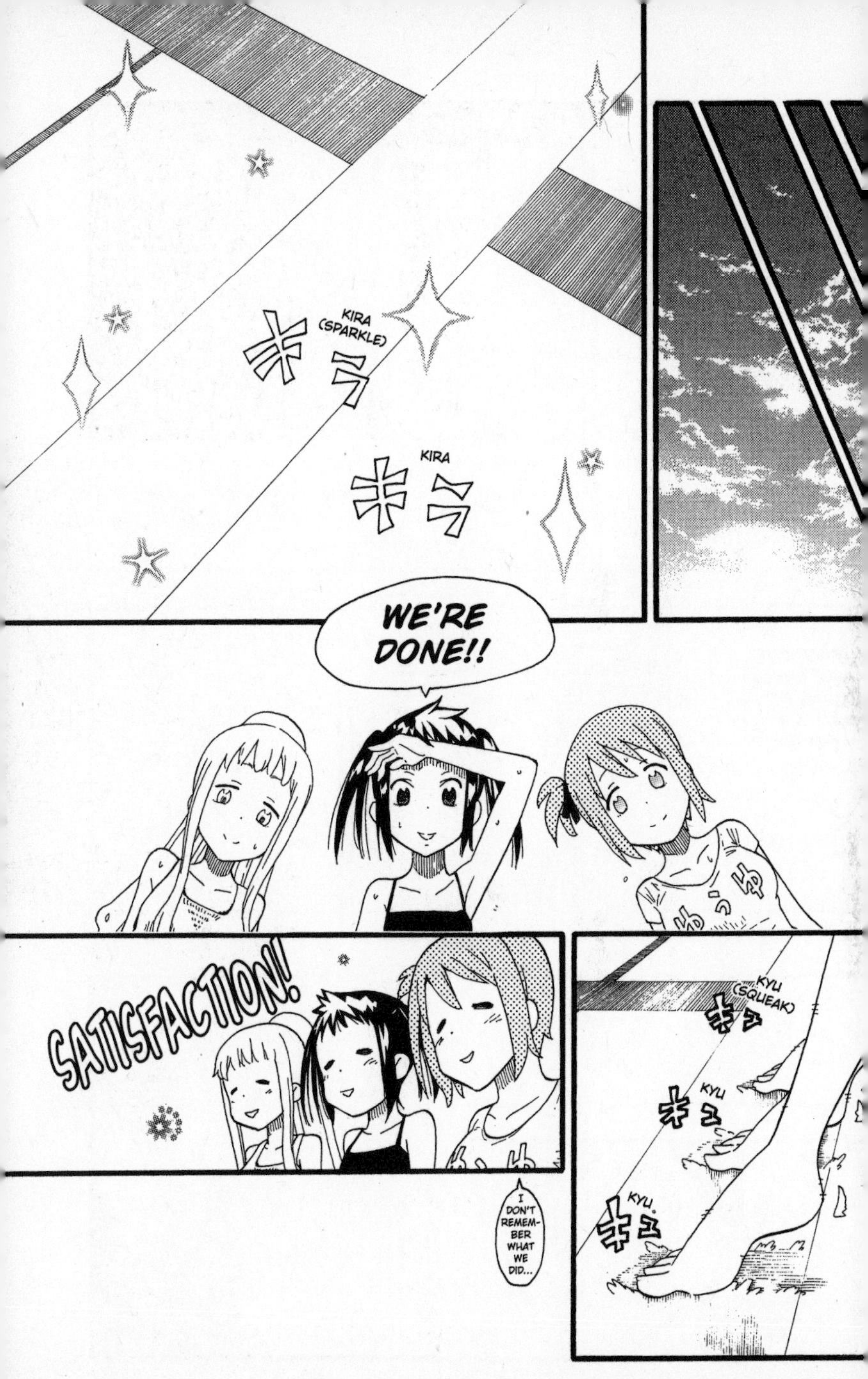

KIRA (SPARKLE)
キラ
KIRA
キラ
WE'RE DONE!!
KYU (SQUEAK)
キュ
KYU
キュ
KYU.
キュ
SATISFACTION!
I DON'T REMEMBER WHAT WE DID...

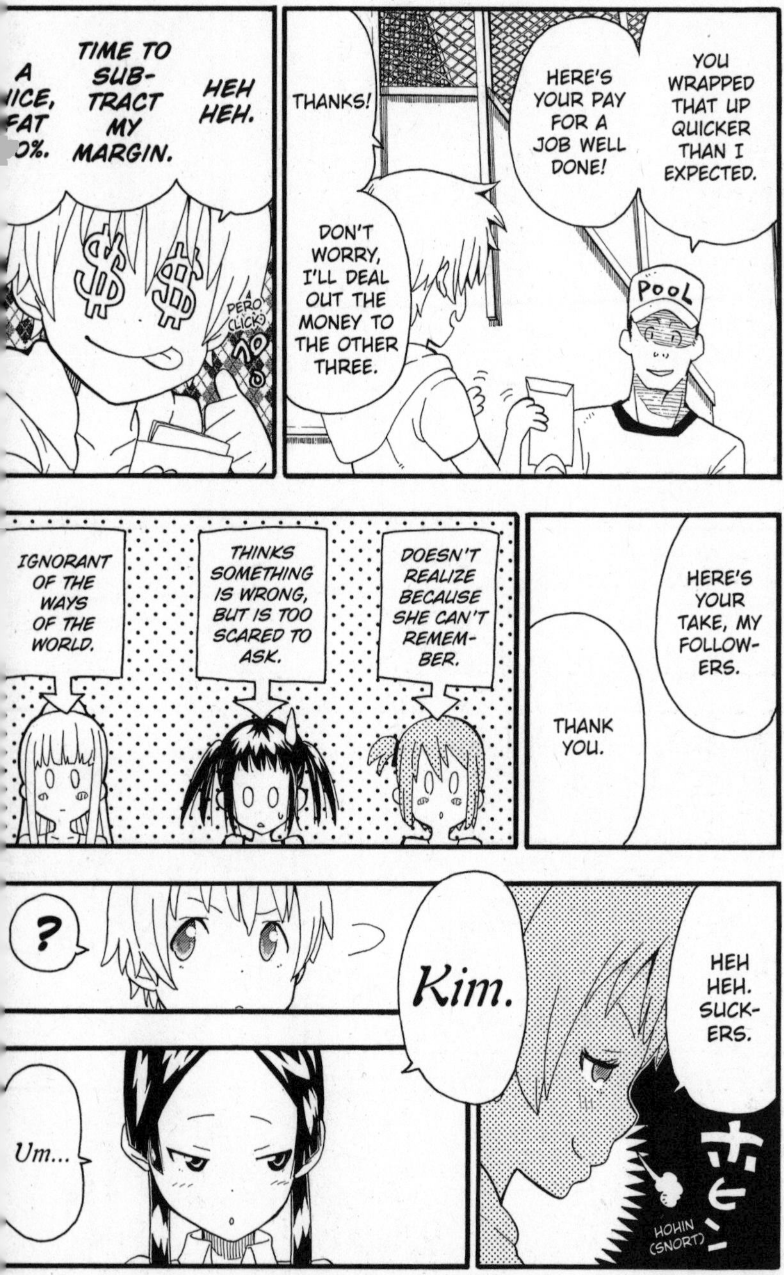
YOU WRAPPED THAT UP QUICKER THAN I EXPECTED.
HERE'S YOUR PAY FOR A JOB WELL DONE!
POOL
THANKS!
DON'T WORRY, I'LL DEAL OUT THE MONEY TO THE OTHER THREE.
HEH HEH.
TIME TO SUB-TRACT MY MARGIN.
PERO (CLICK)
HERE'S YOUR TAKE, MY FOLLOW-ERS.
THANK YOU.
DOESN'T REALIZE BECAUSE SHE CAN'T REMEM-BER.
THINKS SOMETHING IS WRONG, BUT IS TOO SCARED TO ASK.
IGNORANT OF THE WAYS OF THE WORLD.
HEH HEH. SUCK-ERS.
HOHIN (SNORT)
Kim.
?
Um...

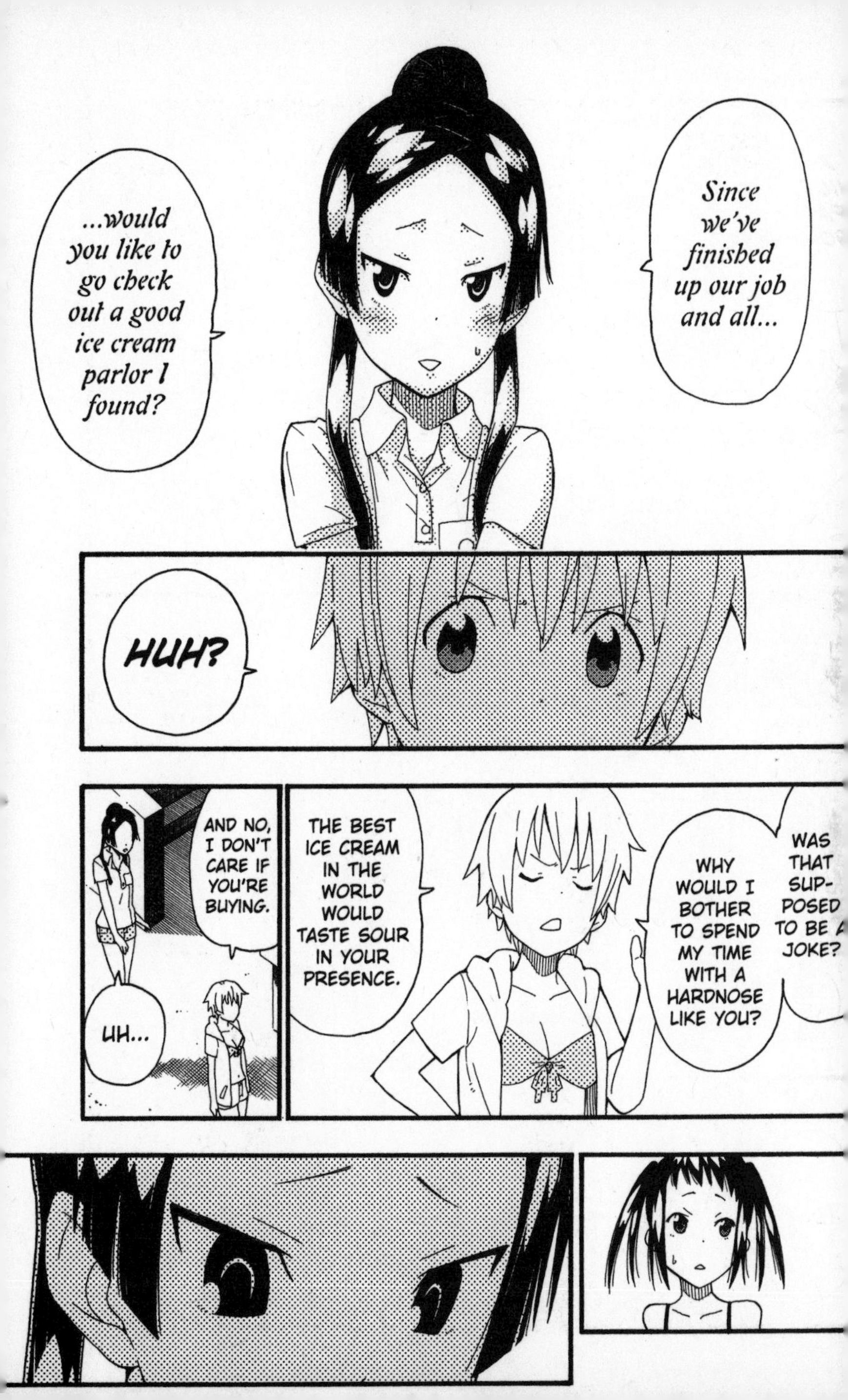
Since we've finished up our job and all...
...would you like to go check out a good ice cream parlor I found?
HUH?
WAS THAT SUP-POSED TO BE A JOKE?
WHY WOULD I BOTHER TO SPEND MY TIME WITH A HARDNOSE LIKE YOU?
THE BEST ICE CREAM IN THE WORLD WOULD TASTE SOUR IN YOUR PRESENCE.
AND NO, I DON'T CARE IF YOU'RE BUYING.
UH...

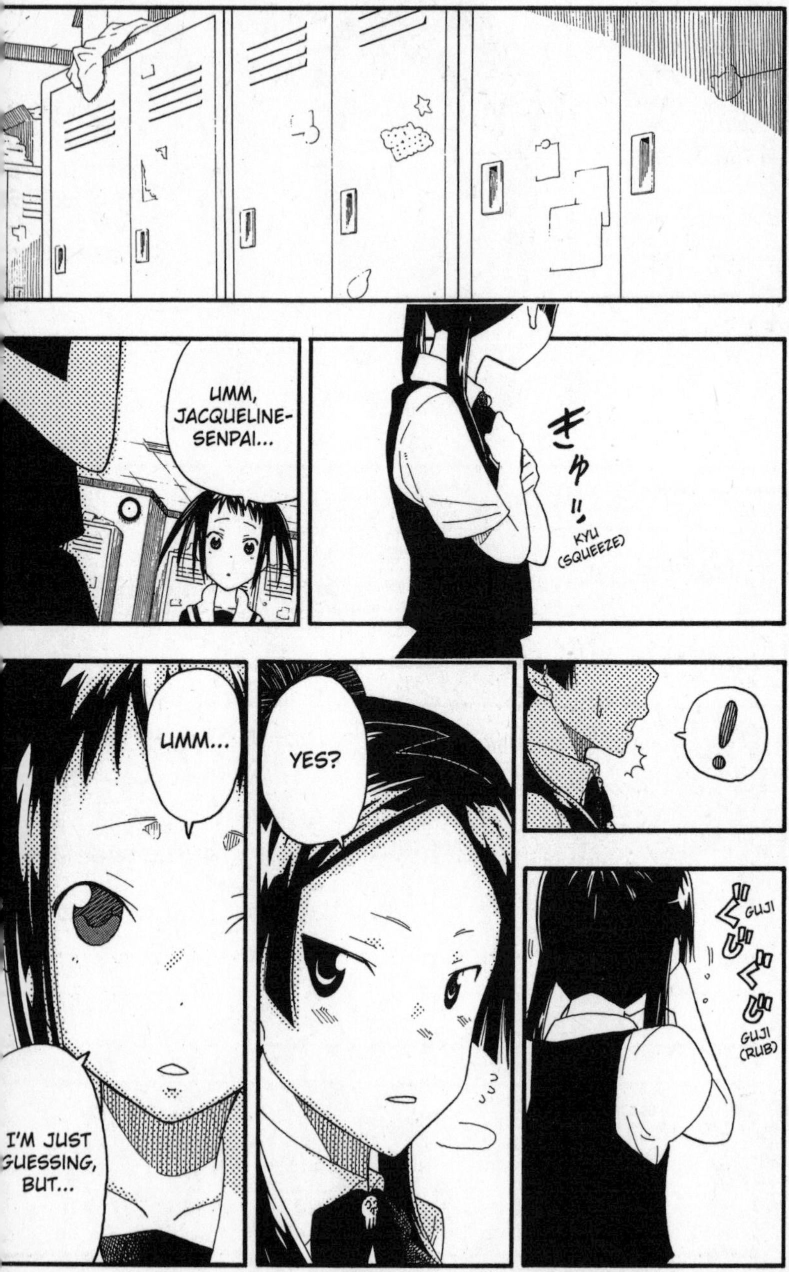

きゅ!!
KYU (SQUEEZE)
UMM, JACQUELINE-SENPAI...
!
ぐじぐじ
GUJI GUJI (RUB)
YES?
UMM...
I'M JUST GUESSING, BUT...

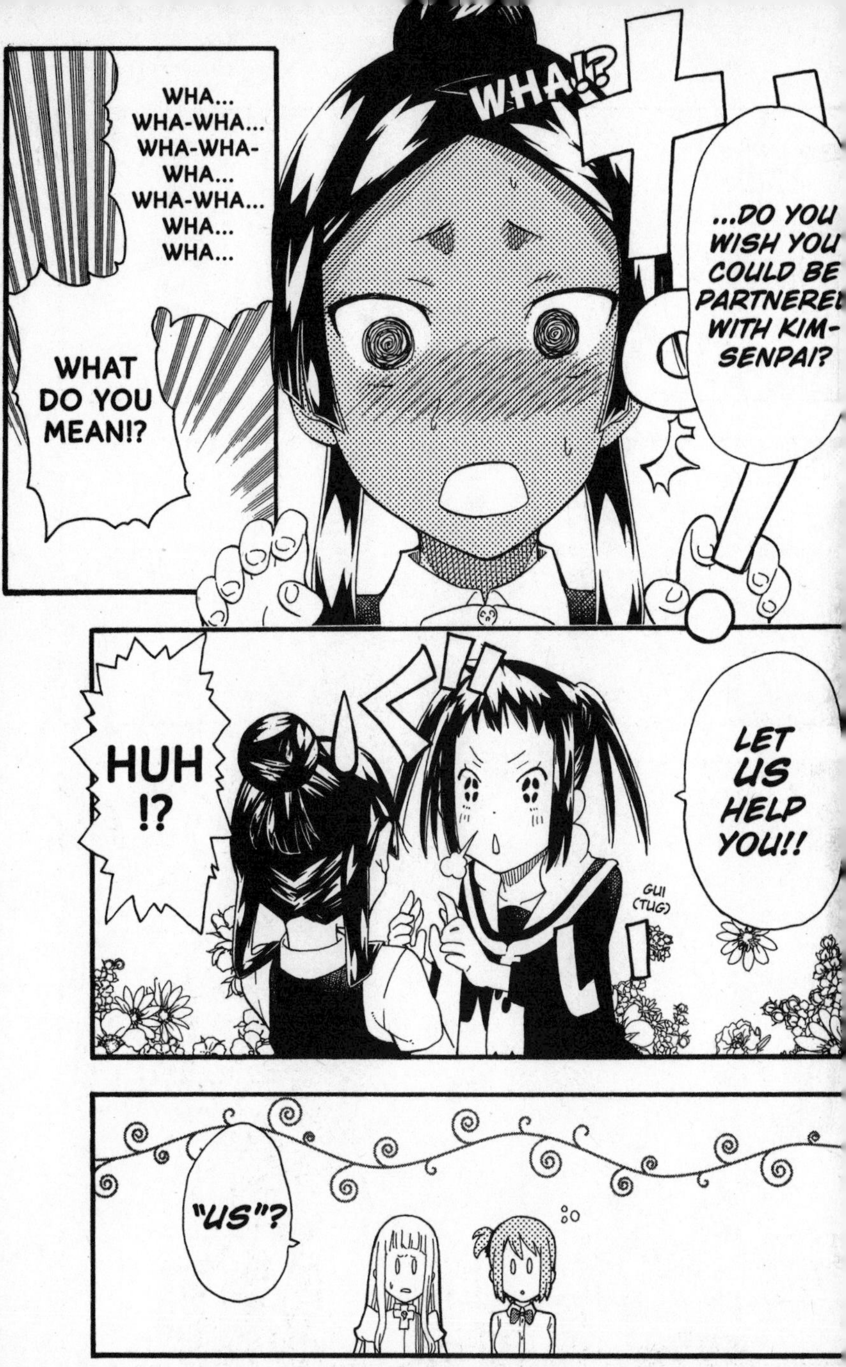
...DO YOU WISH YOU COULD BE PARTNERE WITH KIM-SENPAI?
WHA!?
WHA... WHA-WHA... WHA-WHA-WHA... WHA-WHA... WHA... WHA...
WHAT DO YOU MEAN!?
LET US HELP YOU!!
GUI (TUG)
HUH!?
"US"?

SOUL EATER NOT!

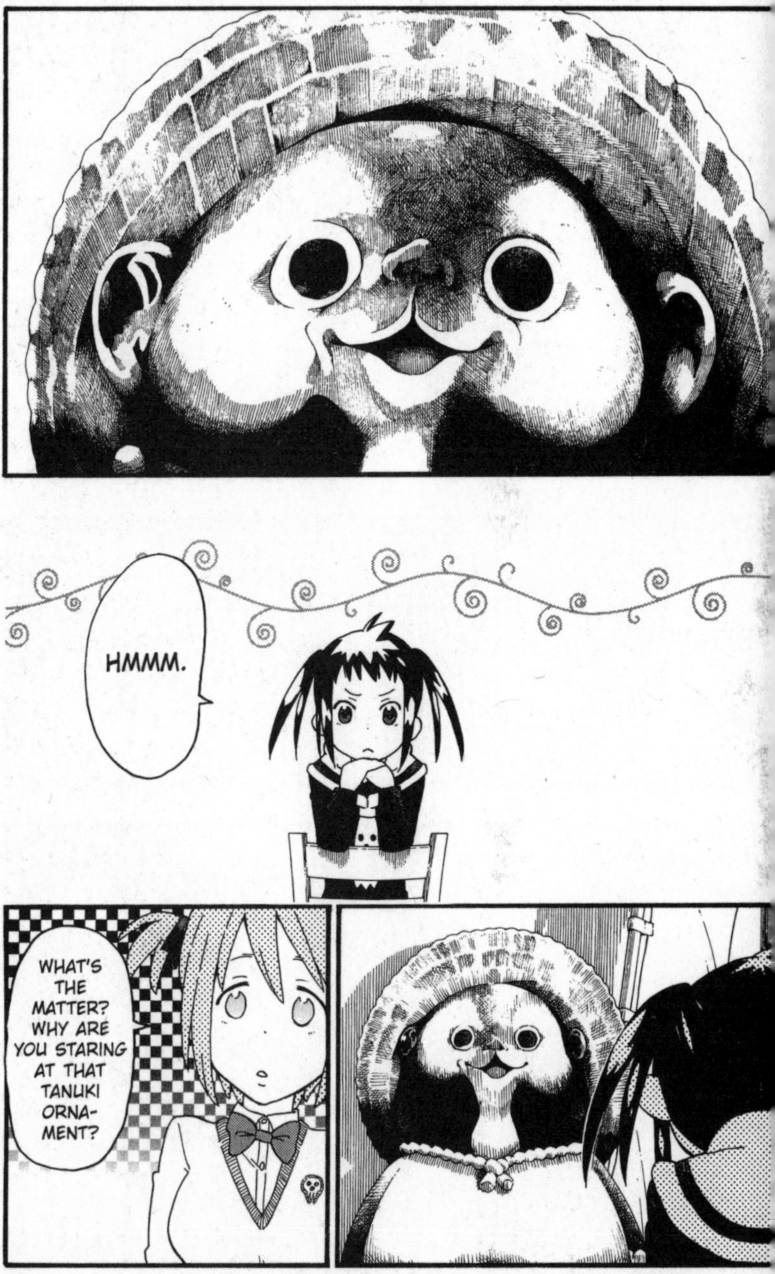
HMMM.
WHAT'S THE MATTER? WHY ARE YOU STARING AT THAT TANUKI ORNAMENT?

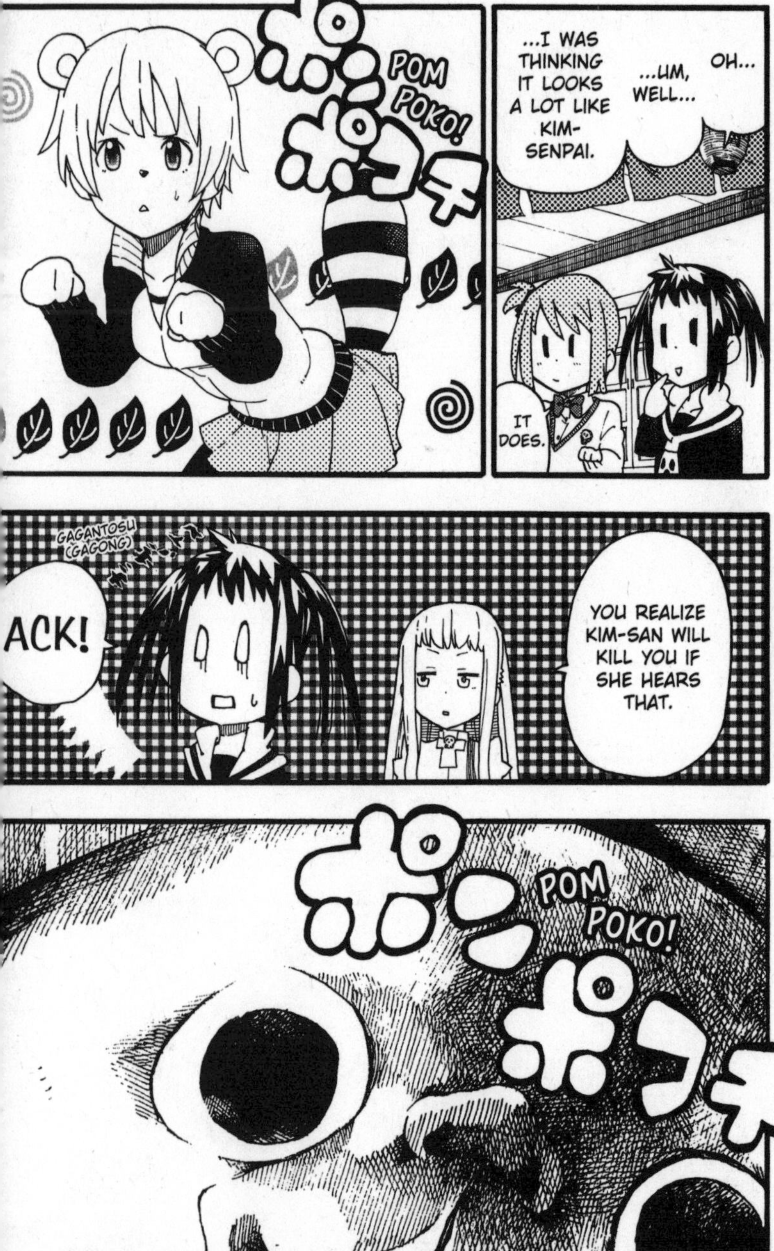
OH...
...UM, WELL...
...I WAS THINKING IT LOOKS A LOT LIKE KIM-SENPAI.
IT DOES.
POM POKO!
YOU REALIZE KIM-SAN WILL KILL YOU IF SHE HEARS THAT.
GAGANTOSU (GAGONG)
ACK!
POM POKO!

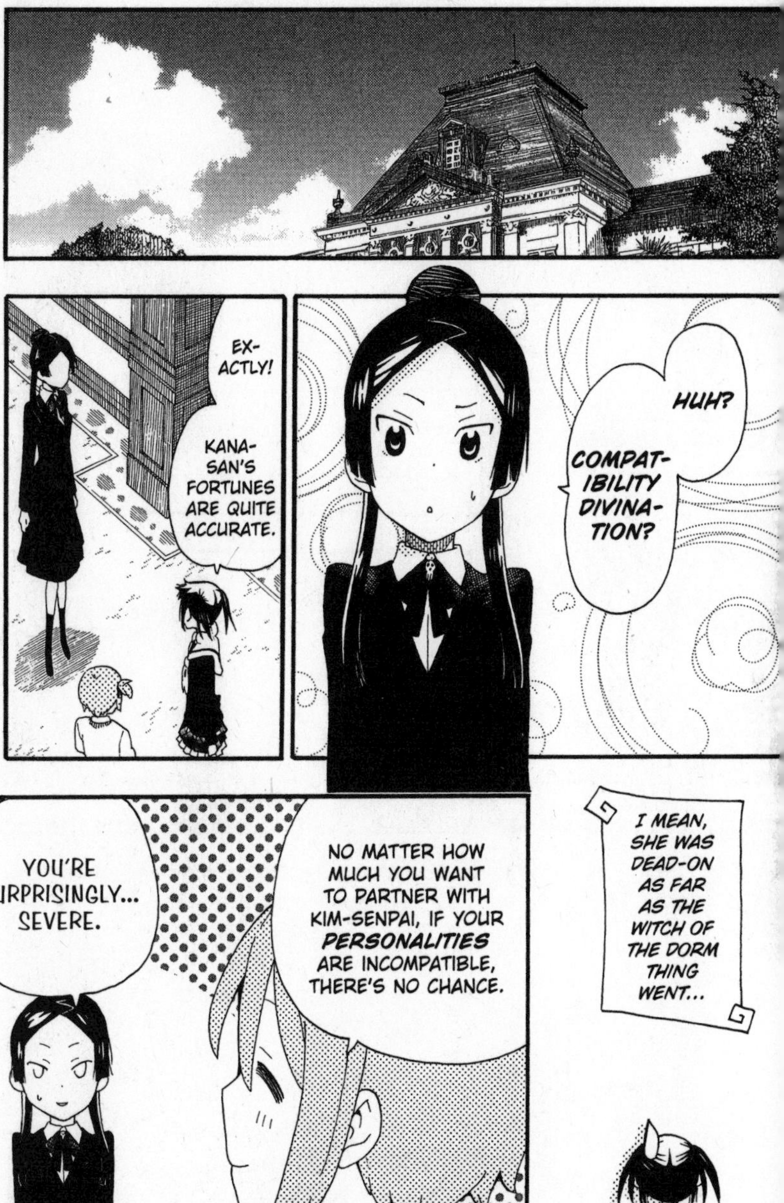
HUH?
COMPATIBILITY DIVINATION?
EXACTLY!
KANA-SAN'S FORTUNES ARE QUITE ACCURATE.
I MEAN, SHE WAS DEAD-ON AS FAR AS THE WITCH OF THE DORM THING WENT...
NO MATTER HOW MUCH YOU WANT TO PARTNER WITH KIM-SENPAI, IF YOUR ***PERSONALITIES*** ARE INCOMPATIBLE, THERE'S NO CHANCE.
YOU'RE SURPRISINGLY... SEVERE.

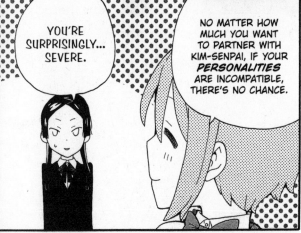

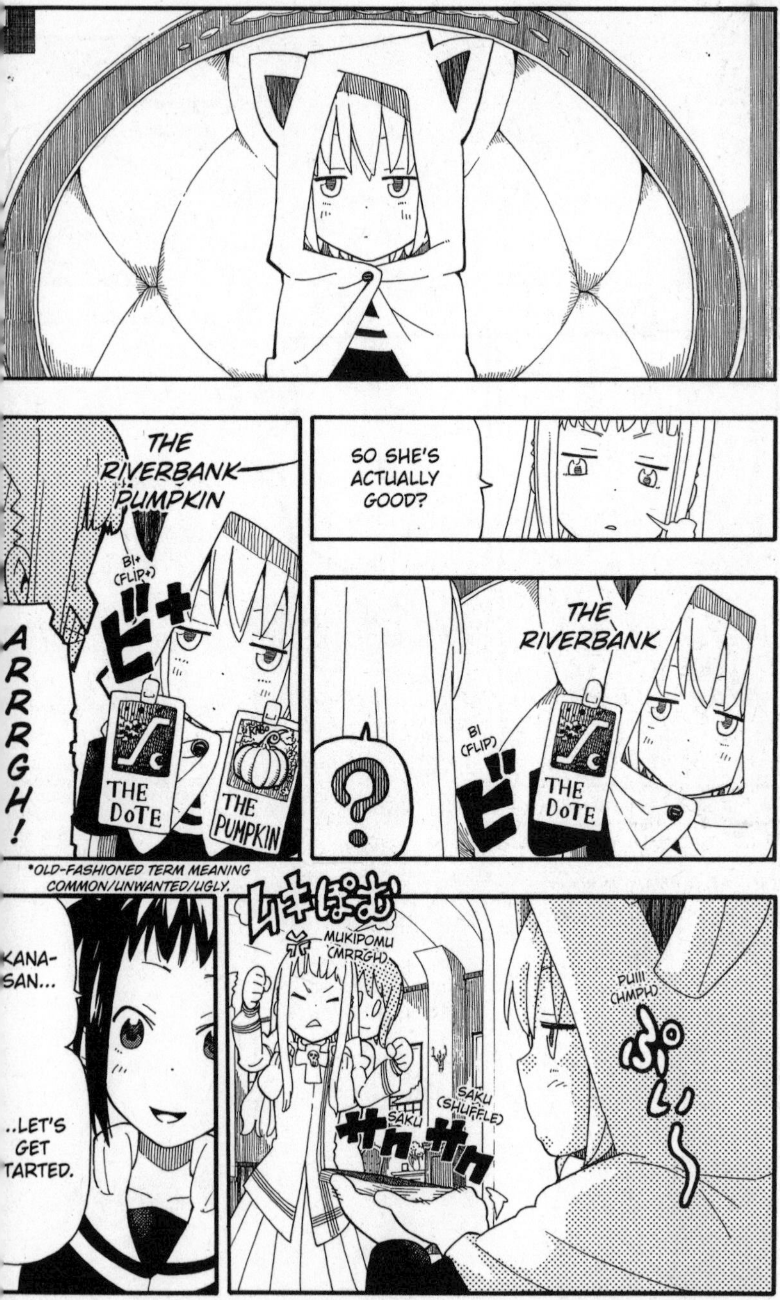

SO SHE'S ACTUALLY GOOD?
THE RIVERBANK
BI (FLIP)
THE DoTE
?
THE RIVERBANK PUMPKIN
BI+ (FLIP+)
THE DoTE
THE PUMPKIN
ARRRGH!
*OLD-FASHIONED TERM MEANING COMMON/UNWANTED/UGLY.
MUKIPOMU (MRRGH)
PUIII (HMPH)
SAKU (SHUFFLE)
SAKU
KANA-SAN...
..LET'S GET TARTED.

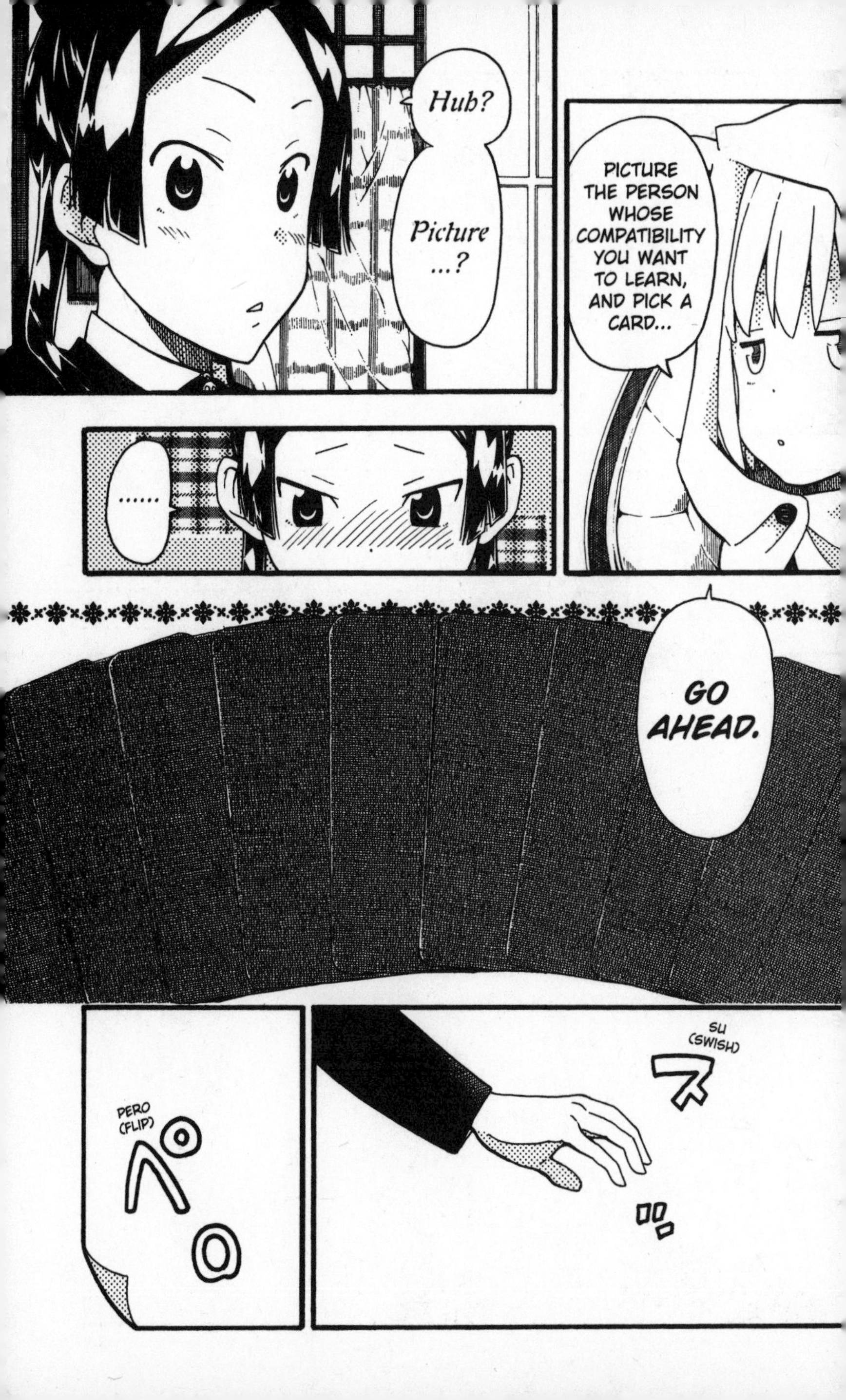
PICTURE THE PERSON WHOSE COMPATIBILITY YOU WANT TO LEARN, AND PICK A CARD...
Huh?
Picture ...?
......
GO AHEAD.
SU (SWISH)
PERO (FLIP)

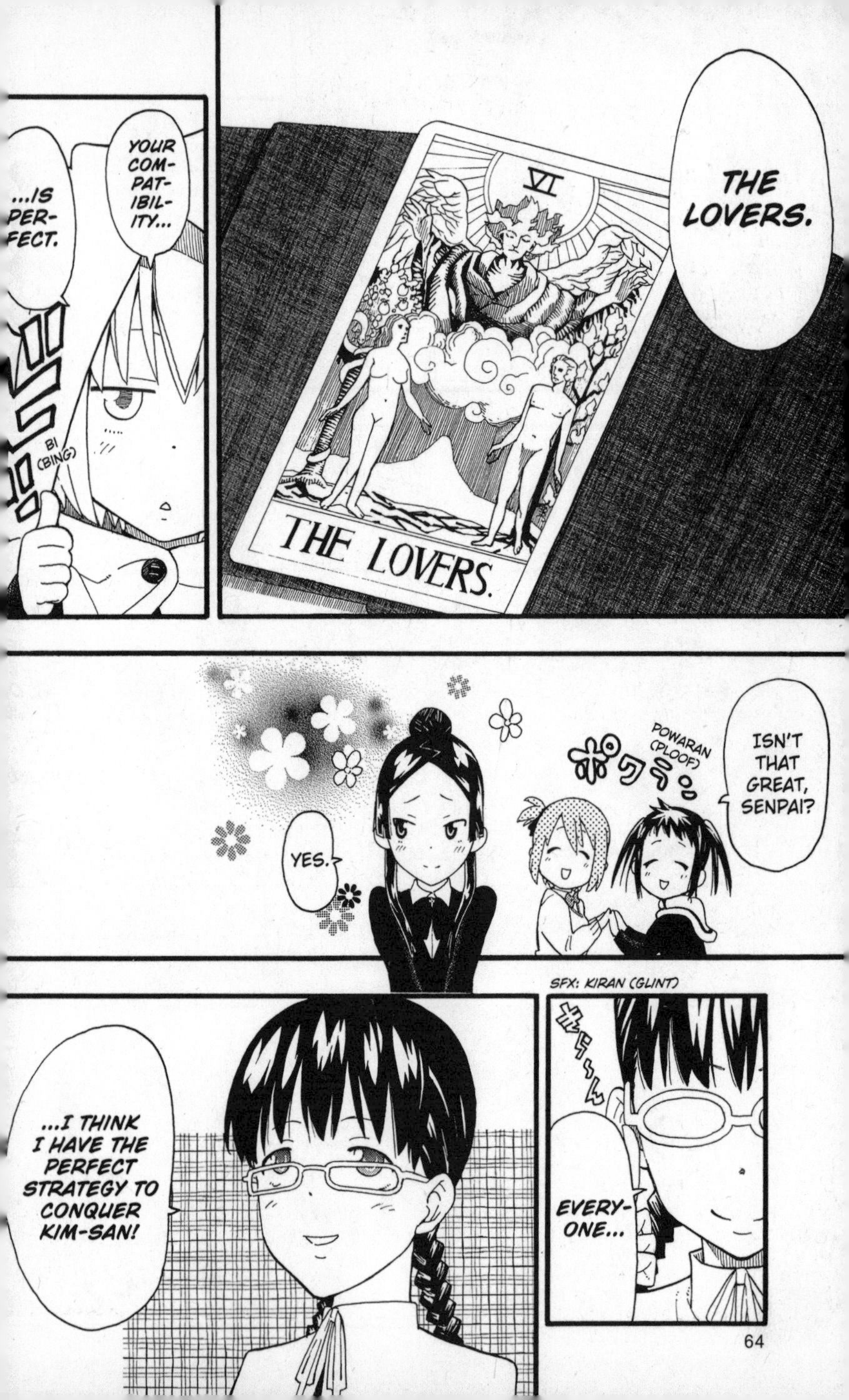
THE LOVERS.
VI
THE LOVERS.
YOUR COMPATIBILITY...
...IS PERFECT.
BI (BING)
POWARAN (PLOOF)
ISN'T THAT GREAT, SENPAI?
YES.
SFX: KIRAN (GLINT)
EVERYONE...
...I THINK I HAVE THE PERFECT STRATEGY TO CONQUER KIM-SAN!

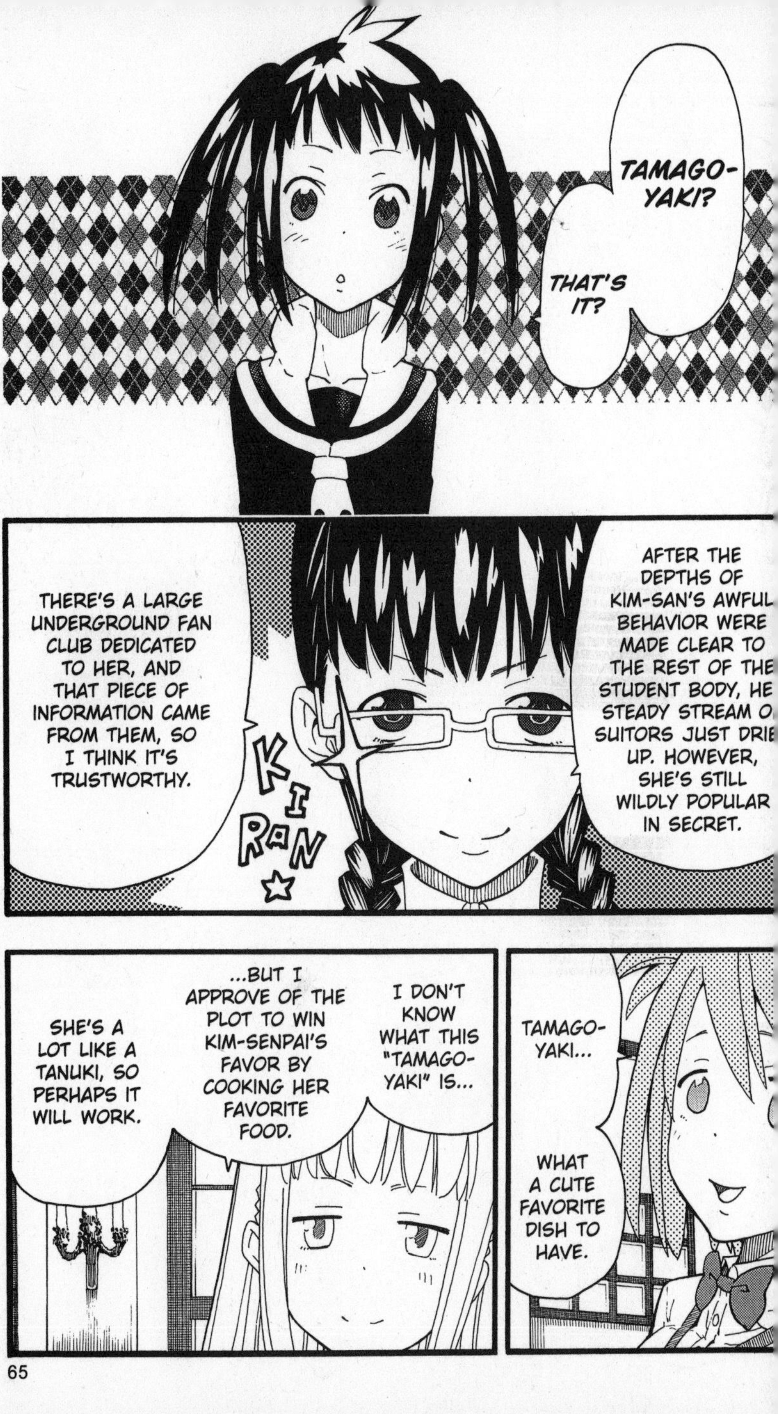

TAMAGO-YAKI?
THAT'S IT?
AFTER THE DEPTHS OF KIM-SAN'S AWFUL BEHAVIOR WERE MADE CLEAR TO THE REST OF THE STUDENT BODY, HE STEADY STREAM O SUITORS JUST DRIE UP. HOWEVER, SHE'S STILL WILDLY POPULAR IN SECRET.
THERE'S A LARGE UNDERGROUND FAN CLUB DEDICATED TO HER, AND THAT PIECE OF INFORMATION CAME FROM THEM, SO I THINK IT'S TRUSTWORTHY.
KIRAN
TAMAGO-YAKI...
WHAT A CUTE FAVORITE DISH TO HAVE.
I DON'T KNOW WHAT THIS "TAMAGO-YAKI" IS...
...BUT I APPROVE OF THE PLOT TO WIN KIM-SENPAI'S FAVOR BY COOKING HER FAVORITE FOOD.
SHE'S A LOT LIKE A TANUKI, SO PERHAPS IT WILL WORK.

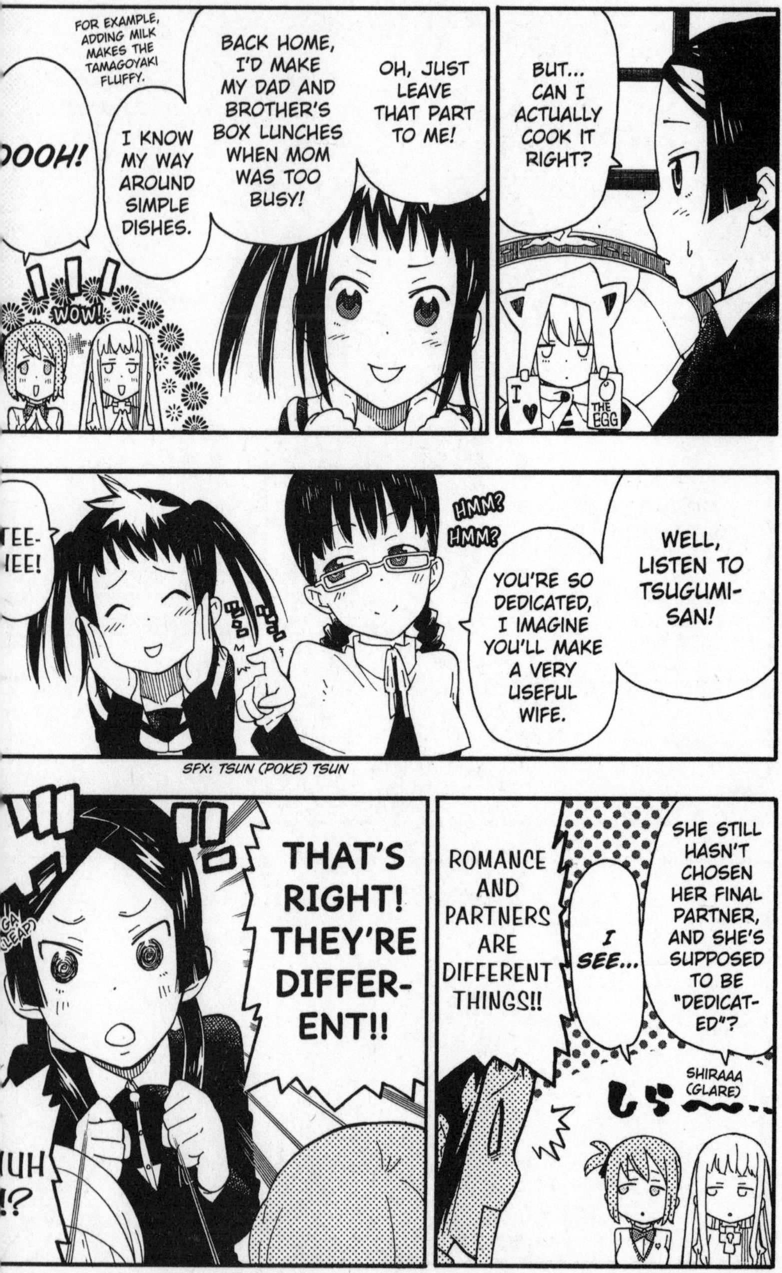
BUT... CAN I ACTUALLY COOK IT RIGHT?
I ♥
THE EGG
OH, JUST LEAVE THAT PART TO ME!
BACK HOME, I'D MAKE MY DAD AND BROTHER'S BOX LUNCHES WHEN MOM WAS TOO BUSY!
I KNOW MY WAY AROUND SIMPLE DISHES.
FOR EXAMPLE, ADDING MILK MAKES THE TAMAGOYAKI FLUFFY.
OOH!
WOW!
WELL, LISTEN TO TSUGUMI-SAN!
YOU'RE SO DEDICATED, I IMAGINE YOU'LL MAKE A VERY USEFUL WIFE.
HMM? HMM?
TEE-HEE!
SFX: TSUN (POKE) TSUN
SHE STILL HASN'T CHOSEN HER FINAL PARTNER, AND SHE'S SUPPOSED TO BE "DEDICATED"?
I SEE...
ROMANCE AND PARTNERS ARE DIFFERENT THINGS!!
SHIRAAA (GLARE)
THAT'S RIGHT! THEY'RE DIFFER-ENT!!

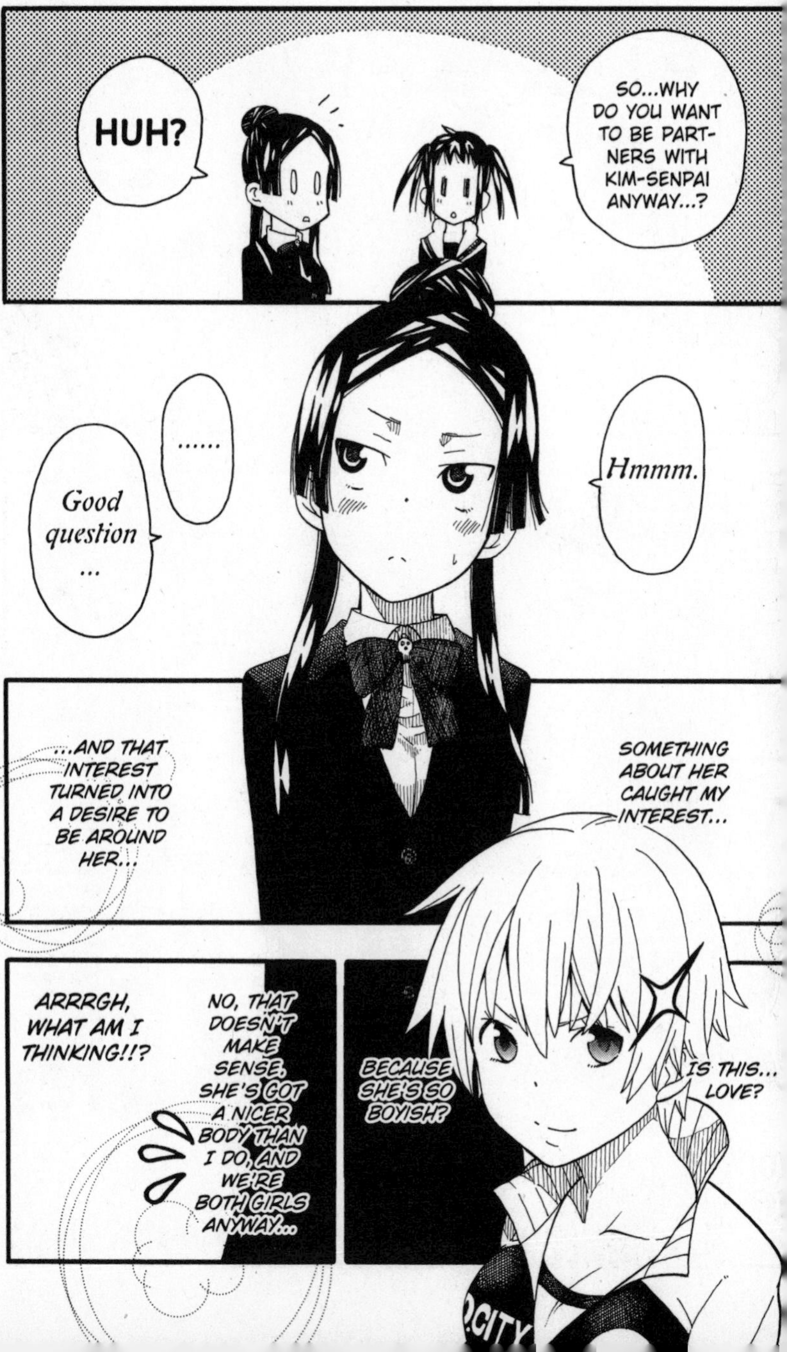
SO...WHY DO YOU WANT TO BE PARTNERS WITH KIM-SENPAI ANYWAY...?
HUH?
Hmmm.
......
Good question ...
SOMETHING ABOUT HER CAUGHT MY INTEREST...
...AND THAT INTEREST TURNED INTO A DESIRE TO BE AROUND HER...
IS THIS... LOVE?
BECAUSE SHE'S SO BOYISH?
NO, THAT DOESN'T MAKE SENSE. SHE'S GOT A NICER BODY THAN I DO, AND WE'RE BOTH GIRLS ANYWAY...
ARRRGH, WHAT AM I THINKING!!?

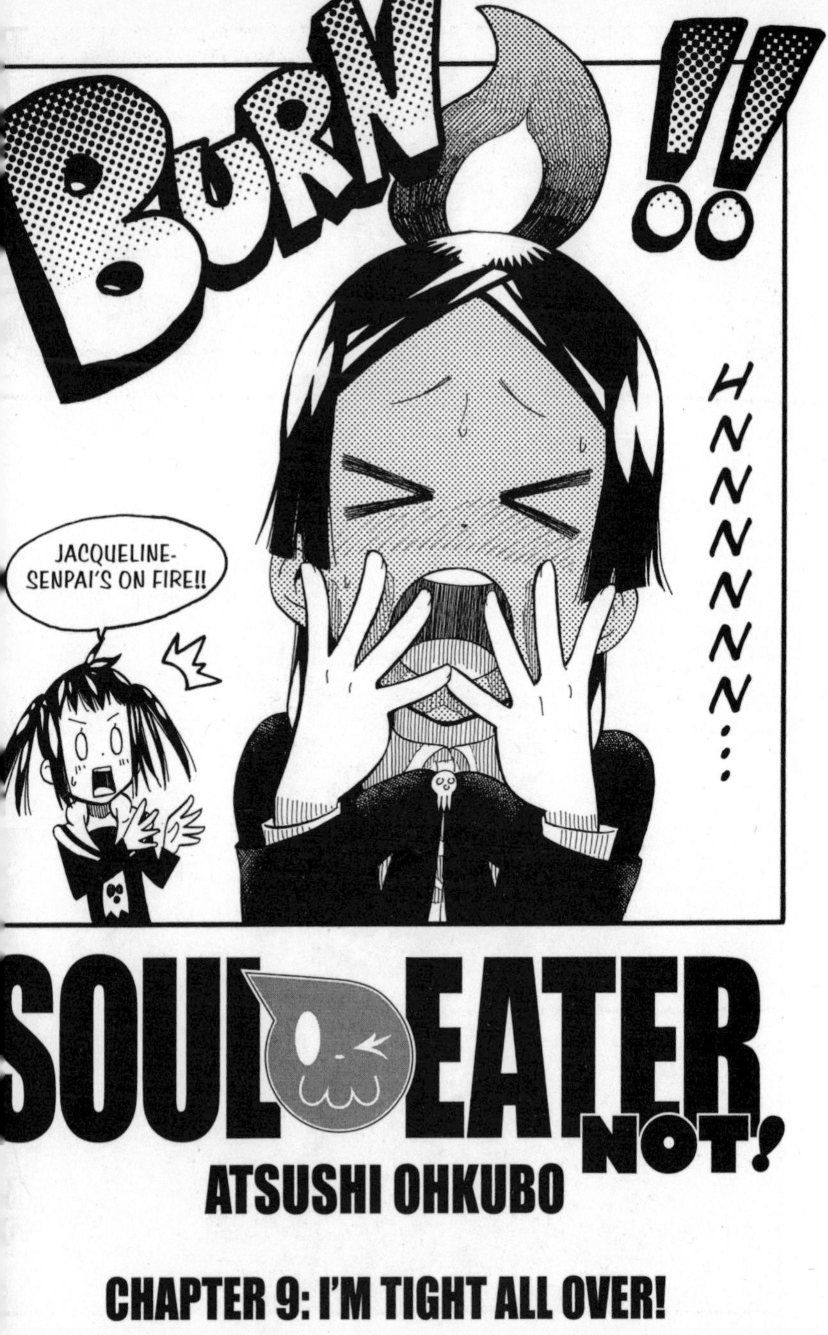
BURN!!
HNNNNNNN...
JACQUELINE-SENPAI'S ON FIRE!!

SOUL EATER NOT!

ATSUSHI OHKUBO

CHAPTER 9: I'M TIGHT ALL OVER!

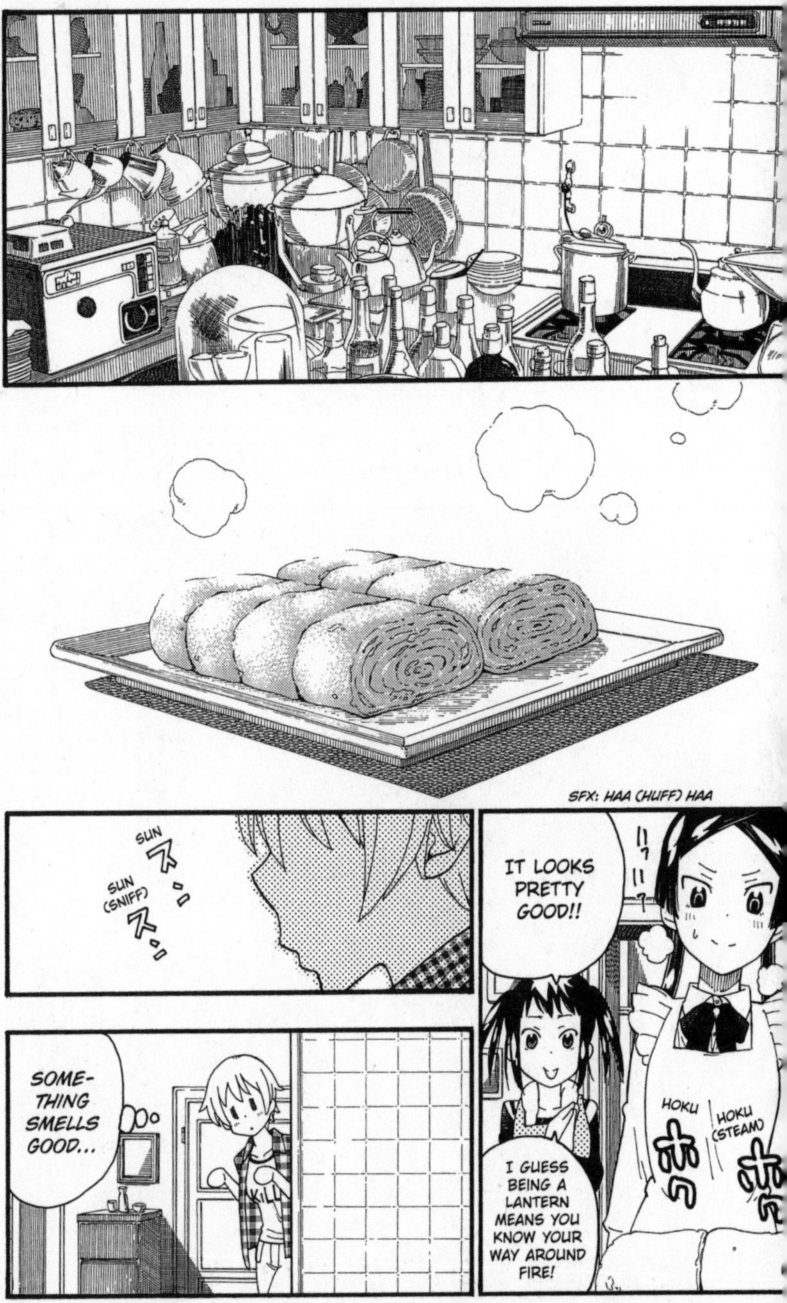
SFX: HAA (HUFF) HAA
IT LOOKS PRETTY GOOD!!
I GUESS BEING A LANTERN MEANS YOU KNOW YOUR WAY AROUND FIRE!
HOKU HOKU (STEAM)
SUN SUN (SNIFF)
SOME-THING SMELLS GOOD...

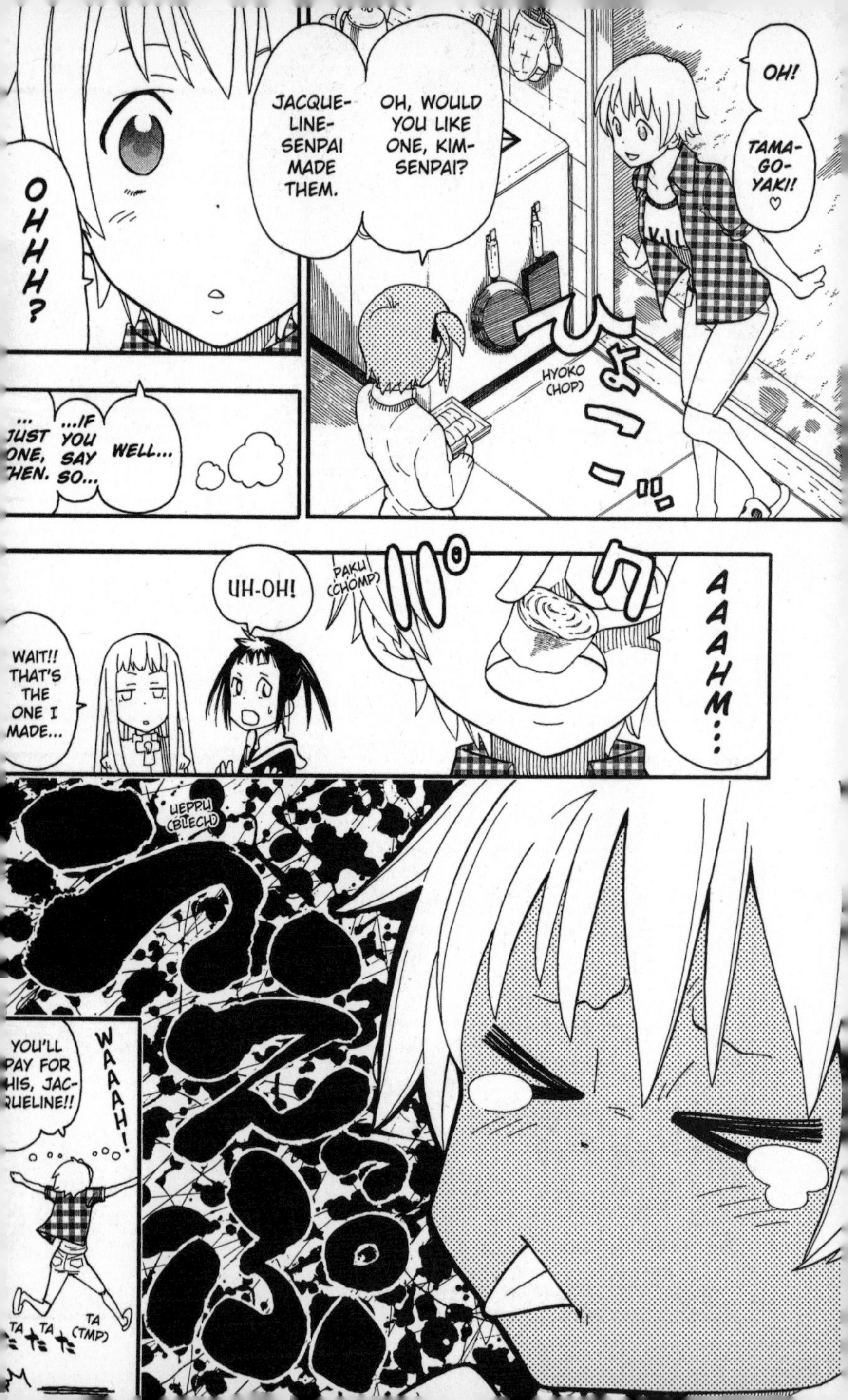
OH!
TAMA-GO-YAKI! ♡
OH, WOULD YOU LIKE ONE, KIM-SENPAI?
JACQUE-LINE-SENPAI MADE THEM.
HYOKO (HOP)
OHHHH?
WELL...
...IF YOU SAY SO...
... JUST ONE, THEN.
AAAHM...
PAKU (CHOMP)
UH-OH!
WAIT!! THAT'S THE ONE I MADE...
UEPPU (BLECH)
WAAAH!
YOU'LL PAY FOR THIS, JAC-QUELINE!!
TA TA TA (TMP)

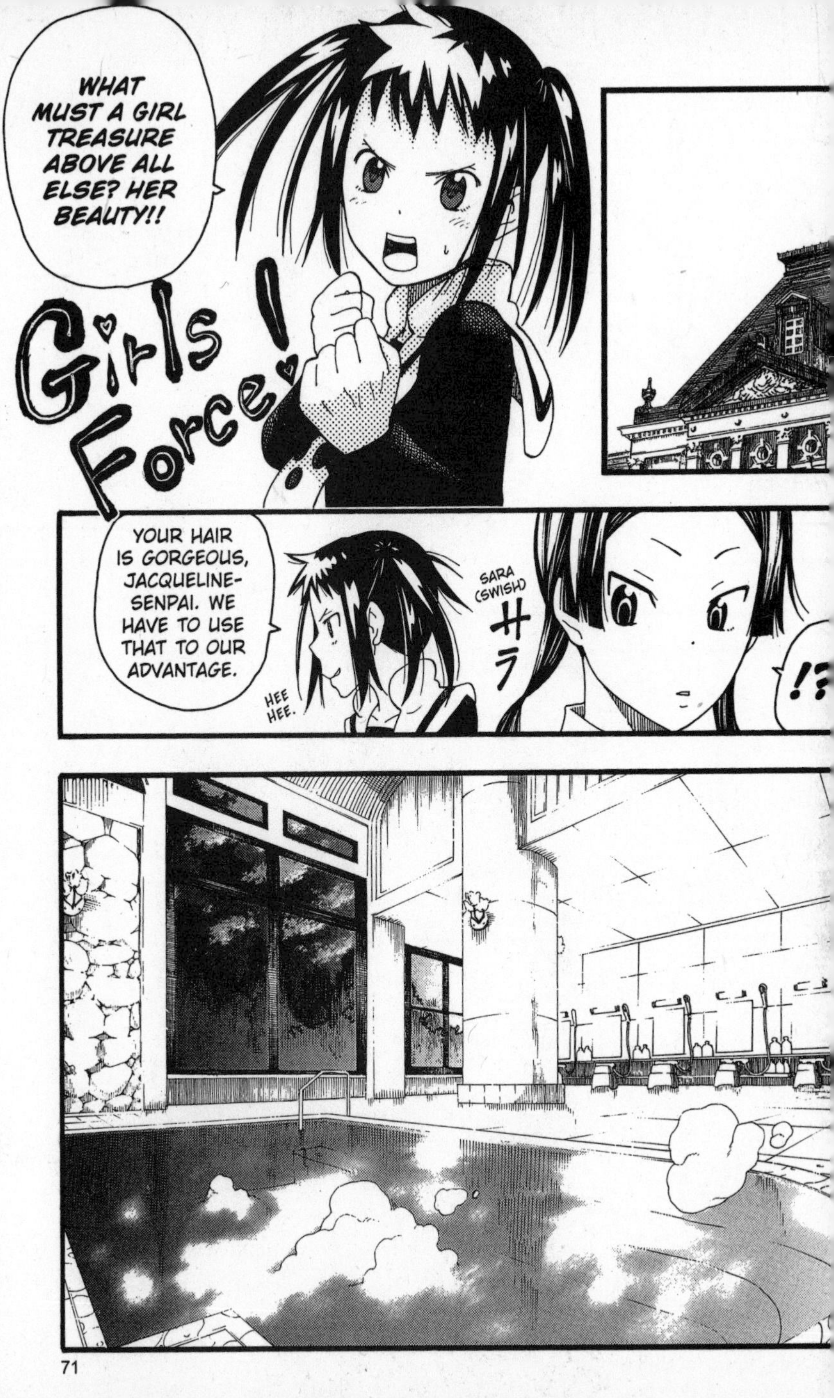
WHAT MUST A GIRL TREASURE ABOVE ALL ELSE? HER BEAUTY!!
Girls Force!
!?
SARA (SWISH)
サラ
YOUR HAIR IS GORGEOUS, JACQUELINE-SENPAI. WE HAVE TO USE THAT TO OUR ADVANTAGE.
HEE HEE.

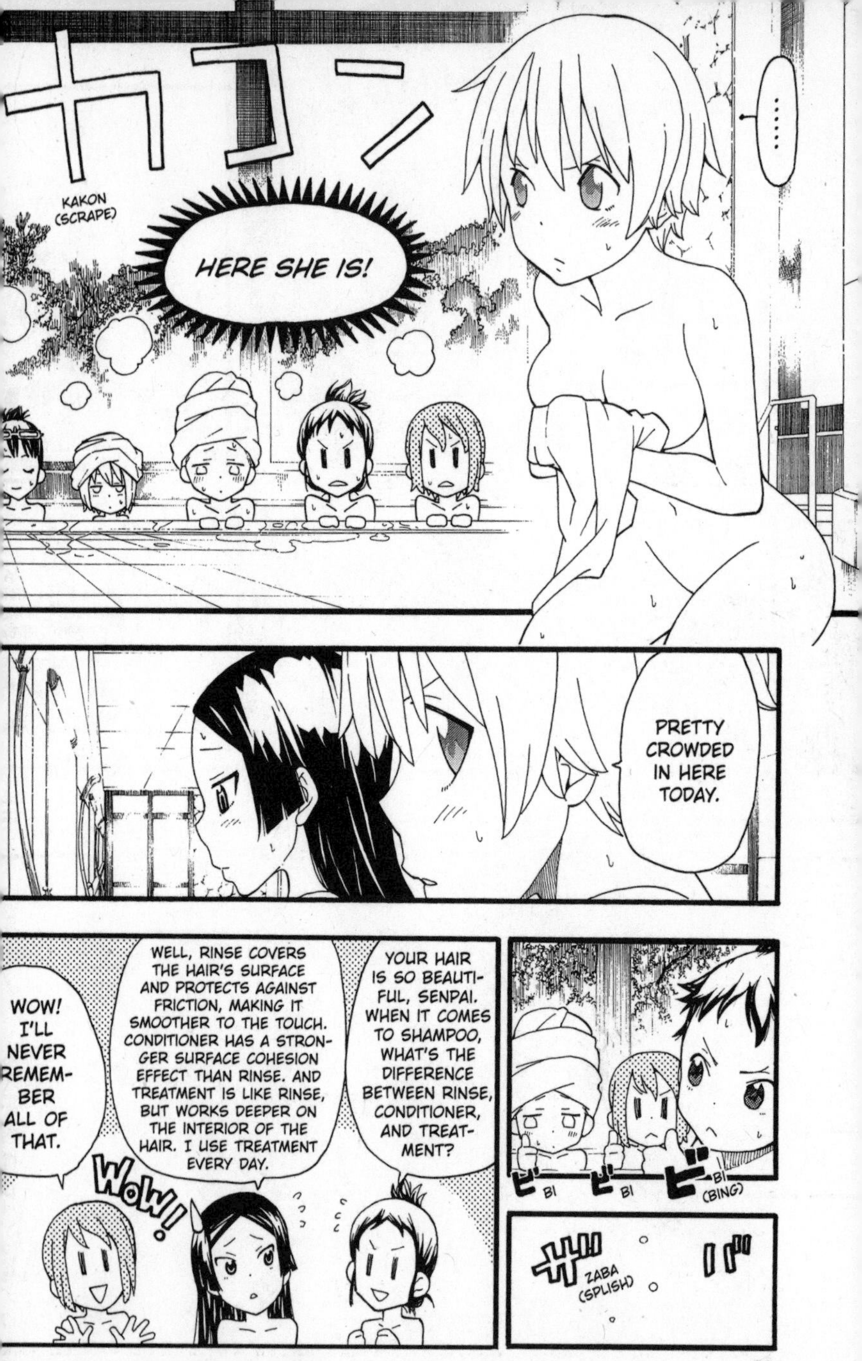
……
KAKON (SCRAPE)
HERE SHE IS!
PRETTY CROWDED IN HERE TODAY.
BI
BI
BI (BING)
ZABA (SPLISH)
YOUR HAIR IS SO BEAUTIFUL, SENPAI. WHEN IT COMES TO SHAMPOO, WHAT'S THE DIFFERENCE BETWEEN RINSE, CONDITIONER, AND TREATMENT?
WELL, RINSE COVERS THE HAIR'S SURFACE AND PROTECTS AGAINST FRICTION, MAKING IT SMOOTHER TO THE TOUCH. CONDITIONER HAS A STRONGER SURFACE COHESION EFFECT THAN RINSE. AND TREATMENT IS LIKE RINSE, BUT WORKS DEEPER ON THE INTERIOR OF THE HAIR. I USE TREATMENT EVERY DAY.
WOW!
WOW! I'LL NEVER REMEMBER ALL OF THAT.

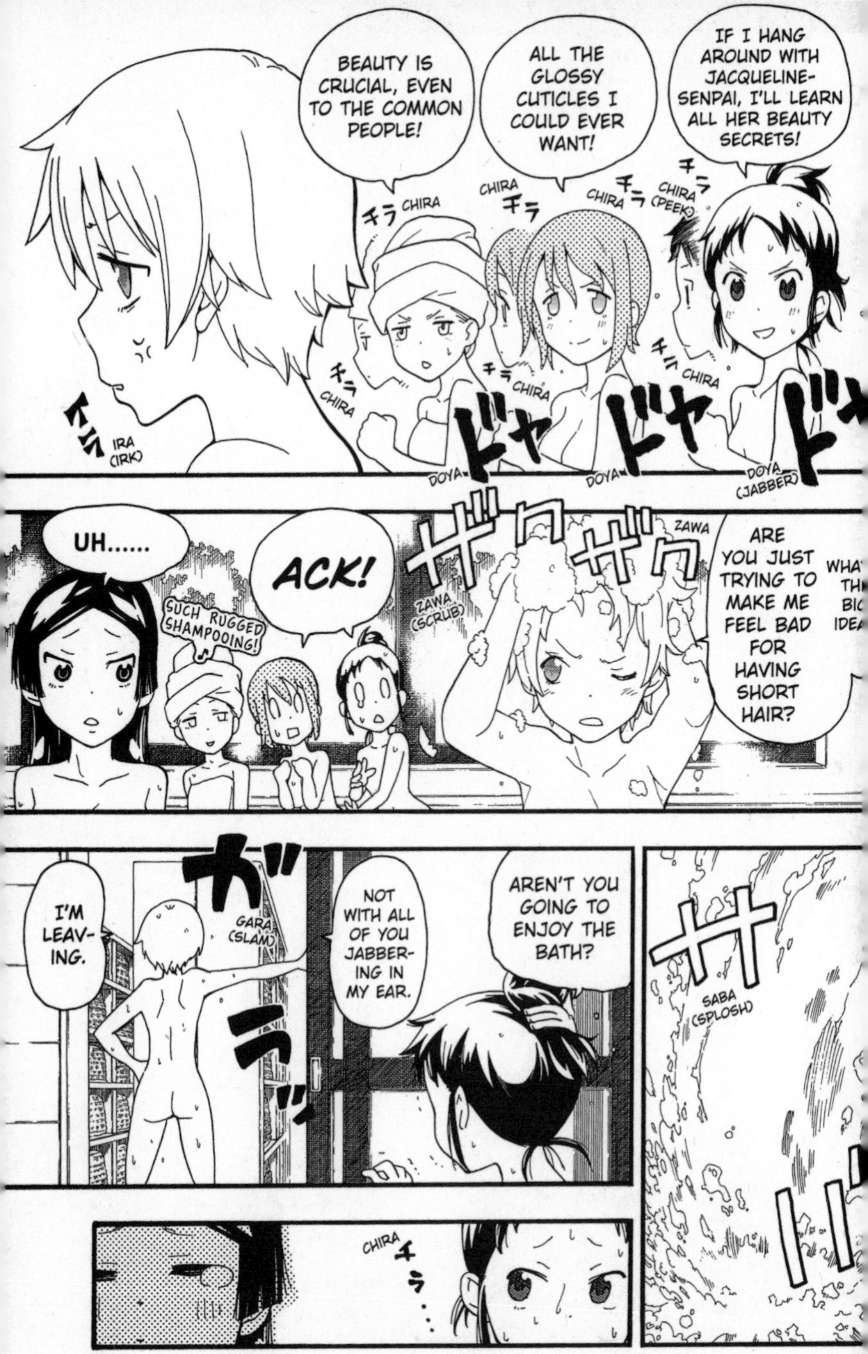
IF I HANG AROUND WITH JACQUELINE-SENPAI, I'LL LEARN ALL HER BEAUTY SECRETS!
ALL THE GLOSSY CUTICLES I COULD EVER WANT!
BEAUTY IS CRUCIAL, EVEN TO THE COMMON PEOPLE!
CHIRA (PEEK)
CHIRA
CHIRA
CHIRA
CHIRA
CHIRA
CHIRA
DOYA (JABBER)
DOYA
DOYA
IRA (IRK)
ARE YOU JUST TRYING TO MAKE ME FEEL BAD FOR HAVING SHORT HAIR?
ZAWA
ZAWA (SCRUB)
ACK!
SUCH RUGGED SHAMPOOING!
UH......
SABA (SPLOSH)
AREN'T YOU GOING TO ENJOY THE BATH?
NOT WITH ALL OF YOU JABBERING IN MY EAR.
GARA (SLAM)
I'M LEAV-ING.
CHIRA

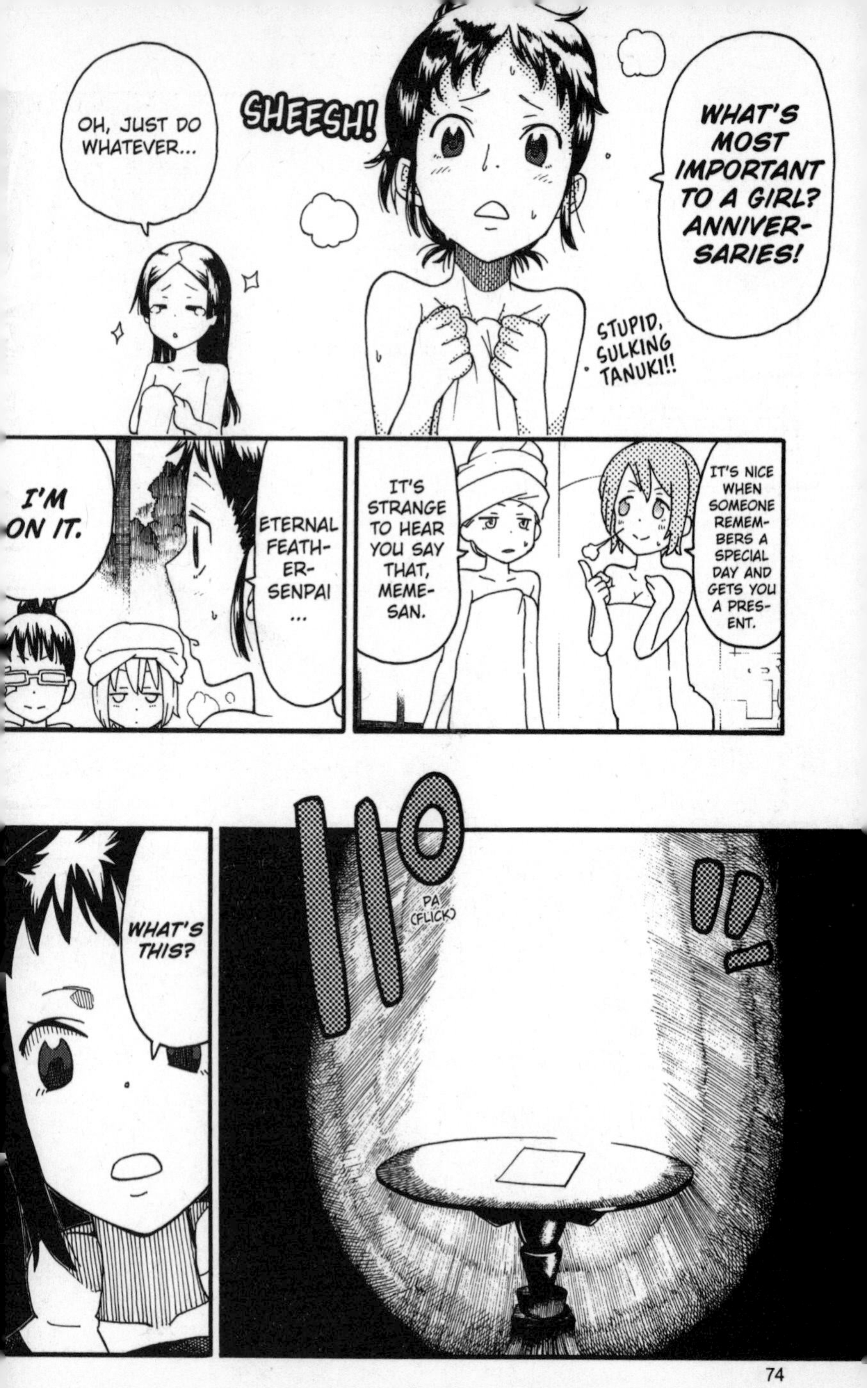
WHAT'S MOST IMPORTANT TO A GIRL? ANNIVER-SARIES!
STUPID, SULKING TANUKI!!
SHEESH!
OH, JUST DO WHATEVER...
IT'S NICE WHEN SOMEONE REMEM-BERS A SPECIAL DAY AND GETS YOU A PRES-ENT.
IT'S STRANGE TO HEAR YOU SAY THAT, MEME-SAN.
ETERNAL FEATH-ER-SENPAI ...
I'M ON IT.
PA (FLICK)
WHAT'S THIS?

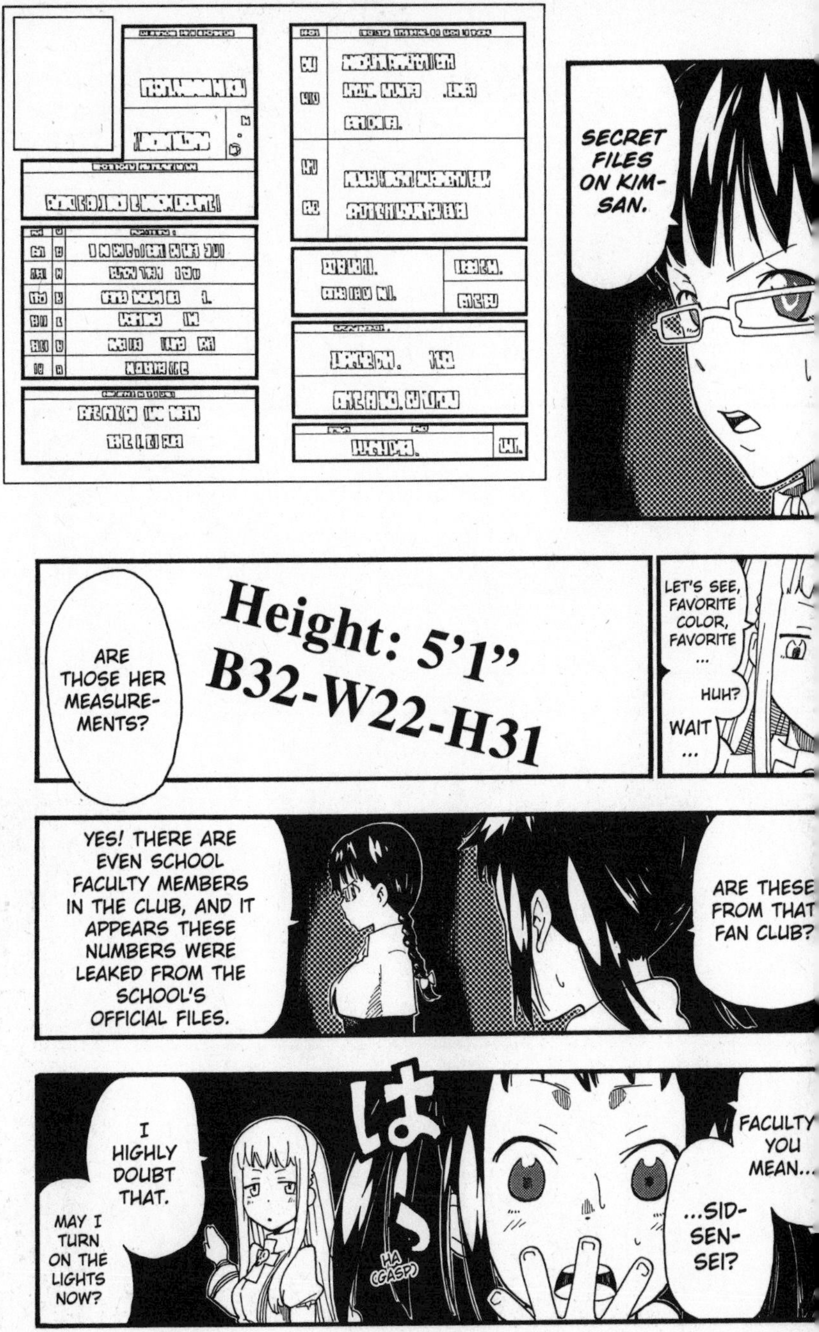
SECRET FILES ON KIM-SAN.
LET'S SEE, FAVORITE COLOR, FAVORITE ...
HUH?
WAIT ...
Height: 5'1"
B32-W22-H31
ARE THOSE HER MEASUREMENTS?
ARE THESE FROM THAT FAN CLUB?
YES! THERE ARE EVEN SCHOOL FACULTY MEMBERS IN THE CLUB, AND IT APPEARS THESE NUMBERS WERE LEAKED FROM THE SCHOOL'S OFFICIAL FILES.
FACULTY YOU MEAN...
...SID-SEN-SEI?
は っ
HA (GASP)
I HIGHLY DOUBT THAT.
MAY I TURN ON THE LIGHTS NOW?

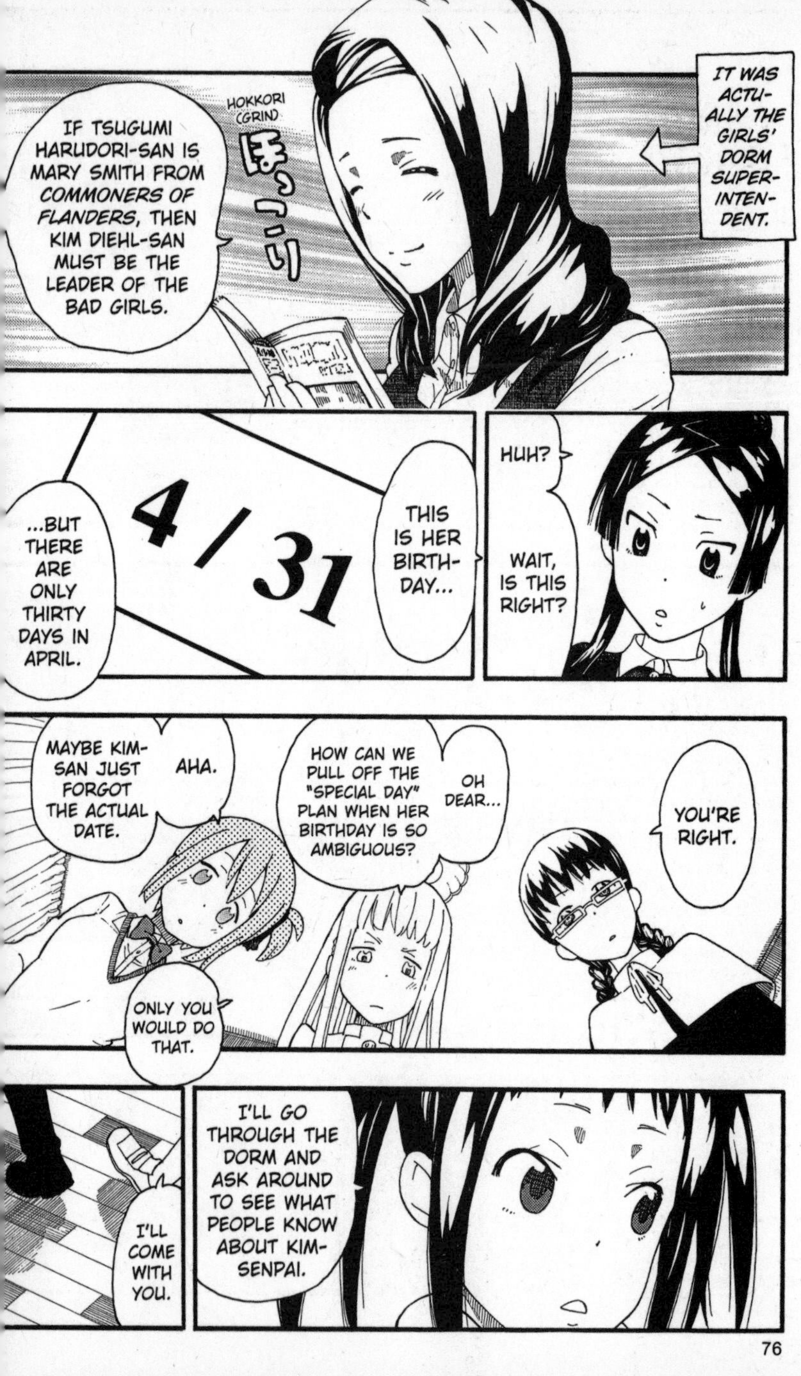
IT WAS ACTUALLY THE GIRLS' DORM SUPERINTENDENT.
HOKKORI (GRIN)
ほっこり
IF TSUGUMI HARUDORI-SAN IS MARY SMITH FROM *COMMONERS OF FLANDERS*, THEN KIM DIEHL-SAN MUST BE THE LEADER OF THE BAD GIRLS.
HUH?
WAIT, IS THIS RIGHT?
THIS IS HER BIRTHDAY...
4 / 31
...BUT THERE ARE ONLY THIRTY DAYS IN APRIL.
YOU'RE RIGHT.
OH DEAR...
HOW CAN WE PULL OFF THE "SPECIAL DAY" PLAN WHEN HER BIRTHDAY IS SO AMBIGUOUS?
AHA.
MAYBE KIM-SAN JUST FORGOT THE ACTUAL DATE.
ONLY YOU WOULD DO THAT.
I'LL GO THROUGH THE DORM AND ASK AROUND TO SEE WHAT PEOPLE KNOW ABOUT KIM-SENPAI.
I'LL COME WITH YOU.

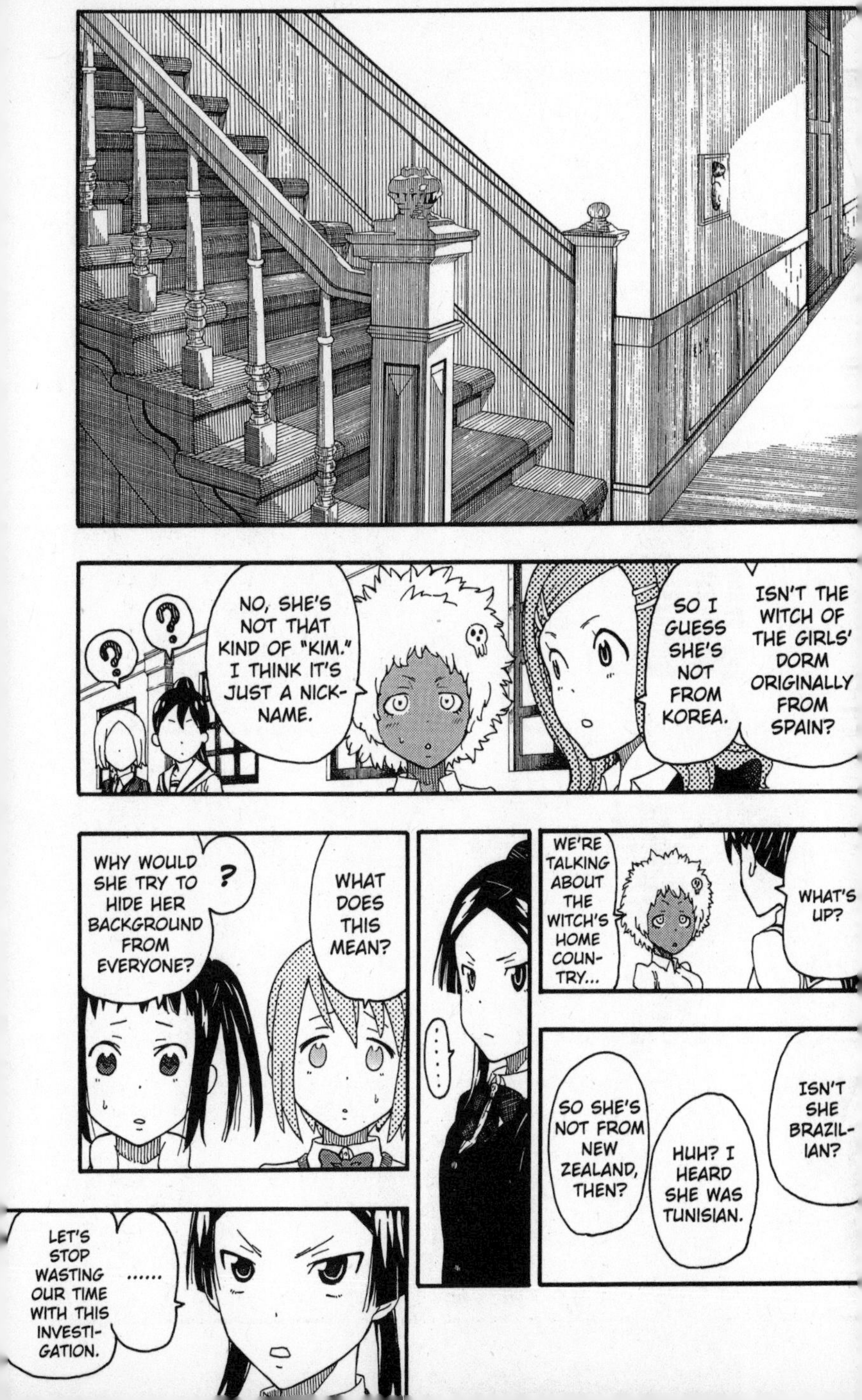
ISN'T THE WITCH OF THE GIRLS' DORM ORIGINALLY FROM SPAIN?
SO I GUESS SHE'S NOT FROM KOREA.
NO, SHE'S NOT THAT KIND OF "KIM." I THINK IT'S JUST A NICK-NAME.
?
?
WHAT'S UP?
WE'RE TALKING ABOUT THE WITCH'S HOME COUN-TRY...
ISN'T SHE BRAZIL-IAN?
HUH? I HEARD SHE WAS TUNISIAN.
SO SHE'S NOT FROM NEW ZEALAND, THEN?
......
WHAT DOES THIS MEAN?
WHY WOULD SHE TRY TO HIDE HER BACKGROUND FROM EVERYONE?
?
......
LET'S STOP WASTING OUR TIME WITH THIS INVESTI-GATION.

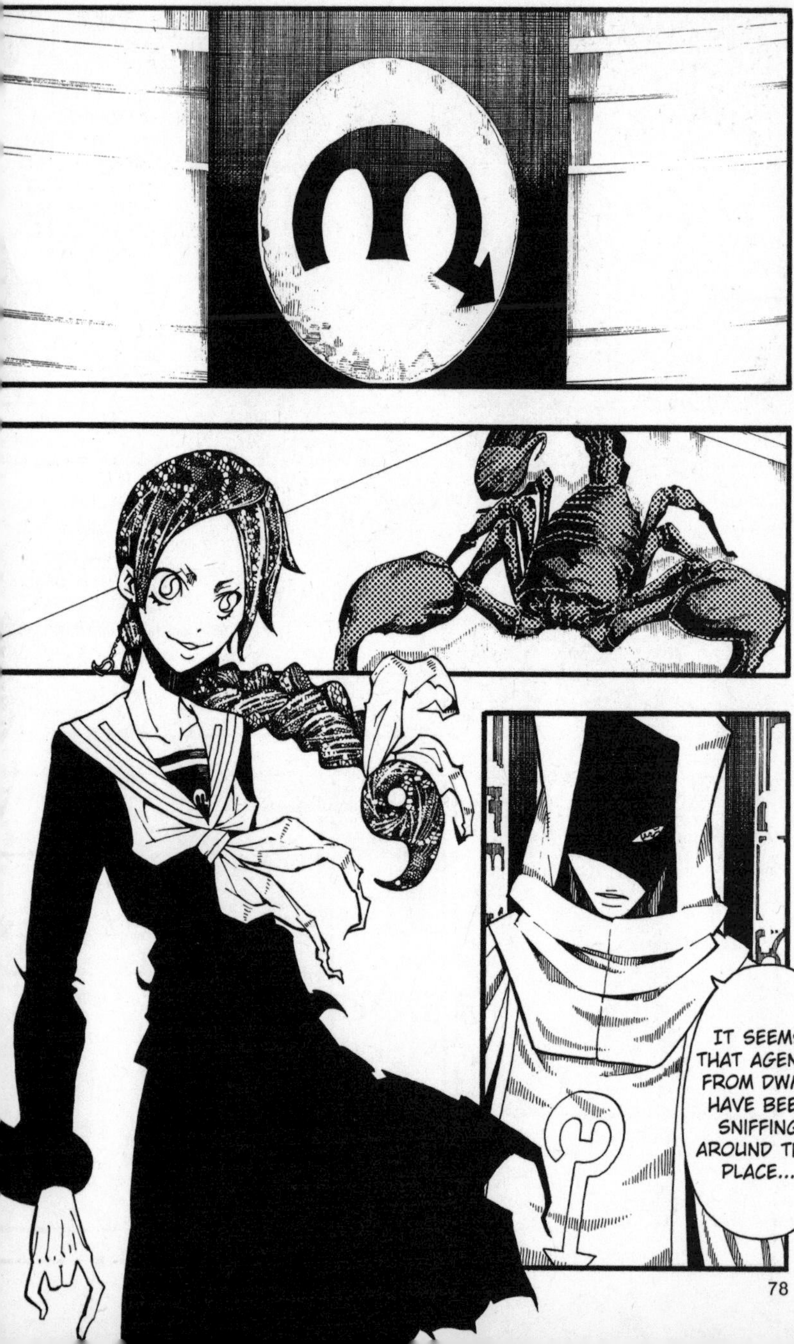
IT SEEMS THAT AGENTS FROM DWMA HAVE BEEN SNIFFING AROUND THIS PLACE...

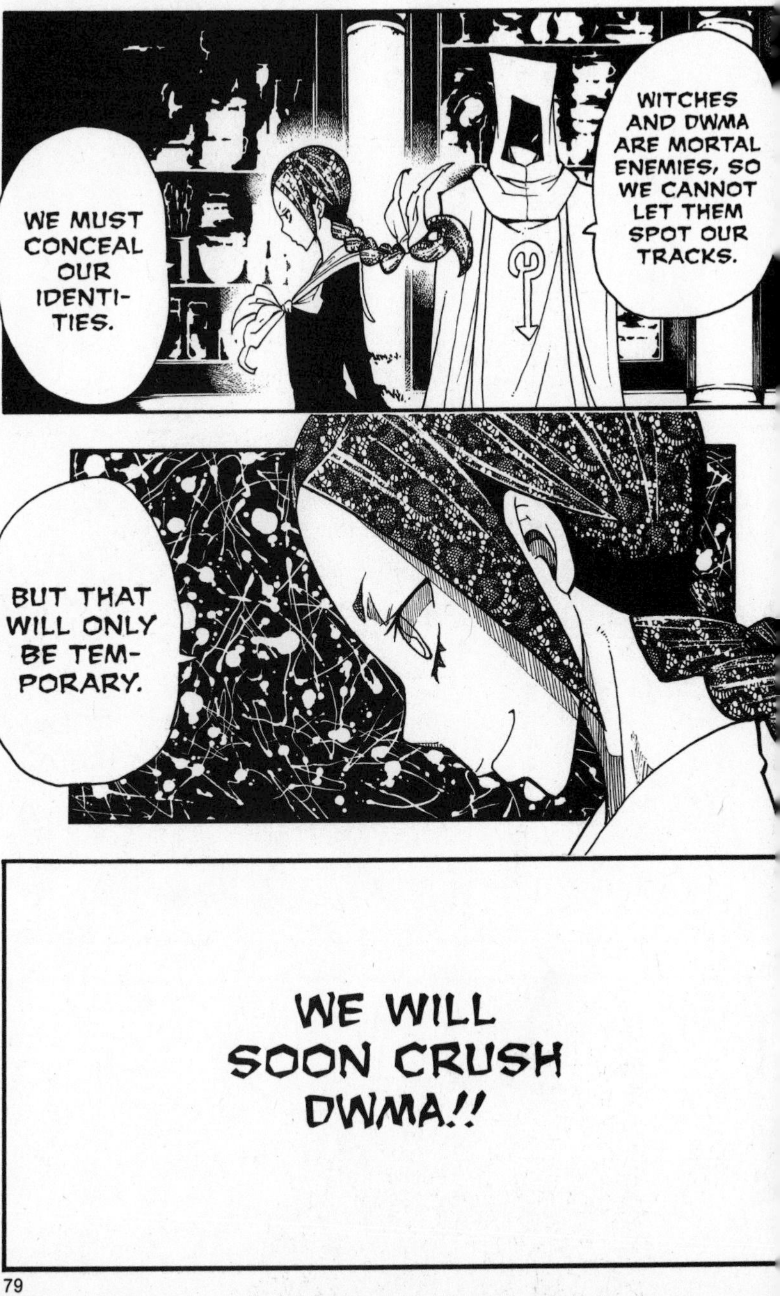
WITCHES AND DWMA ARE MORTAL ENEMIES, SO WE CANNOT LET THEM SPOT OUR TRACKS.
WE MUST CONCEAL OUR IDENTITIES.
BUT THAT WILL ONLY BE TEMPORARY.
WE WILL SOON CRUSH DWMA!!

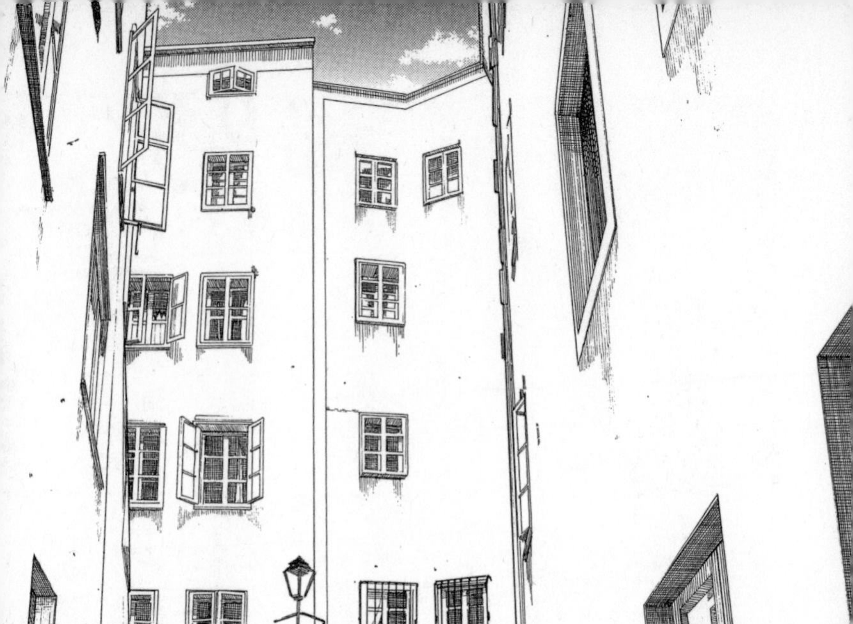
POTSUN
(THMP)
ポツ

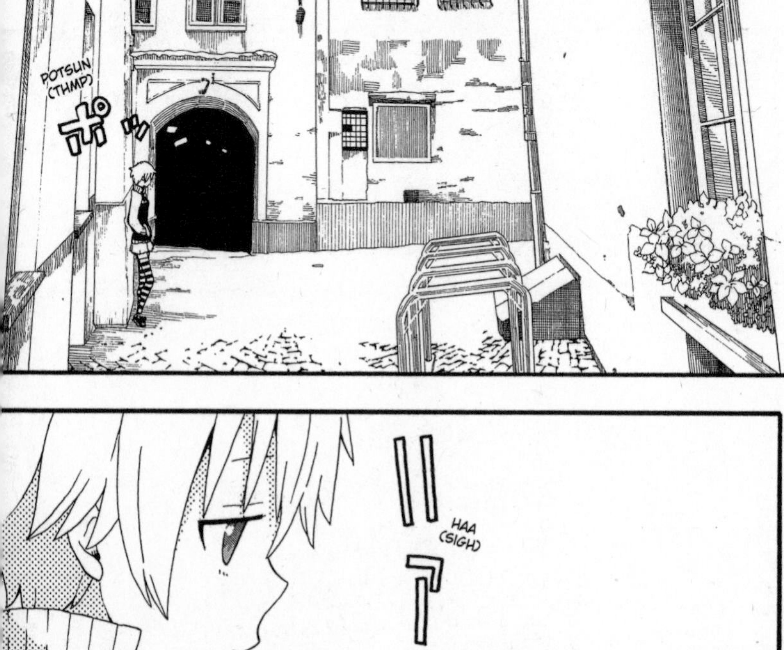
HAA
(SIGH)
はァ

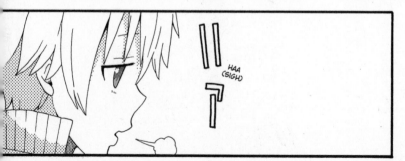

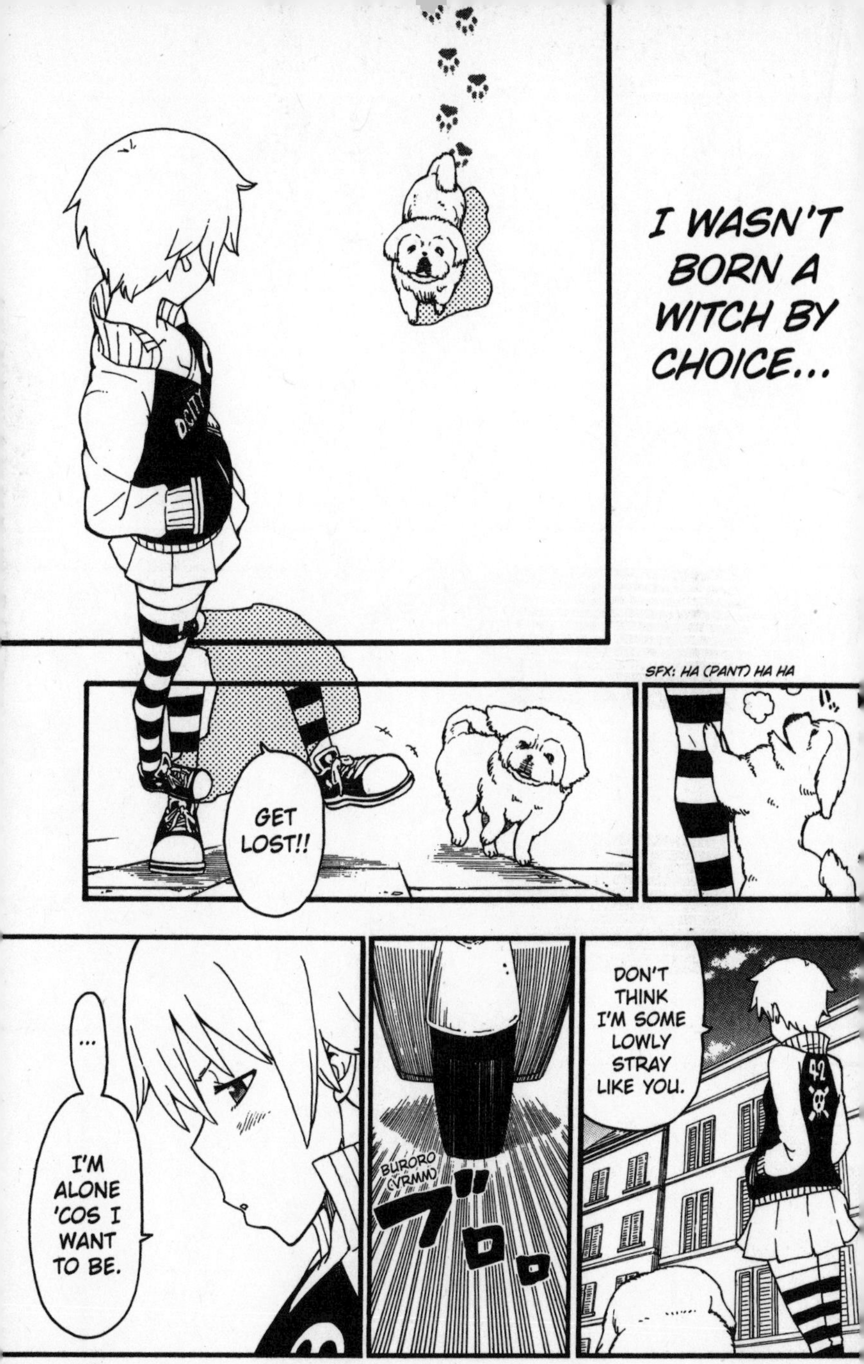
I WASN'T BORN A WITCH BY CHOICE...
SFX: HA (PANT) HA HA
GET LOST!!
DON'T THINK I'M SOME LOWLY STRAY LIKE YOU.
...
BURORO (VRMM)
...
I'M ALONE 'COS I WANT TO BE.

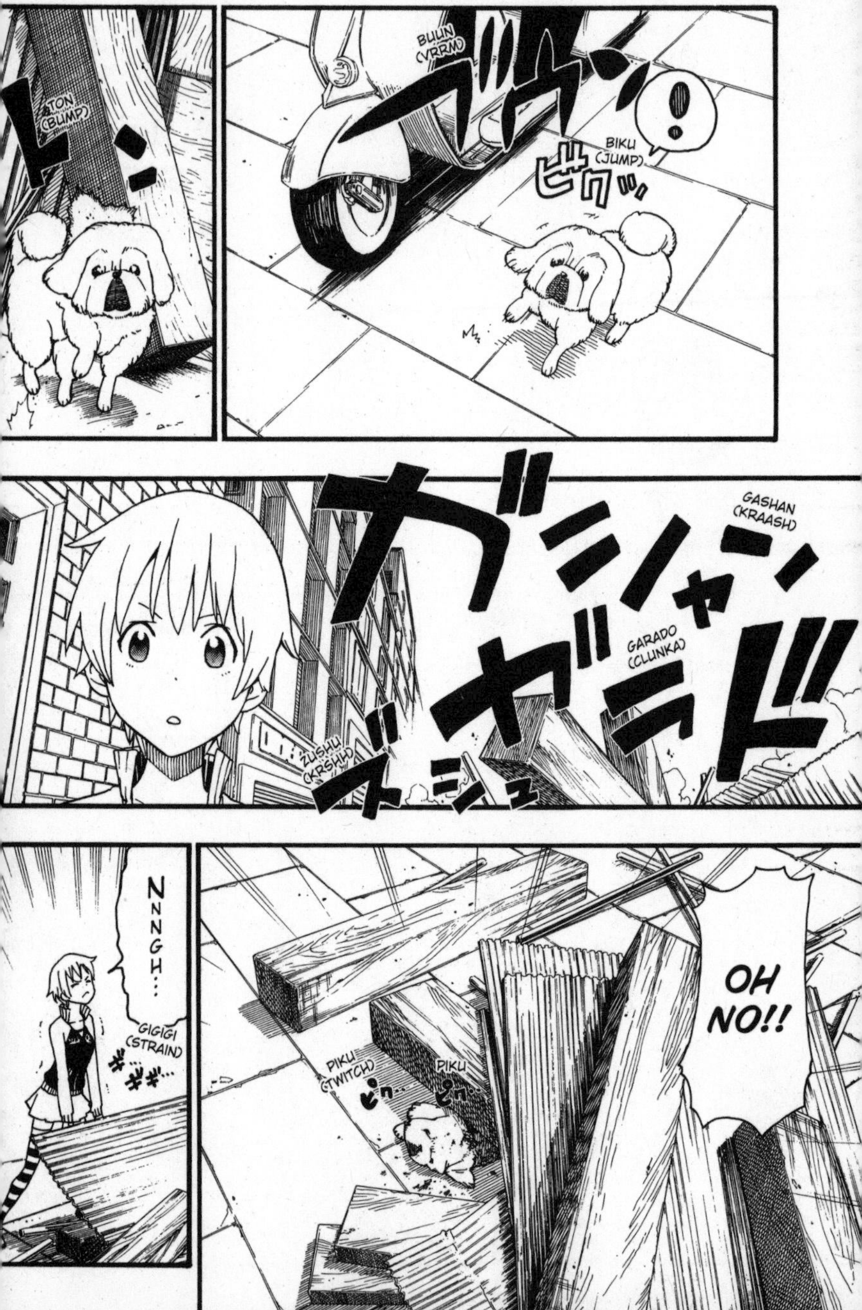
BUUN (VRRM)
!
BIKU (JUMP)
TON (BUMP)
GASHAN (KRAASH)
GARADO (CLUNKA)
ZUSHU (KRSHH)
OH NO!!
PIKU
PIKU (TWITCH)
NNNGH...
GIGIGI (STRAIN)

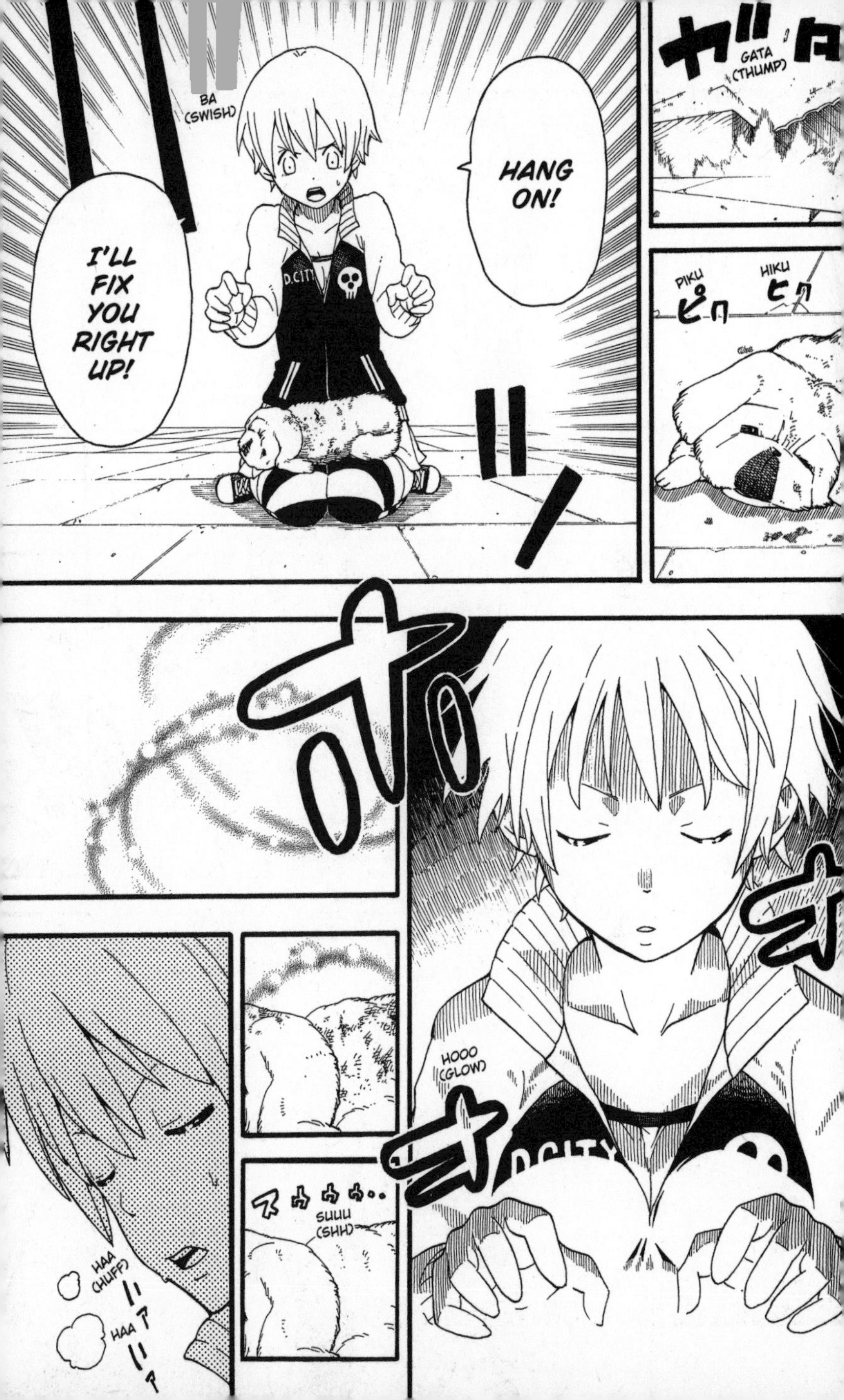
GATA (THUMP)
PIKU
HIKU
HANG ON!
BA (SWISH)
I'LL FIX YOU RIGHT UP!
HOOO (GLOW)
SUUU (SHH)
HAA (HUFF)
HAA

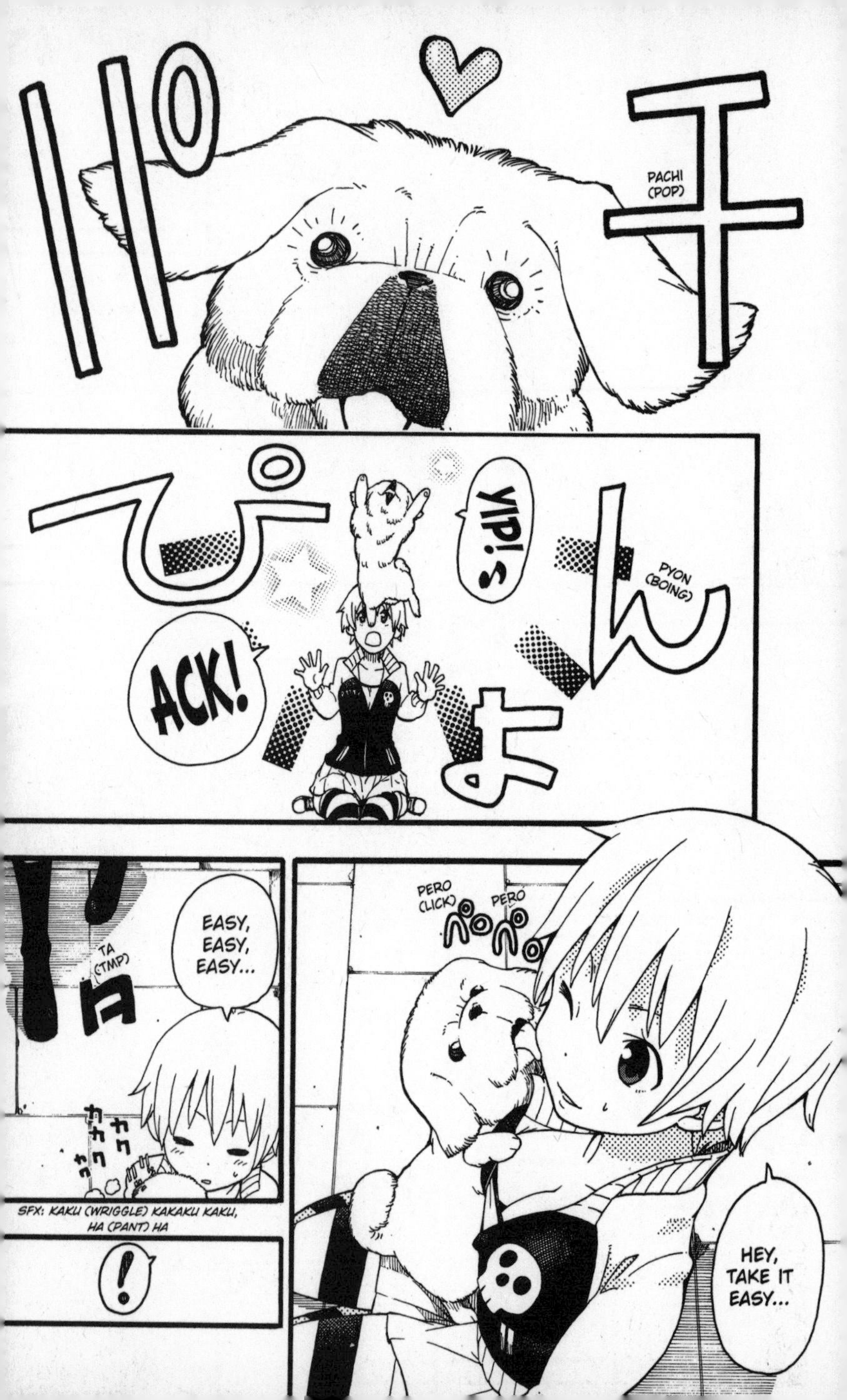
PACHI (POP)
PYON (BOING)
YIP!
ACK!
PERO (LICK) PERO
HEY, TAKE IT EASY...
TA (TMP)
EASY, EASY, EASY...
SFX: KAKU (WRIGGLE) KAKAKU KAKU, HA (PANT) HA
!

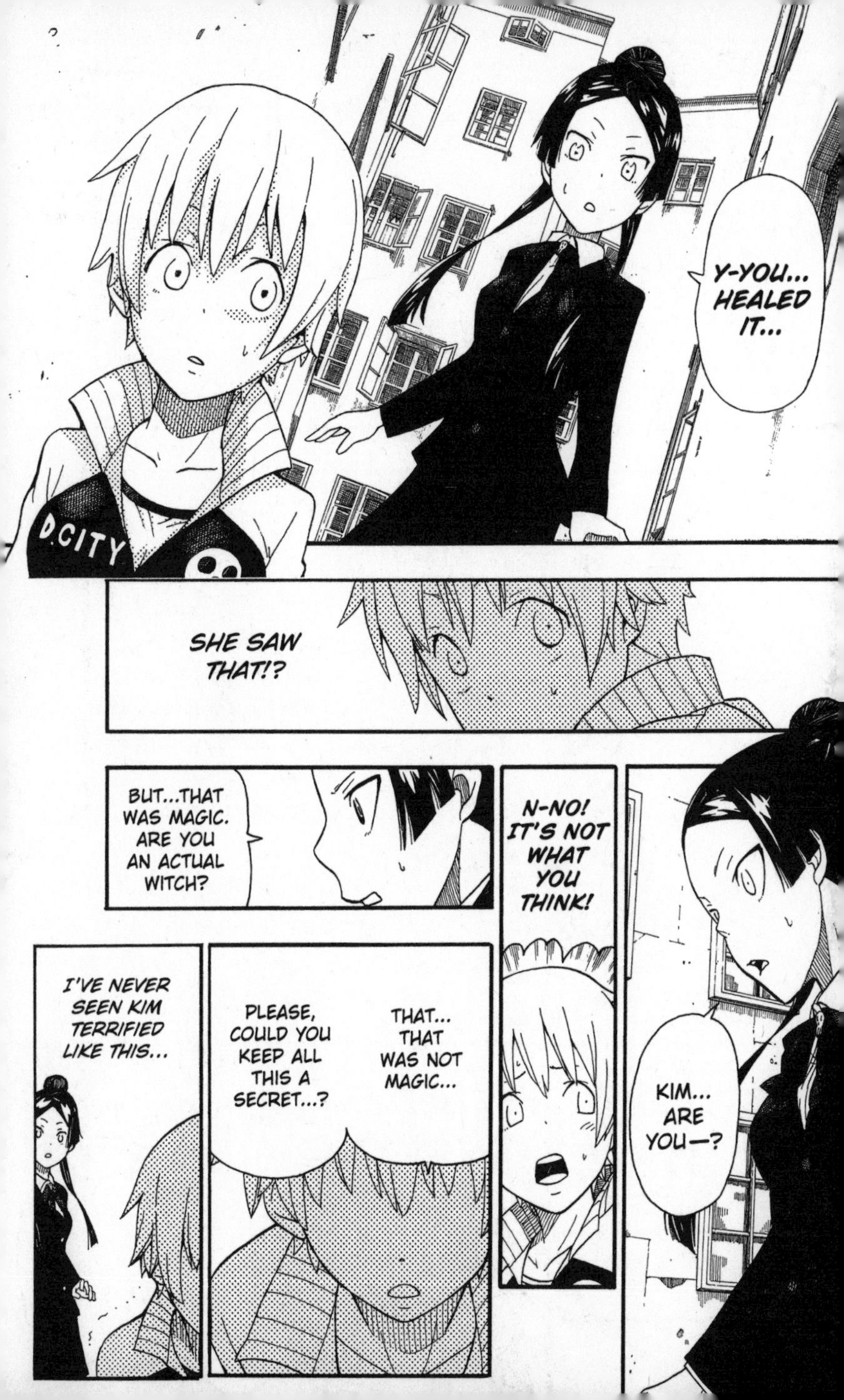
Y-YOU... HEALED IT...
SHE SAW THAT!?
KIM... ARE YOU—?
N-NO! IT'S NOT WHAT YOU THINK!
BUT...THAT WAS MAGIC. ARE YOU AN ACTUAL WITCH?
THAT... THAT WAS NOT MAGIC...
PLEASE, COULD YOU KEEP ALL THIS A SECRET...?
I'VE NEVER SEEN KIM TERRIFIED LIKE THIS...
D.CITY

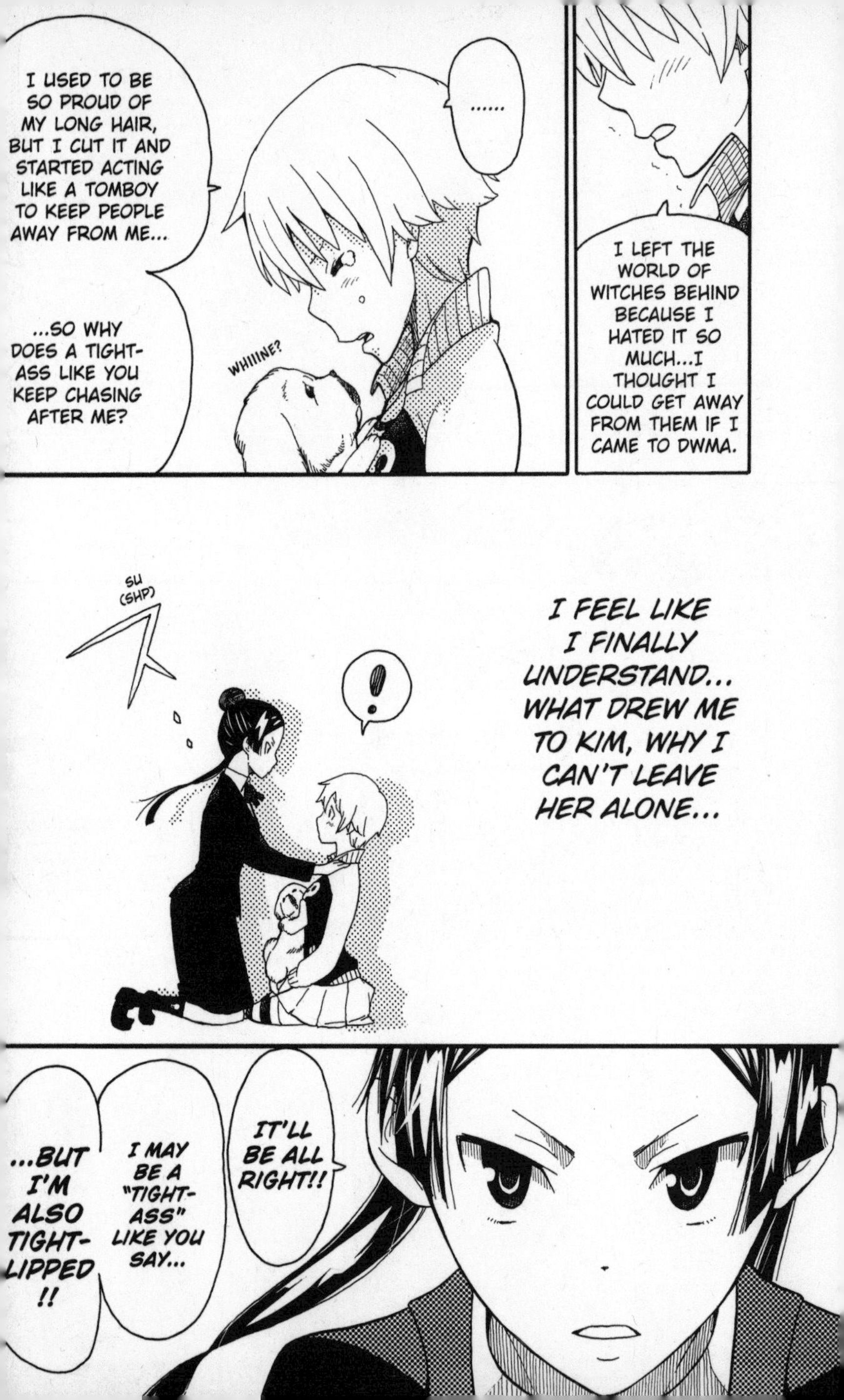

I LEFT THE WORLD OF WITCHES BEHIND BECAUSE I HATED IT SO MUCH...I THOUGHT I COULD GET AWAY FROM THEM IF I CAME TO DWMA.
......
I USED TO BE SO PROUD OF MY LONG HAIR, BUT I CUT IT AND STARTED ACTING LIKE A TOMBOY TO KEEP PEOPLE AWAY FROM ME...
WHIIINE?
...SO WHY DOES A TIGHT-ASS LIKE YOU KEEP CHASING AFTER ME?
I FEEL LIKE I FINALLY UNDERSTAND... WHAT DREW ME TO KIM, WHY I CAN'T LEAVE HER ALONE...
!
SU (SHP)
IT'LL BE ALL RIGHT!!
I MAY BE A "TIGHT-ASS" LIKE YOU SAY...
...BUT I'M ALSO TIGHT-LIPPED!!

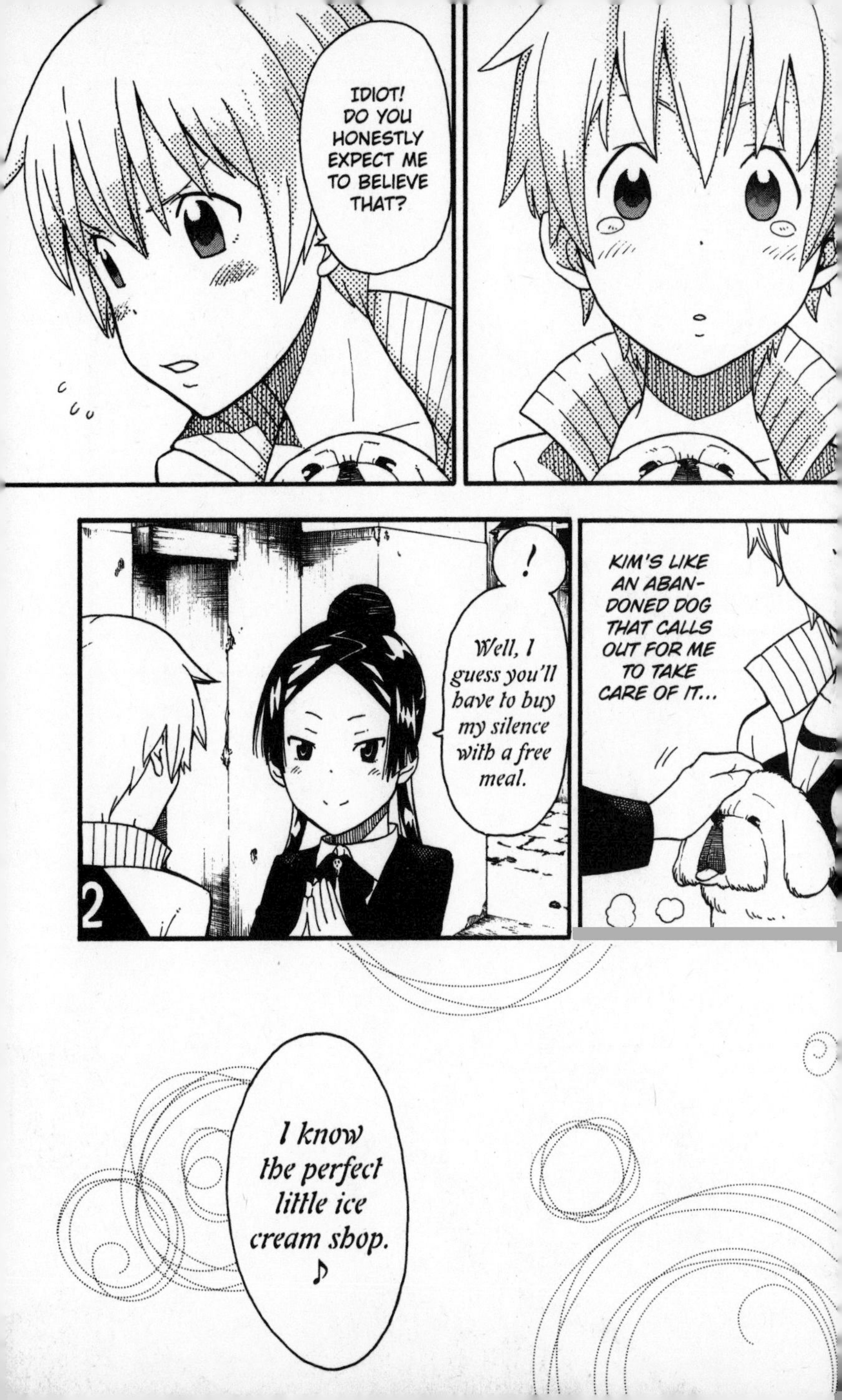
IDIOT! DO YOU HONESTLY EXPECT ME TO BELIEVE THAT?
KIM'S LIKE AN ABAN-DONED DOG THAT CALLS OUT FOR ME TO TAKE CARE OF IT...
!
Well, I guess you'll have to buy my silence with a free meal.
2
I know the perfect little ice cream shop. ♪

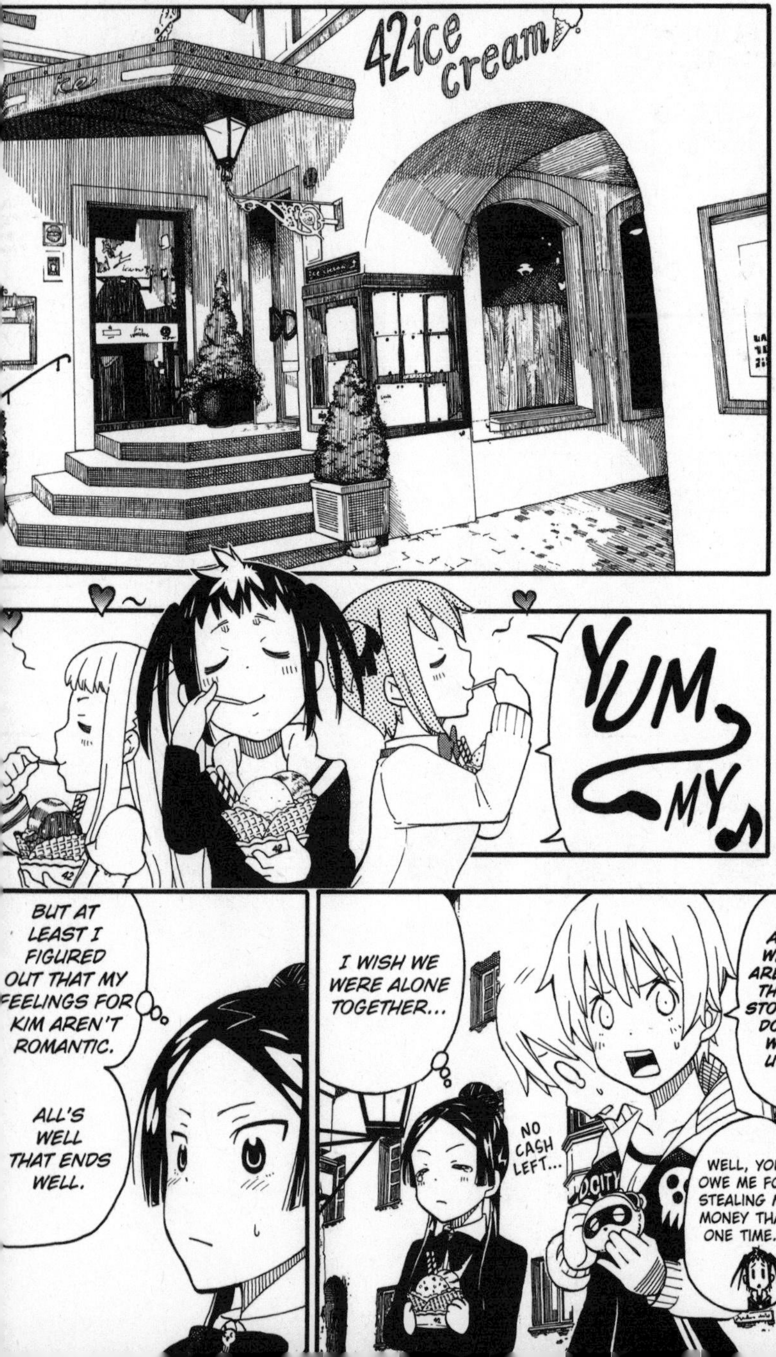

42 ice cream
YUMMY
AND WHAT ARE THE THREE STOOGES DOING WITH US!?
I WISH WE WERE ALONE TOGETHER...
NO CASH LEFT...
WELL, YOU OWE ME FOR STEALING MY MONEY THAT ONE TIME...
BUT AT LEAST I FIGURED OUT THAT MY FEELINGS FOR KIM AREN'T ROMANTIC.
ALL'S WELL THAT ENDS WELL.

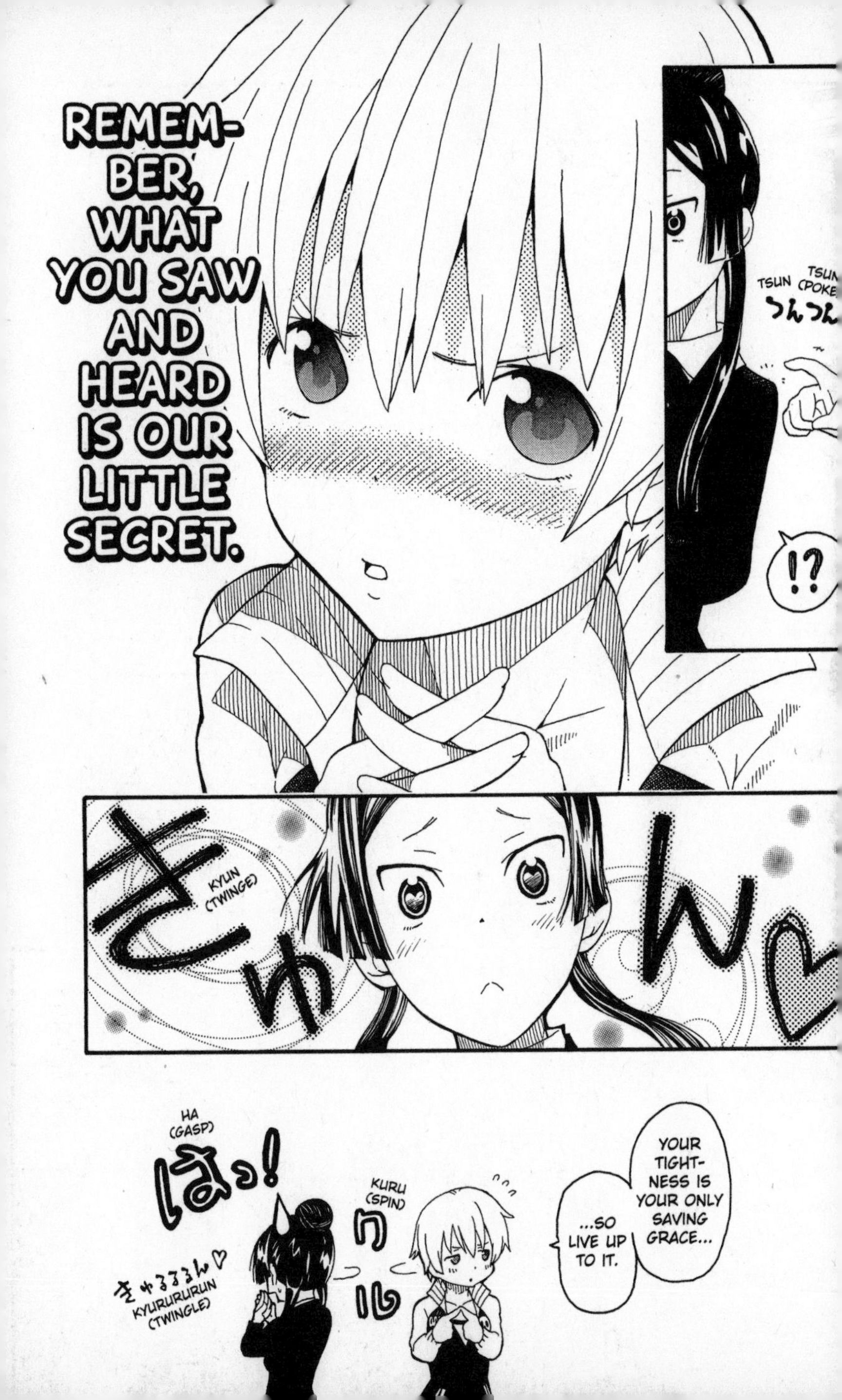

TSUN TSUN (POKE
つんつん
!?
REMEMBER, WHAT YOU SAW AND HEARD IS OUR LITTLE SECRET.
きゅん♡
KYUN (TWINGE)
YOUR TIGHTNESS IS YOUR ONLY SAVING GRACE...
...SO LIVE UP TO IT.
KURU (SPIN)
はっ!
HA (GASP)
きゅるるるん♡
KYURURURUN (TWINGLE)

SOUL EATER NOT!

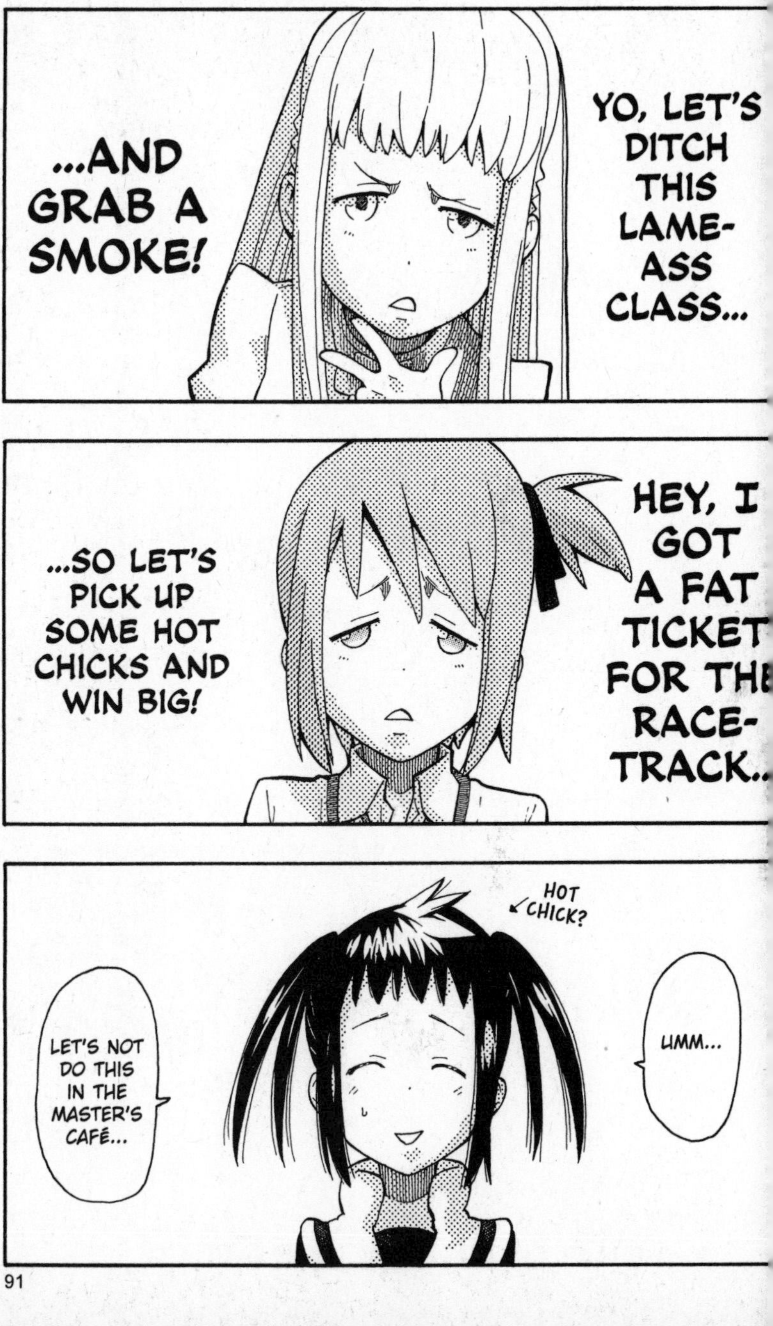
YO, LET'S DITCH THIS LAME-ASS CLASS...
...AND GRAB A SMOKE!
HEY, I GOT A FAT TICKET FOR THE RACE-TRACK...
...SO LET'S PICK UP SOME HOT CHICKS AND WIN BIG!
HOT CHICK?
UMM...
LET'S NOT DO THIS IN THE MASTER'S CAFÉ...

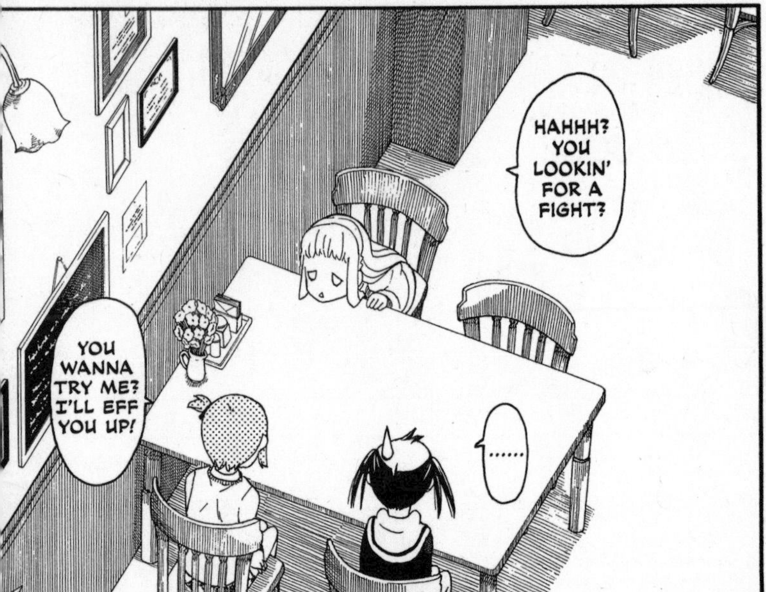
HAHHH? YOU LOOKIN' FOR A FIGHT?
YOU WANNA TRY ME? I'LL EFF YOU UP!
......

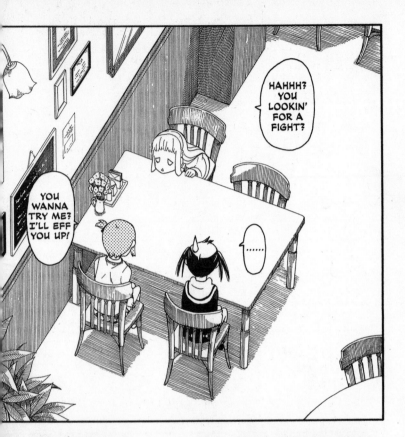

SOUL EATER NOT!

CHAPTER 10: FIGHTING STREET

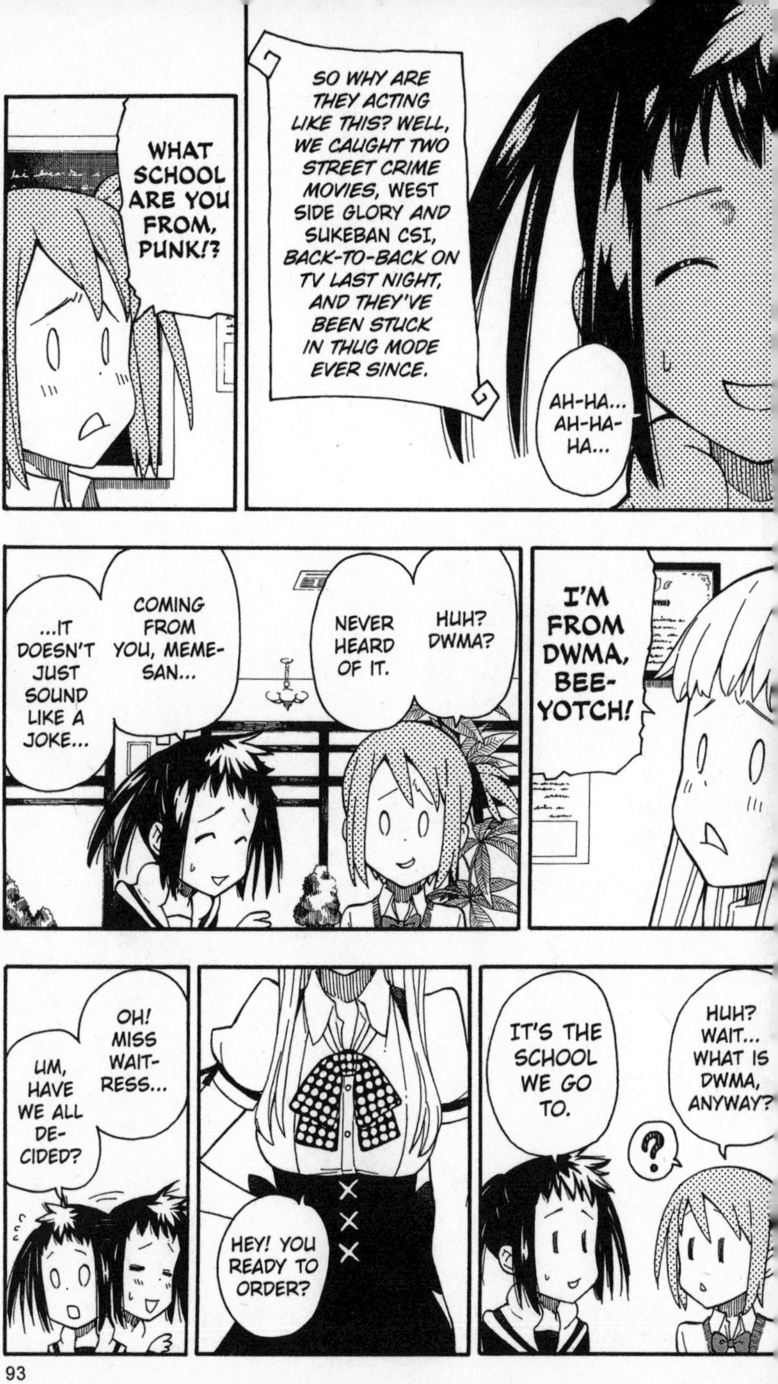
SO WHY ARE THEY ACTING LIKE THIS? WELL, WE CAUGHT TWO STREET CRIME MOVIES, WEST SIDE GLORY AND SUKEBAN CSI, BACK-TO-BACK ON TV LAST NIGHT, AND THEY'VE BEEN STUCK IN THUG MODE EVER SINCE.
AH-HA... AH-HA-HA...
WHAT SCHOOL ARE YOU FROM, PUNK!?
I'M FROM DWMA, BEE-YOTCH!
HUH? DWMA?
NEVER HEARD OF IT.
COMING FROM YOU, MEME-SAN...
...IT DOESN'T JUST SOUND LIKE A JOKE...
HUH? WAIT... WHAT IS DWMA, ANYWAY?
?
IT'S THE SCHOOL WE GO TO.
HEY! YOU READY TO ORDER?
OH! MISS WAITRESS...
UM, HAVE WE ALL DECIDED?

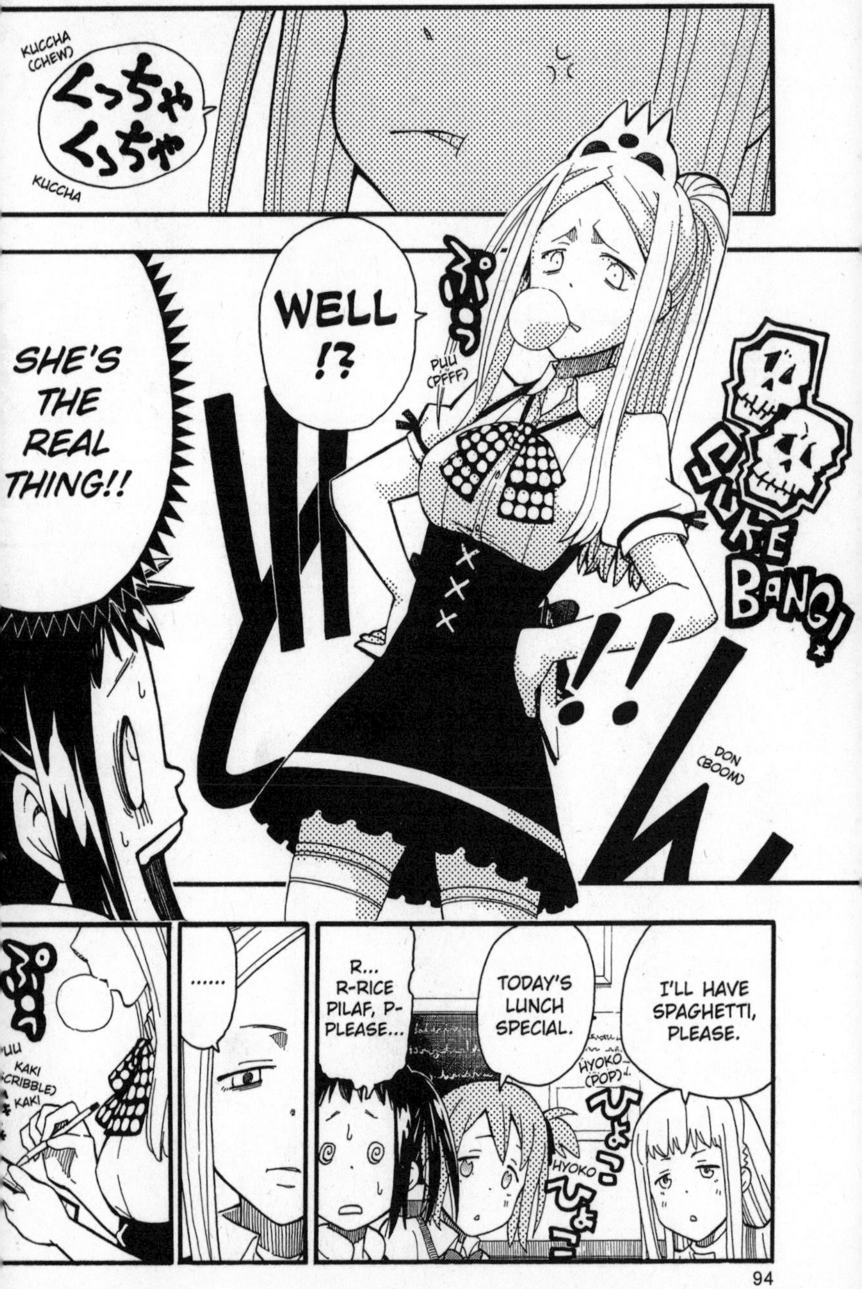
KUCCHA (CHEW)
くっちゃ くっちゃ
KUCCHA
SUKE BANG!
WELL !?
ぷぅ
PUU (PFFF)
SHE'S THE REAL THING!!
DON (BOOM)
I'LL HAVE SPAGHETTI, PLEASE.
HYOKO (POP)
ひょこ
TODAY'S LUNCH SPECIAL.
HYOKO
ひょこ
R... R-RICE PILAF, P-PLEASE...
......
ぷぅ
UU
KAKI
SCRIBBLE)
KAKI

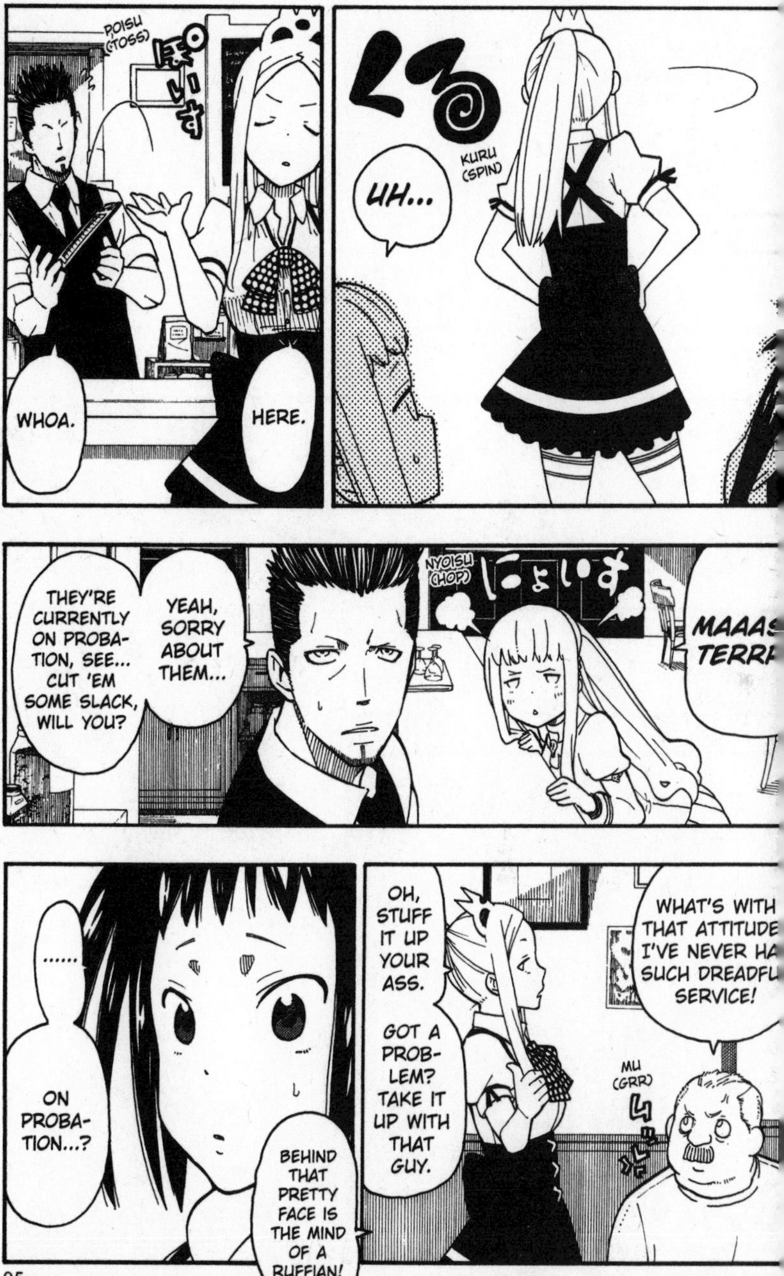
くる
KURU (SPIN)
UH...
ぽいす
POISU (TOSS)
HERE.
WHOA.
MAAAS
TERR
にょいす
NYOISU (CHOP)
YEAH, SORRY ABOUT THEM...
THEY'RE CURRENTLY ON PROBA-TION, SEE... CUT 'EM SOME SLACK, WILL YOU?
WHAT'S WITH THAT ATTITUDE
I'VE NEVER HA
SUCH DREADF
SERVICE!
MU (GRR)
ムッ
OH, STUFF IT UP YOUR ASS.
GOT A PROB-LEM? TAKE IT UP WITH THAT GUY.
......
ON PROBA-TION...?
BEHIND THAT PRETTY FACE IS THE MIND OF A RUFFIAN!

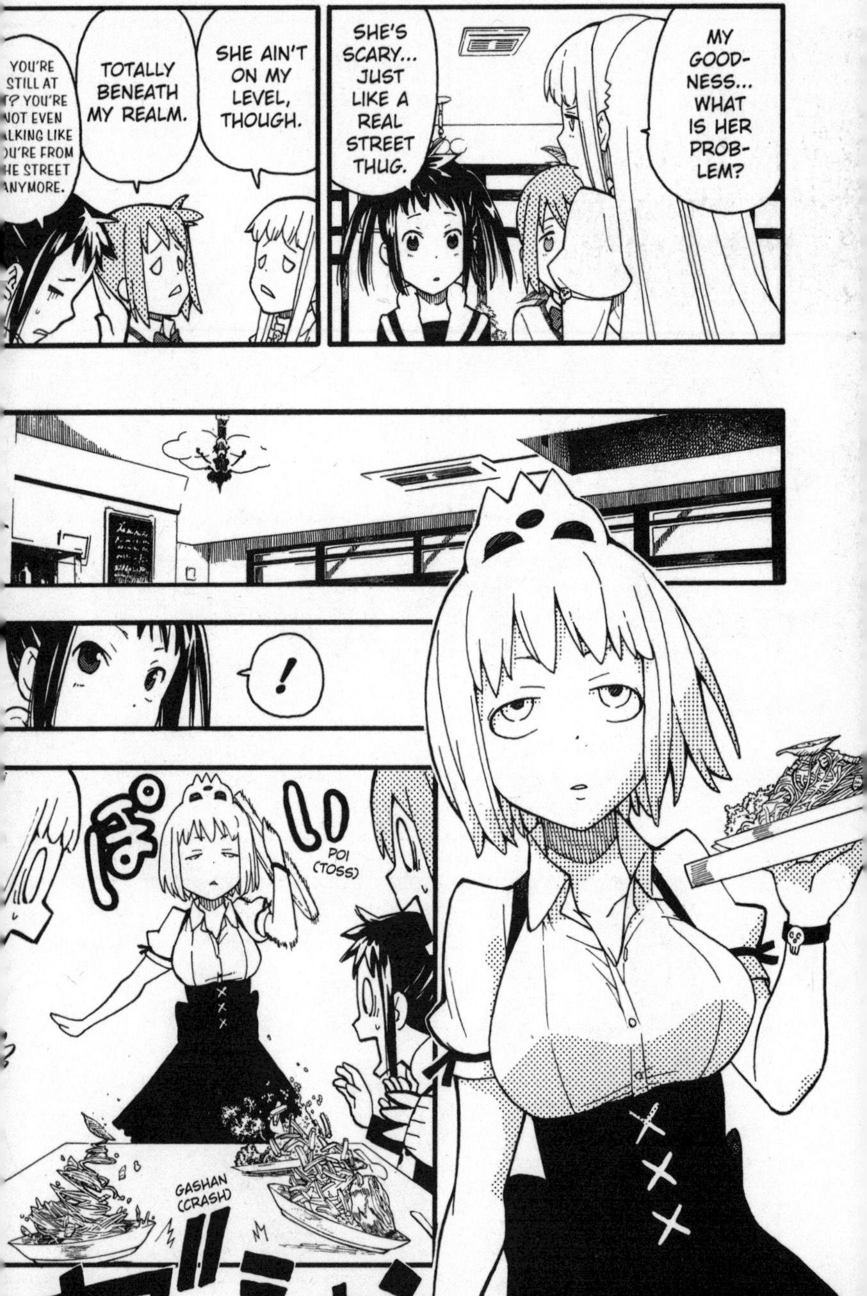
MY GOODNESS... WHAT IS HER PROBLEM?
SHE'S SCARY... JUST LIKE A REAL STREET THUG.
SHE AIN'T ON MY LEVEL, THOUGH.
TOTALLY BENEATH MY REALM.
YOU'RE STILL AT T? YOU'RE NOT EVEN ALKING LIKE U'RE FROM HE STREET ANYMORE.
!
ぽい
POI (TOSS)
ガシャン
GASHAN (CRASH)

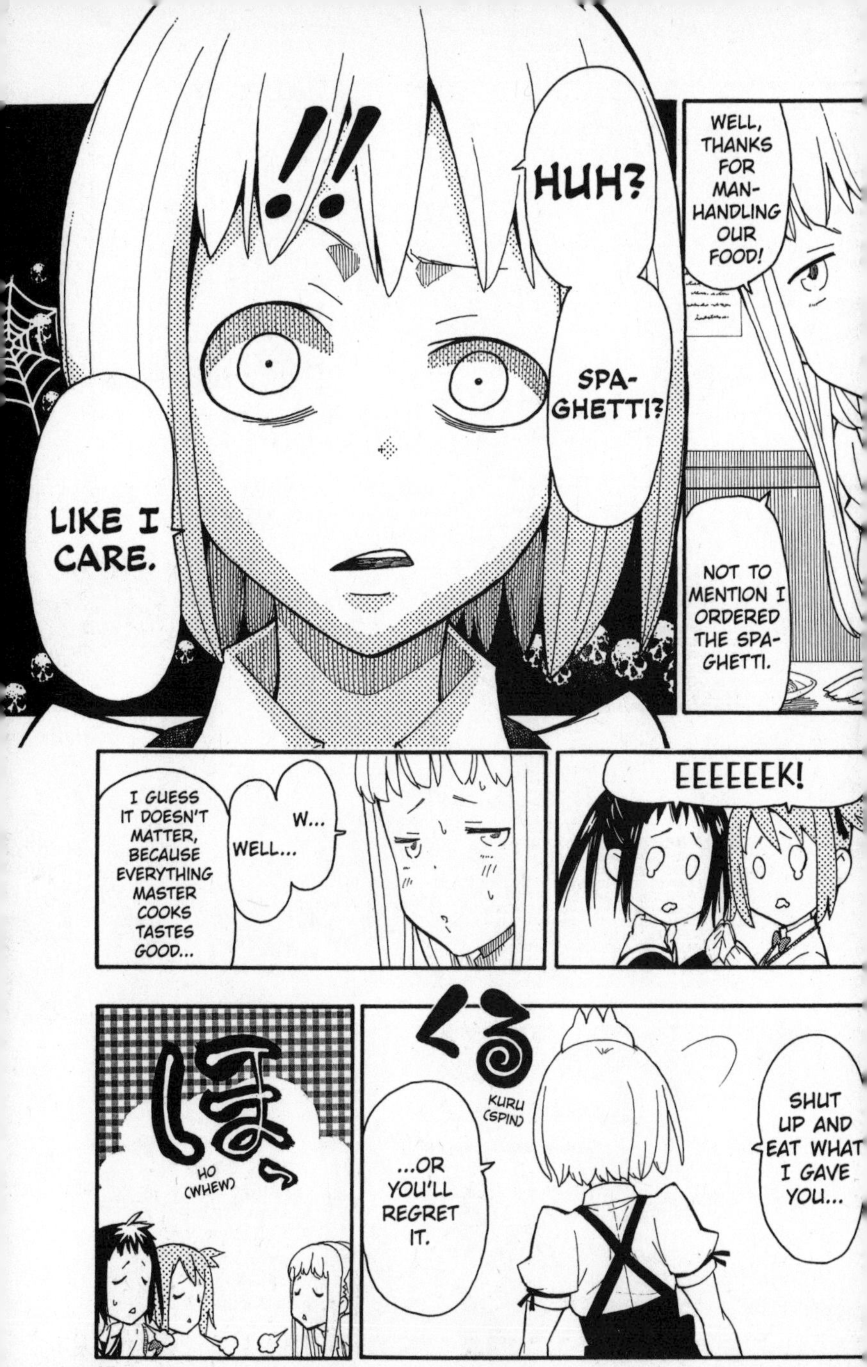
WELL, THANKS FOR MAN-HANDLING OUR FOOD!
NOT TO MENTION I ORDERED THE SPA-GHETTI.
!!
HUH?
SPA-GHETTI?
LIKE I CARE.
EEEEEEK!
W... WELL...
I GUESS IT DOESN'T MATTER, BECAUSE EVERYTHING MASTER COOKS TASTES GOOD...
SHUT UP AND EAT WHAT I GAVE YOU...
くる
KURU (SPIN)
...OR YOU'LL REGRET IT.
ほっ
HO (WHEW)

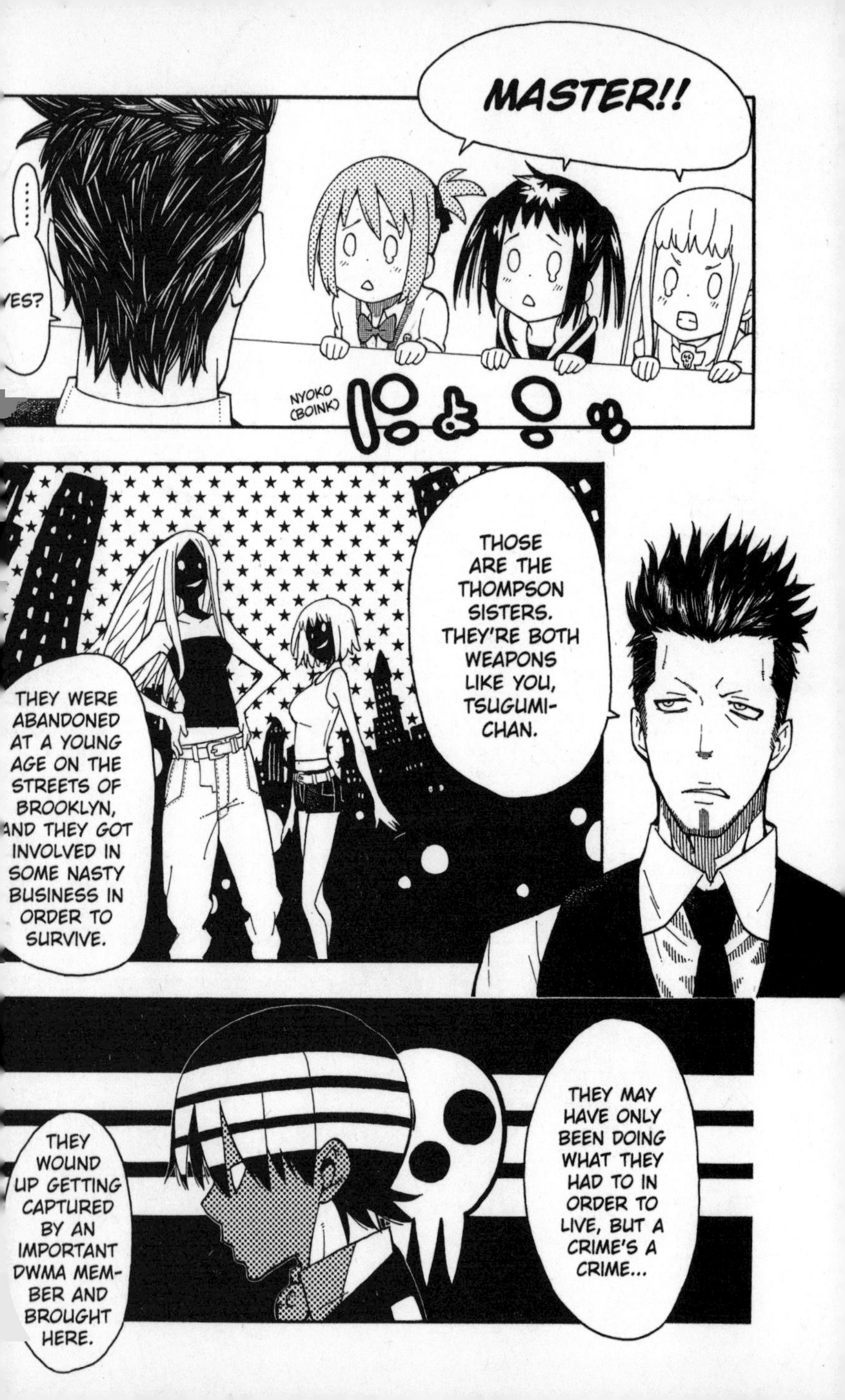
MASTER!!
......
YES?
NYOKO (BOINK)
THOSE ARE THE THOMPSON SISTERS. THEY'RE BOTH WEAPONS LIKE YOU, TSUGUMI-CHAN.
THEY WERE ABANDONED AT A YOUNG AGE ON THE STREETS OF BROOKLYN, AND THEY GOT INVOLVED IN SOME NASTY BUSINESS IN ORDER TO SURVIVE.
THEY MAY HAVE ONLY BEEN DOING WHAT THEY HAD TO IN ORDER TO LIVE, BUT A CRIME'S A CRIME...
THEY WOUND UP GETTING CAPTURED BY AN IMPORTANT DWMA MEM-BER AND BROUGHT HERE.

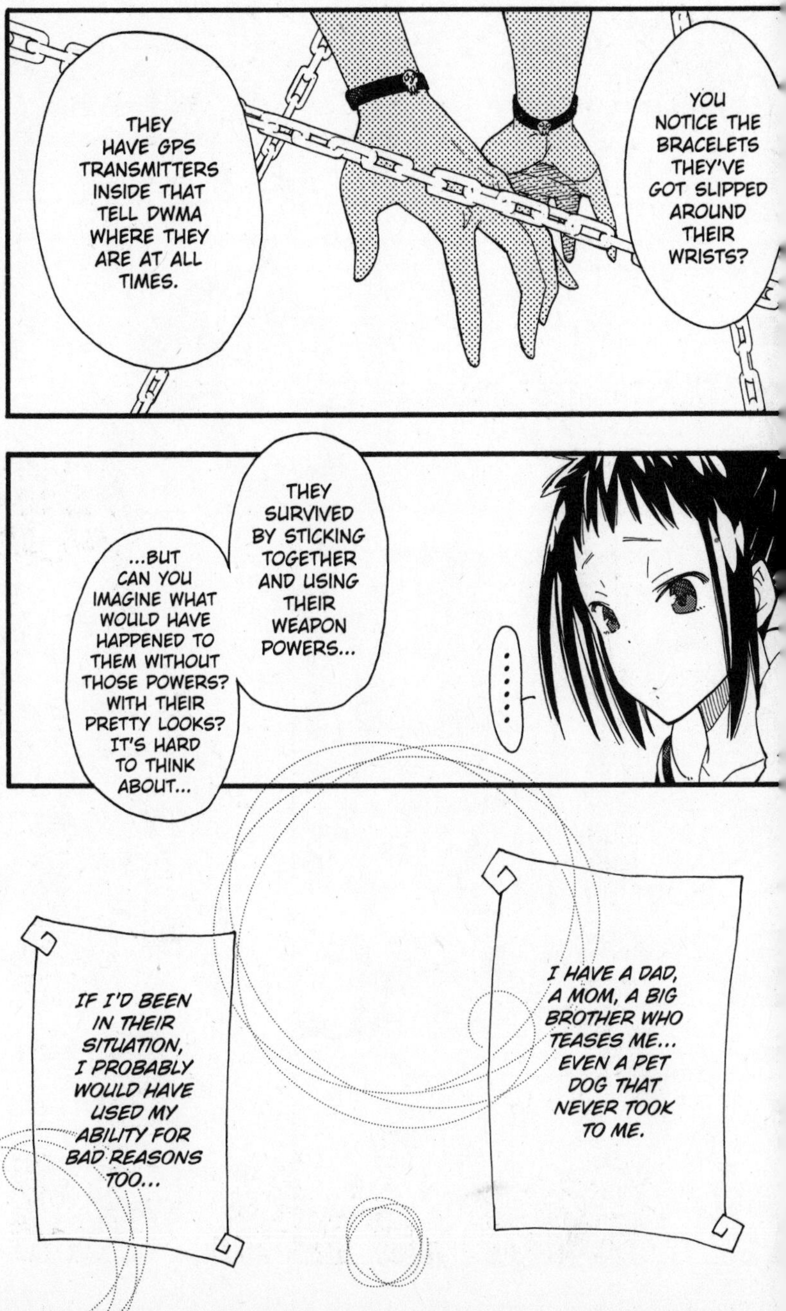
YOU NOTICE THE BRACELETS THEY'VE GOT SLIPPED AROUND THEIR WRISTS?
THEY HAVE GPS TRANSMITTERS INSIDE THAT TELL DWMA WHERE THEY ARE AT ALL TIMES.
THEY SURVIVED BY STICKING TOGETHER AND USING THEIR WEAPON POWERS...
...BUT CAN YOU IMAGINE WHAT WOULD HAVE HAPPENED TO THEM WITHOUT THOSE POWERS? WITH THEIR PRETTY LOOKS? IT'S HARD TO THINK ABOUT...
......
I HAVE A DAD, A MOM, A BIG BROTHER WHO TEASES ME... EVEN A PET DOG THAT NEVER TOOK TO ME.
IF I'D BEEN IN THEIR SITUATION, I PROBABLY WOULD HAVE USED MY ABILITY FOR BAD REASONS TOO...

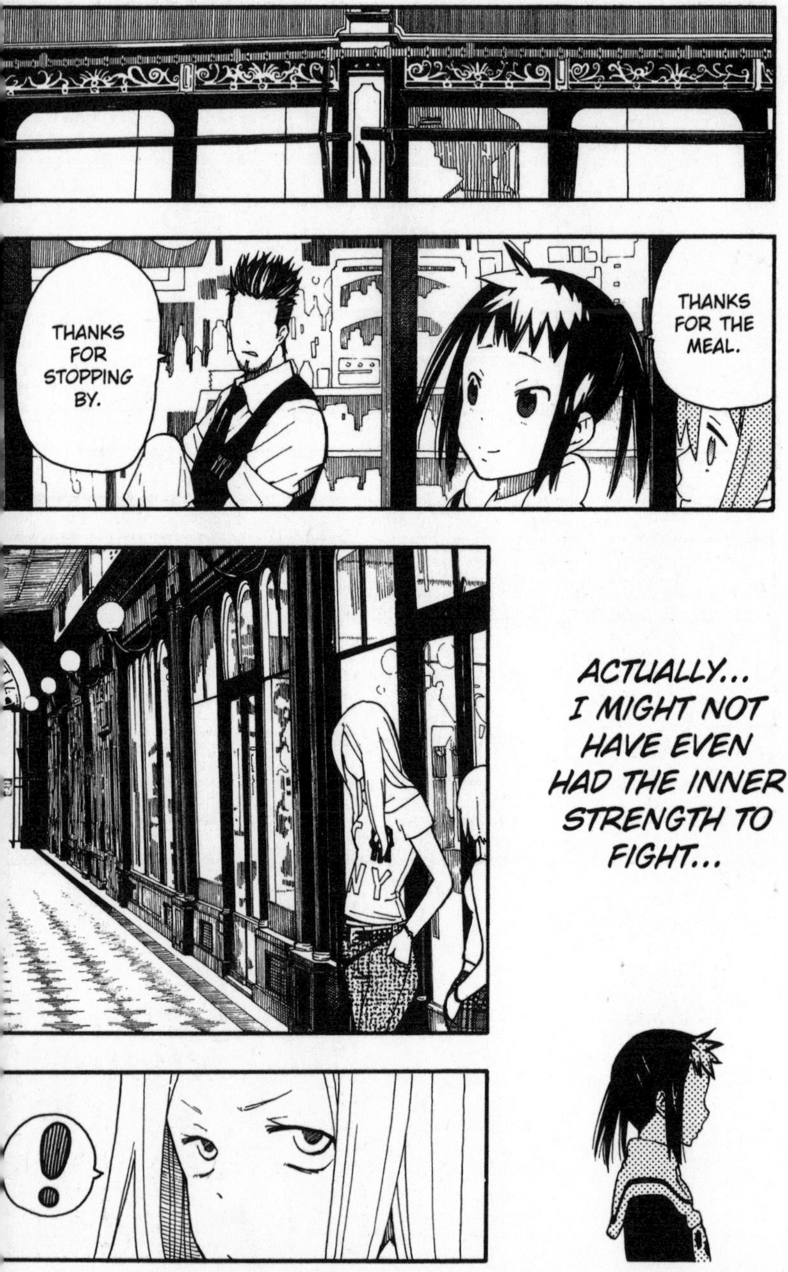
THANKS FOR THE MEAL.
THANKS FOR STOPPING BY.
ACTUALLY... I MIGHT NOT HAVE EVEN HAD THE INNER STRENGTH TO FIGHT...
!

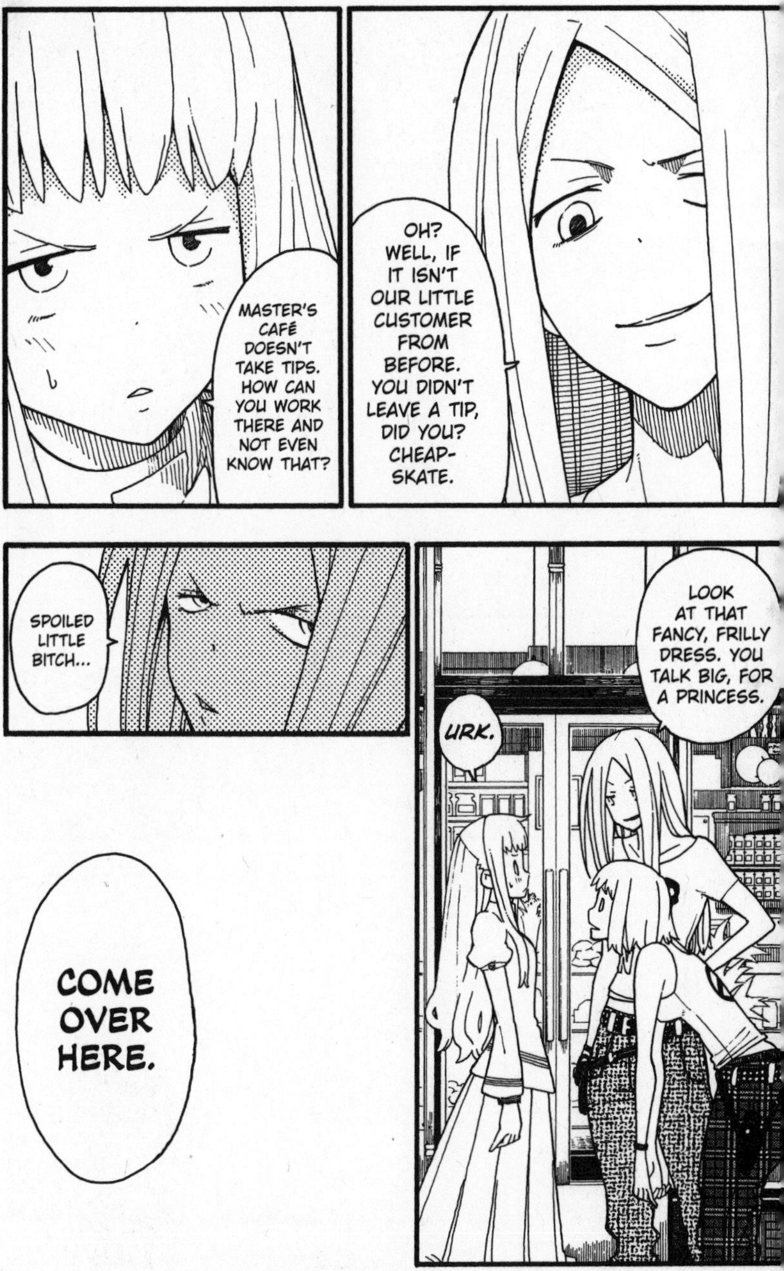
OH? WELL, IF IT ISN'T OUR LITTLE CUSTOMER FROM BEFORE. YOU DIDN'T LEAVE A TIP, DID YOU? CHEAP-SKATE.
MASTER'S CAFÉ DOESN'T TAKE TIPS. HOW CAN YOU WORK THERE AND NOT EVEN KNOW THAT?
LOOK AT THAT FANCY, FRILLY DRESS. YOU TALK BIG, FOR A PRINCESS.
URK.
SPOILED LITTLE BITCH...
COME OVER HERE.

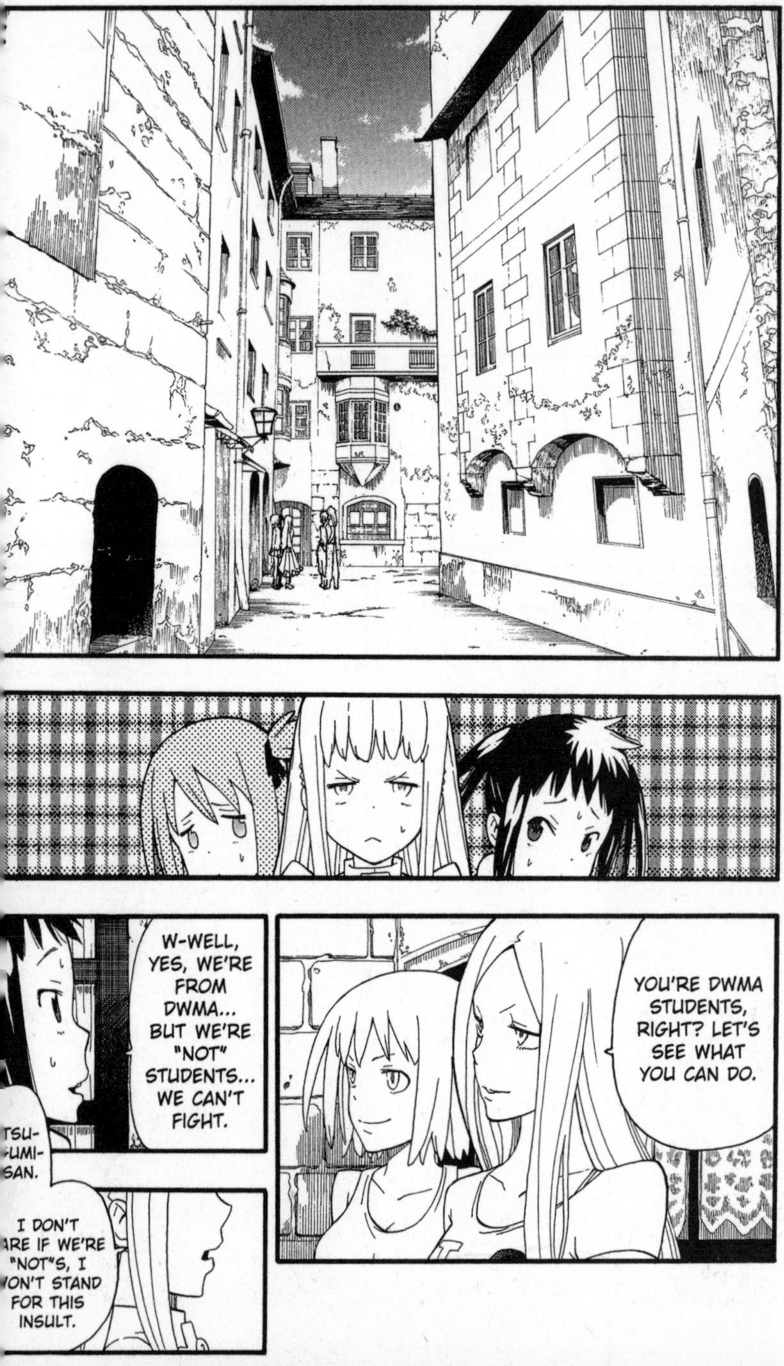

YOU'RE DWMA STUDENTS, RIGHT? LET'S SEE WHAT YOU CAN DO.
W-WELL, YES, WE'RE FROM DWMA... BUT WE'RE "NOT" STUDENTS... WE CAN'T FIGHT.
TSU-UMI-SAN.
I DON'T ARE IF WE'RE "NOT"S, I ON'T STAND FOR THIS INSULT.

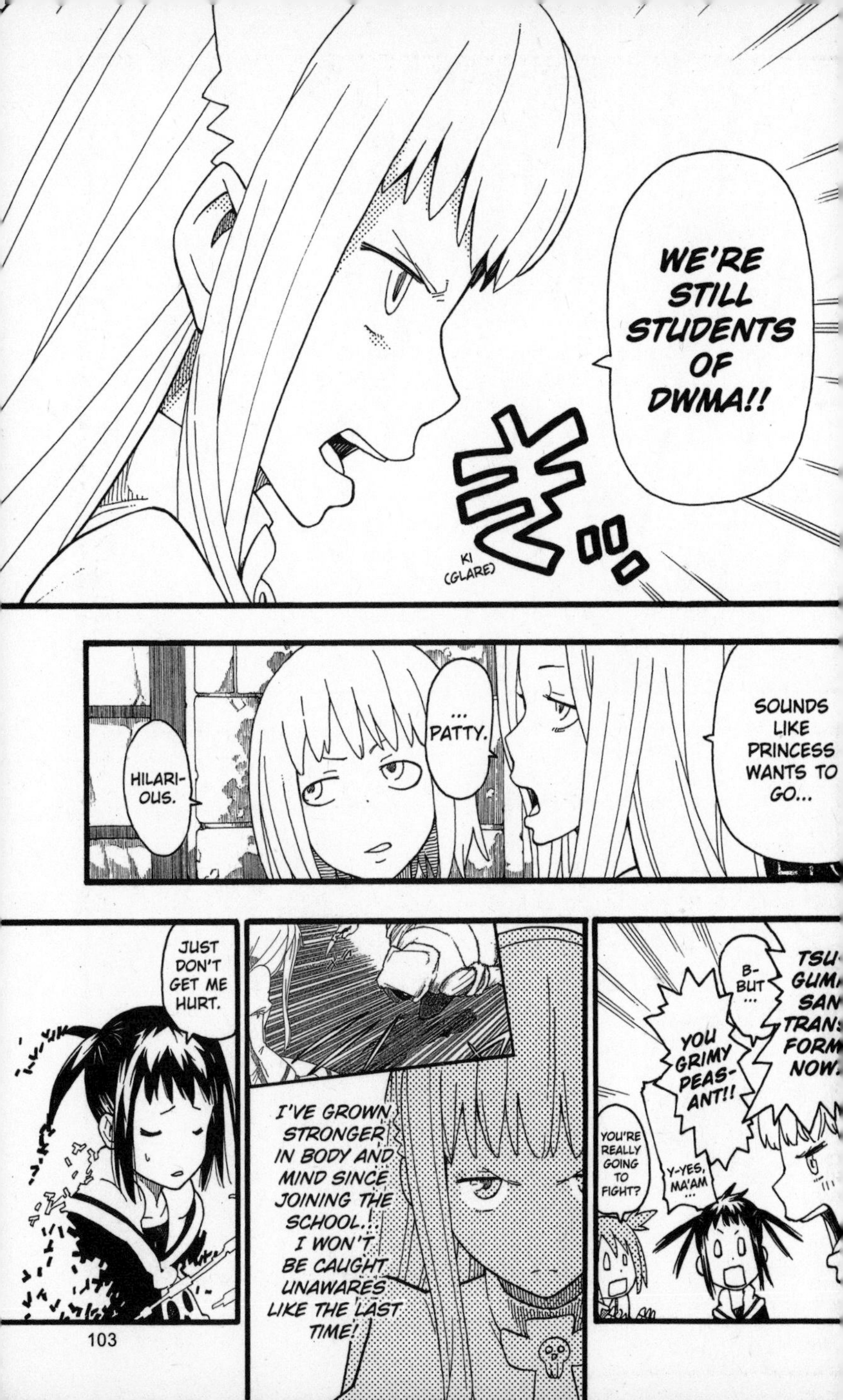
WE'RE STILL STUDENTS OF DWMA!!
KI (GLARE)
SOUNDS LIKE PRINCESS WANTS TO GO...
... PATTY.
HILARI-OUS.
TSU-GUM SAN TRANS FORM NOW.
B-BUT ...
YOU GRIMY PEAS-ANT!!
Y-YES, MA'AM ...
YOU'RE REALLY GOING TO FIGHT?
I'VE GROWN STRONGER IN BODY AND MIND SINCE JOINING THE SCHOOL...! I WON'T BE CAUGHT UNAWARES LIKE THE LAST TIME!
JUST DON'T GET ME HURT.

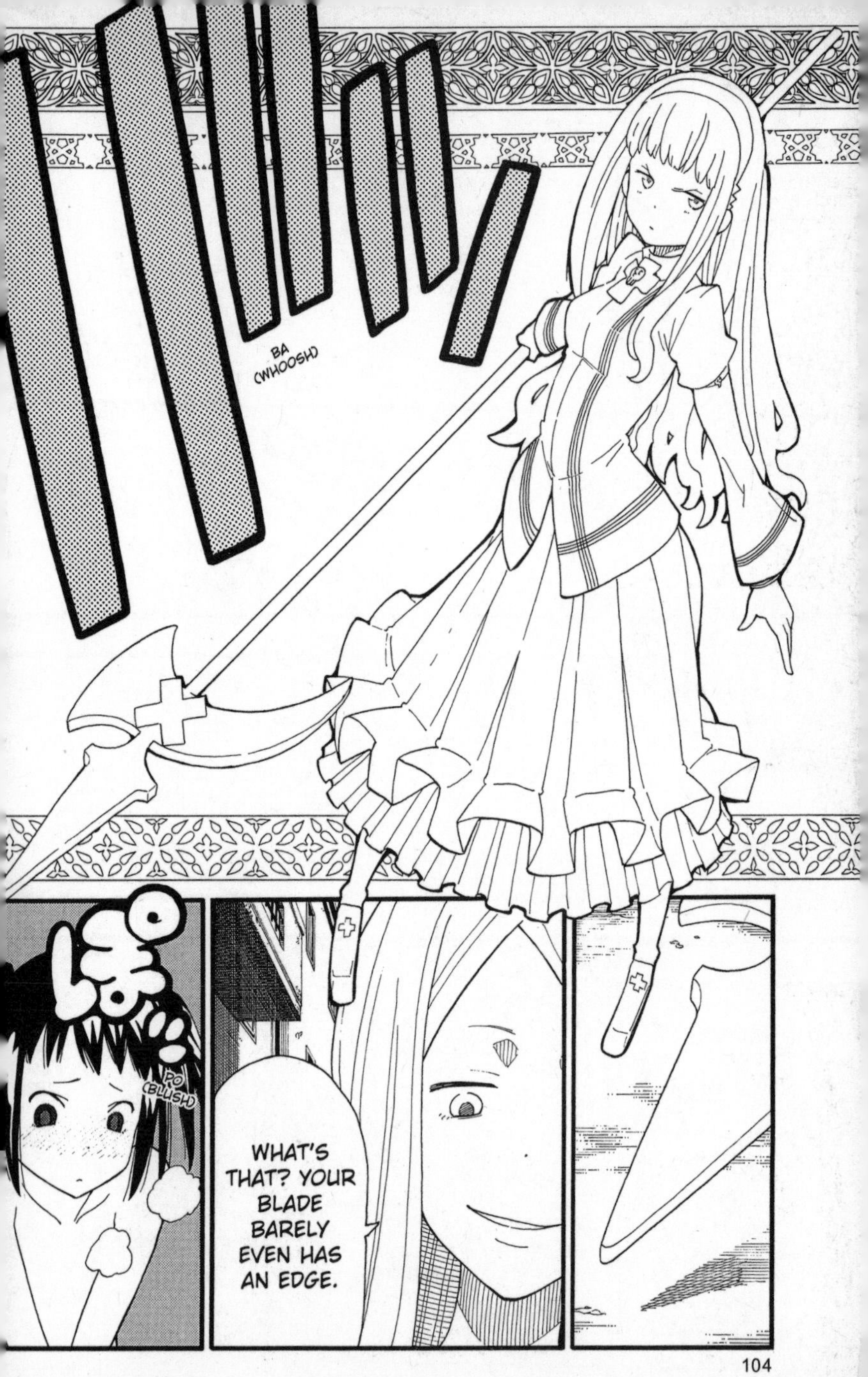
BA
(WHOOSH)
PO
(BLUSH)
WHAT'S THAT? YOUR BLADE BARELY EVEN HAS AN EDGE.

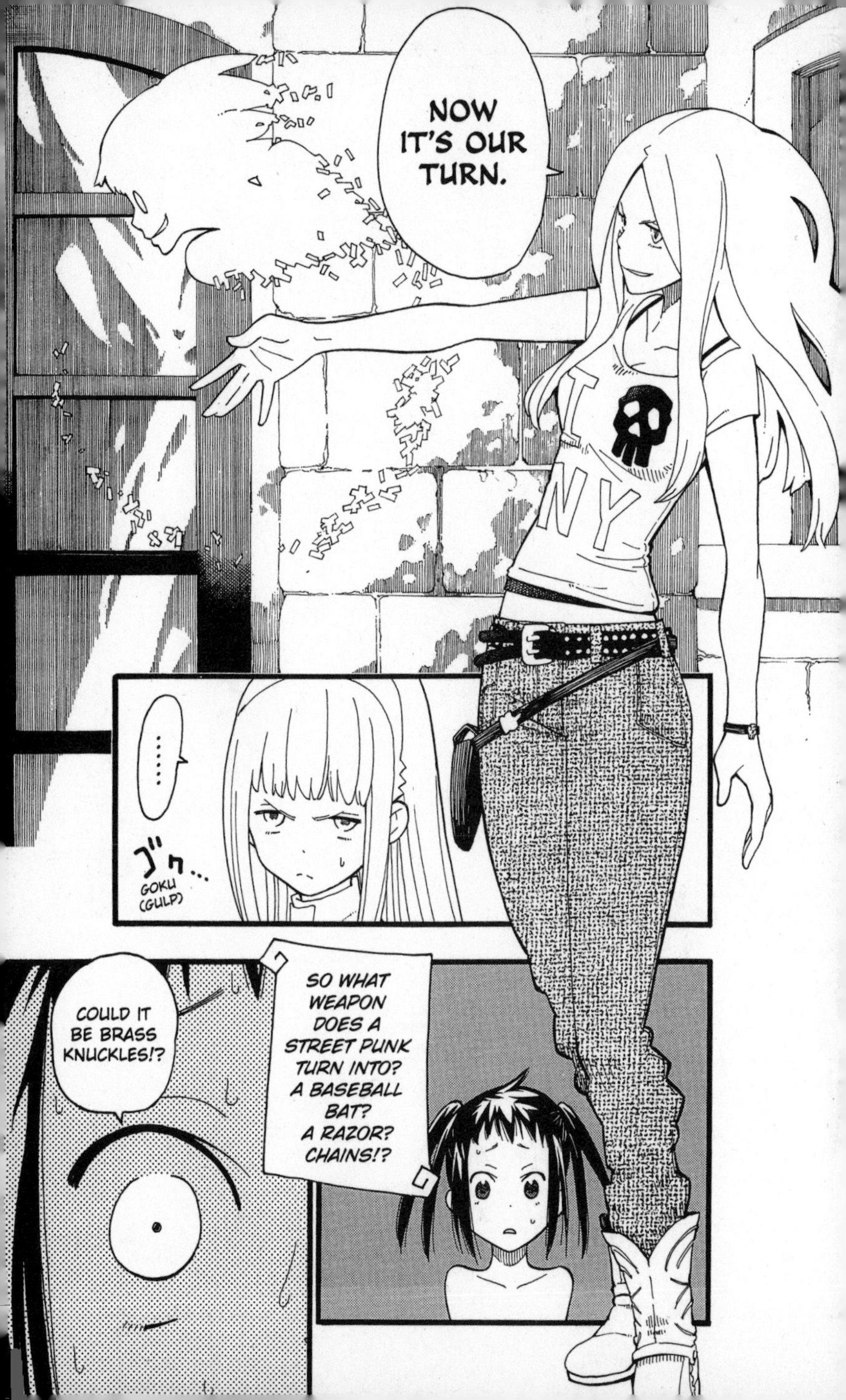
NOW IT'S OUR TURN.
......
ゴク...
GOKU (GULP)
SO WHAT WEAPON DOES A STREET PUNK TURN INTO? A BASEBALL BAT? A RAZOR? CHAINS!?
COULD IT BE BRASS KNUCKLES!?

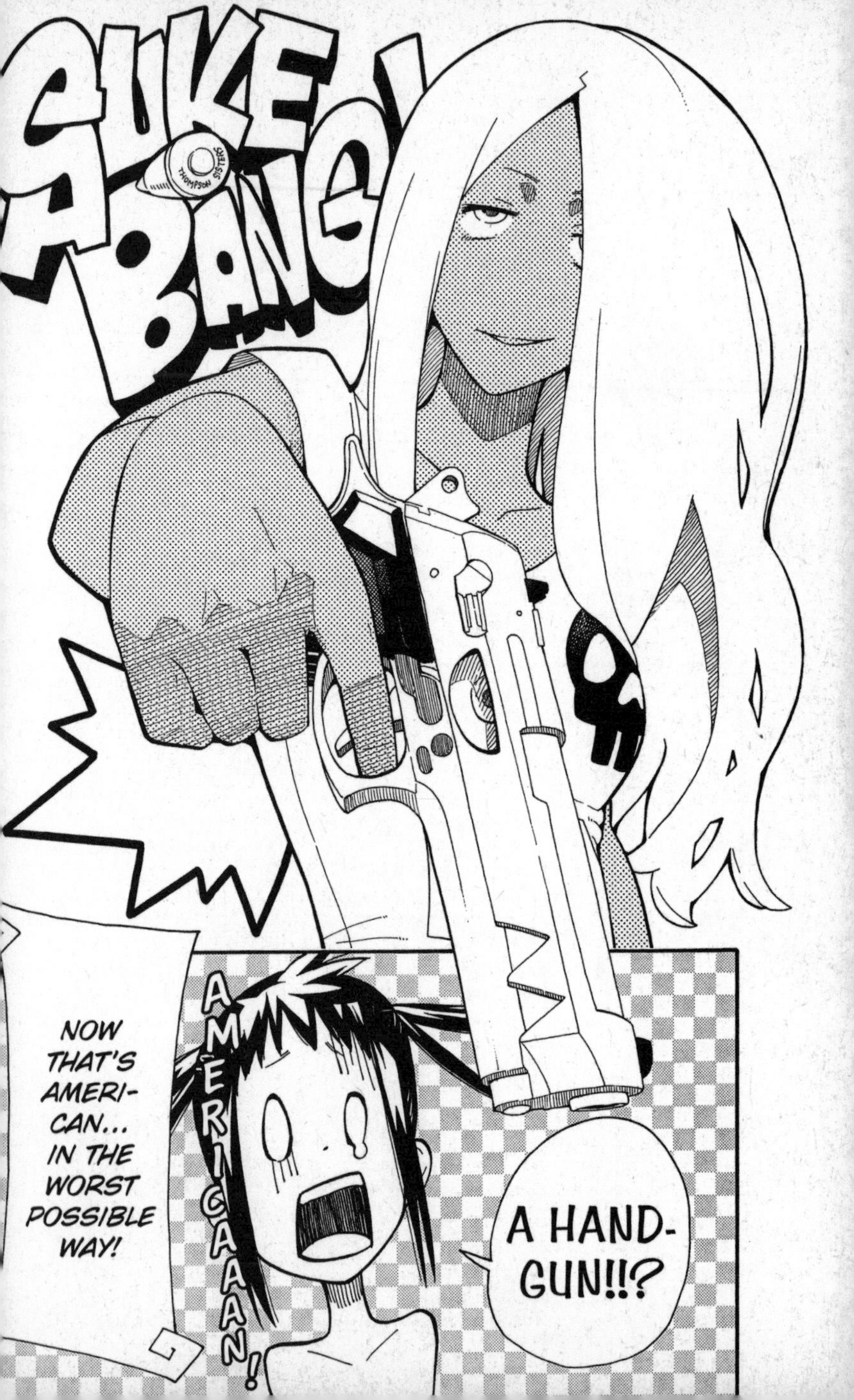
SUKE BANG
THOMPSON SISTERS
A HAND-GUN!!?
AMERICAAAAN!
NOW THAT'S AMERI-CAN... IN THE WORST POSSIBLE WAY!

SOUL EATER NOT!

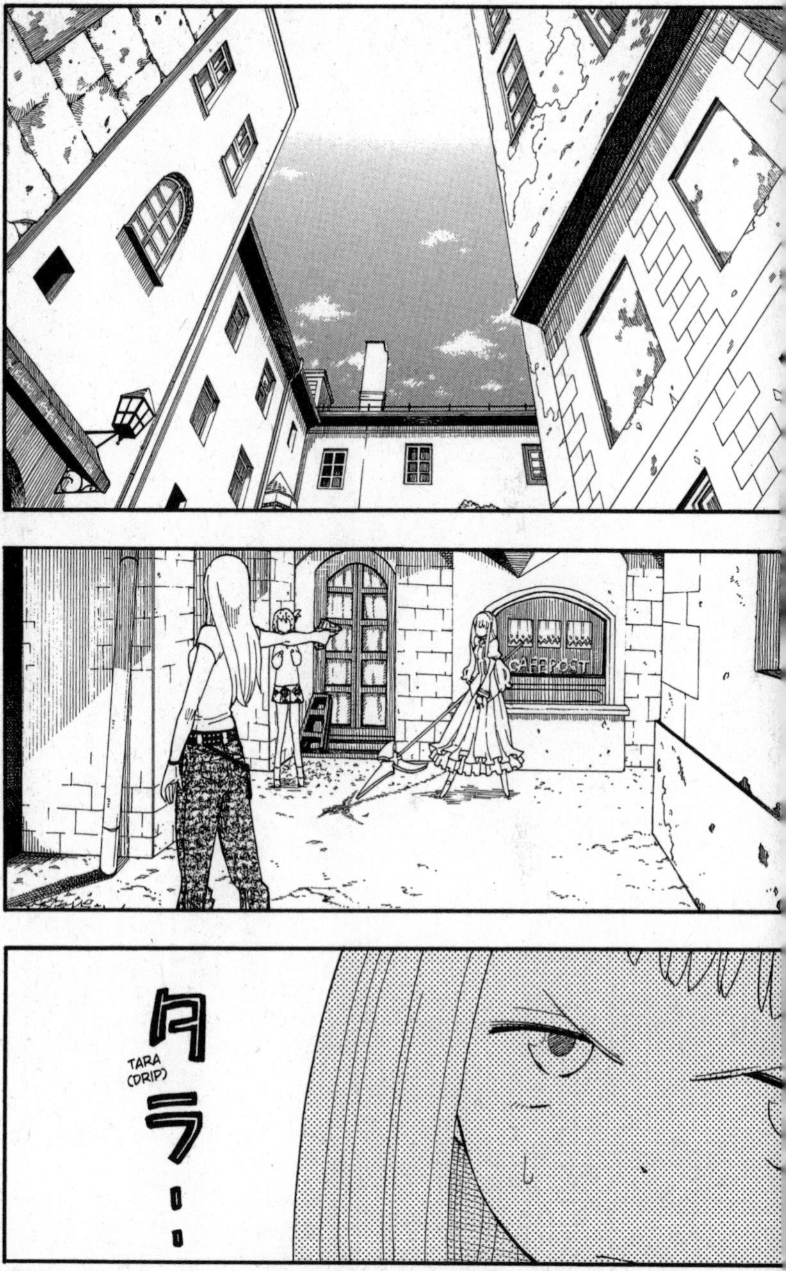
CAFE POST
タラ‥
TARA (DRIP)

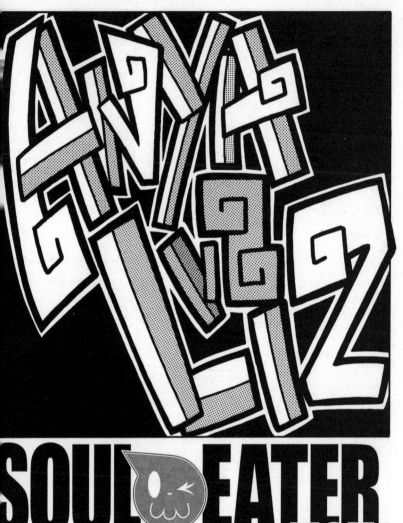

SOUL EATER NOT!

CHAPTER 11: SF2!

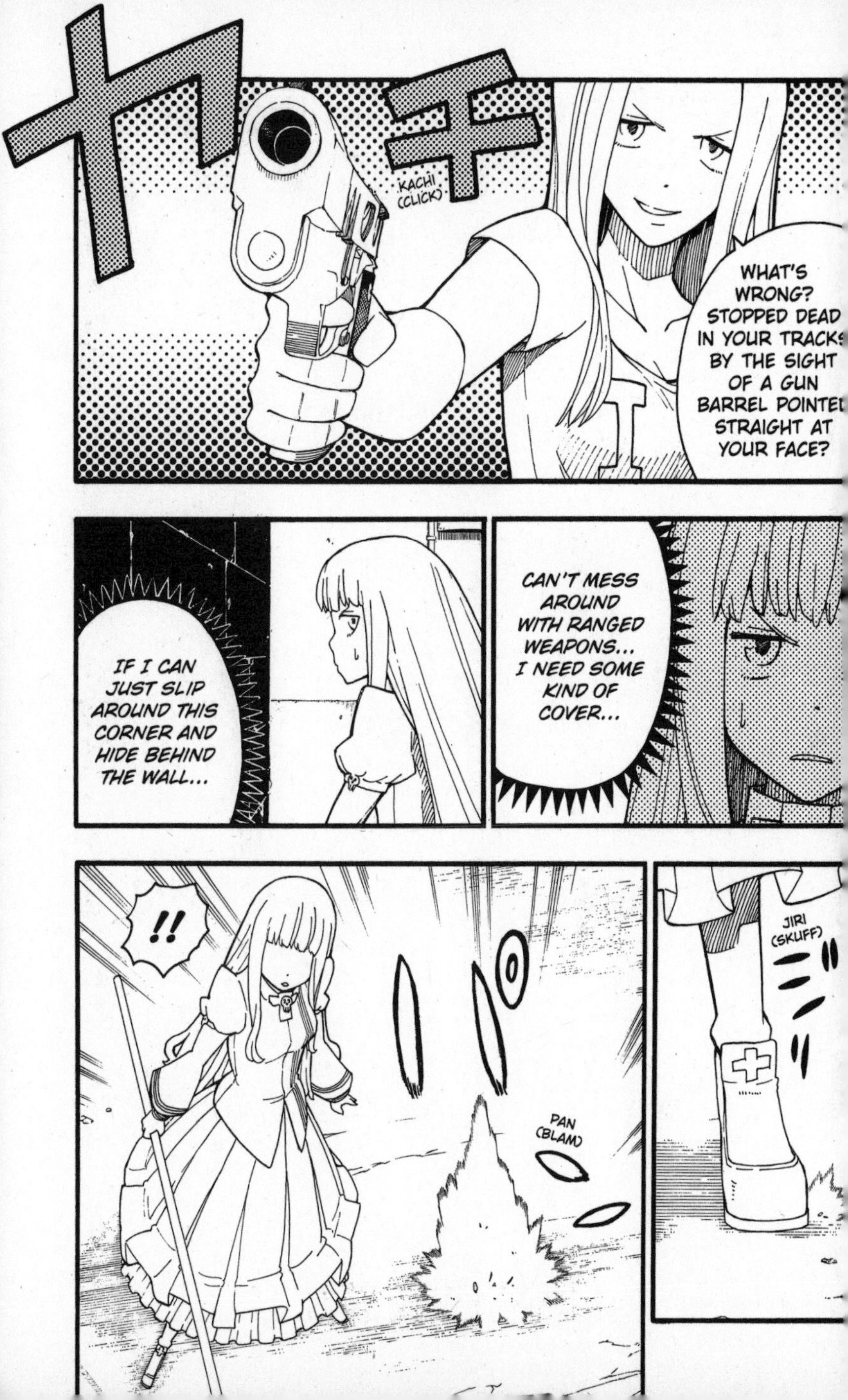
KACHI (CLICK)
WHAT'S WRONG? STOPPED DEAD IN YOUR TRACKS BY THE SIGHT OF A GUN BARREL POINTED STRAIGHT AT YOUR FACE?
CAN'T MESS AROUND WITH RANGED WEAPONS... I NEED SOME KIND OF COVER...
IF I CAN JUST SLIP AROUND THIS CORNER AND HIDE BEHIND THE WALL...
JIRI (SKUFF)
!!
PAN (BLAM)

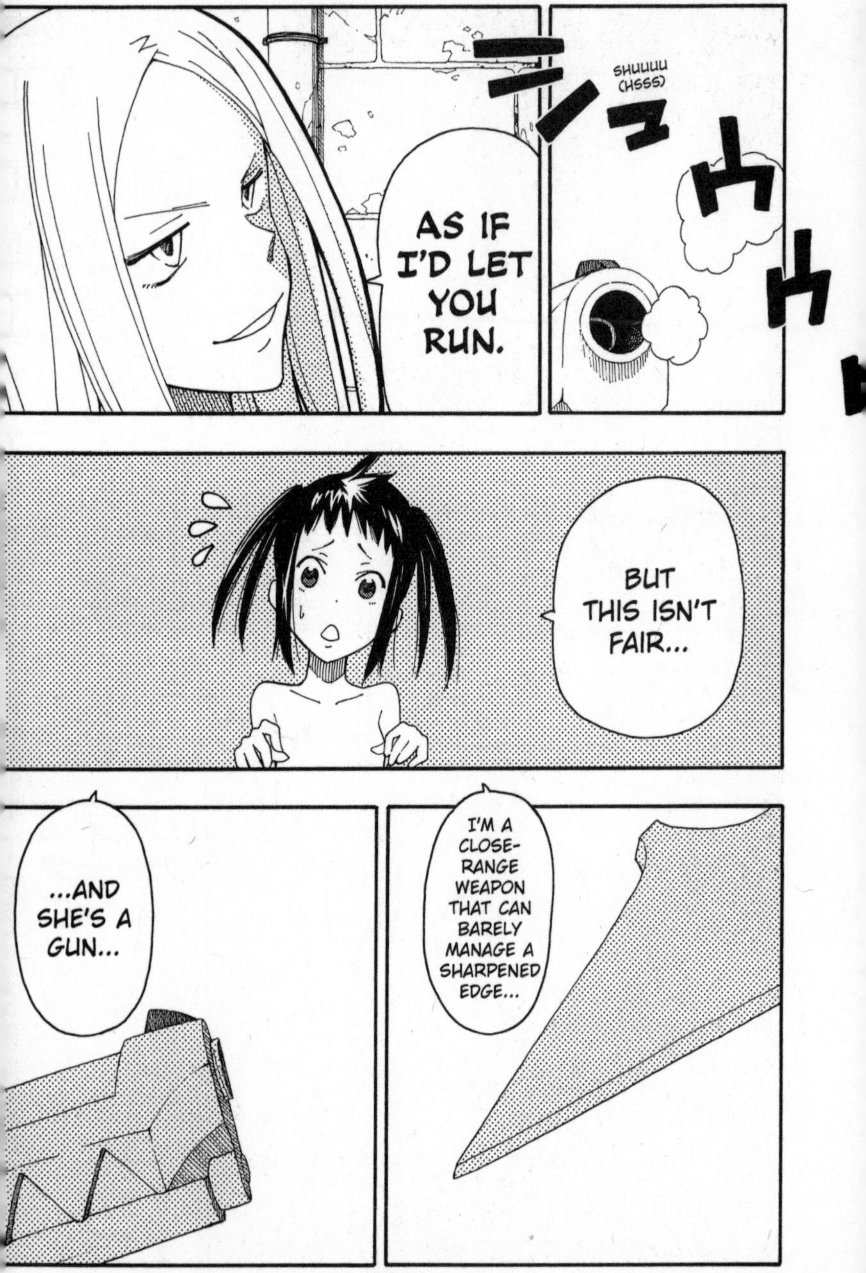
シュウウ
SHUUUU (HSSS)
AS IF I'D LET YOU RUN.
BUT THIS ISN'T FAIR...
I'M A CLOSE-RANGE WEAPON THAT CAN BARELY MANAGE A SHARPENED EDGE...
...AND SHE'S A GUN...

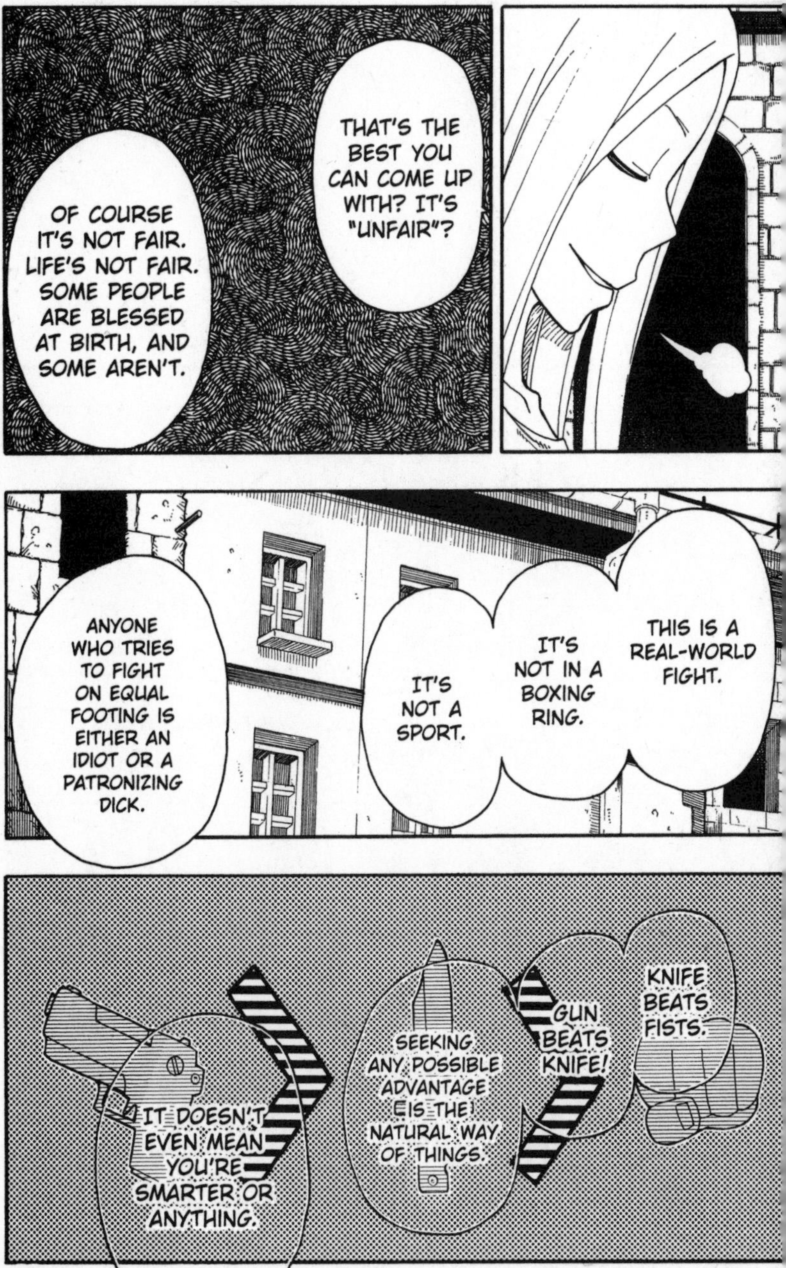
THAT'S THE BEST YOU CAN COME UP WITH? IT'S "UNFAIR"?
OF COURSE IT'S NOT FAIR. LIFE'S NOT FAIR. SOME PEOPLE ARE BLESSED AT BIRTH, AND SOME AREN'T.
THIS IS A REAL-WORLD FIGHT.
IT'S NOT IN A BOXING RING.
IT'S NOT A SPORT.
ANYONE WHO TRIES TO FIGHT ON EQUAL FOOTING IS EITHER AN IDIOT OR A PATRONIZING DICK.
KNIFE BEATS FISTS.
GUN BEATS KNIFE!
SEEKING ANY POSSIBLE ADVANTAGE IS THE NATURAL WAY OF THINGS.
IT DOESN'T EVEN MEAN YOU'RE SMARTER OR ANYTHING.

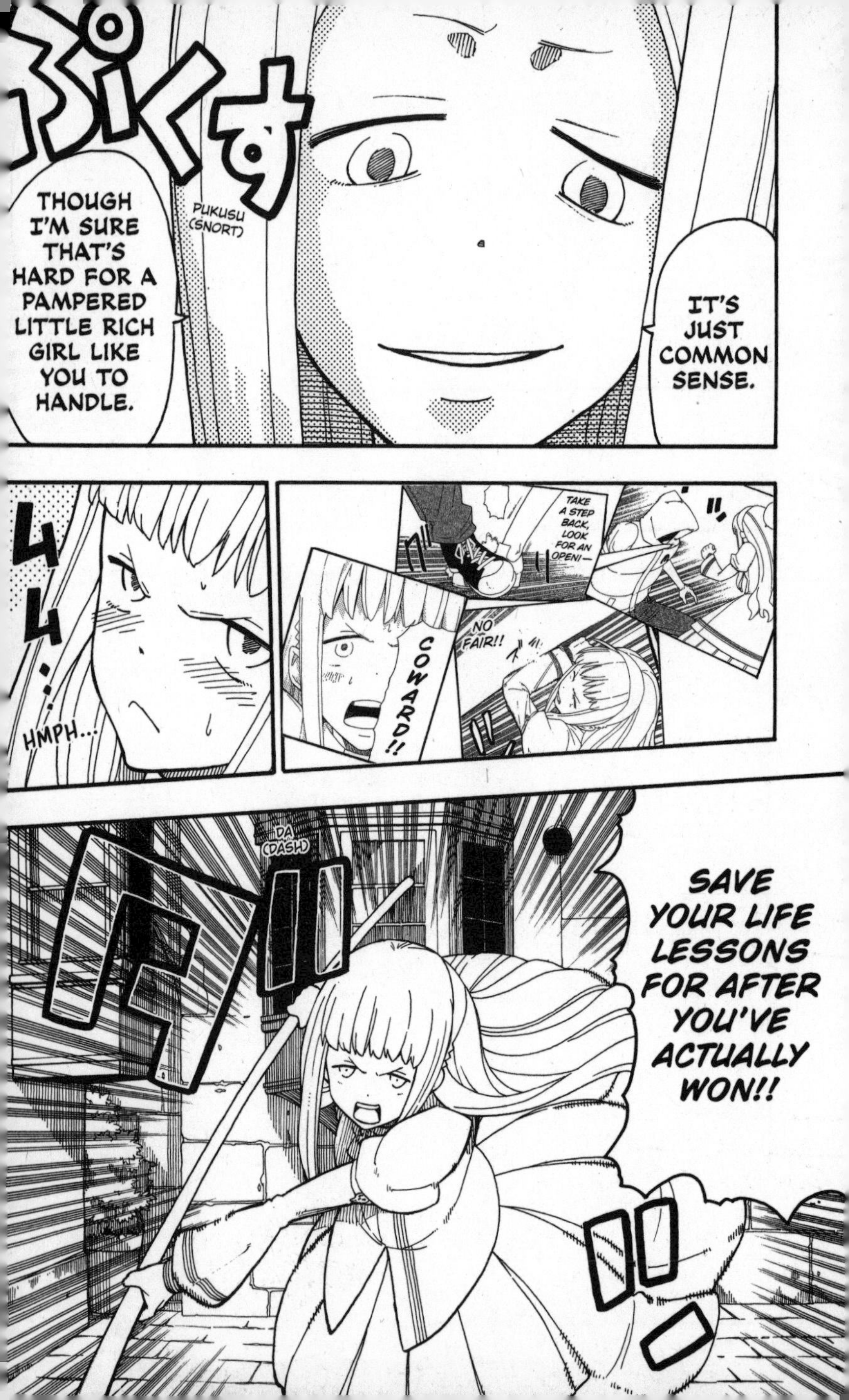

ぷくす
PUKUSU (SNORT)
IT'S JUST COMMON SENSE.
THOUGH I'M SURE THAT'S HARD FOR A PAMPERED LITTLE RICH GIRL LIKE YOU TO HANDLE.
TAKE A STEP BACK, LOOK FOR AN OPEN!—
NO FAIR!!
COWARD!!
HMPH...
SAVE YOUR LIFE LESSONS FOR AFTER YOU'VE ACTUALLY WON!!
DA (DASH)

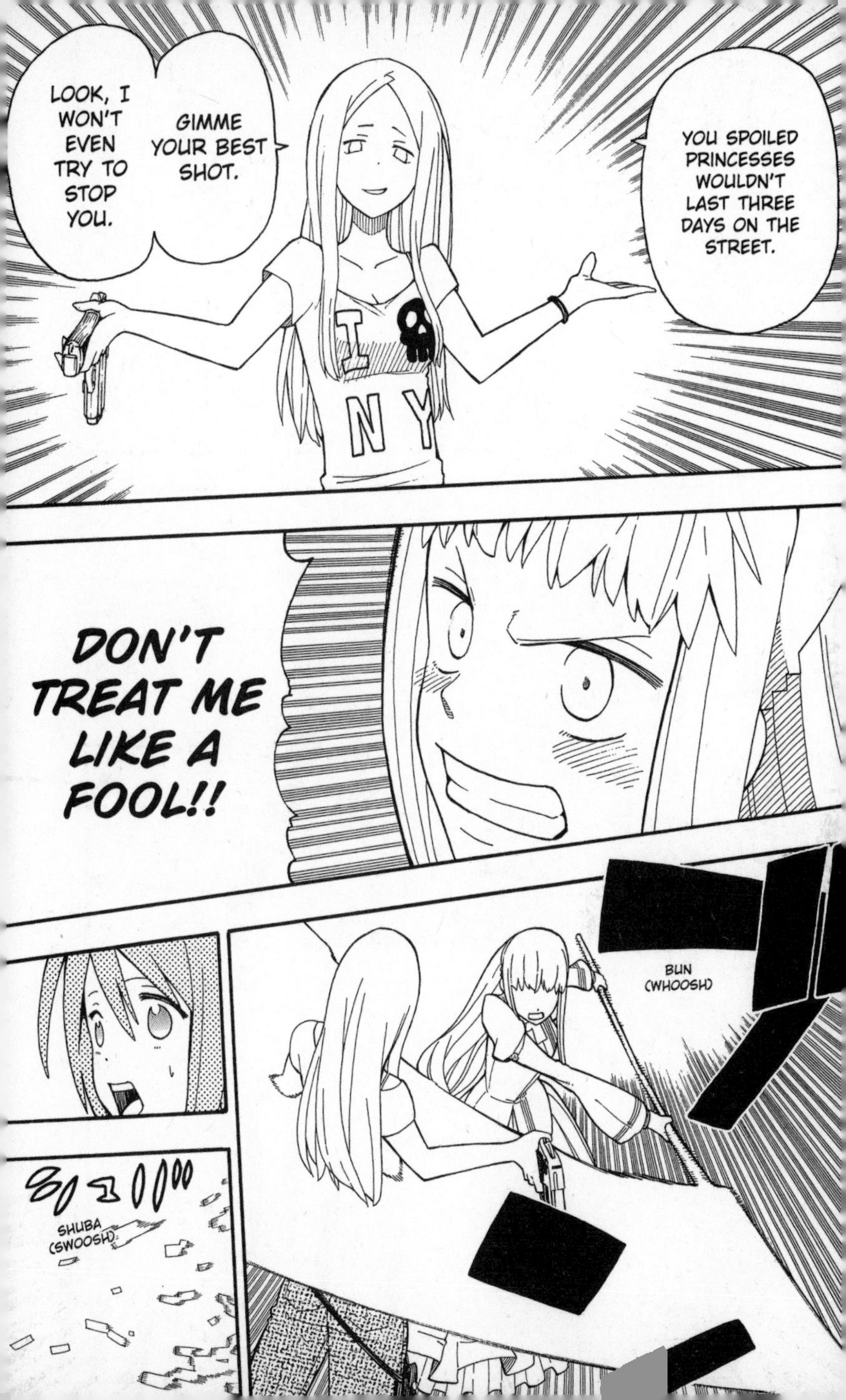

YOU SPOILED PRINCESSES WOULDN'T LAST THREE DAYS ON THE STREET.
GIMME YOUR BEST SHOT.
LOOK, I WON'T EVEN TRY TO STOP YOU.
DON'T TREAT ME LIKE A FOOL!!
BUN (WHOOSH)
SHUBA (SWOOSH)

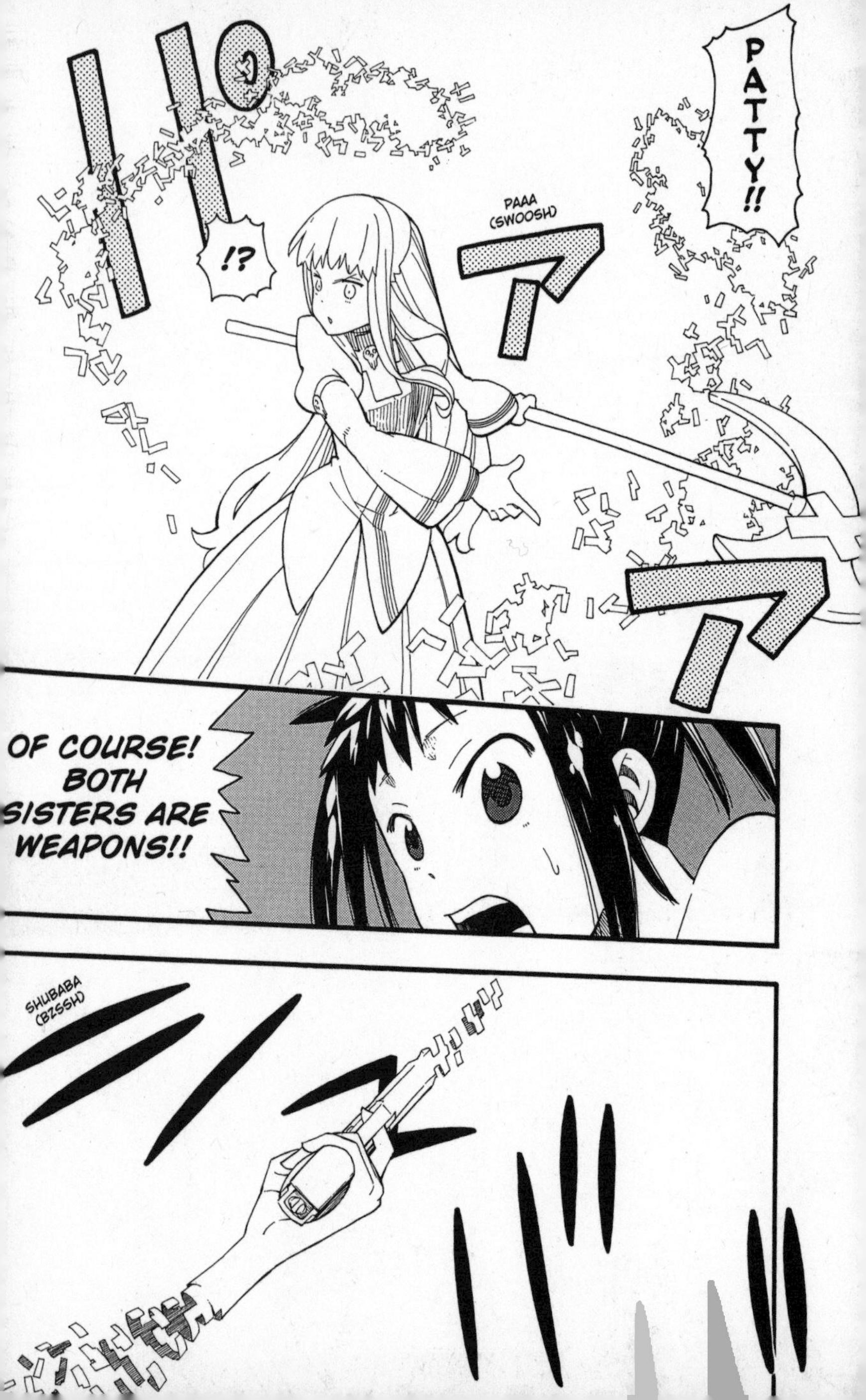
PATTY!!
PAAA (SWOOSH)
!?
OF COURSE! BOTH SISTERS ARE WEAPONS!!
SHUBABA (BZSSH)

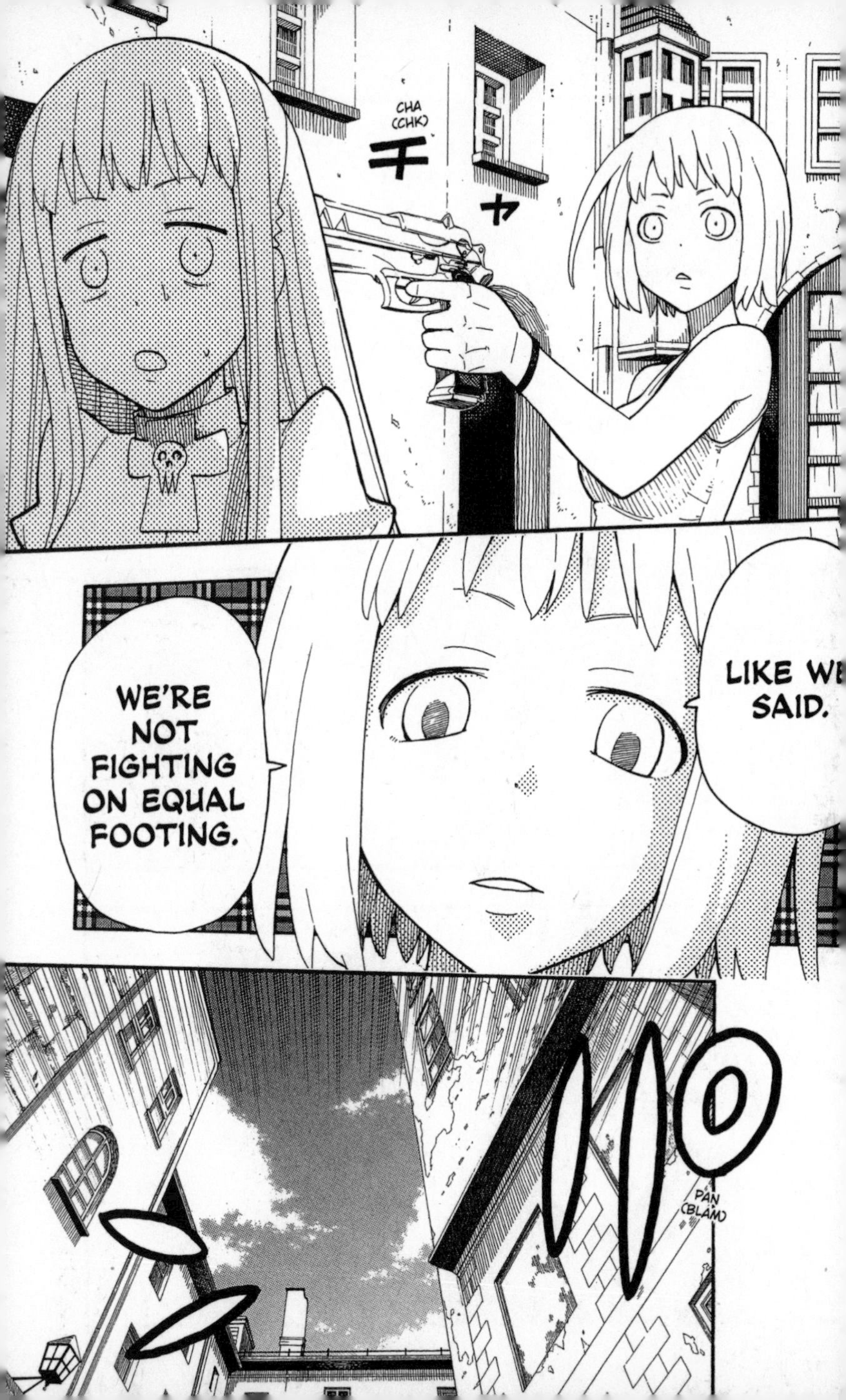

CHA (CHK)
チャ
LIKE WE SAID.
WE'RE NOT FIGHTING ON EQUAL FOOTING.
PAN (BLAM)

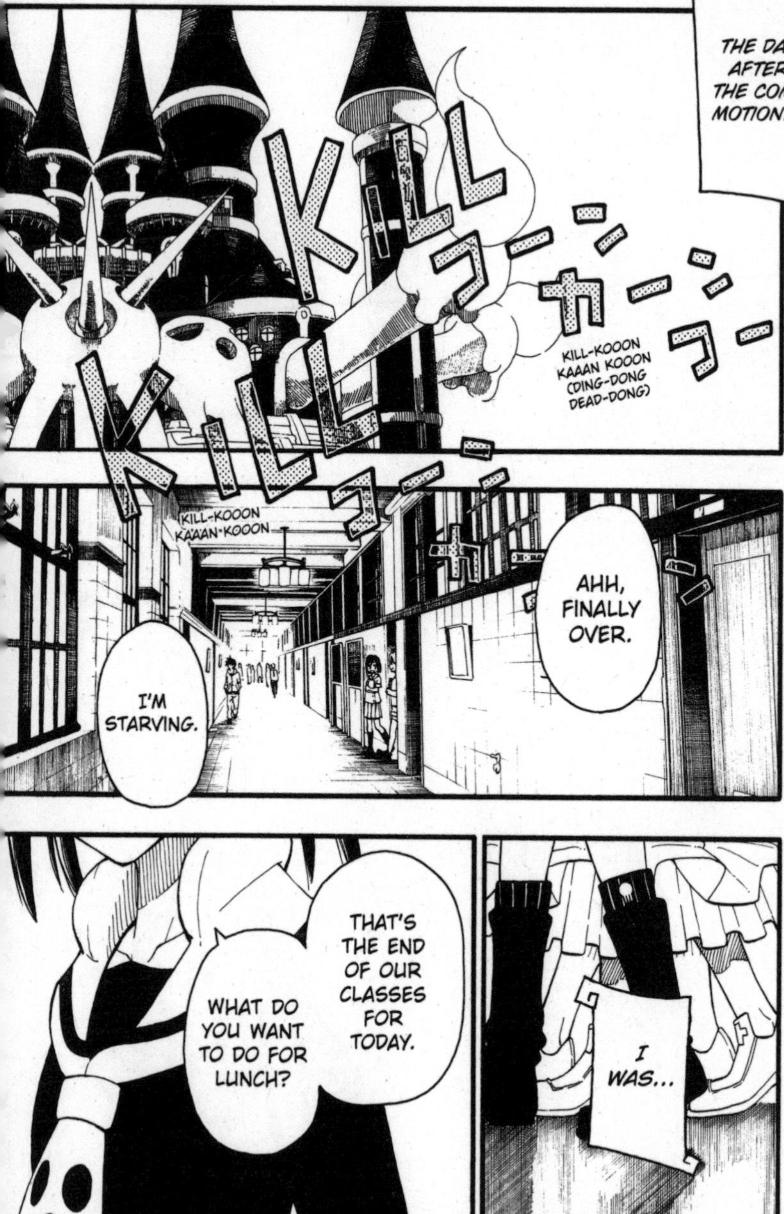
THE DAY AFTER THE COM- MOTION...
KILL
KILL
KILL-KOOON KAAAN KOOON (DING-DONG DEAD-DONG)
AHH, FINALLY OVER.
KILL-KOOON KAAAN-KOOON
I'M STARVING.
I WAS...
THAT'S THE END OF OUR CLASSES FOR TODAY.
WHAT DO YOU WANT TO DO FOR LUNCH?

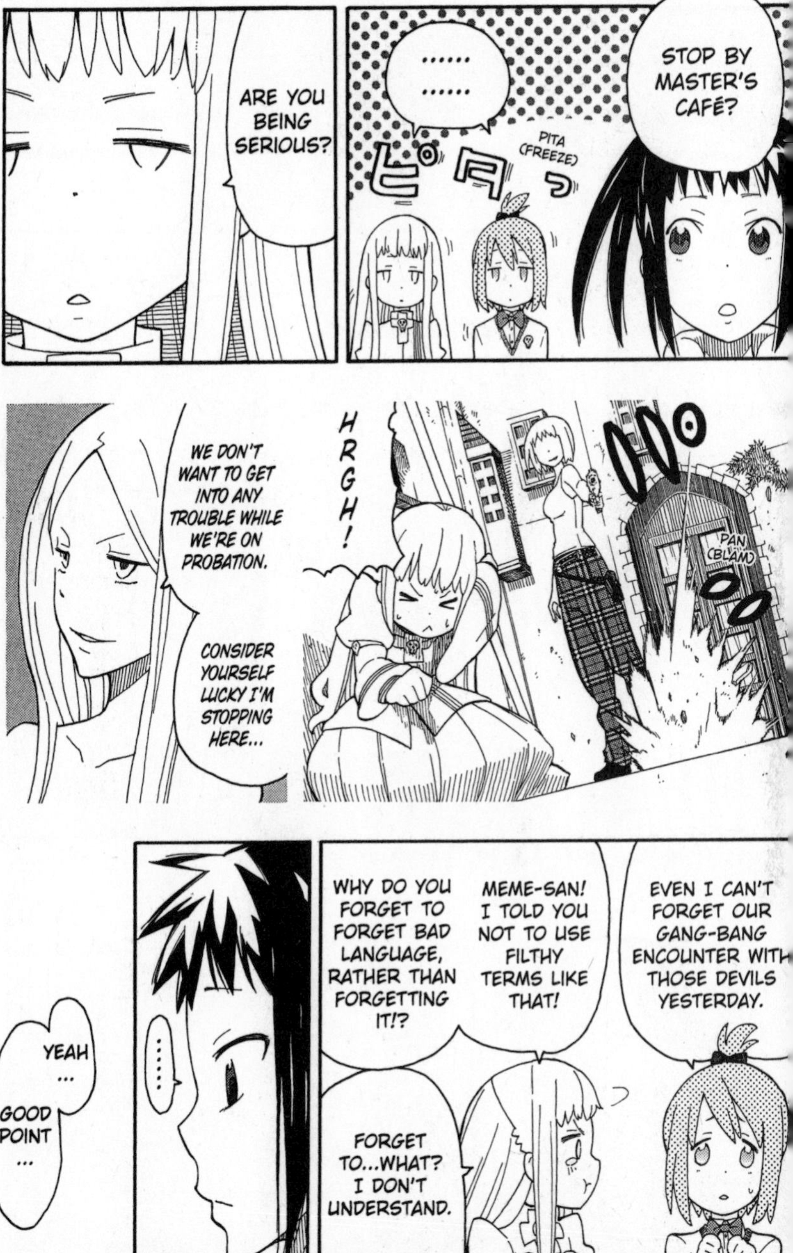
STOP BY MASTER'S CAFÉ?
......
......
ピタッ
PITA (FREEZE)
ARE YOU BEING SERIOUS?
HRGH!
PAN (BLAM)
WE DON'T WANT TO GET INTO ANY TROUBLE WHILE WE'RE ON PROBATION.
CONSIDER YOURSELF LUCKY I'M STOPPING HERE...
EVEN I CAN'T FORGET OUR GANG-BANG ENCOUNTER WITH THOSE DEVILS YESTERDAY.
MEME-SAN! I TOLD YOU NOT TO USE FILTHY TERMS LIKE THAT!
WHY DO YOU FORGET TO FORGET BAD LANGUAGE, RATHER THAN FORGETTING IT!?
FORGET TO...WHAT? I DON'T UNDERSTAND.
......
YEAH ... GOOD POINT ...

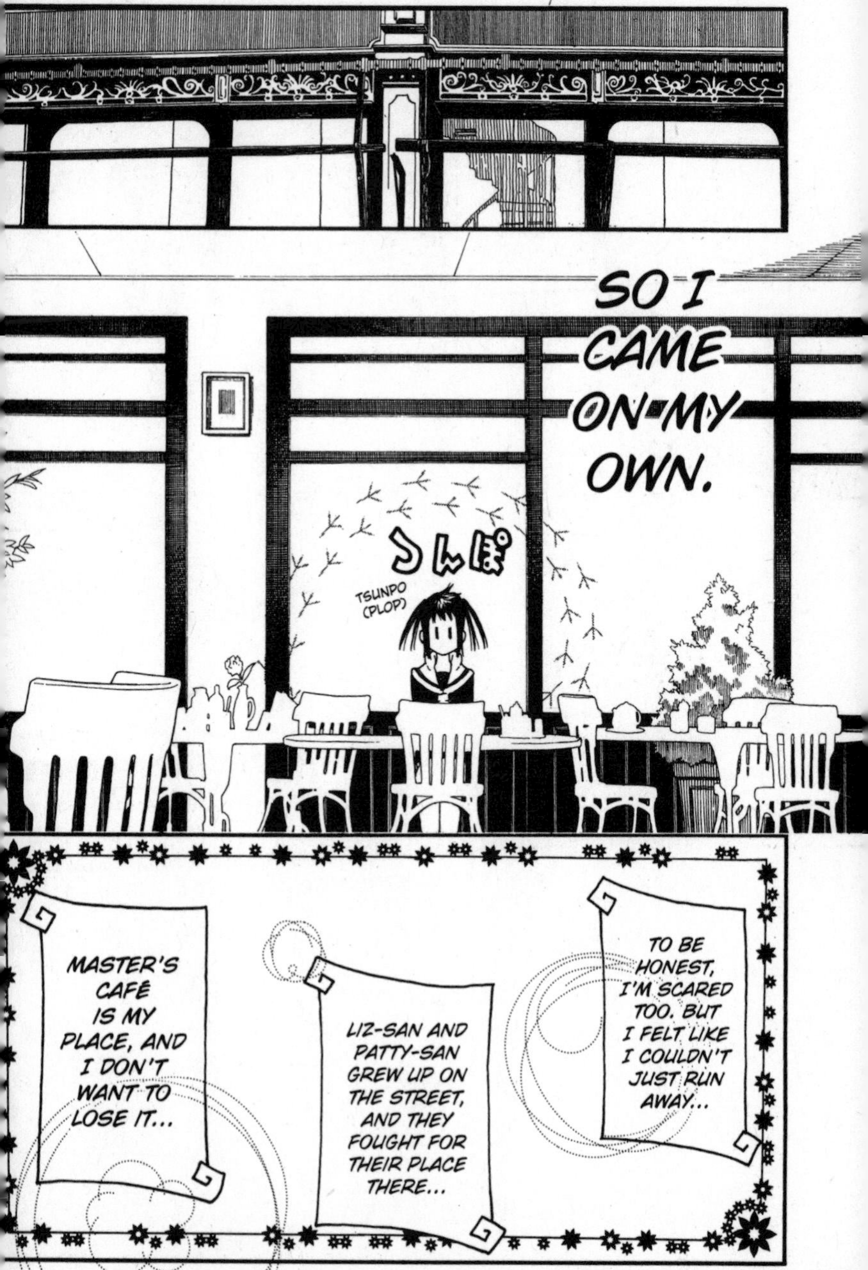
SO I CAME ON MY OWN.
つんぽ
TSUNPO (PLOP)
TO BE HONEST, I'M SCARED TOO. BUT I FELT LIKE I COULDN'T JUST RUN AWAY...
LIZ-SAN AND PATTY-SAN GREW UP ON THE STREET, AND THEY FOUGHT FOR THEIR PLACE THERE...
MASTER'S CAFÉ IS MY PLACE, AND I DON'T WANT TO LOSE IT...

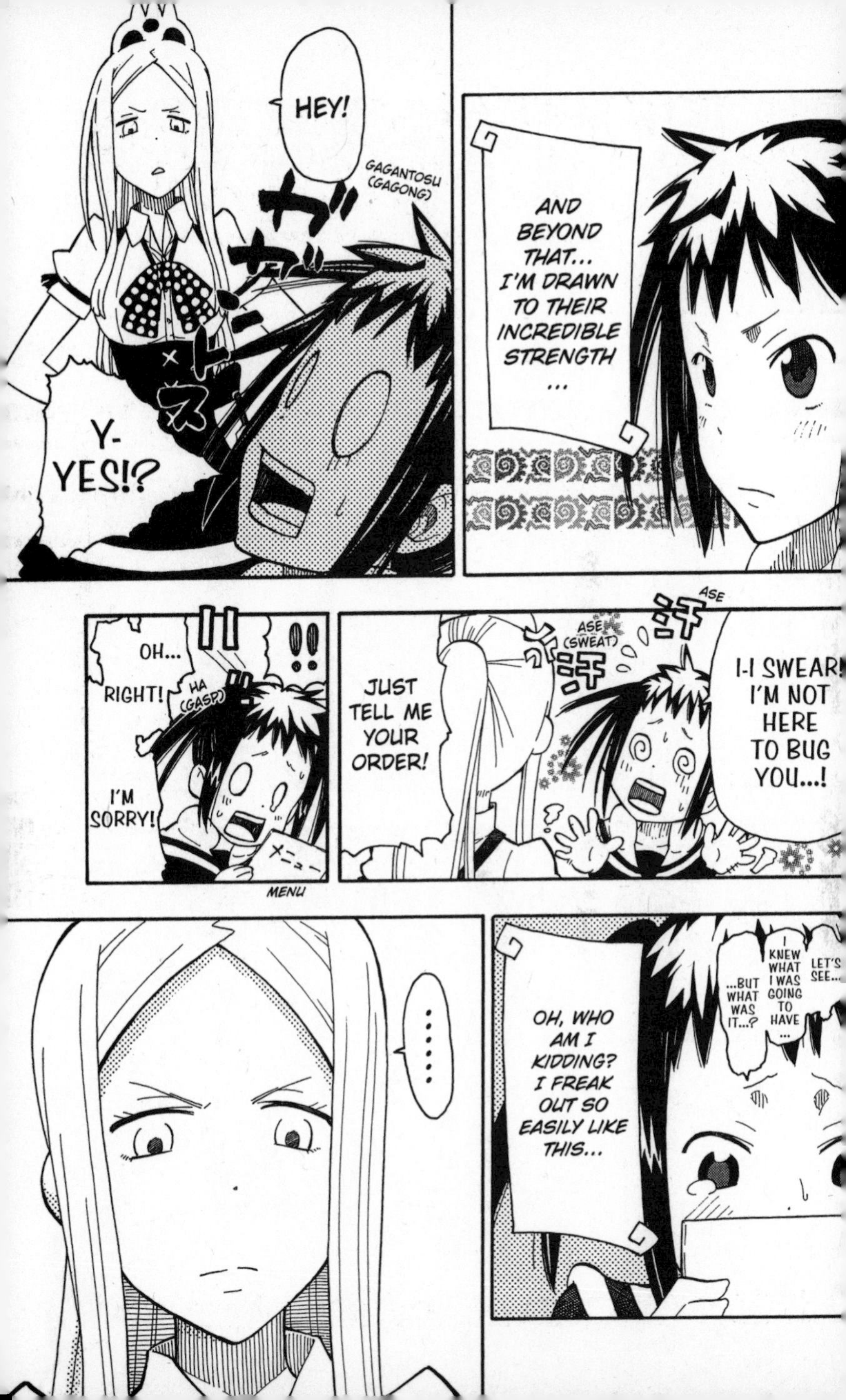
AND BEYOND THAT... I'M DRAWN TO THEIR INCREDIBLE STRENGTH...
HEY!
GAGANTOSU (GAGONG)
Y-YES!?
I-I SWEAR! I'M NOT HERE TO BUG YOU...!
ASE
ASE (SWEAT)
JUST TELL ME YOUR ORDER!
OH... RIGHT!
HA (GASP)
I'M SORRY!
MENU
LET'S SEE...
I KNEW WHAT I WAS GOING TO HAVE...
...BUT WHAT WAS IT...?
OH, WHO AM I KIDDING? I FREAK OUT SO EASILY LIKE THIS...
......

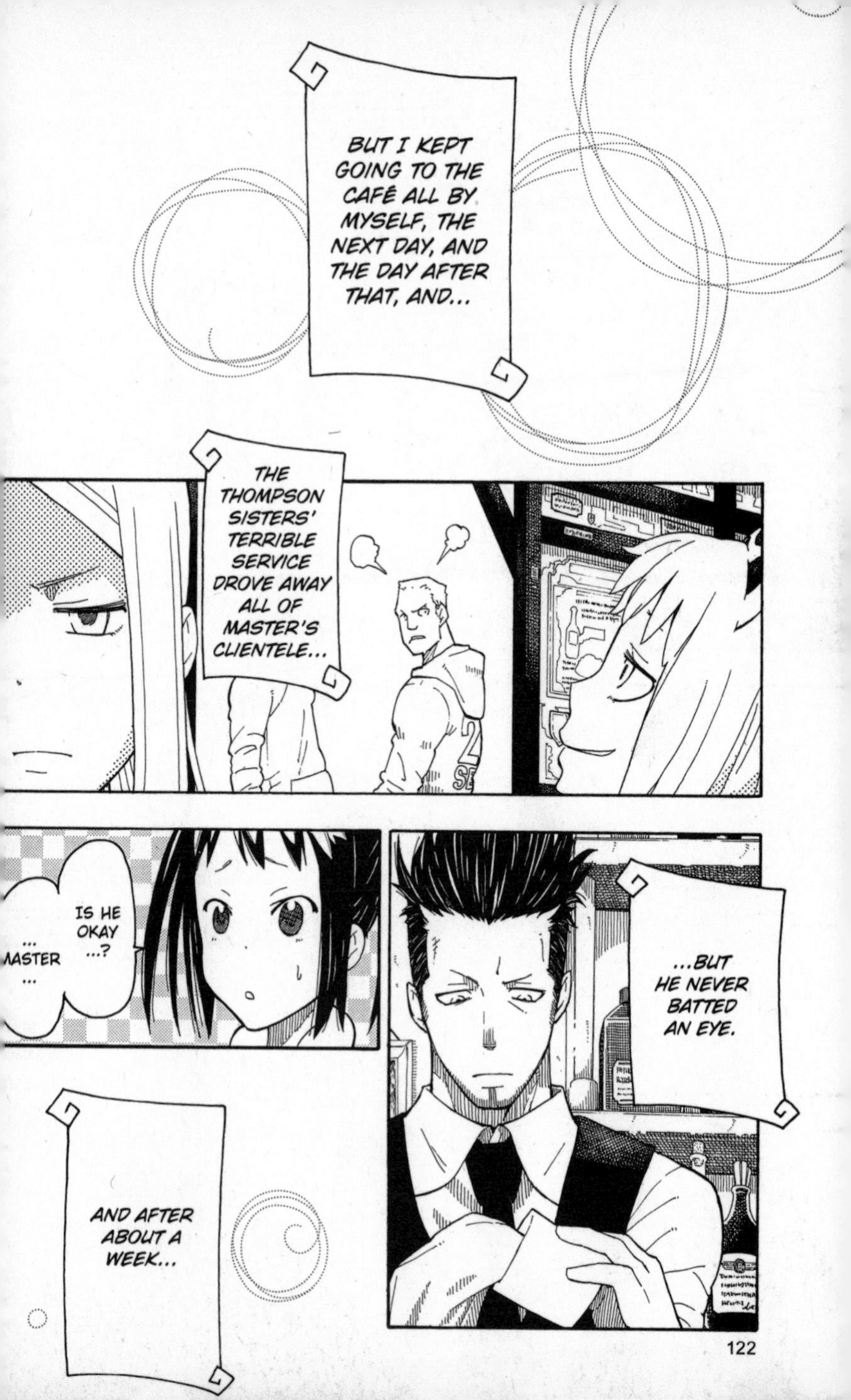
BUT I KEPT GOING TO THE CAFÉ ALL BY MYSELF, THE NEXT DAY, AND THE DAY AFTER THAT, AND...
THE THOMPSON SISTERS' TERRIBLE SERVICE DROVE AWAY ALL OF MASTER'S CLIENTELE...
...BUT HE NEVER BATTED AN EYE.
... MASTER ... IS HE OKAY ...?
AND AFTER ABOUT A WEEK...

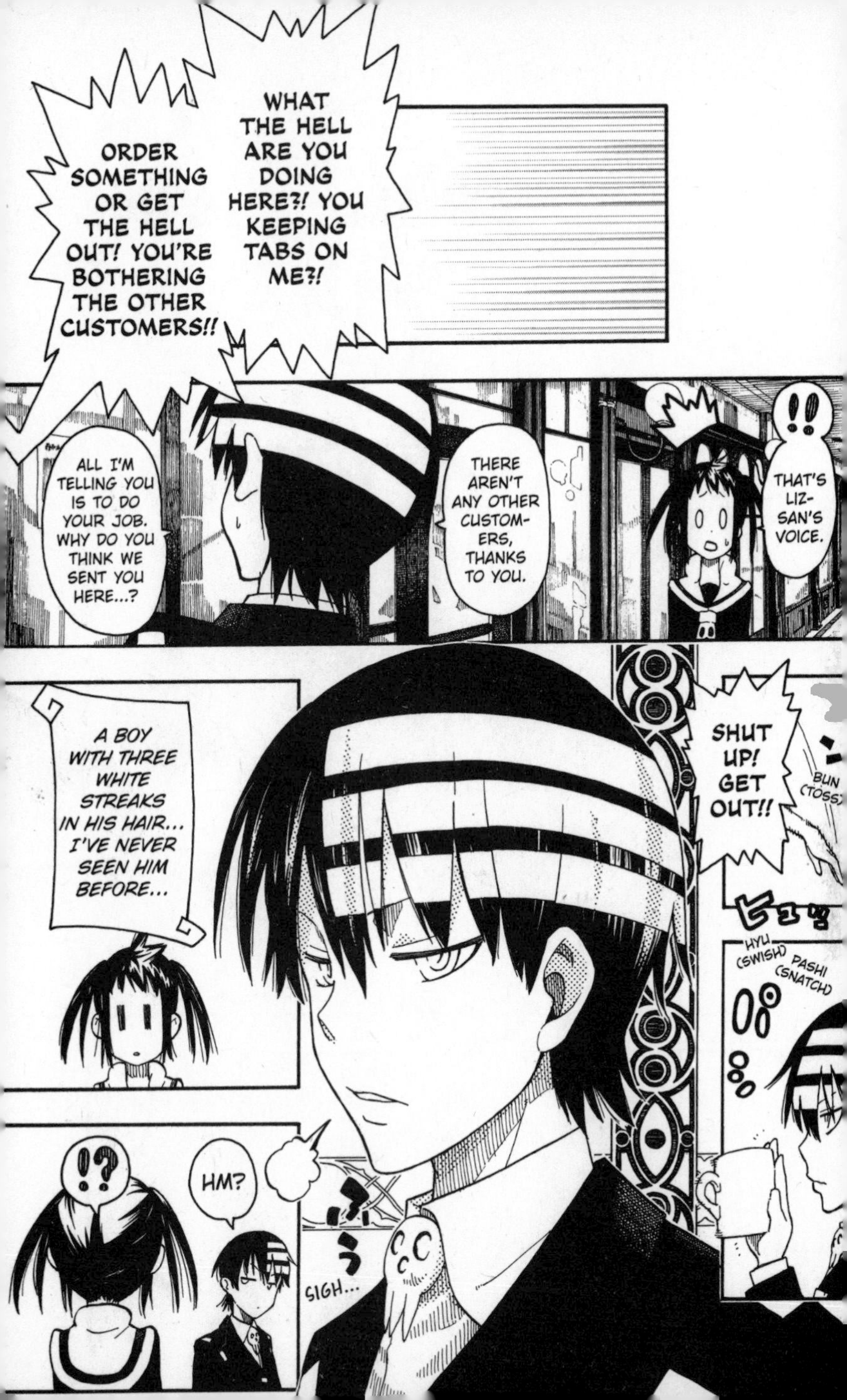
WHAT THE HELL ARE YOU DOING HERE?! YOU KEEPING TABS ON ME?!
ORDER SOMETHING OR GET THE HELL OUT! YOU'RE BOTHERING THE OTHER CUSTOMERS!!
!!
THAT'S LIZ-SAN'S VOICE.
THERE AREN'T ANY OTHER CUSTOMERS, THANKS TO YOU.
ALL I'M TELLING YOU IS TO DO YOUR JOB. WHY DO YOU THINK WE SENT YOU HERE...?
SHUT UP! GET OUT!!
BUN (TOSS)
HYU (SWISH)
PASHI (SNATCH)
SIGH...
A BOY WITH THREE WHITE STREAKS IN HIS HAIR... I'VE NEVER SEEN HIM BEFORE...
HM?
!?

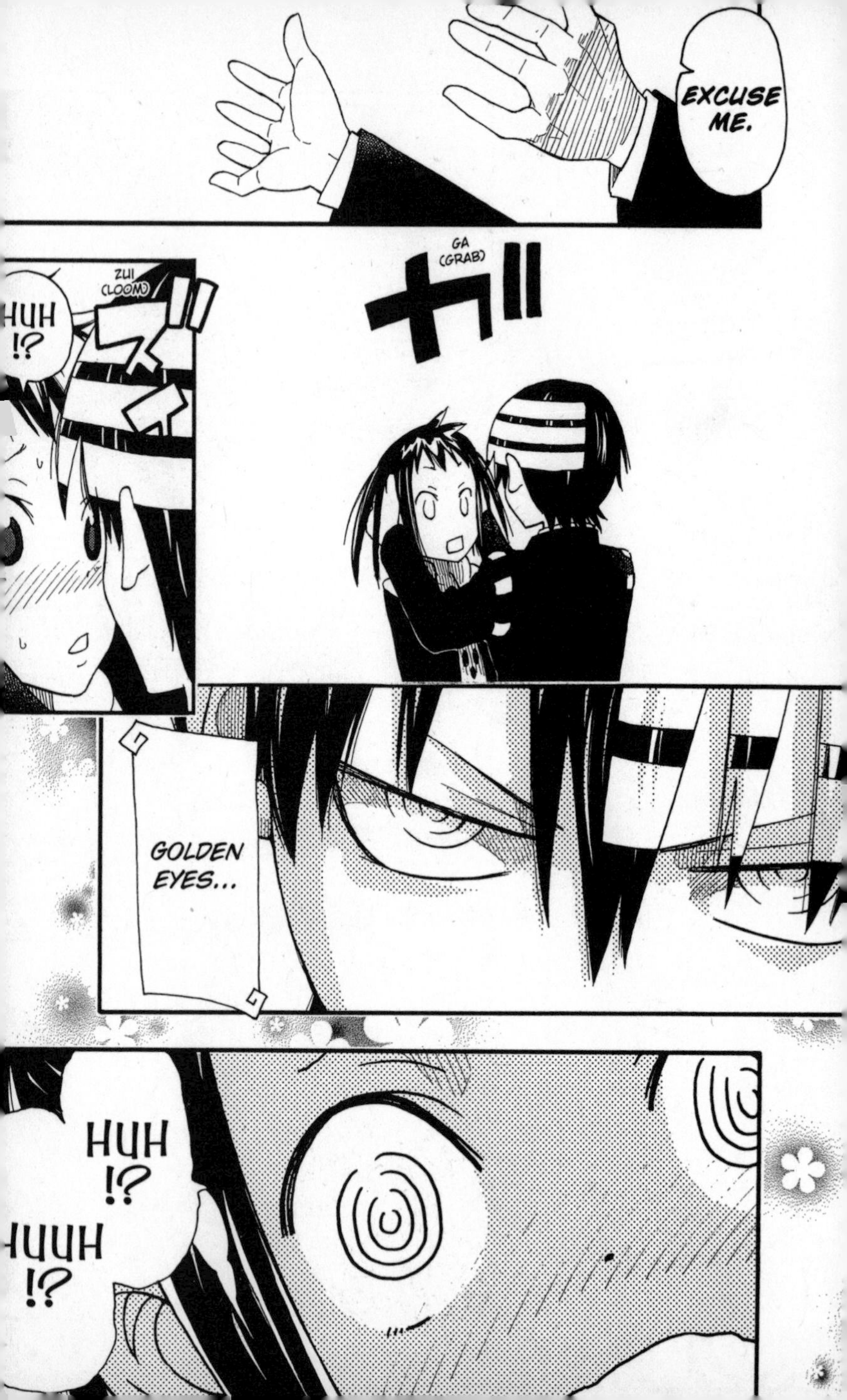
EXCUSE ME.
GA (GRAB)
ZUI (LOOM)
HUH !?
GOLDEN EYES...
HUH !?
HUUH !?

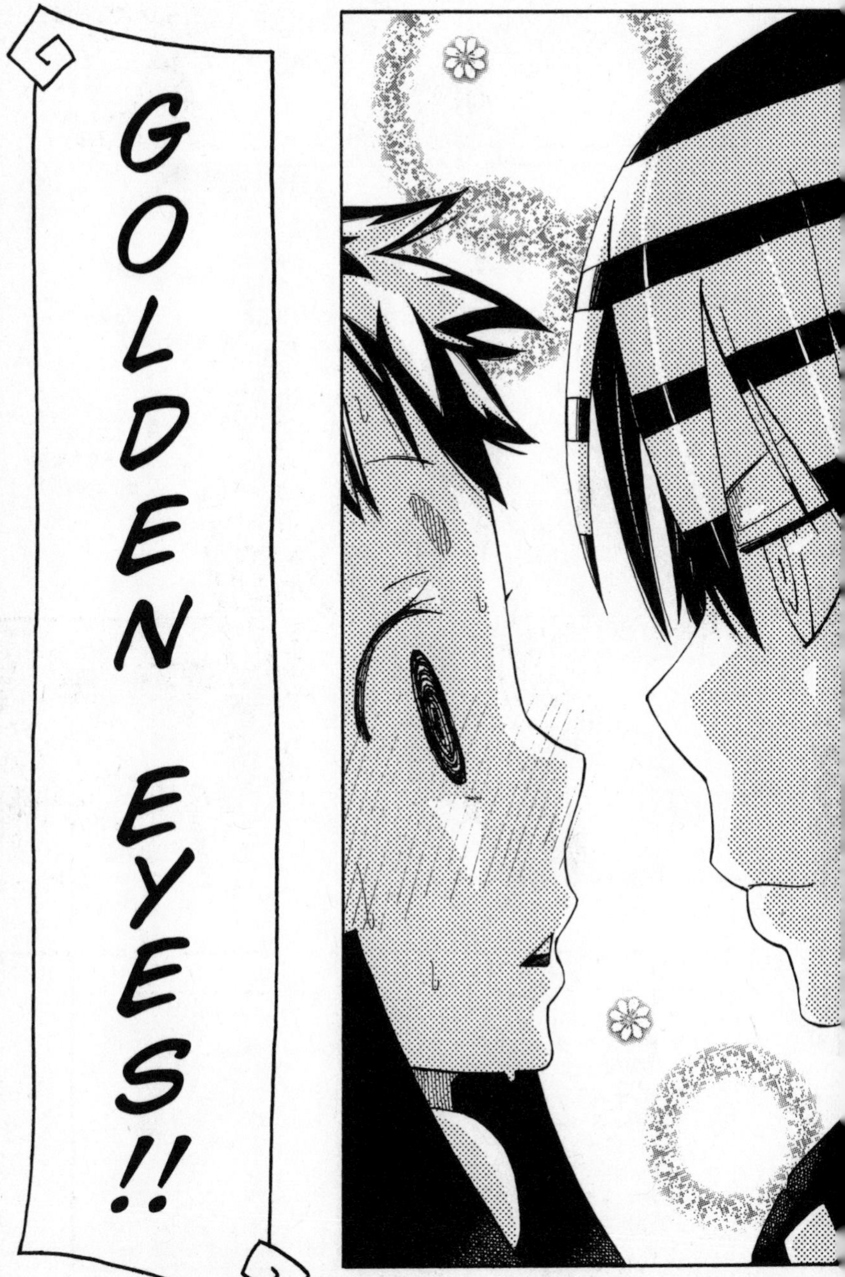
GOLDEN EYES!!

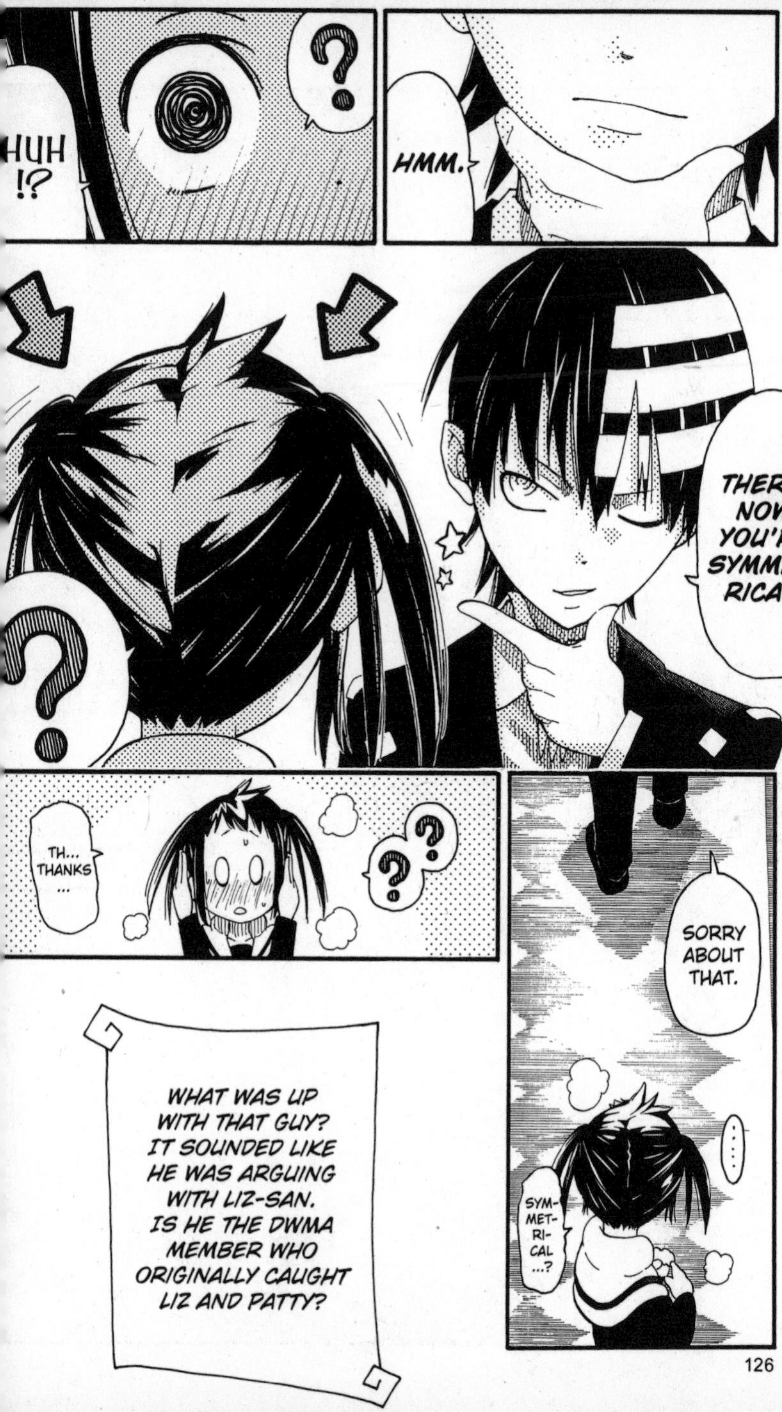
HMM.
?
HUH!?
THERE. NOW YOU'RE SYMMETRICAL.
?
SORRY ABOUT THAT.
......
SYMMETRICAL...?
??
TH... THANKS...
WHAT WAS UP WITH THAT GUY? IT SOUNDED LIKE HE WAS ARGUING WITH LIZ-SAN. IS HE THE DWMA MEMBER WHO ORIGINALLY CAUGHT LIZ AND PATTY?

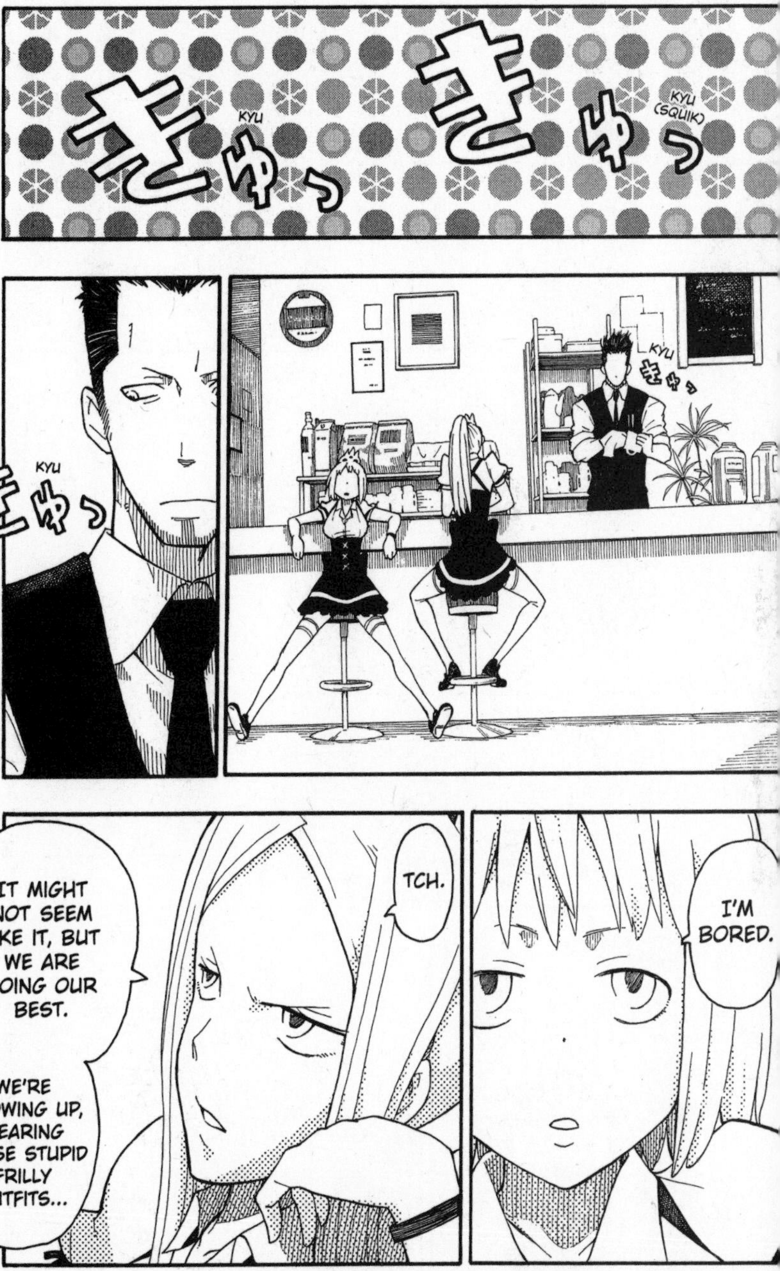
きゅっ
KYU (SQUIK)
きゅっ
KYU
きゅっ
KYU
きゅっ
KYU
I'M BORED.
TCH.
IT MIGHT NOT SEEM LIKE IT, BUT WE ARE DOING OUR BEST.
WE'RE SHOWING UP, WEARING THESE STUPID FRILLY OUTFITS...

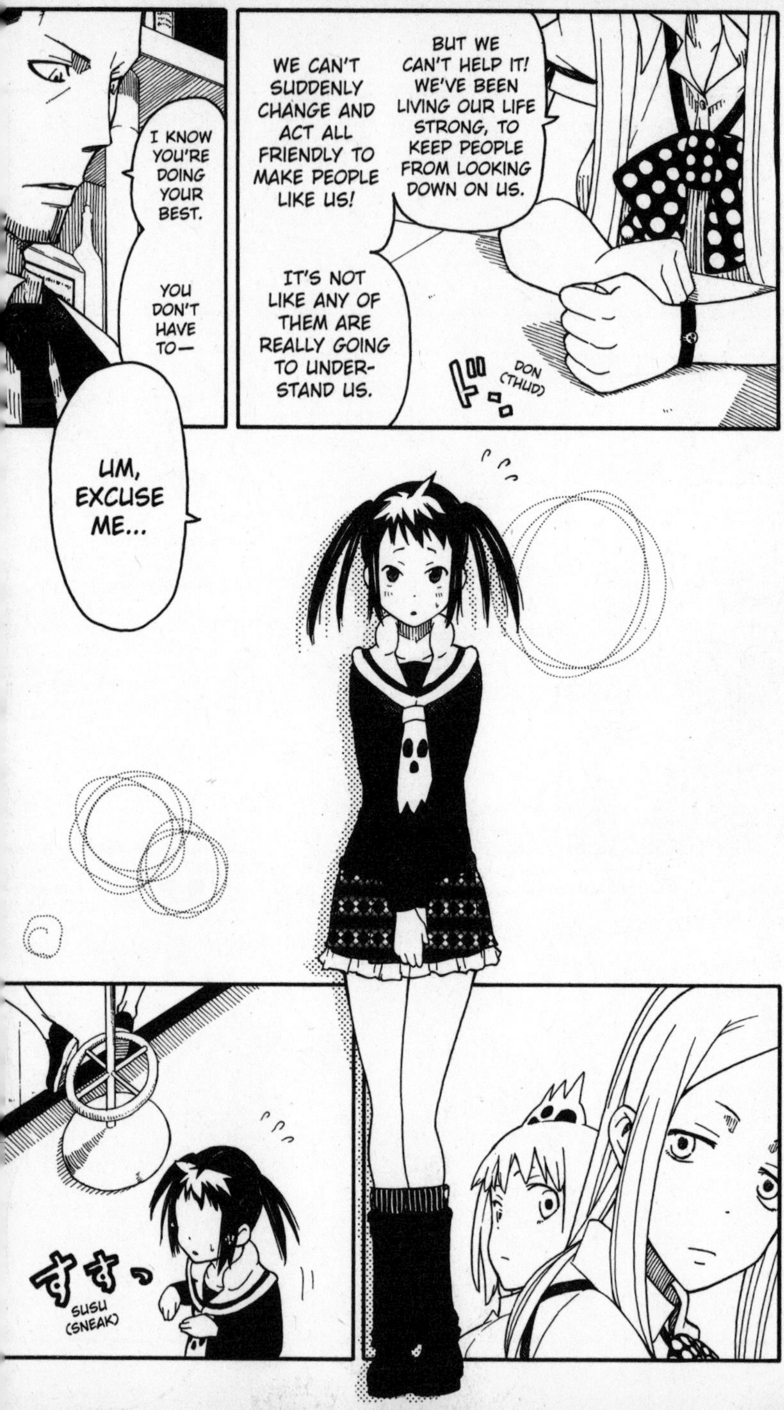
BUT WE CAN'T HELP IT! WE'VE BEEN LIVING OUR LIFE STRONG, TO KEEP PEOPLE FROM LOOKING DOWN ON US.
WE CAN'T SUDDENLY CHANGE AND ACT ALL FRIENDLY TO MAKE PEOPLE LIKE US!
IT'S NOT LIKE ANY OF THEM ARE REALLY GOING TO UNDER-STAND US.
ドン
DON (THUD)
I KNOW YOU'RE DOING YOUR BEST.
YOU DON'T HAVE TO—
UM, EXCUSE ME...
すすっ
SUSU (SNEAK)

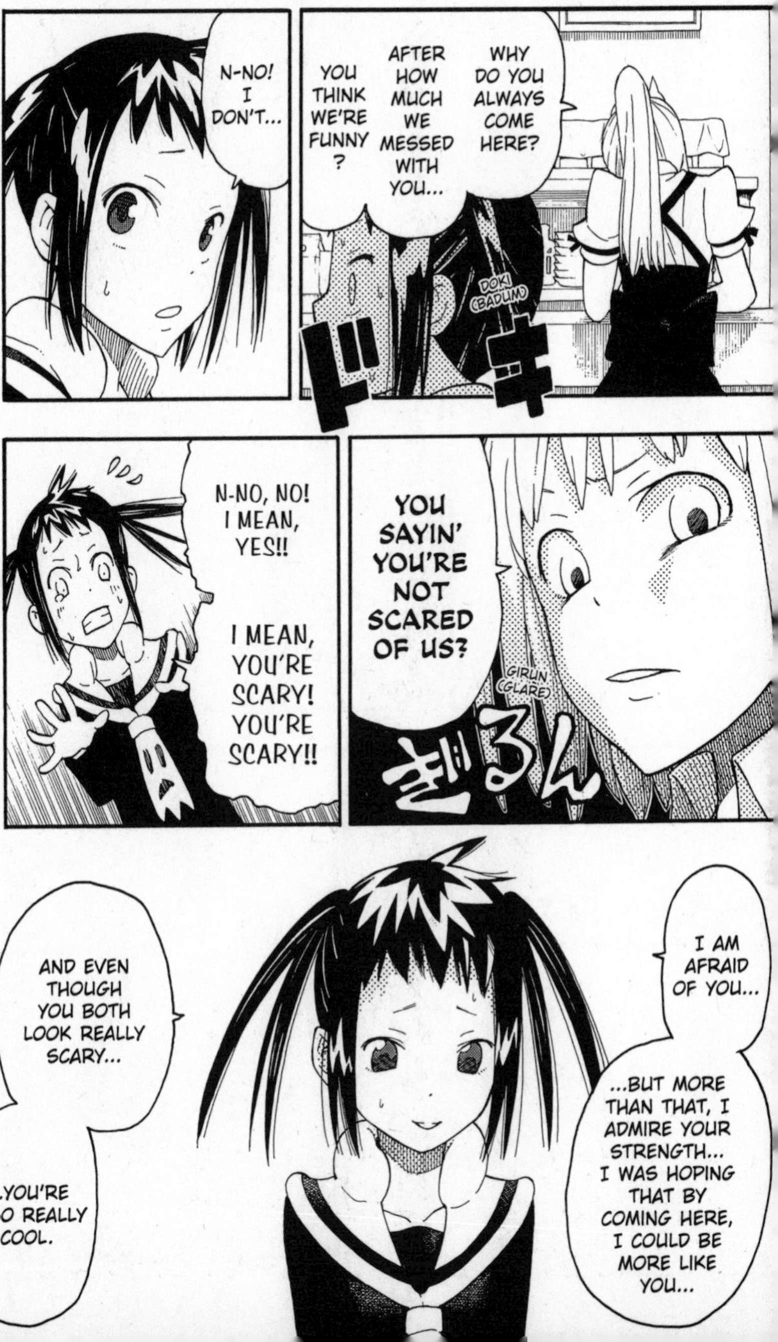
WHY DO YOU ALWAYS COME HERE?
AFTER HOW MUCH WE MESSED WITH YOU...
YOU THINK WE'RE FUNNY?
DOKI (BADUM)
N-NO! I DON'T...
YOU SAYIN' YOU'RE NOT SCARED OF US?
GIRUN (GLARE)
N-NO, NO! I MEAN, YES!!
I MEAN, YOU'RE SCARY! YOU'RE SCARY!!
I AM AFRAID OF YOU...
...BUT MORE THAN THAT, I ADMIRE YOUR STRENGTH... I WAS HOPING THAT BY COMING HERE, I COULD BE MORE LIKE YOU...
AND EVEN THOUGH YOU BOTH LOOK REALLY SCARY...
...YOU'RE ALSO REALLY COOL.

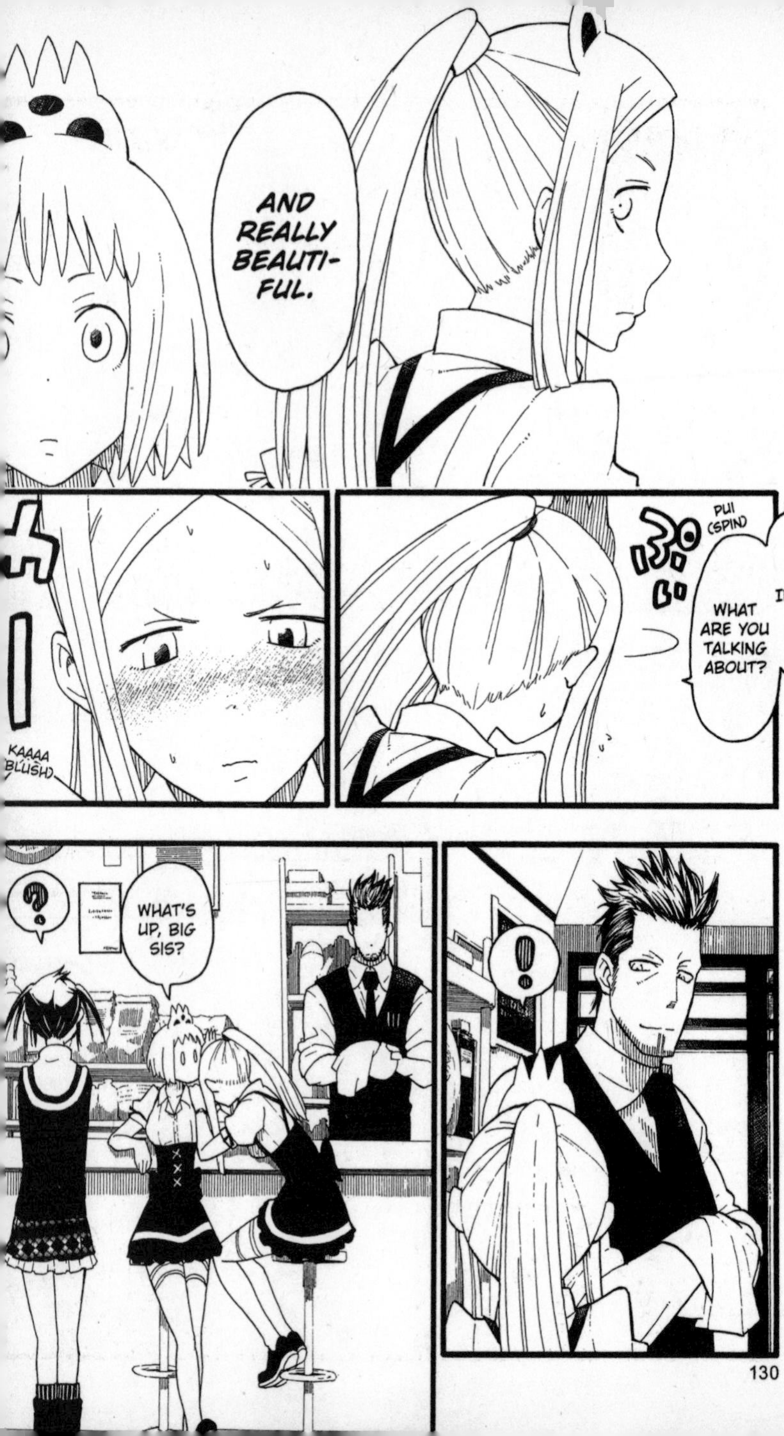
AND REALLY BEAUTI-FUL.
PUI (SPIN)
I- IDIOT.
WHAT ARE YOU TALKING ABOUT?
KAAAA (BLUSH)
WHAT'S UP, BIG SIS?

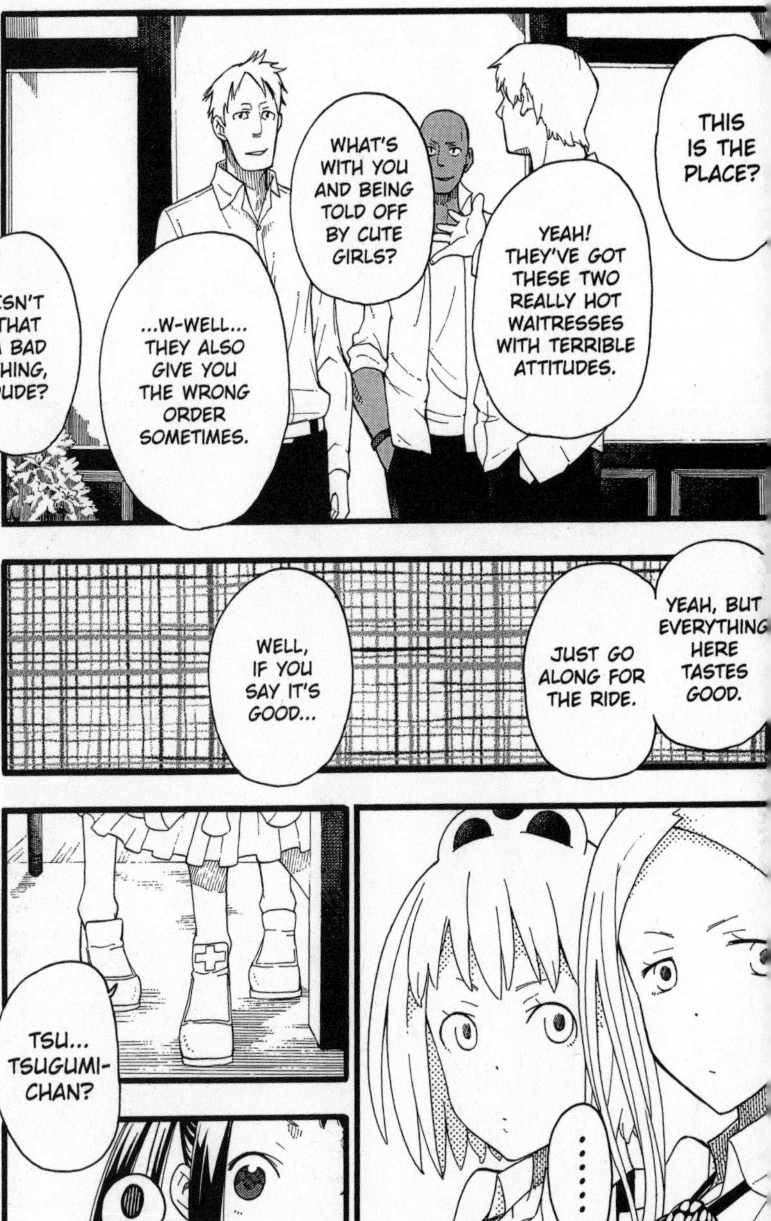
THIS IS THE PLACE?
YEAH! THEY'VE GOT THESE TWO REALLY HOT WAITRESSES WITH TERRIBLE ATTITUDES.
WHAT'S WITH YOU AND BEING TOLD OFF BY CUTE GIRLS?
...W-WELL... THEY ALSO GIVE YOU THE WRONG ORDER SOMETIMES.
ISN'T THAT A BAD THING, DUDE?
YEAH, BUT EVERYTHING HERE TASTES GOOD.
JUST GO ALONG FOR THE RIDE.
WELL, IF YOU SAY IT'S GOOD...
......
TSU... TSUGUMI-CHAN?
!

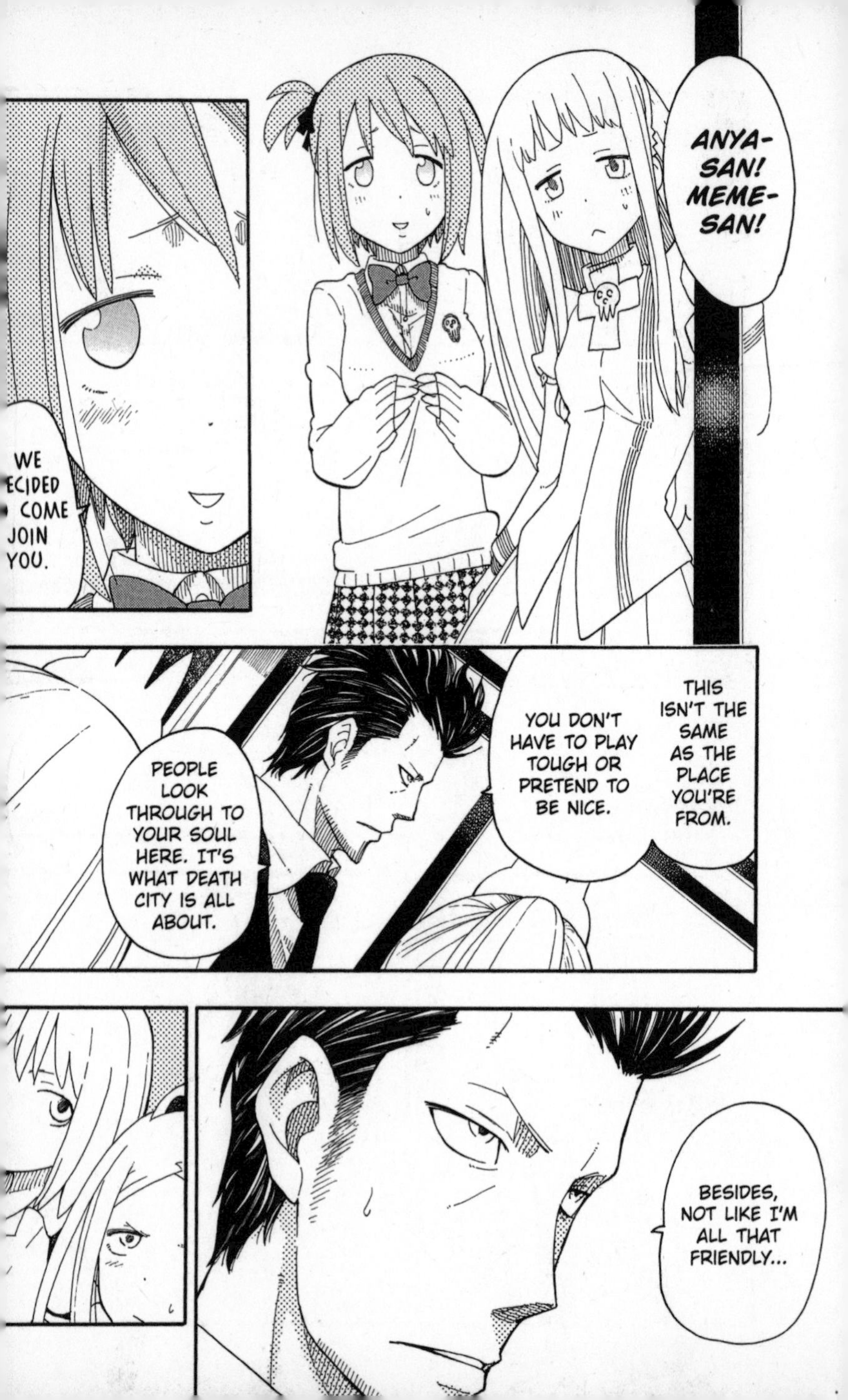
ANYA-SAN! MEME-SAN!
WE ECIDED COME JOIN YOU.
THIS ISN'T THE SAME AS THE PLACE YOU'RE FROM.
YOU DON'T HAVE TO PLAY TOUGH OR PRETEND TO BE NICE.
PEOPLE LOOK THROUGH TO YOUR SOUL HERE. IT'S WHAT DEATH CITY IS ALL ABOUT.
BESIDES, NOT LIKE I'M ALL THAT FRIENDLY...

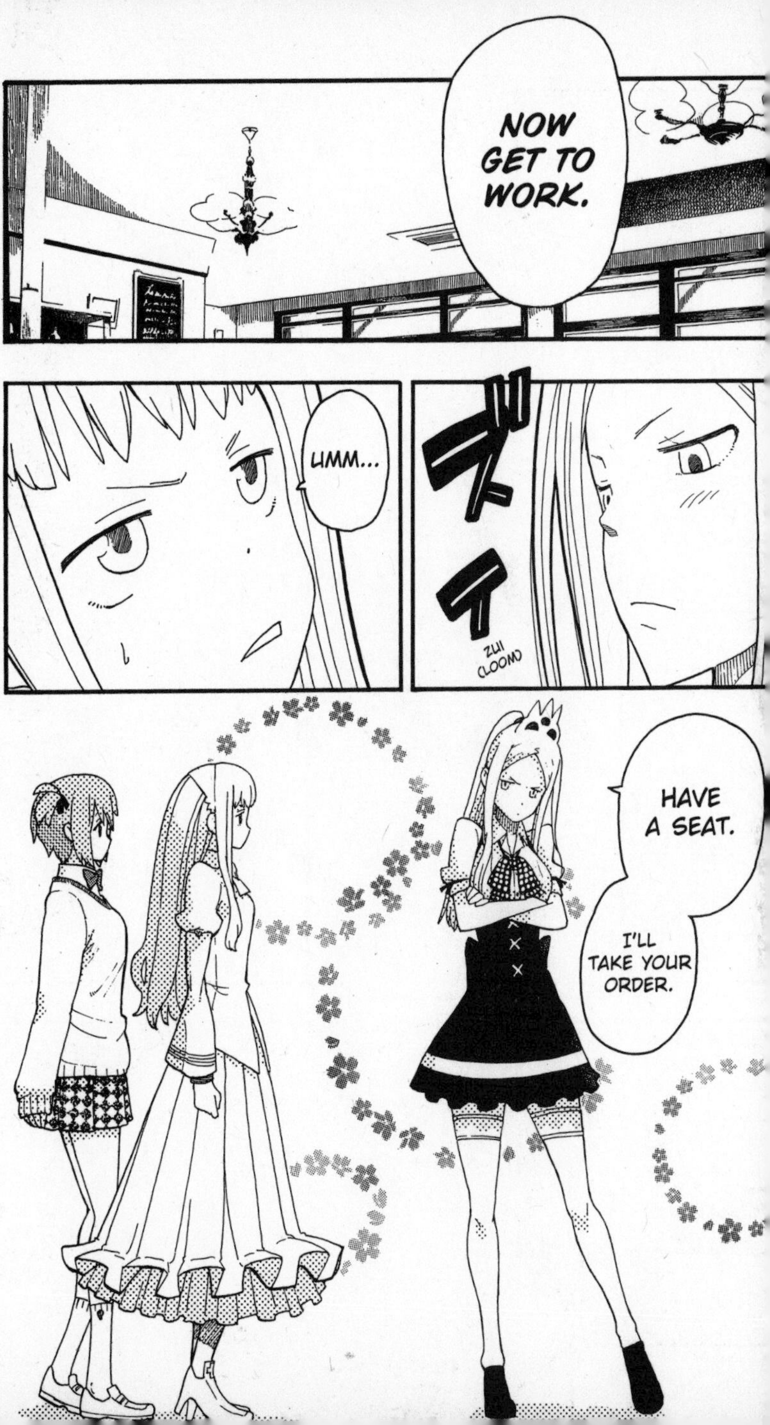
NOW GET TO WORK.
ZUI (LOOM)
UMM...
HAVE A SEAT.
I'LL TAKE YOUR ORDER.

SURE
YOU DON'T
MEAN, "I'LL
DECIDE YOUR
ORDER"?

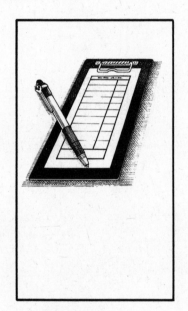

HA-HA-HA,
MAYBE.

SOUL EATER NOT!

SOUL EATER NOT

CHAPTER 12: STUDY GROUP!

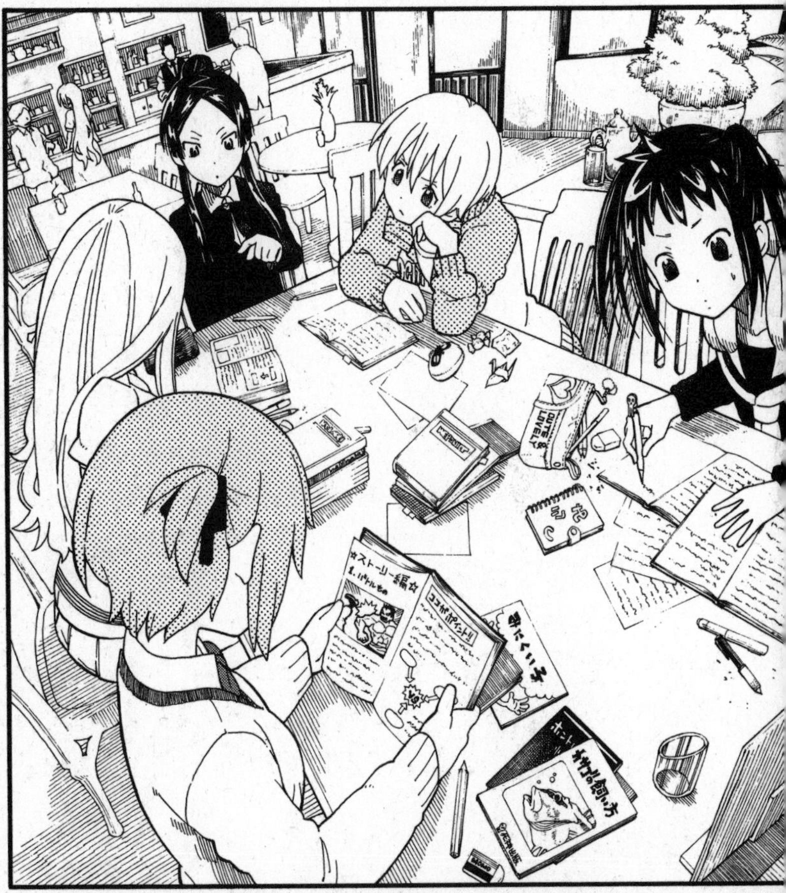
☆ストーリー編☆
ココがポイント!!
CUTE & LOVELY

TSUGUMI'S NOTEBOOK: TSUGUMI   MEME'S BOOK: STORY SECTION 1. BATTLES / WATCH OUT FOR THIS!
OTHER BOOKS: THE UGLY CHILD, HOW TO RAISE ROCKFISH

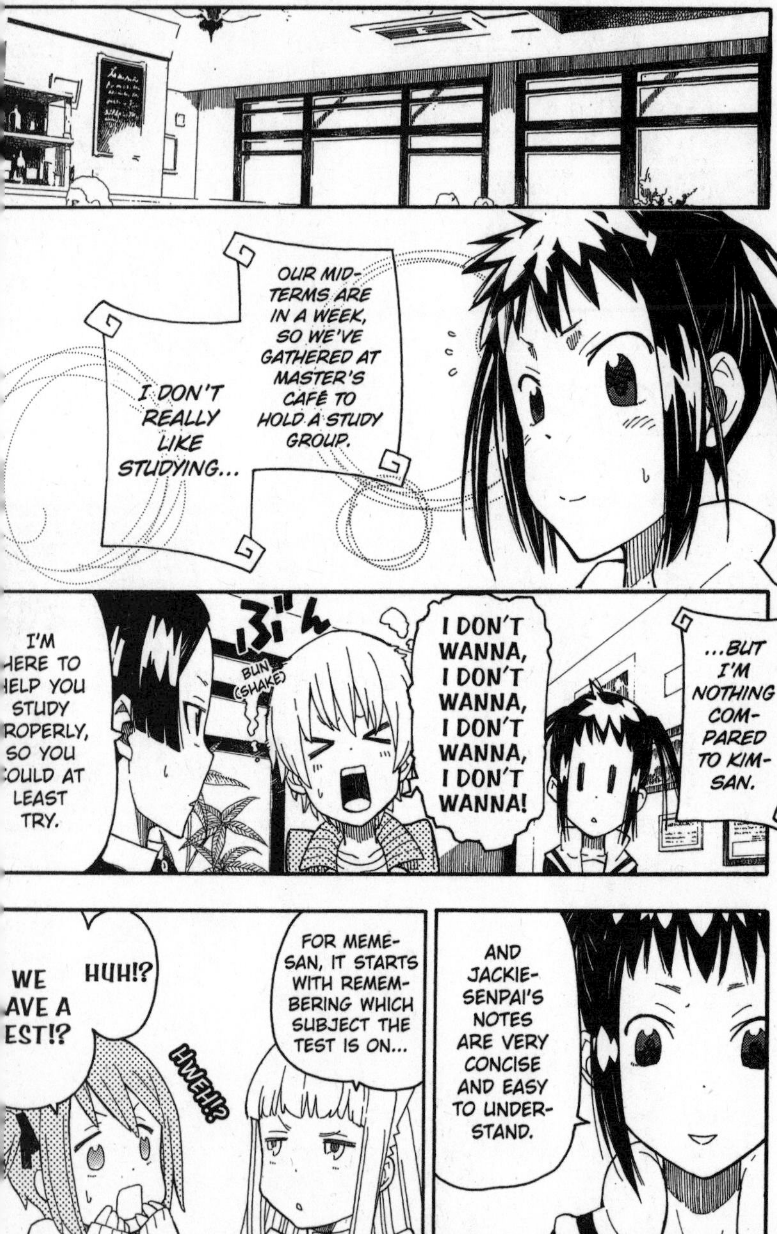
OUR MID-TERMS ARE IN A WEEK, SO WE'VE GATHERED AT MASTER'S CAFÉ TO HOLD A STUDY GROUP.
I DON'T REALLY LIKE STUDYING...
...BUT I'M NOTHING COMPARED TO KIM-SAN.
I DON'T WANNA, I DON'T WANNA, I DON'T WANNA, I DON'T WANNA!
ぶん
BUN (SHAKE)
I'M HERE TO HELP YOU STUDY ROPERLY, SO YOU OULD AT LEAST TRY.
AND JACKIE-SENPAI'S NOTES ARE VERY CONCISE AND EASY TO UNDERSTAND.
FOR MEME-SAN, IT STARTS WITH REMEMBERING WHICH SUBJECT THE TEST IS ON...
HUH!?
WE AVE A EST!?
HWEH!?

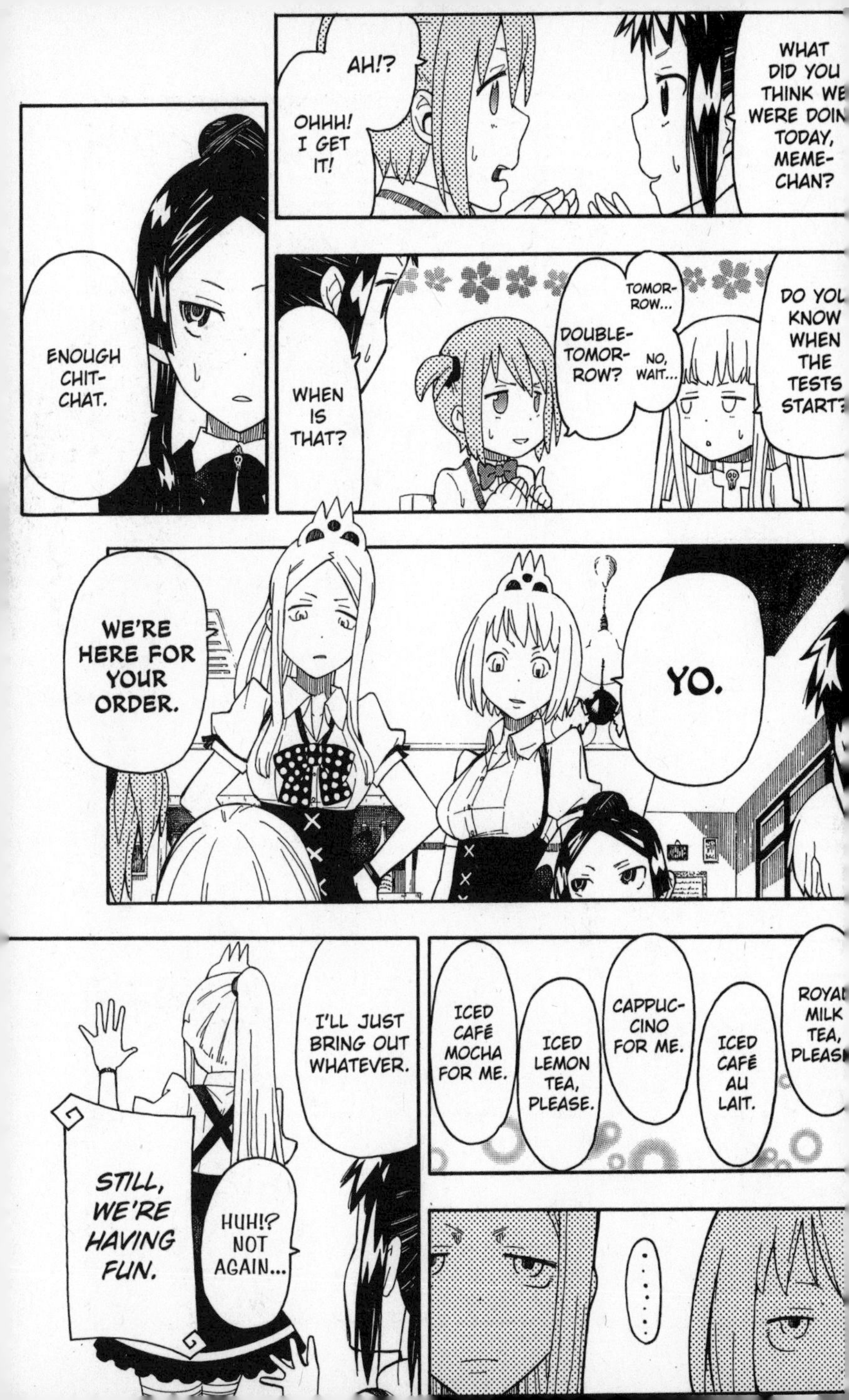
WHAT DID YOU THINK WE WERE DOING TODAY, MEME-CHAN?
AH!?
OHHH! I GET IT!
DO YOU KNOW WHEN THE TESTS START?
TOMORROW...
DOUBLE-TOMORROW? NO, WAIT...
WHEN IS THAT?
ENOUGH CHIT-CHAT.
YO.
WE'RE HERE FOR YOUR ORDER.
ROYAL MILK TEA, PLEASE.
ICED CAFÉ AU LAIT.
CAPPUCCINO FOR ME.
ICED LEMON TEA, PLEASE.
ICED CAFÉ MOCHA FOR ME.
......
I'LL JUST BRING OUT WHATEVER.
HUH!? NOT AGAIN...
STILL, WE'RE HAVING FUN.

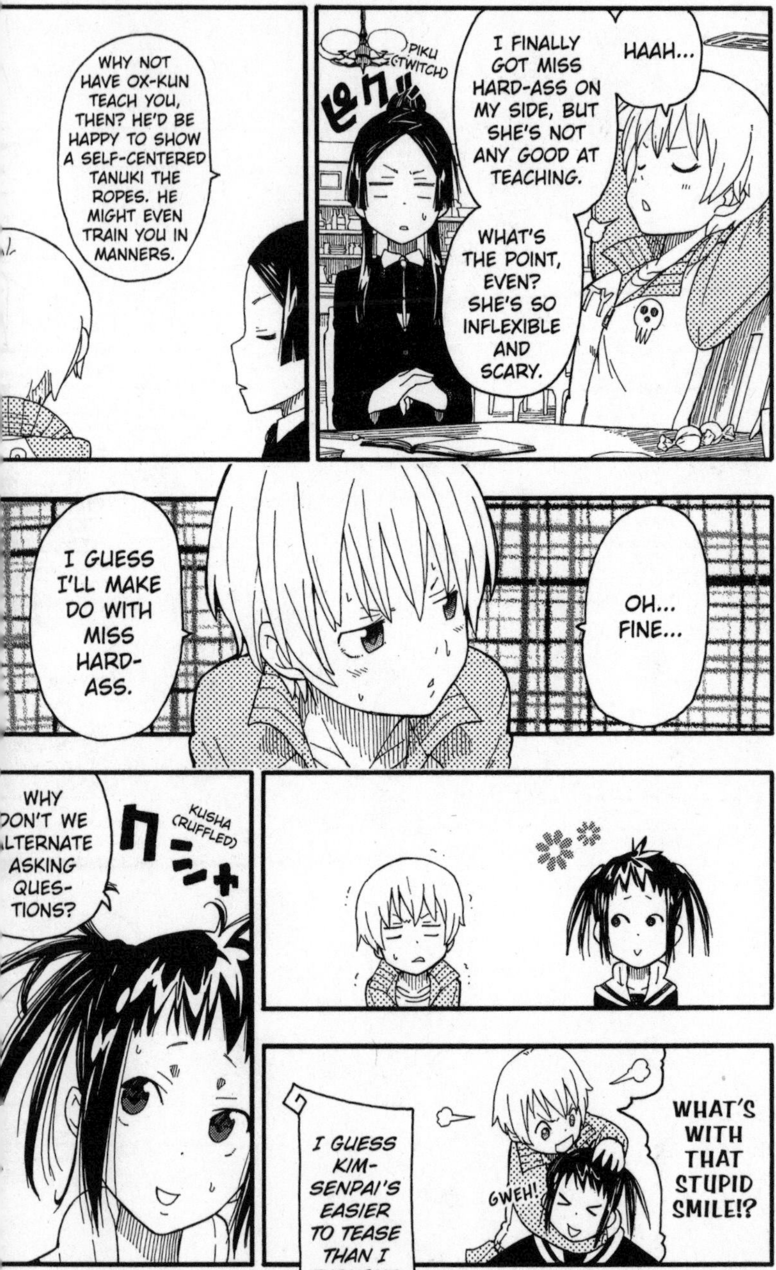
HAAH...
I FINALLY GOT MISS HARD-ASS ON MY SIDE, BUT SHE'S NOT ANY GOOD AT TEACHING.
WHAT'S THE POINT, EVEN? SHE'S SO INFLEXIBLE AND SCARY.
PIKU (TWITCH)
WHY NOT HAVE OX-KUN TEACH YOU, THEN? HE'D BE HAPPY TO SHOW A SELF-CENTERED TANUKI THE ROPES. HE MIGHT EVEN TRAIN YOU IN MANNERS.
OH... FINE...
I GUESS I'LL MAKE DO WITH MISS HARD-ASS.
WHAT'S WITH THAT STUPID SMILE!?
GWEH!
I GUESS KIM-SENPAI'S EASIER TO TEASE THAN I THOUGHT.
WHY ON'T WE LTERNATE ASKING QUESTIONS?
KUSHA (RUFFLED)

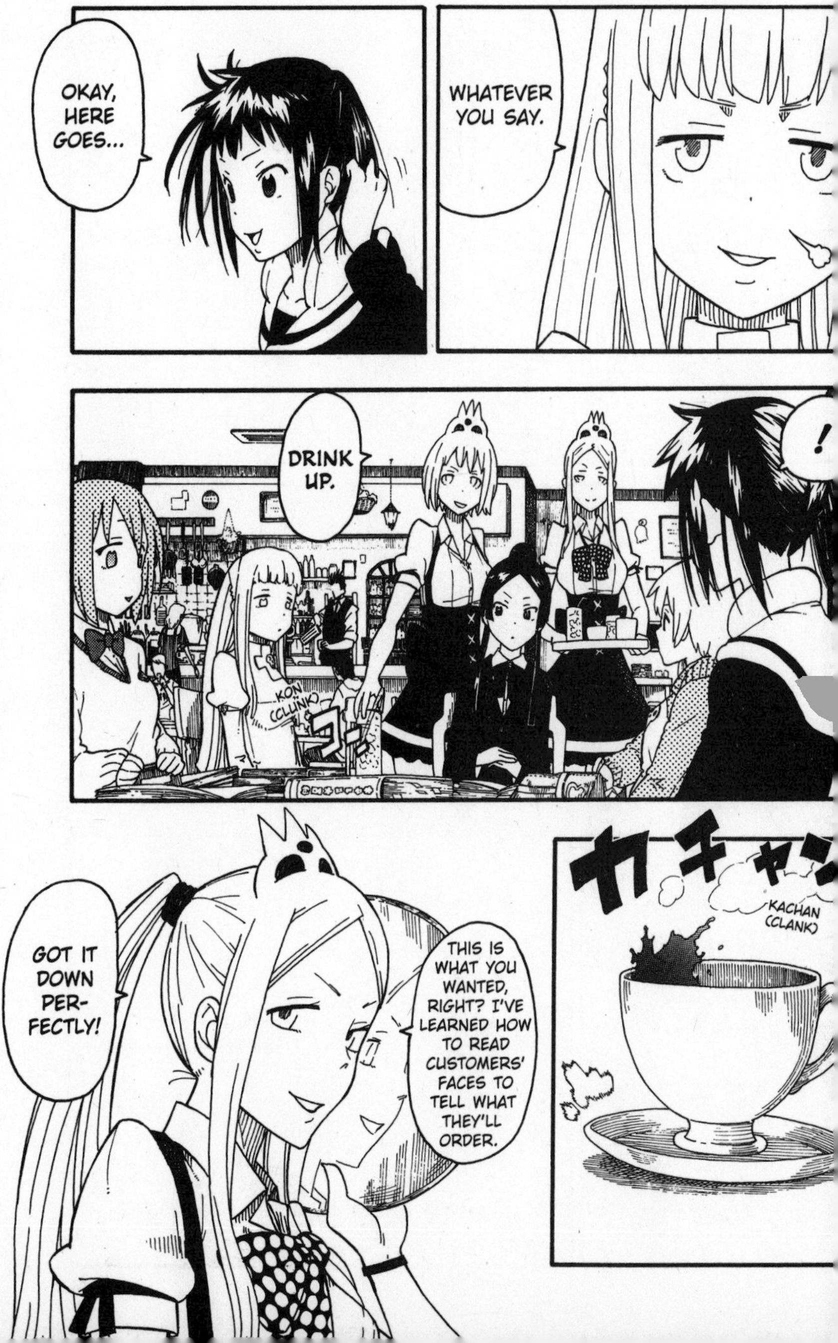
WHATEVER YOU SAY.
OKAY, HERE GOES...
!
DRINK UP.
KON (CLINK)
KACHAN (CLANK)
THIS IS WHAT YOU WANTED, RIGHT? I'VE LEARNED HOW TO READ CUSTOMERS' FACES TO TELL WHAT THEY'LL ORDER.
GOT IT DOWN PER-FECTLY!

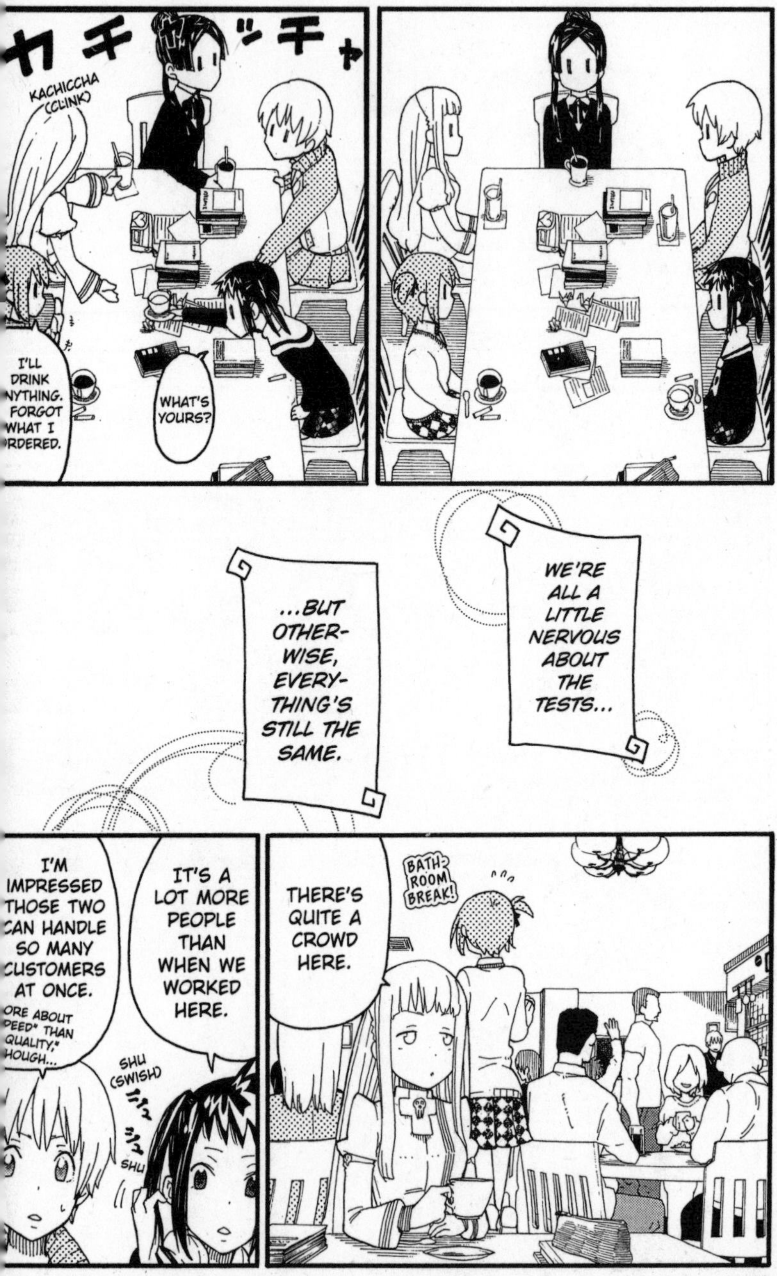

カチッチャ
KACHICCHA (CLINK)
WHAT'S YOURS?
I'LL DRINK NYTHING. FORGOT WHAT I RDERED.
WE'RE ALL A LITTLE NERVOUS ABOUT THE TESTS...
...BUT OTHERWISE, EVERYTHING'S STILL THE SAME.
BATH-ROOM BREAK!
THERE'S QUITE A CROWD HERE.
IT'S A LOT MORE PEOPLE THAN WHEN WE WORKED HERE.
I'M IMPRESSED THOSE TWO CAN HANDLE SO MANY CUSTOMERS AT ONCE.
ORE ABOUT "PEED" THAN QUALITY," HOUGH...
SHU (SWISH)
SHU

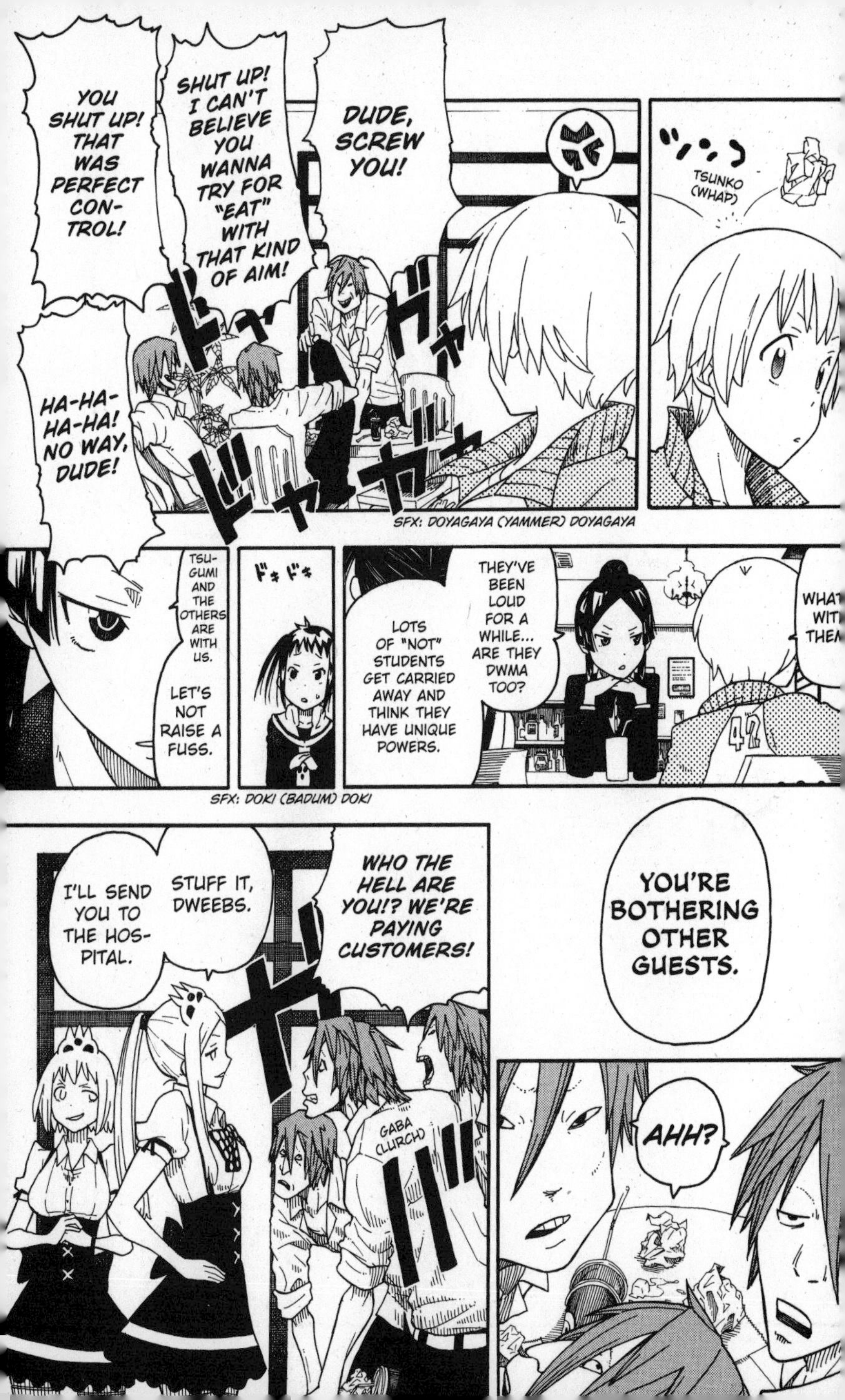
TSUNKO (WHAP)
DUDE, SCREW YOU!
SHUT UP! I CAN'T BELIEVE YOU WANNA TRY FOR "EAT" WITH THAT KIND OF AIM!
YOU SHUT UP! THAT WAS PERFECT CON-TROL!
HA-HA-HA-HA! NO WAY, DUDE!
SFX: DOYAGAYA (YAMMER) DOYAGAYA
WHAT WIT THEM
THEY'VE BEEN LOUD FOR A WHILE... ARE THEY DWMA TOO?
LOTS OF "NOT" STUDENTS GET CARRIED AWAY AND THINK THEY HAVE UNIQUE POWERS.
TSU-GUMI AND THE OTHERS ARE WITH US.
LET'S NOT RAISE A FUSS.
SFX: DOKI (BADUM) DOKI
YOU'RE BOTHERING OTHER GUESTS.
AHH?
WHO THE HELL ARE YOU!? WE'RE PAYING CUSTOMERS!
GABA (LURCH)
STUFF IT, DWEEBS.
I'LL SEND YOU TO THE HOS-PITAL.

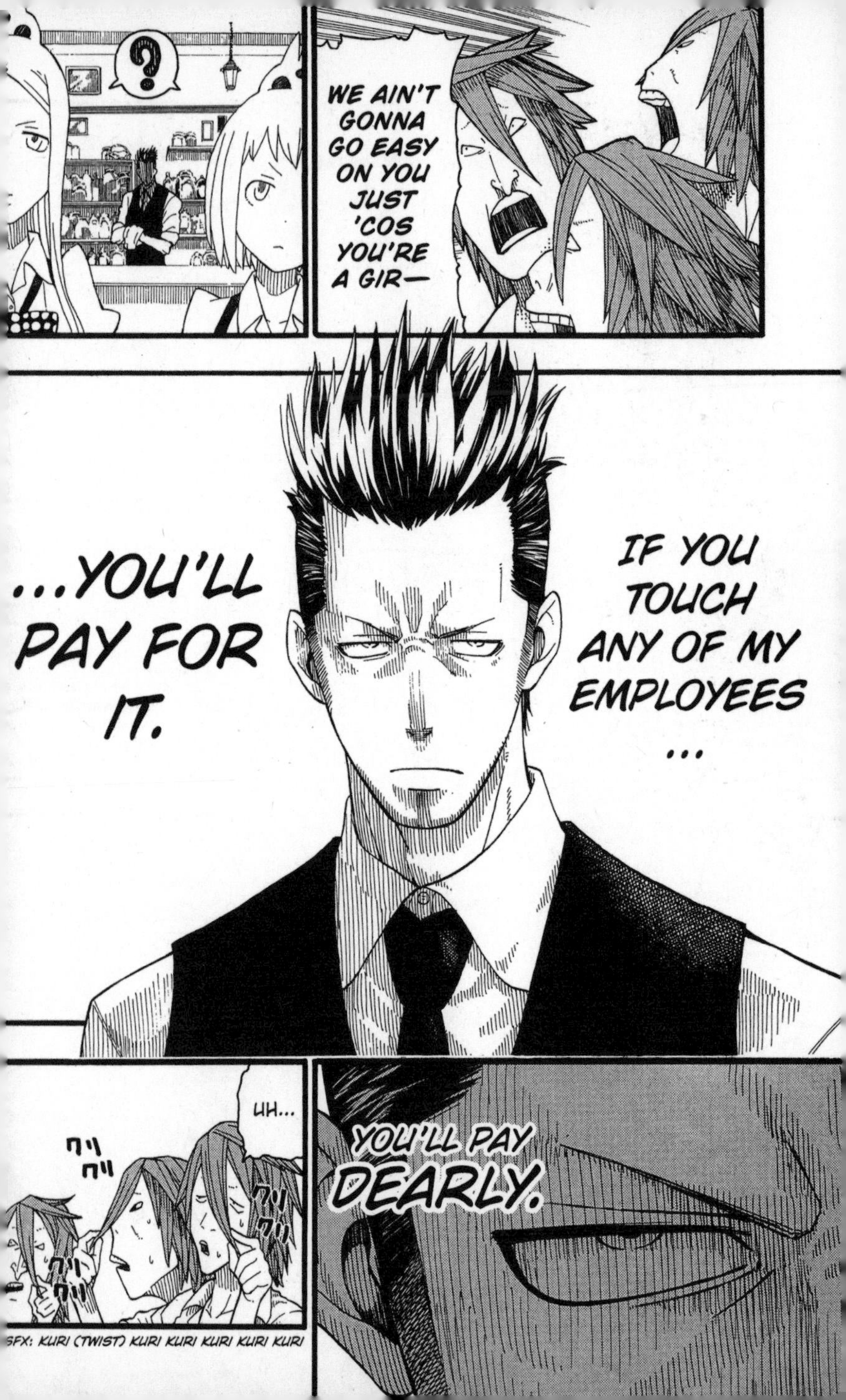
WE AIN'T GONNA GO EASY ON YOU JUST 'COS YOU'RE A GIR—
?
IF YOU TOUCH ANY OF MY EMPLOYEES ...
...YOU'LL PAY FOR IT.
YOU'LL PAY DEARLY.
UH...
SFX: KURI (TWIST) KURI KURI KURI KURI KURI

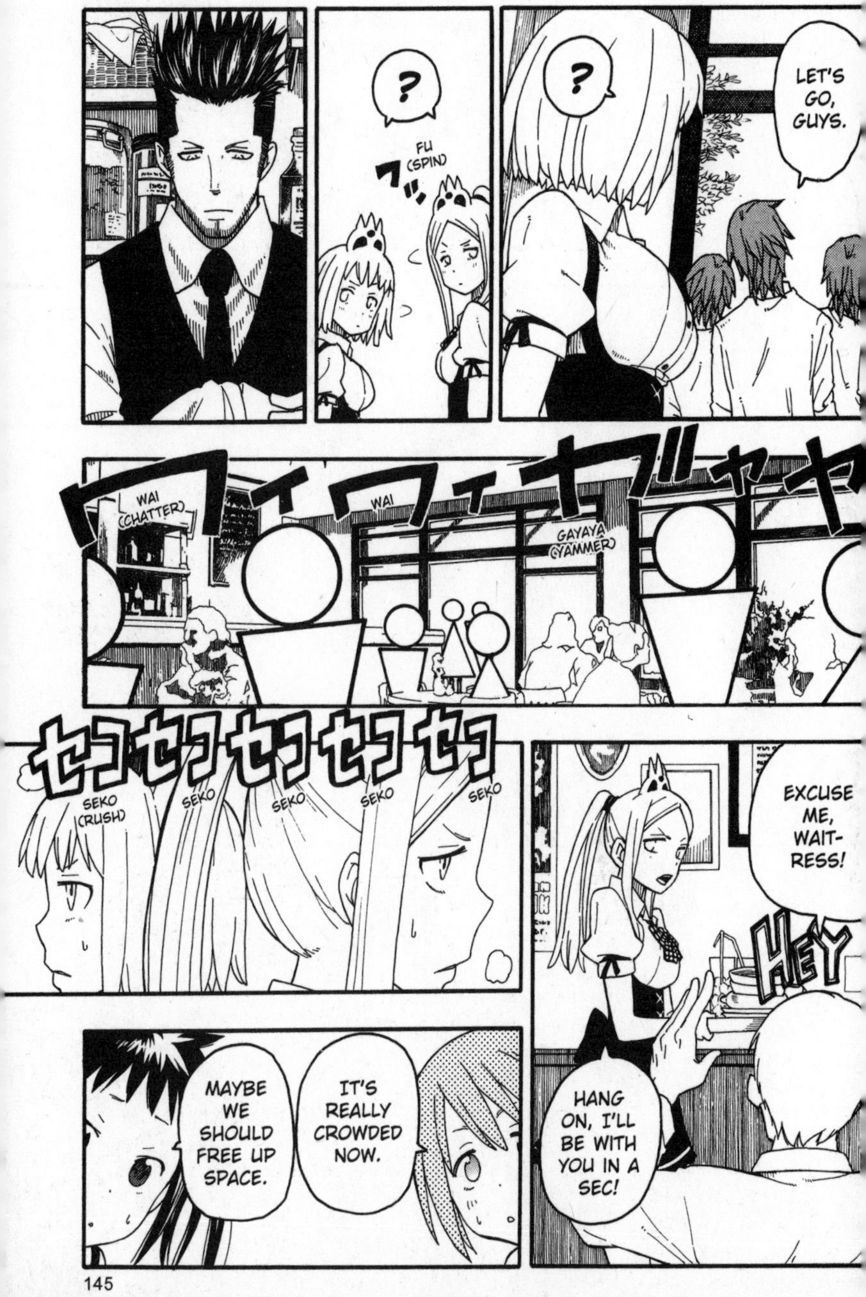
LET'S GO, GUYS.
?
?
FU (SPIN)
WAI (CHATTER)
WAI
GAYAYA (YAMMER)
EXCUSE ME, WAIT-RESS!
HEY
HANG ON, I'LL BE WITH YOU IN A SEC!
SEKO (CRUSH)
SEKO
SEKO
SEKO
SEKO
IT'S REALLY CROWDED NOW.
MAYBE WE SHOULD FREE UP SPACE.

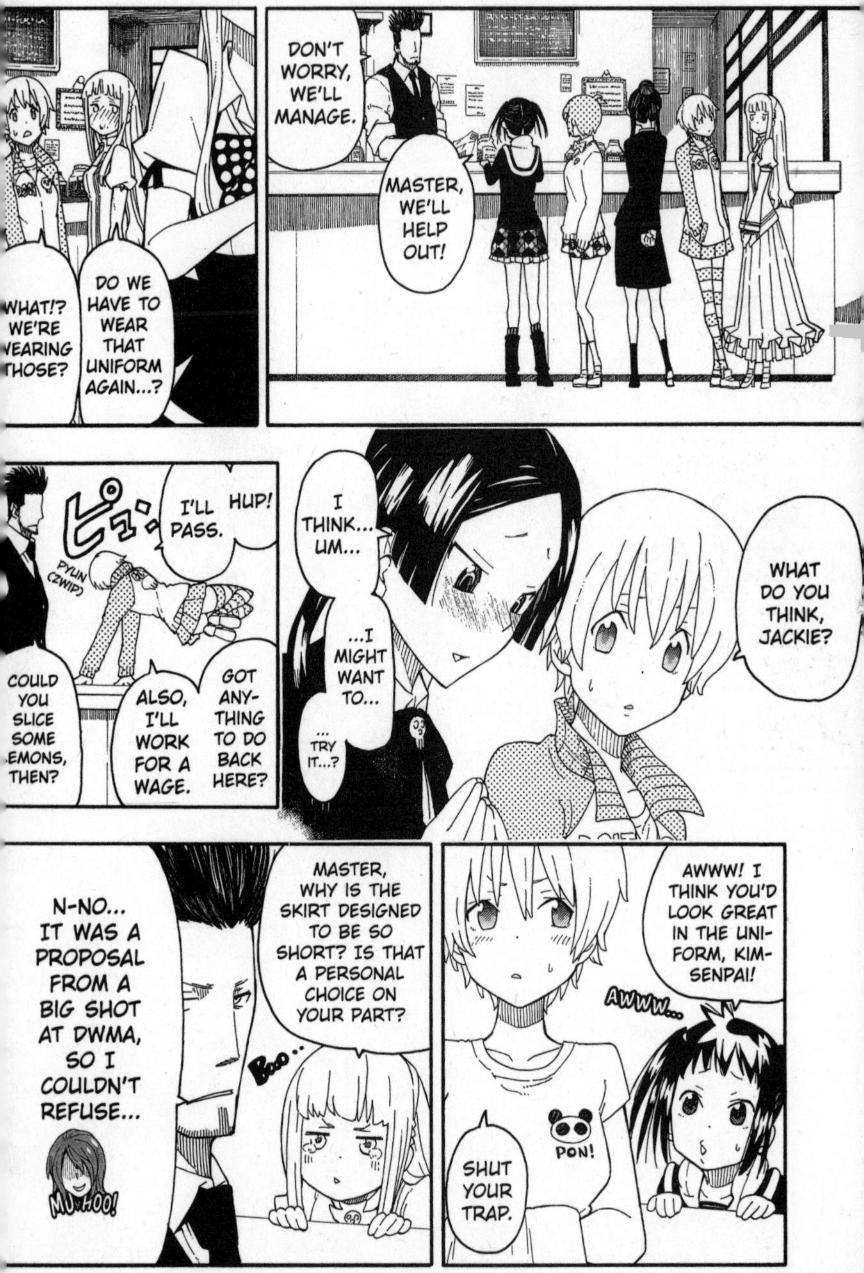
DON'T WORRY, WE'LL MANAGE.
MASTER, WE'LL HELP OUT!
DO WE HAVE TO WEAR THAT UNIFORM AGAIN...?
WHAT!? WE'RE WEARING THOSE?
WHAT DO YOU THINK, JACKIE?
I THINK... UM...
...I MIGHT WANT TO...
...TRY IT...?
HUP!
I'LL PASS.
ピュ
PYUN (ZWIP)
GOT ANYTHING TO DO BACK HERE?
ALSO, I'LL WORK FOR A WAGE.
COULD YOU SLICE SOME LEMONS, THEN?
AWWW! I THINK YOU'D LOOK GREAT IN THE UNIFORM, KIM-SENPAI!
AWWW...
PON!
SHUT YOUR TRAP.
MASTER, WHY IS THE SKIRT DESIGNED TO BE SO SHORT? IS THAT A PERSONAL CHOICE ON YOUR PART?
BOO..
N-NO... IT WAS A PROPOSAL FROM A BIG SHOT AT DWMA, SO I COULDN'T REFUSE...
MU-HOO!

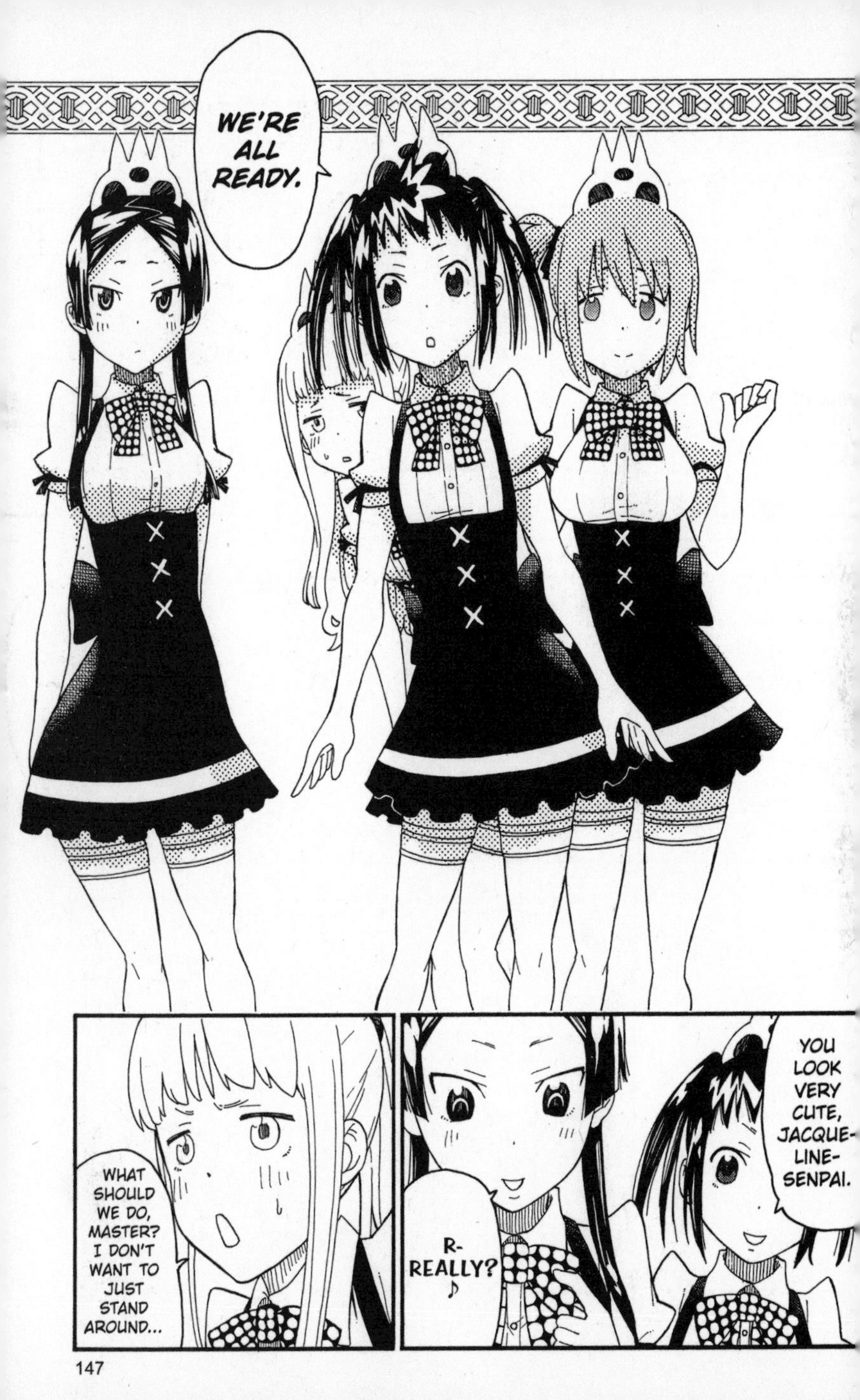
WE'RE ALL READY.
YOU LOOK VERY CUTE, JACQUE-LINE-SENPAI.
R-REALLY? ♪
WHAT SHOULD WE DO, MASTER? I DON'T WANT TO JUST STAND AROUND...

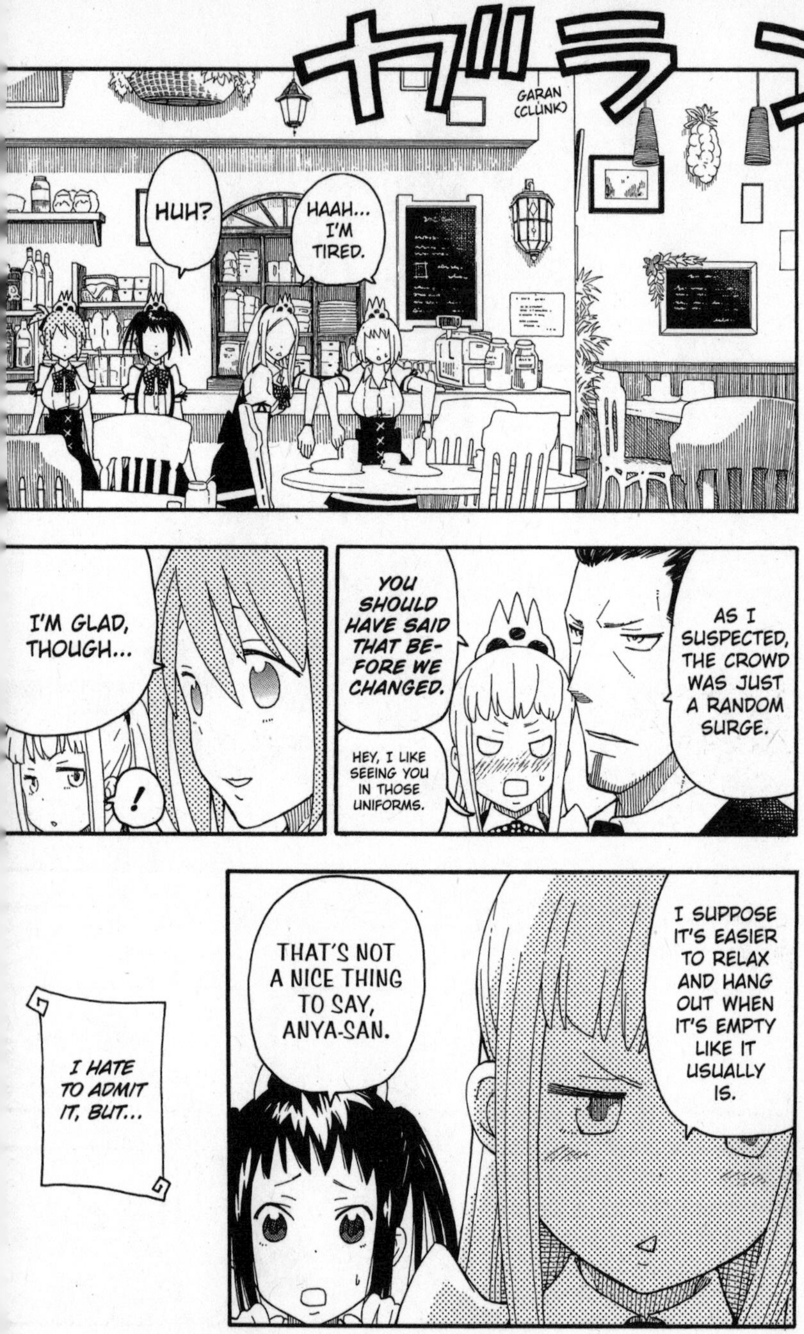
GARAN (CLUNK)
HAAH... I'M TIRED.
HUH?
AS I SUSPECTED, THE CROWD WAS JUST A RANDOM SURGE.
YOU SHOULD HAVE SAID THAT BE-FORE WE CHANGED.
HEY, I LIKE SEEING YOU IN THOSE UNIFORMS.
I'M GLAD, THOUGH...
I SUPPOSE IT'S EASIER TO RELAX AND HANG OUT WHEN IT'S EMPTY LIKE IT USUALLY IS.
THAT'S NOT A NICE THING TO SAY, ANYA-SAN.
I HATE TO ADMIT IT, BUT...

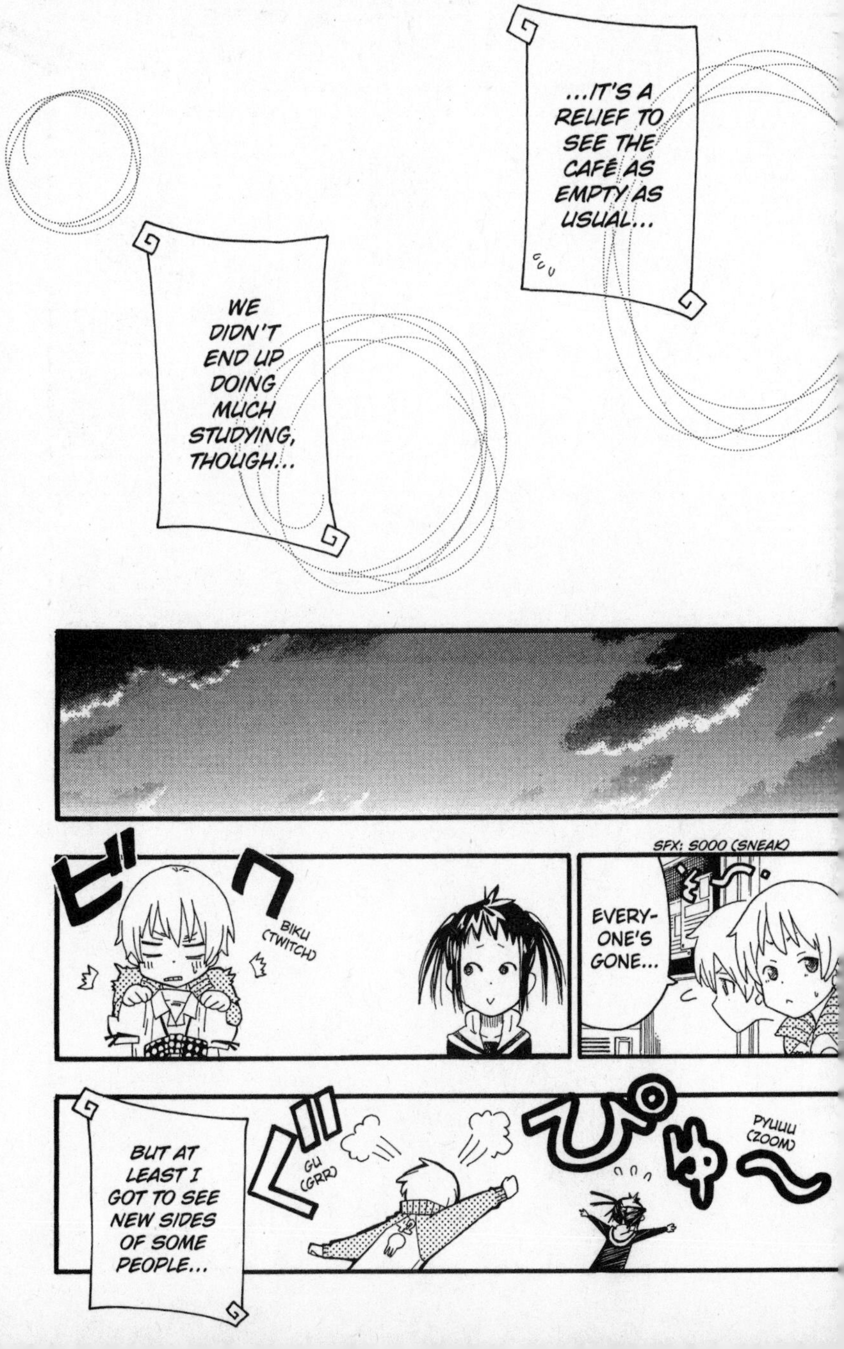
...IT'S A RELIEF TO SEE THE CAFÉ AS EMPTY AS USUAL...
WE DIDN'T END UP DOING MUCH STUDYING, THOUGH...
SFX: SOOO (SNEAK)
EVERY-ONE'S GONE...
BIKU (TWITCH)
PYUUU (ZOOM)
GU (GRR)
BUT AT LEAST I GOT TO SEE NEW SIDES OF SOME PEOPLE...

SOUL EATER NOT!

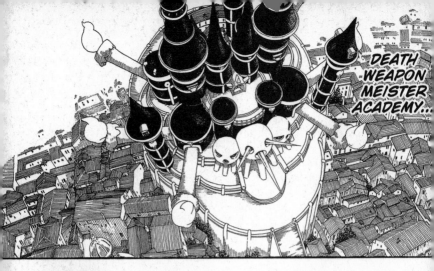

DEATH WEAPON MEISTER ACADEMY...

HUH?

THIS WA TSUGUM SAN!

KUI (TUG)

I THINK WE SHOULD GO THIS WAY. WHAT ABOUT YOU, TSUGUMI-CHAN?

HUH?

KUI

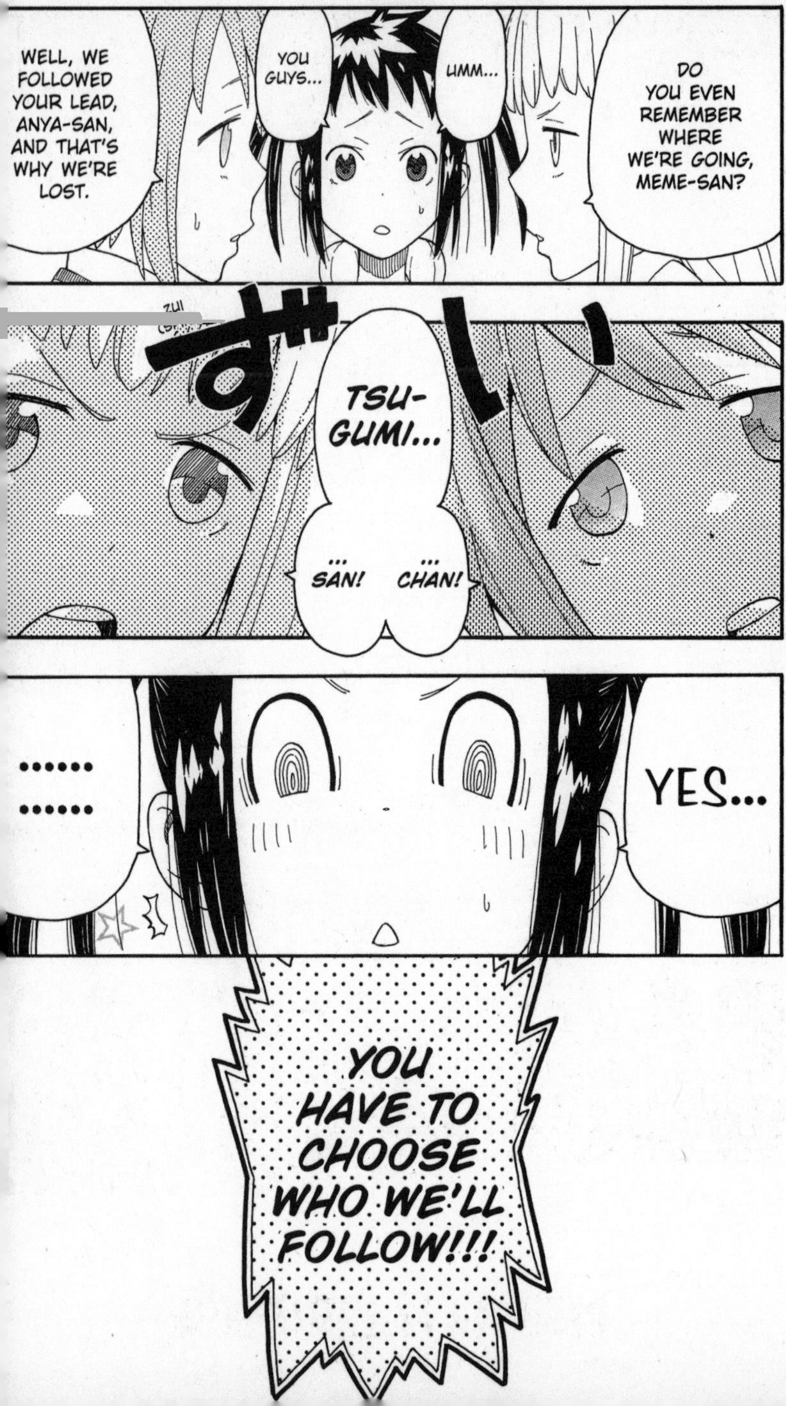

DO YOU EVEN REMEMBER WHERE WE'RE GOING, MEME-SAN?
UMM...
YOU GUYS...
WELL, WE FOLLOWED YOUR LEAD, ANYA-SAN, AND THAT'S WHY WE'RE LOST.
ずい
ZUI
TSU-GUMI...
...CHAN!
...SAN!
YES...
....
YOU HAVE TO CHOOSE WHO WE'LL FOLLOW!!!

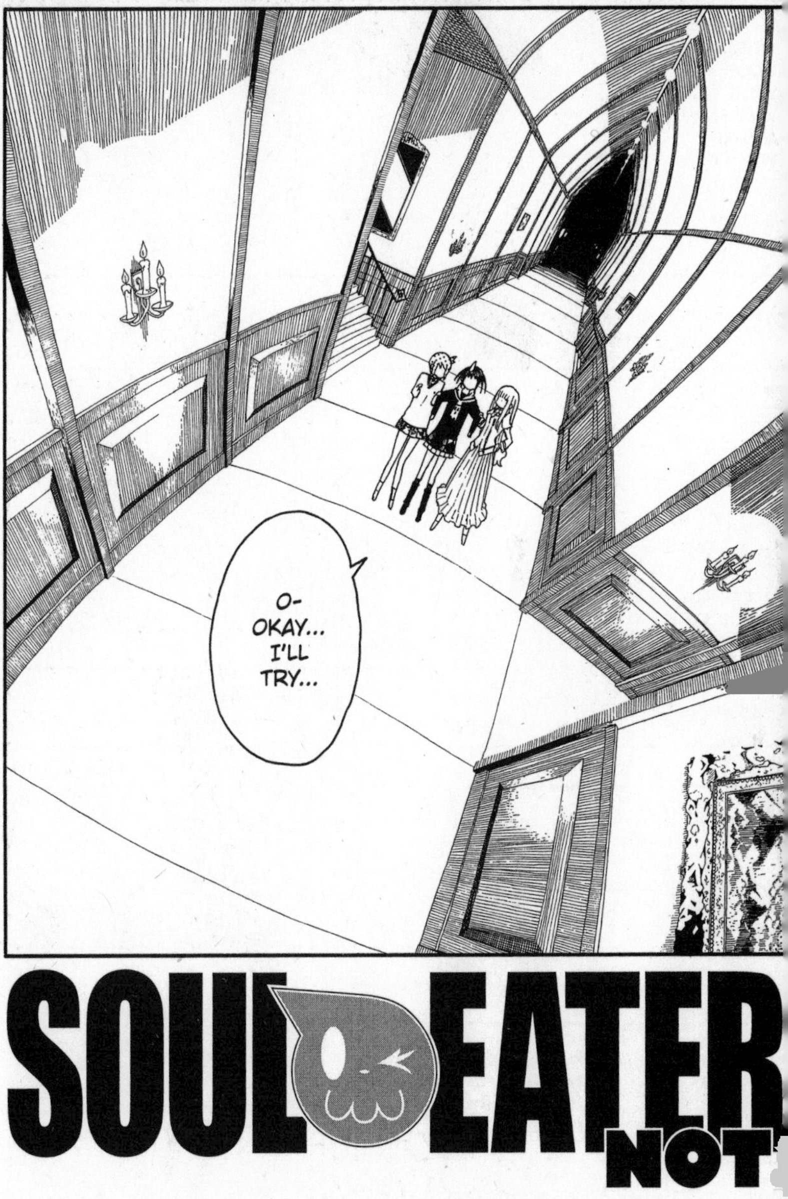
O-OKAY... I'LL TRY...

SOUL EATER NOT

CHAPTER 13: LABYRINTH!

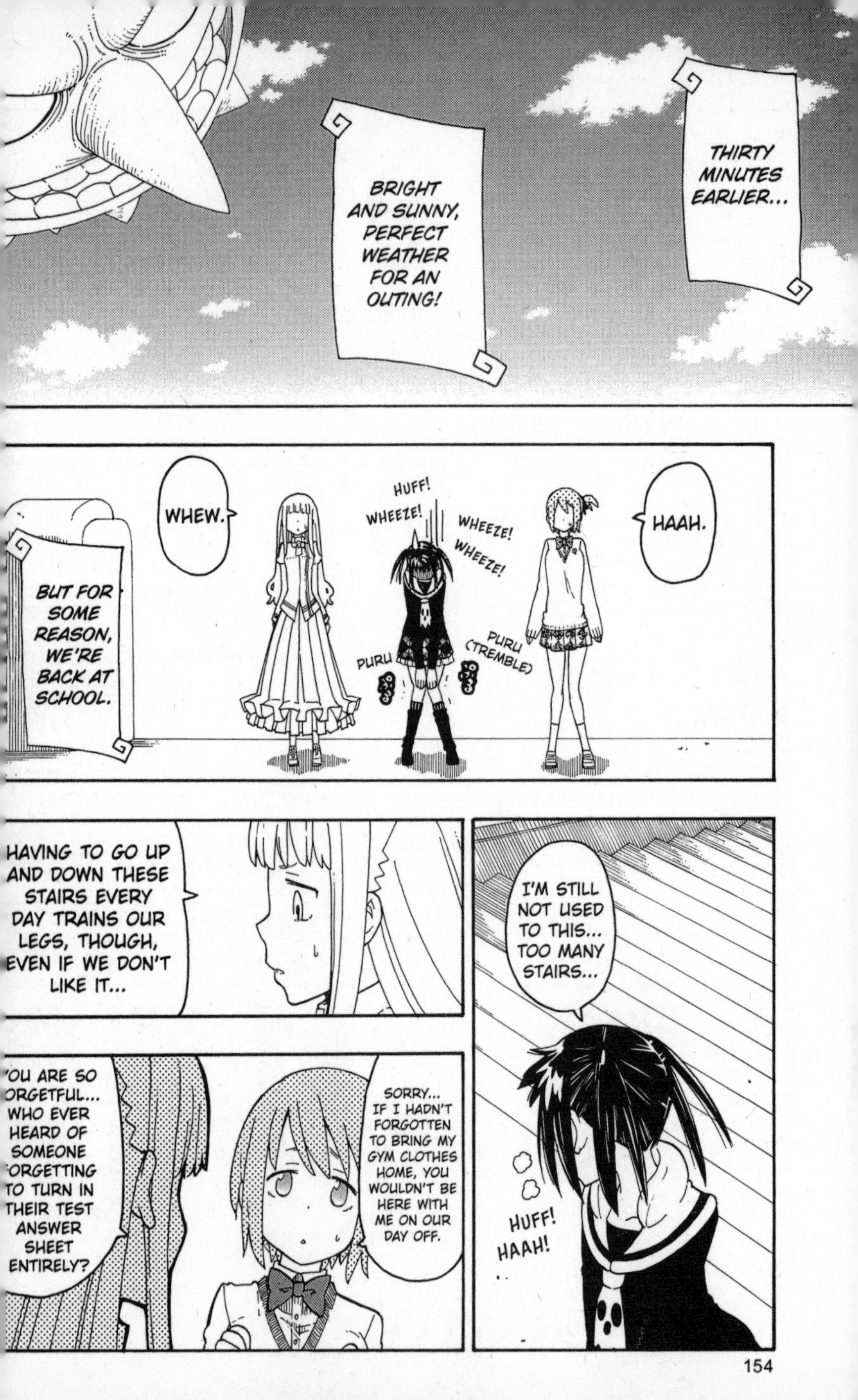
THIRTY MINUTES EARLIER...
BRIGHT AND SUNNY, PERFECT WEATHER FOR AN OUTING!
HAAH.
PURU (TREMBLE)
WHEEZE! WHEEZE!
HUFF! WHEEZE!
PURU
WHEW.
BUT FOR SOME REASON, WE'RE BACK AT SCHOOL.
I'M STILL NOT USED TO THIS... TOO MANY STAIRS...
HUFF! HAAH!
HAVING TO GO UP AND DOWN THESE STAIRS EVERY DAY TRAINS OUR LEGS, THOUGH, EVEN IF WE DON'T LIKE IT...
SORRY... IF I HADN'T FORGOTTEN TO BRING MY GYM CLOTHES HOME, YOU WOULDN'T BE HERE WITH ME ON OUR DAY OFF.
OU ARE SO ORGETFUL... WHO EVER HEARD OF SOMEONE ORGETTING TO TURN IN THEIR TEST ANSWER SHEET ENTIRELY?

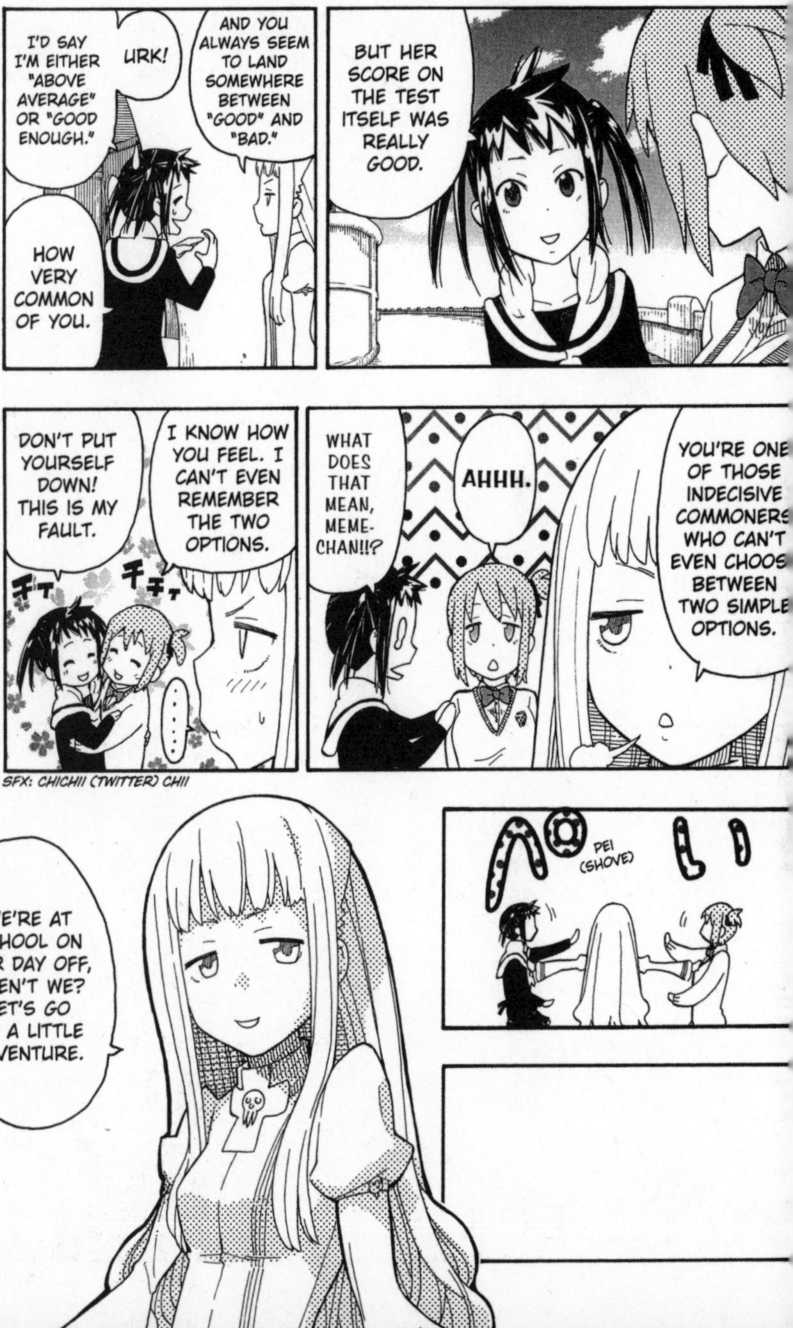
BUT HER SCORE ON THE TEST ITSELF WAS REALLY GOOD.
AND YOU ALWAYS SEEM TO LAND SOMEWHERE BETWEEN "GOOD" AND "BAD."
URK!
I'D SAY I'M EITHER "ABOVE AVERAGE" OR "GOOD ENOUGH."
HOW VERY COMMON OF YOU.
YOU'RE ONE OF THOSE INDECISIVE COMMONERS WHO CAN'T EVEN CHOOS BETWEEN TWO SIMPLE OPTIONS.
AHHH.
WHAT DOES THAT MEAN, MEME-CHAN!!?
I KNOW HOW YOU FEEL. I CAN'T EVEN REMEMBER THE TWO OPTIONS.
DON'T PUT YOURSELF DOWN! THIS IS MY FAULT.
チチィ
チィ
......
PEI (SHOVE)
WE'RE AT SCHOOL ON OUR DAY OFF, AREN'T WE? LET'S GO ON A LITTLE ADVENTURE.
SFX: CHICHII (TWITTER) CHII

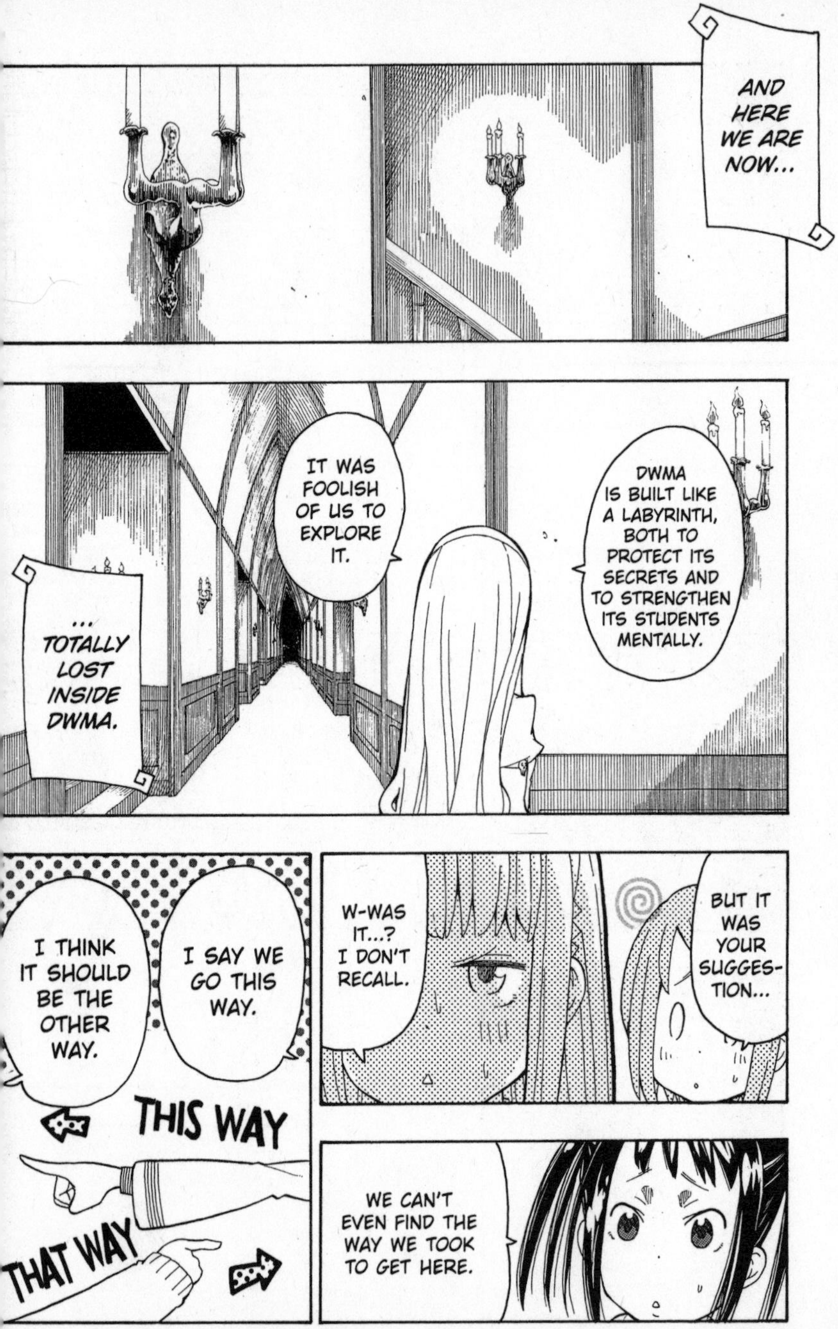
AND HERE WE ARE NOW...
DWMA IS BUILT LIKE A LABYRINTH, BOTH TO PROTECT ITS SECRETS AND TO STRENGTHEN ITS STUDENTS MENTALLY.
IT WAS FOOLISH OF US TO EXPLORE IT.
...TOTALLY LOST INSIDE DWMA.
BUT IT WAS YOUR SUGGES-TION...
W-WAS IT...? I DON'T RECALL.
WE CAN'T EVEN FIND THE WAY WE TOOK TO GET HERE.
I SAY WE GO THIS WAY.
I THINK IT SHOULD BE THE OTHER WAY.
THIS WAY
THAT WAY

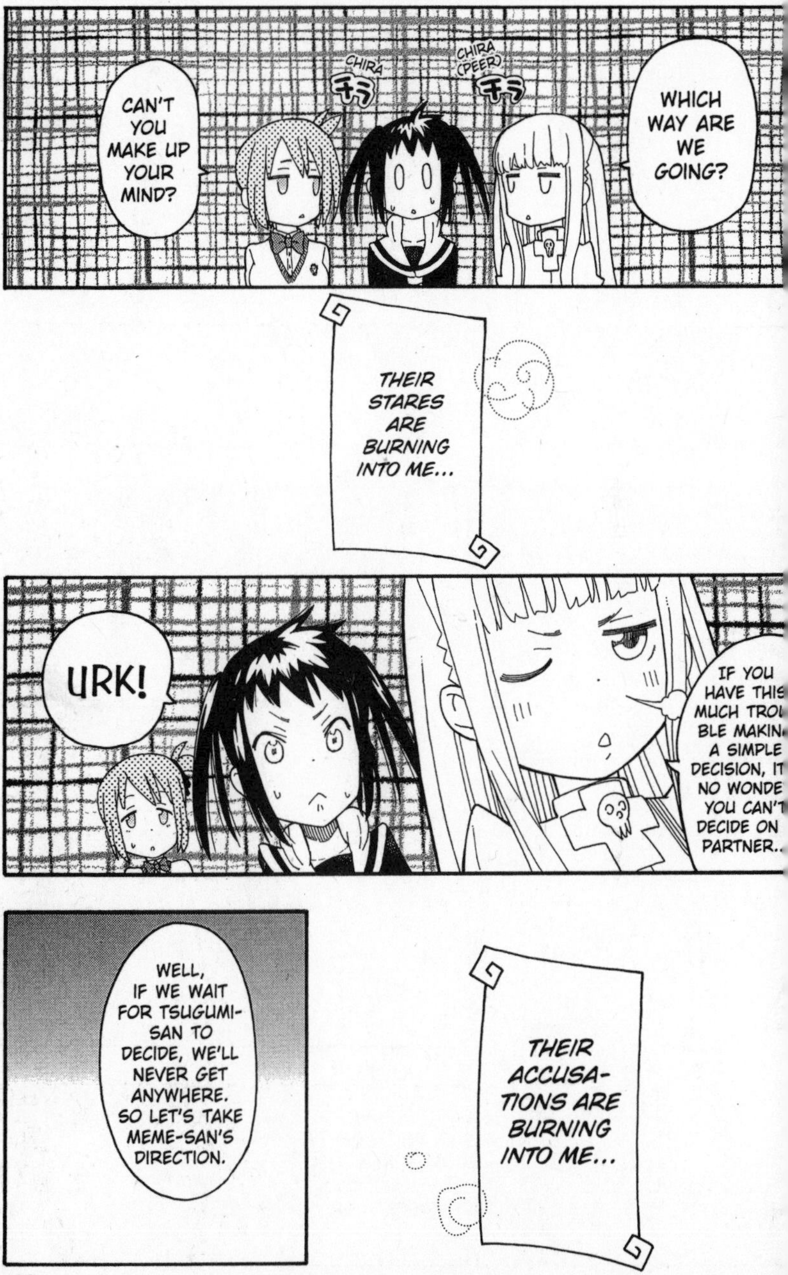
WHICH WAY ARE WE GOING?
CHIRA (PEER)
チラ
CHIRA
チラ
CAN'T YOU MAKE UP YOUR MIND?
THEIR STARES ARE BURNING INTO ME...
IF YOU HAVE THIS MUCH TRO BLE MAKIN A SIMPLE DECISION, IT NO WONDE YOU CAN'T DECIDE ON PARTNER..
URK!
THEIR ACCUSA-TIONS ARE BURNING INTO ME...
WELL, IF WE WAIT FOR TSUGUMI-SAN TO DECIDE, WE'LL NEVER GET ANYWHERE. SO LET'S TAKE MEME-SAN'S DIRECTION.

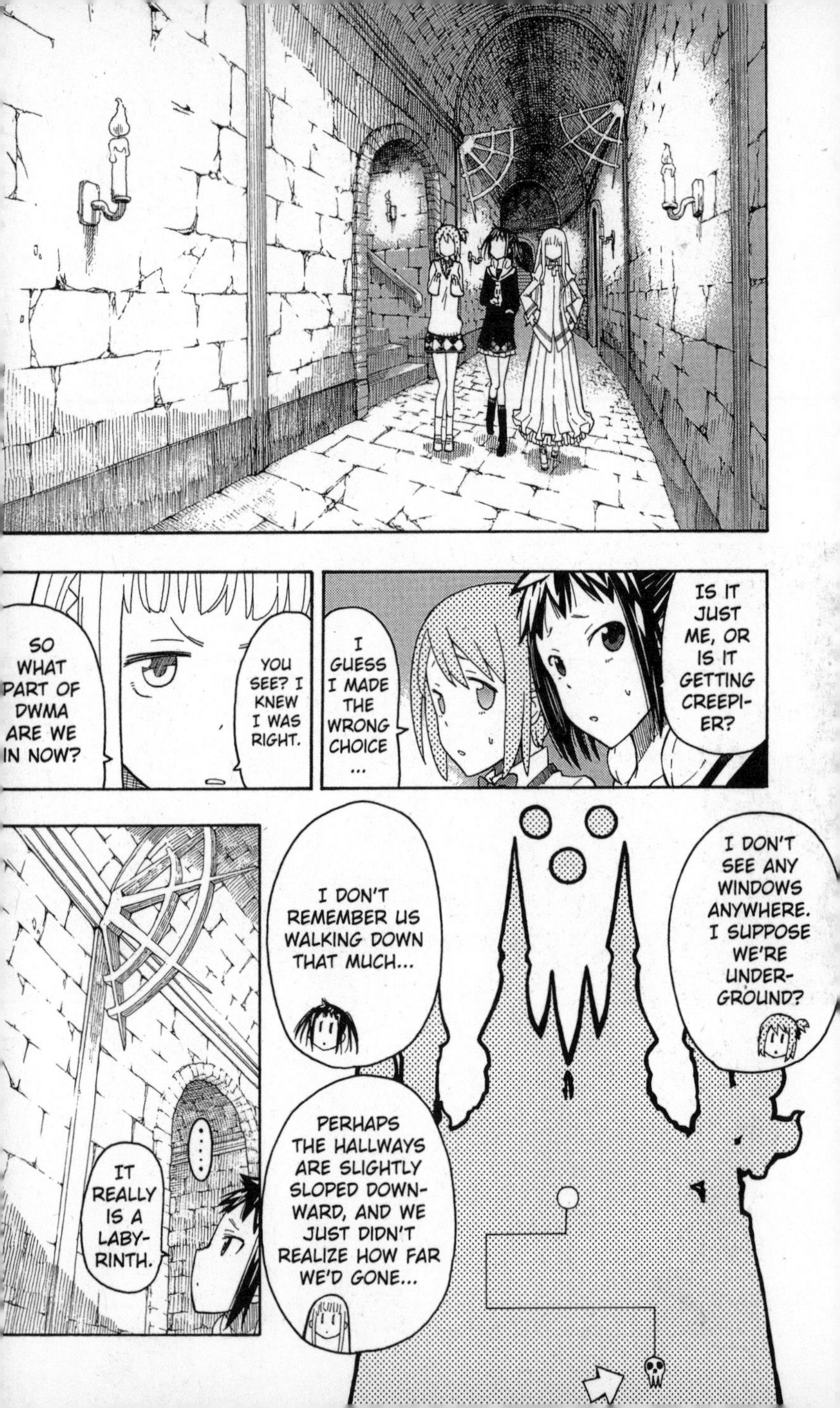
IS IT JUST ME, OR IS IT GETTING CREEPIER?
I GUESS I MADE THE WRONG CHOICE ...
YOU SEE? I KNEW I WAS RIGHT.
SO WHAT PART OF DWMA ARE WE IN NOW?
I DON'T SEE ANY WINDOWS ANYWHERE. I SUPPOSE WE'RE UNDERGROUND?
I DON'T REMEMBER US WALKING DOWN THAT MUCH...
PERHAPS THE HALLWAYS ARE SLIGHTLY SLOPED DOWNWARD, AND WE JUST DIDN'T REALIZE HOW FAR WE'D GONE...
...
IT REALLY IS A LABYRINTH.

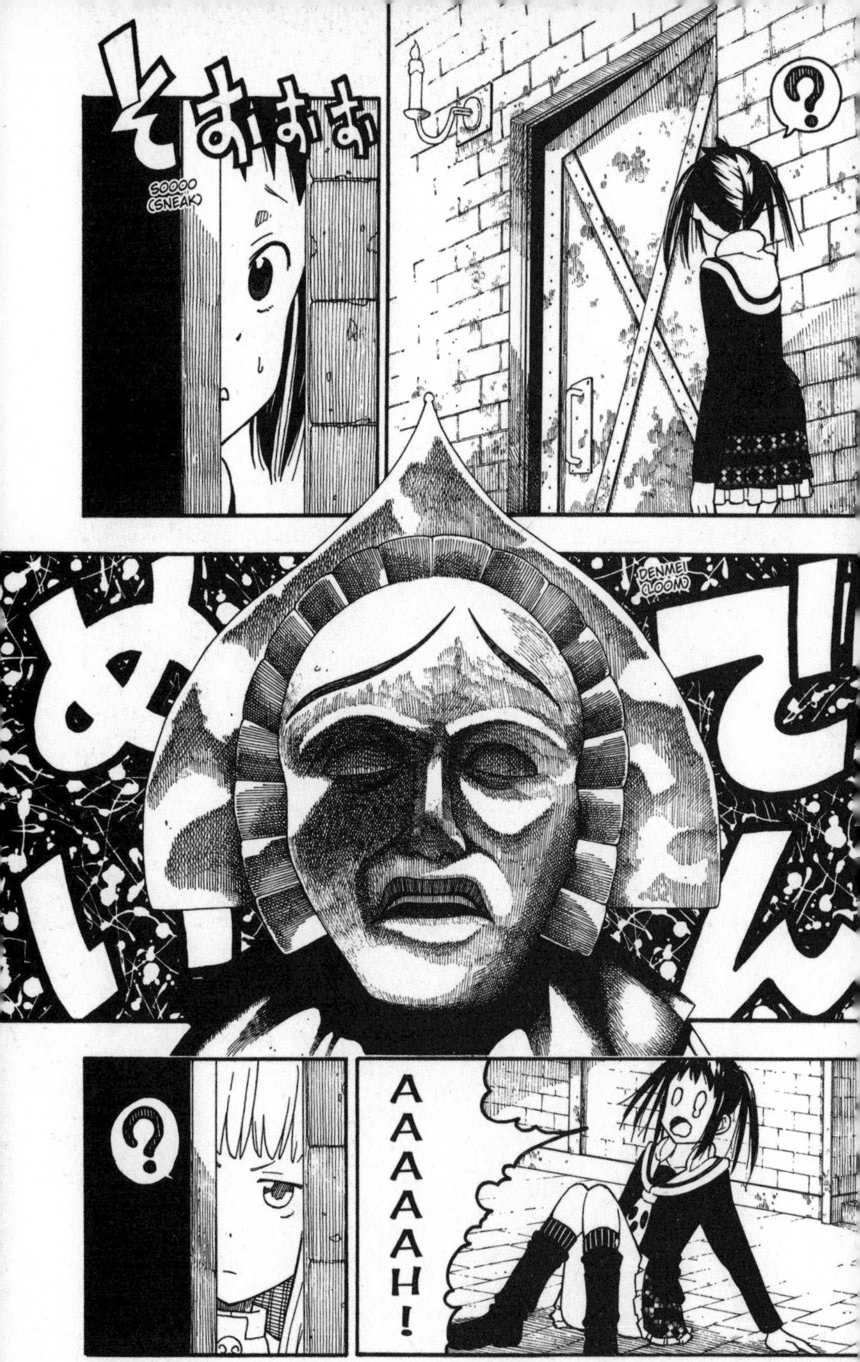
?
そぉぉぉ
SOOOO (SNEAK)
でんめい
DENMEI (LOOM)
AAAAAAH!
?

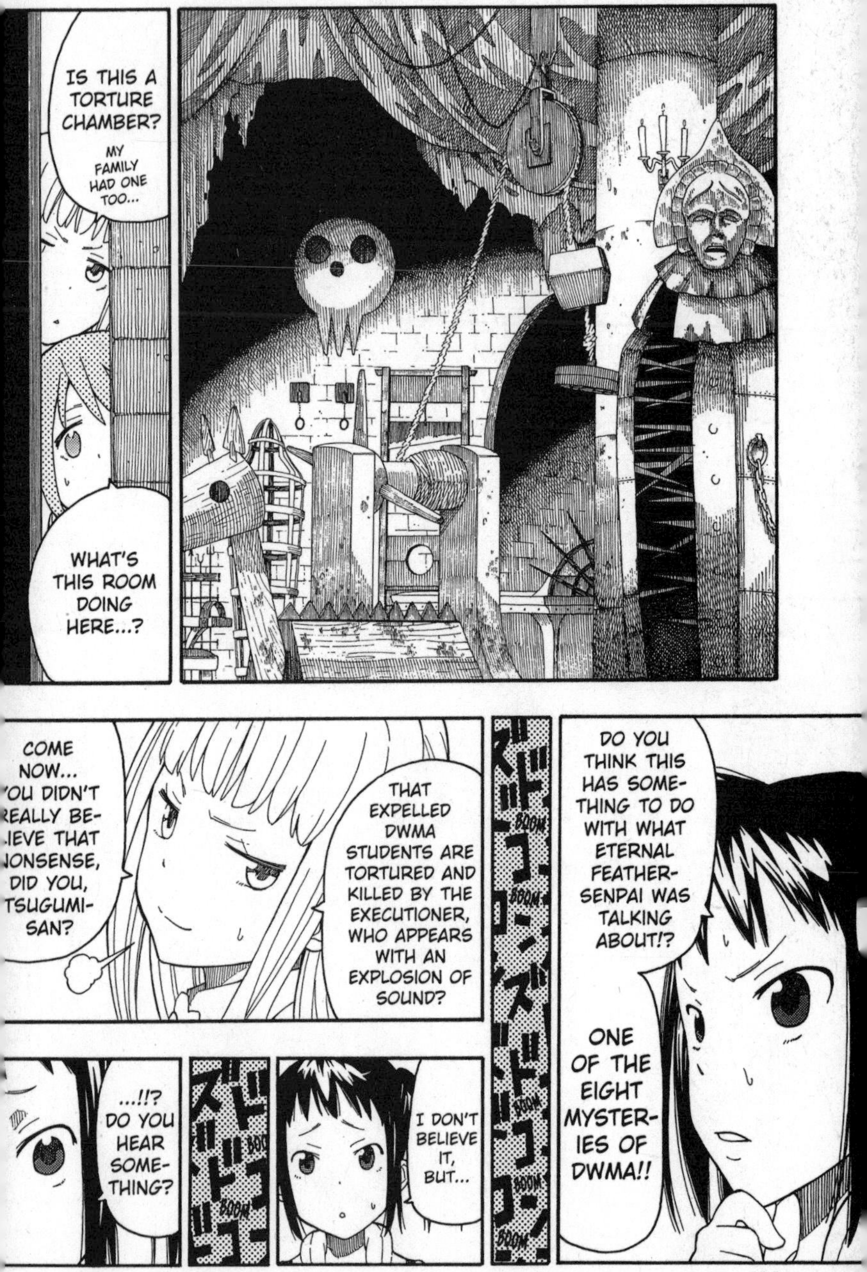
IS THIS A TORTURE CHAMBER?
MY FAMILY HAD ONE TOO...
WHAT'S THIS ROOM DOING HERE...?
DO YOU THINK THIS HAS SOMETHING TO DO WITH WHAT ETERNAL FEATHER-SENPAI WAS TALKING ABOUT!?
ONE OF THE EIGHT MYSTERIES OF DWMA!!
BOOM BOOM BOOM BOOM
THAT EXPELLED DWMA STUDENTS ARE TORTURED AND KILLED BY THE EXECUTIONER, WHO APPEARS WITH AN EXPLOSION OF SOUND?
COME NOW... 'OU DIDN'T REALLY BE-IEVE THAT NONSENSE, DID YOU, TSUGUMI-SAN?
I DON'T BELIEVE IT, BUT...
BOOM BOOM
...!!? DO YOU HEAR SOMETHING?

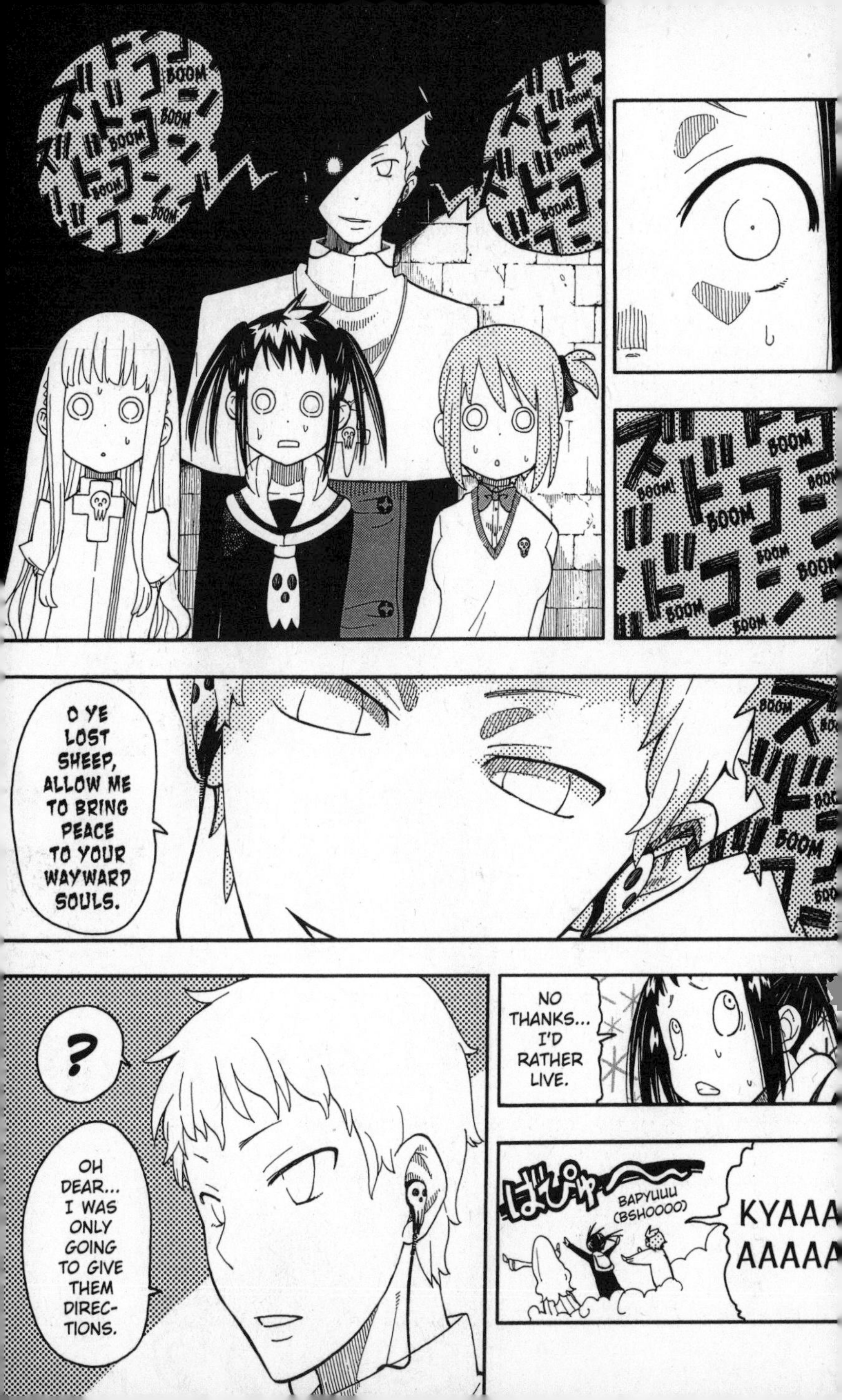
BOOM BOOM BOOM BOOM BOOM BOOM BOOM BOOM
BOOM BOOM BOOM BOOM BOOM BOOM BOOM BOOM BOOM
BOOM BOOM BOOM BOOM BOOM
O YE LOST SHEEP, ALLOW ME TO BRING PEACE TO YOUR WAYWARD SOULS.
NO THANKS... I'D RATHER LIVE.
ばぴゅ〜
BAPYUUU (BSHOOOO)
KYAAAAAAAA
?
OH DEAR... I WAS ONLY GOING TO GIVE THEM DIRECTIONS.

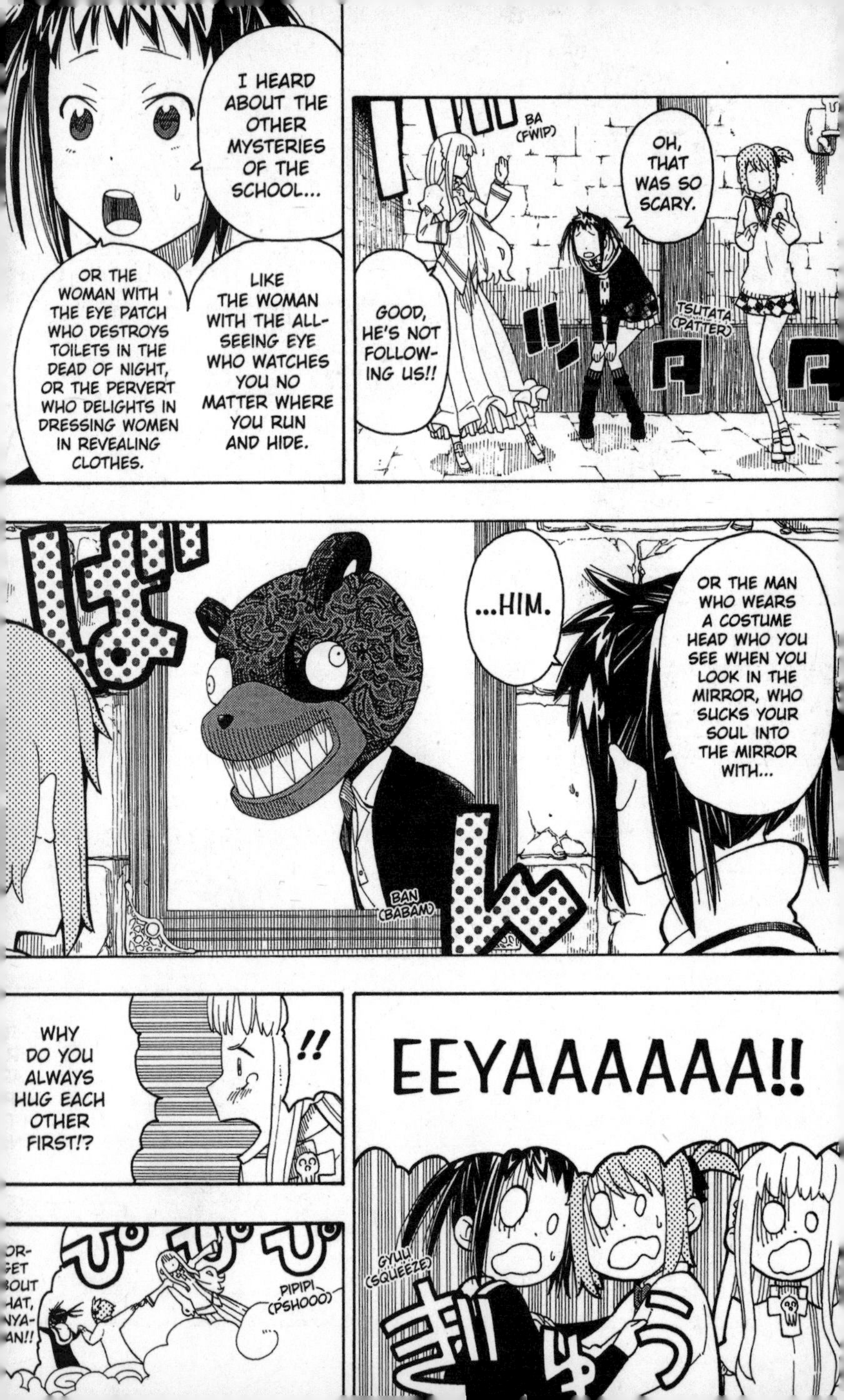
BA (FWIP)
OH, THAT WAS SO SCARY.
GOOD, HE'S NOT FOLLOW-ING US!!
TSUTATA (PATTER)
I HEARD ABOUT THE OTHER MYSTERIES OF THE SCHOOL...
LIKE THE WOMAN WITH THE ALL-SEEING EYE WHO WATCHES YOU NO MATTER WHERE YOU RUN AND HIDE.
OR THE WOMAN WITH THE EYE PATCH WHO DESTROYS TOILETS IN THE DEAD OF NIGHT, OR THE PERVERT WHO DELIGHTS IN DRESSING WOMEN IN REVEALING CLOTHES.
OR THE MAN WHO WEARS A COSTUME HEAD WHO YOU SEE WHEN YOU LOOK IN THE MIRROR, WHO SUCKS YOUR SOUL INTO THE MIRROR WITH...
...HIM.
BAN (BABAM)
EEYAAAAAAA!!
GYUU (SQUEEZE)
WHY DO YOU ALWAYS HUG EACH OTHER FIRST!?
!!
PIPIPI (PSHOOO)
OR-GET BOUT HAT, NYA-AN!!

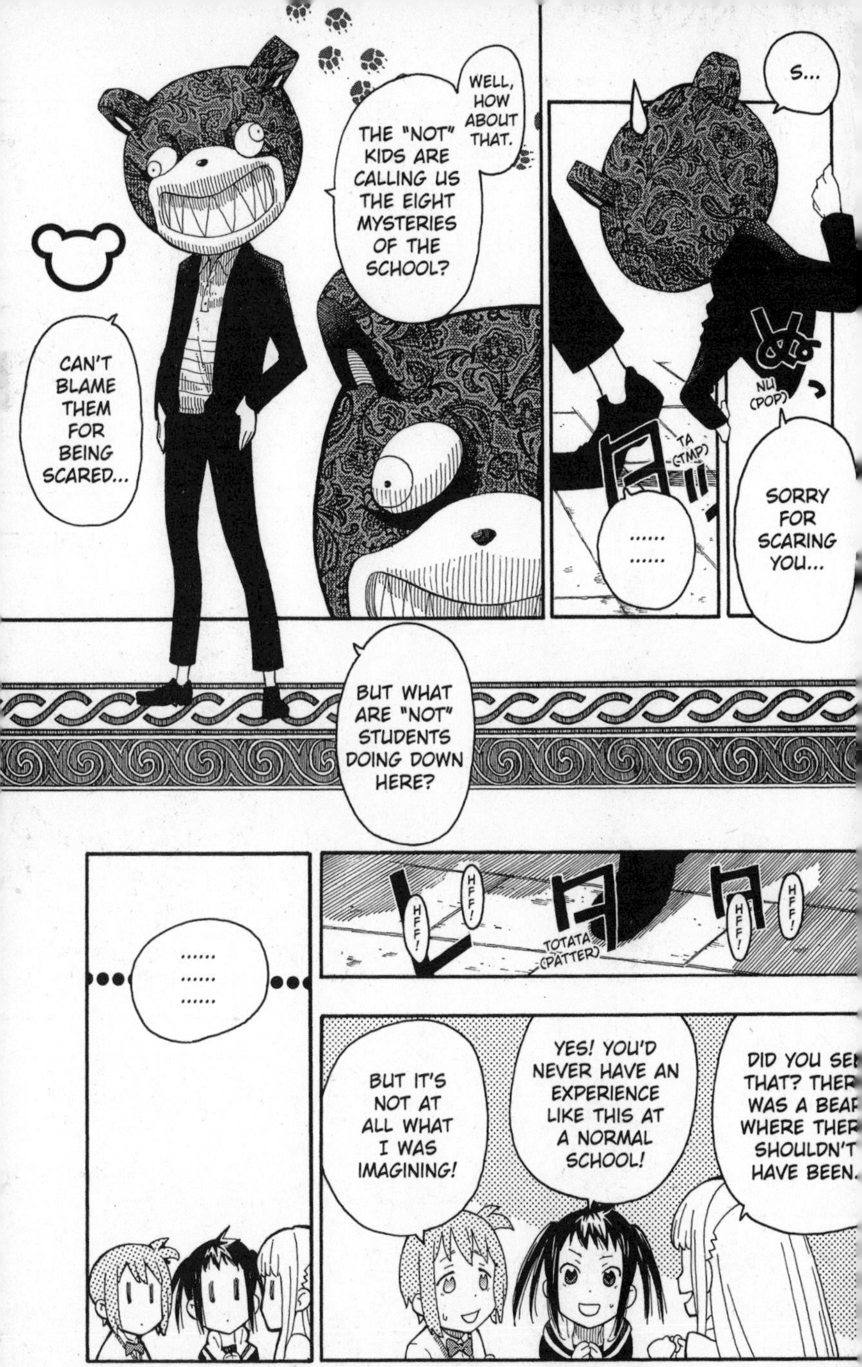
S...
NU (POP)
TA (TMP)
......
......
SORRY FOR SCARING YOU...
WELL, HOW ABOUT THAT.
THE "NOT" KIDS ARE CALLING US THE EIGHT MYSTERIES OF THE SCHOOL?
CAN'T BLAME THEM FOR BEING SCARED...
BUT WHAT ARE "NOT" STUDENTS DOING DOWN HERE?
HFF!
HFF!
TOTATA (PATTER)
HFF!
HFF!
DID YOU SE THAT? THER WAS A BEAF WHERE THER SHOULDN'T HAVE BEEN.
YES! YOU'D NEVER HAVE AN EXPERIENCE LIKE THIS AT A NORMAL SCHOOL!
BUT IT'S NOT AT ALL WHAT I WAS IMAGINING!
......
......
......

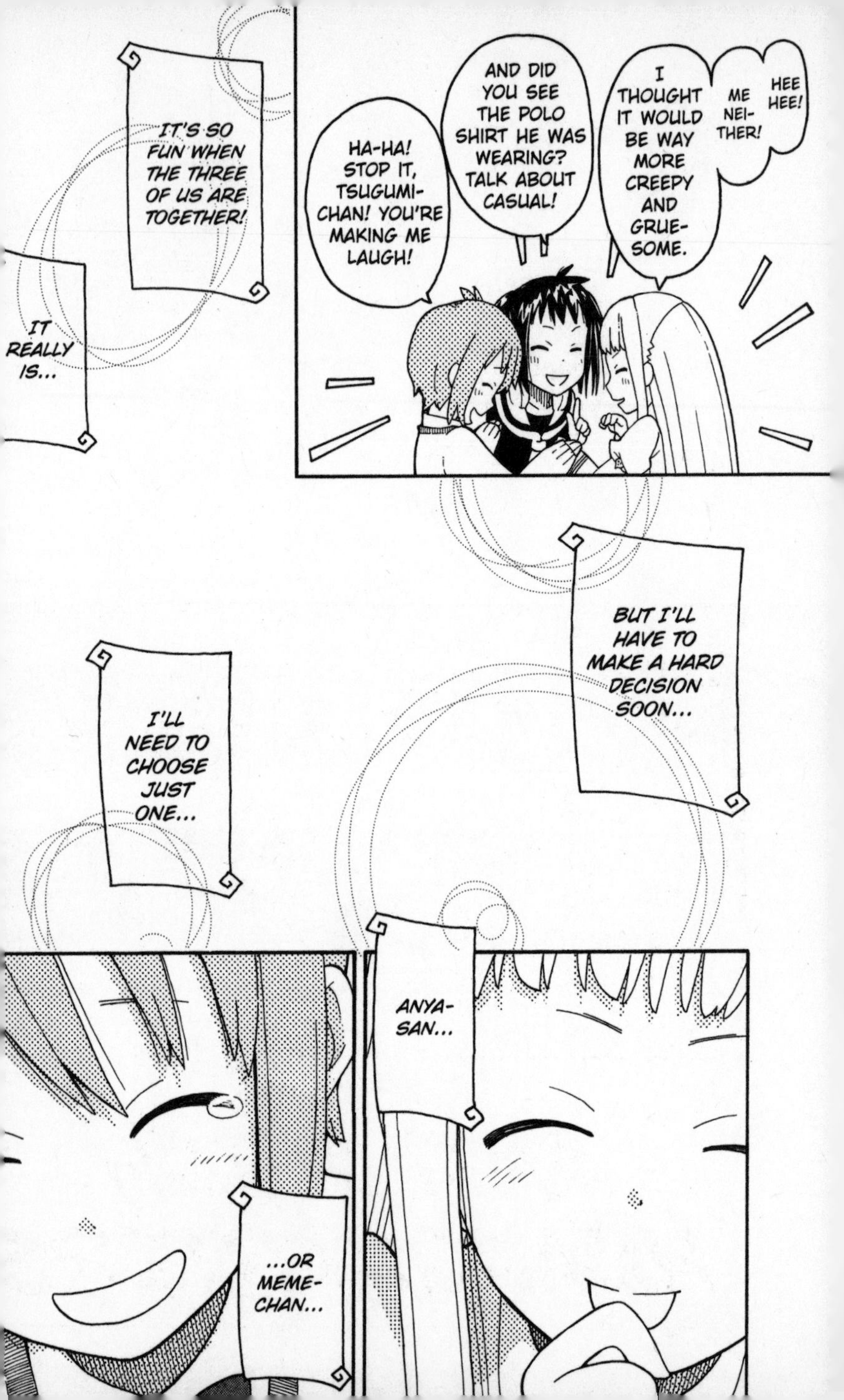
I THOUGHT IT WOULD BE WAY MORE CREEPY AND GRUESOME.
ME NEITHER!
HEE HEE!
AND DID YOU SEE THE POLO SHIRT HE WAS WEARING? TALK ABOUT CASUAL!
HA-HA! STOP IT, TSUGUMI-CHAN! YOU'RE MAKING ME LAUGH!
IT'S SO FUN WHEN THE THREE OF US ARE TOGETHER!
IT REALLY IS...
BUT I'LL HAVE TO MAKE A HARD DECISION SOON...
I'LL NEED TO CHOOSE JUST ONE...
ANYA-SAN...
...OR MEME-CHAN...

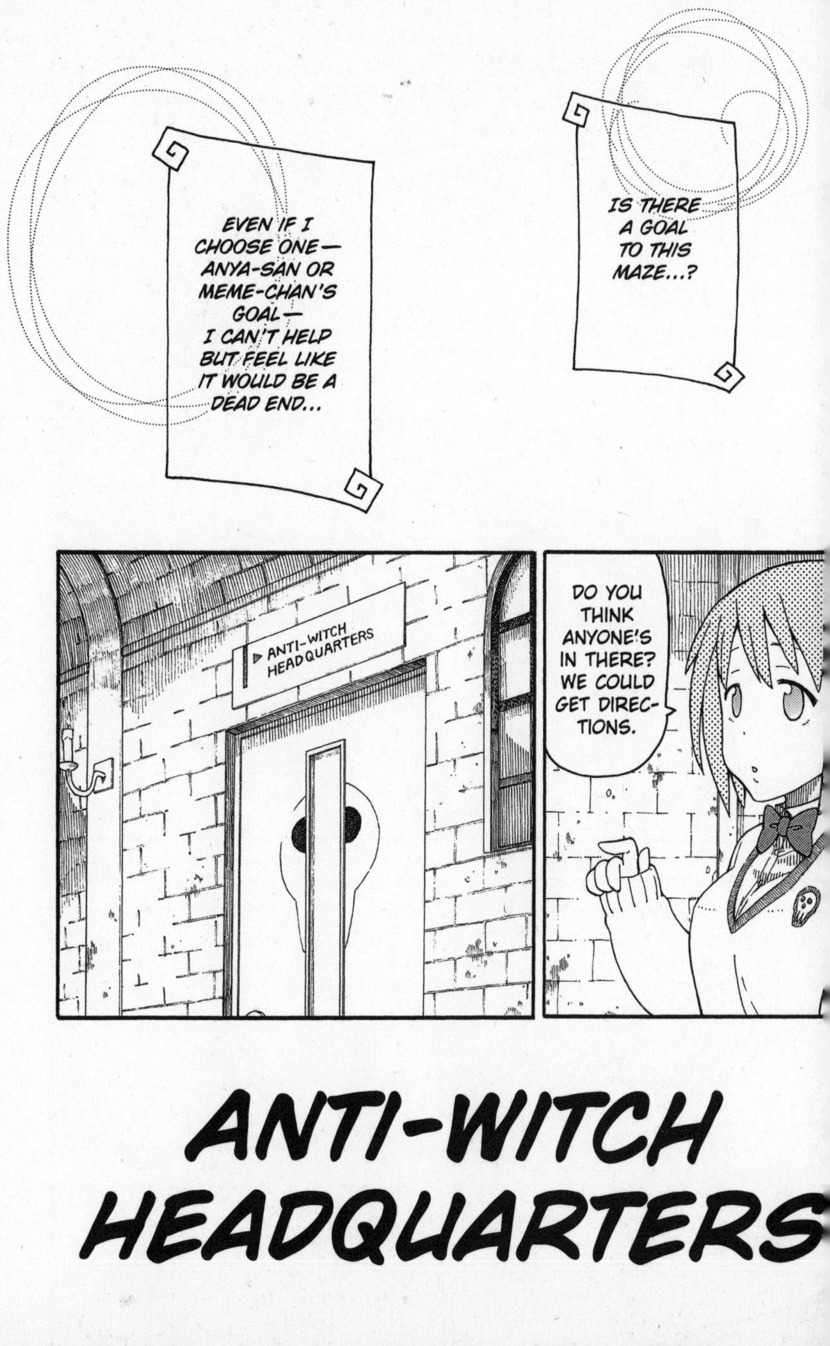
IS THERE A GOAL TO THIS MAZE...?
EVEN IF I CHOOSE ONE—ANYA-SAN OR MEME-CHAN'S GOAL—I CAN'T HELP BUT FEEL LIKE IT WOULD BE A DEAD END...
DO YOU THINK ANYONE'S IN THERE? WE COULD GET DIRECTIONS.
ANTI-WITCH HEADQUARTERS
ANTI-WITCH HEADQUARTERS

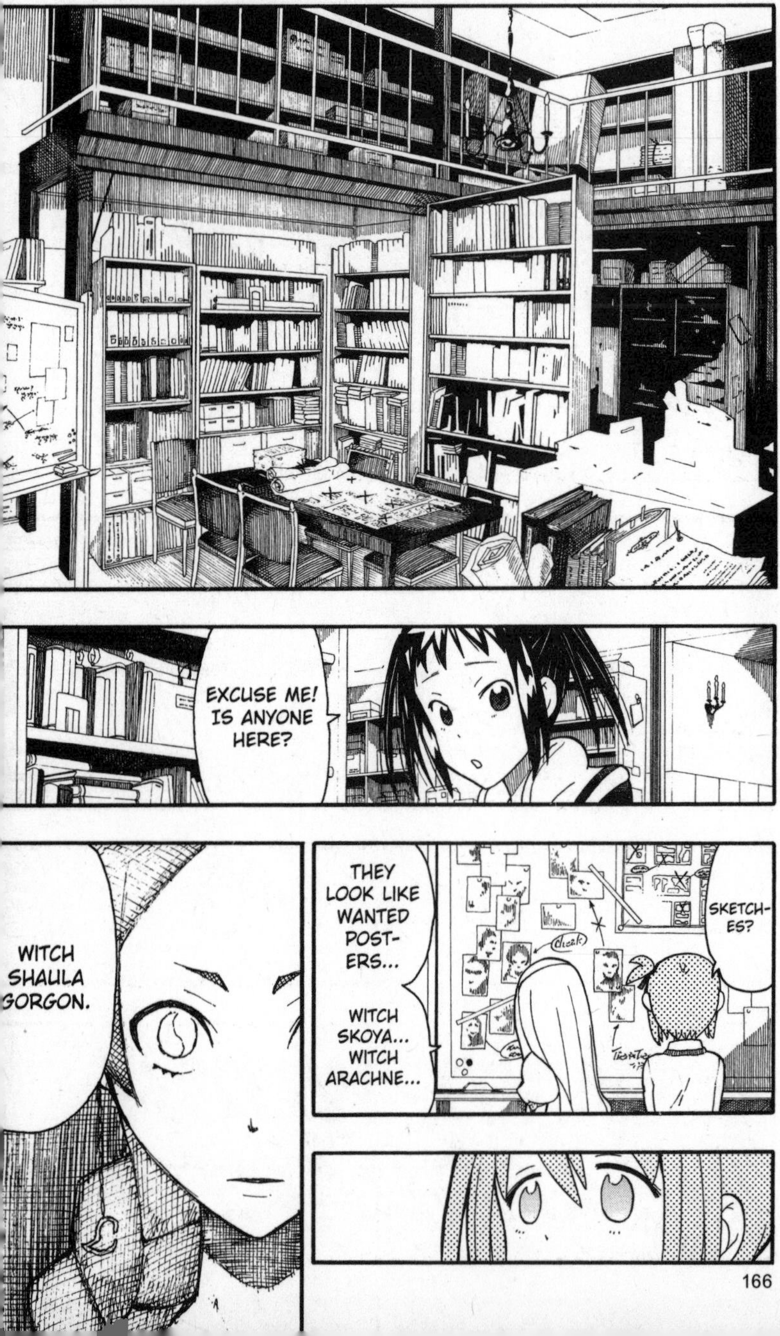
EXCUSE ME! IS ANYONE HERE?
SKETCH-ES?
THEY LOOK LIKE WANTED POST-ERS...
WITCH SKOYA... WITCH ARACHNE...
WITCH SHAULA GORGON.

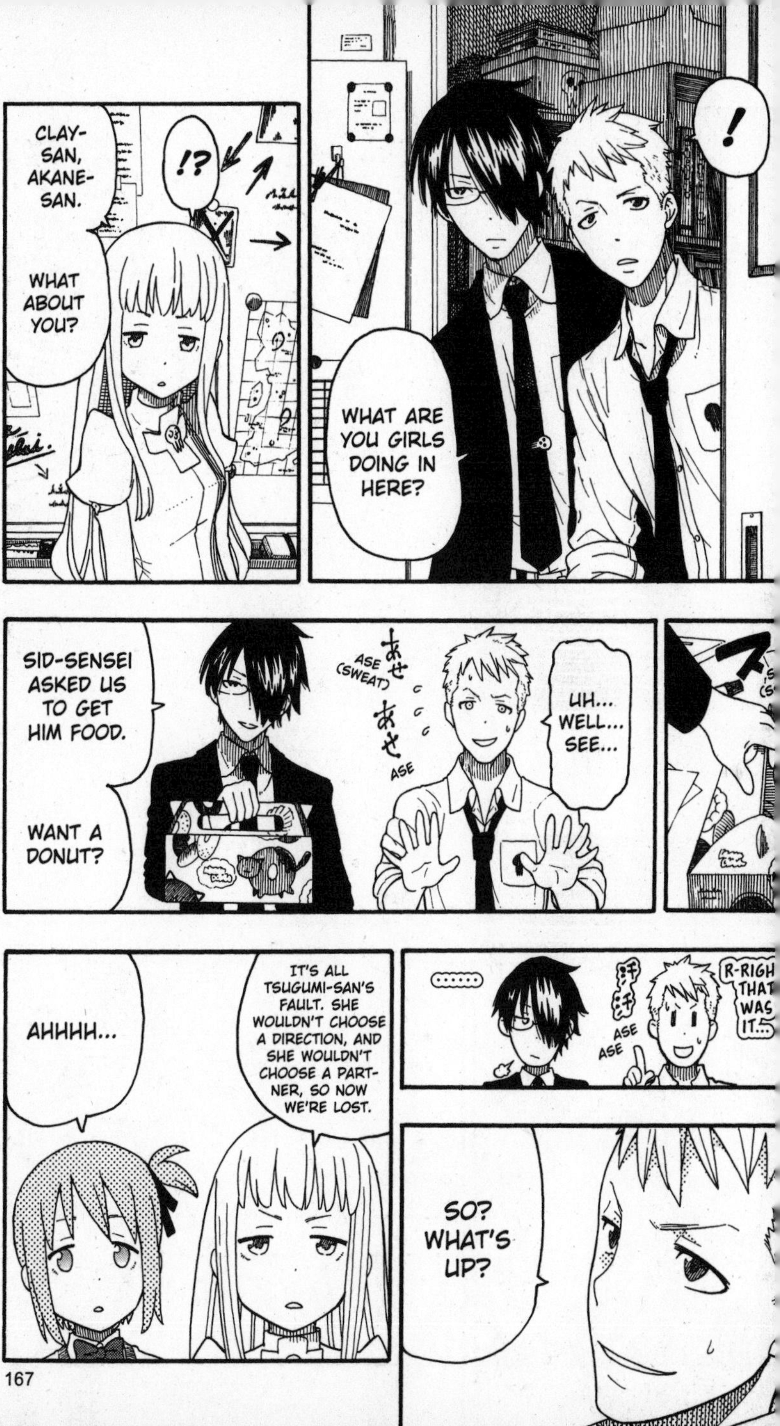
!
WHAT ARE YOU GIRLS DOING IN HERE?
!?
CLAY-SAN, AKANE-SAN.
WHAT ABOUT YOU?
UH... WELL... SEE...
あせ ASE (SWEAT)
あせ ASE
SID-SENSEI ASKED US TO GET HIM FOOD.
WANT A DONUT?
R-RIGH THAT WAS IT...
汗汗 ASE ASE
......
SO? WHAT'S UP?
IT'S ALL TSUGUMI-SAN'S FAULT. SHE WOULDN'T CHOOSE A DIRECTION, AND SHE WOULDN'T CHOOSE A PARTNER, SO NOW WE'RE LOST.
AHHHH...

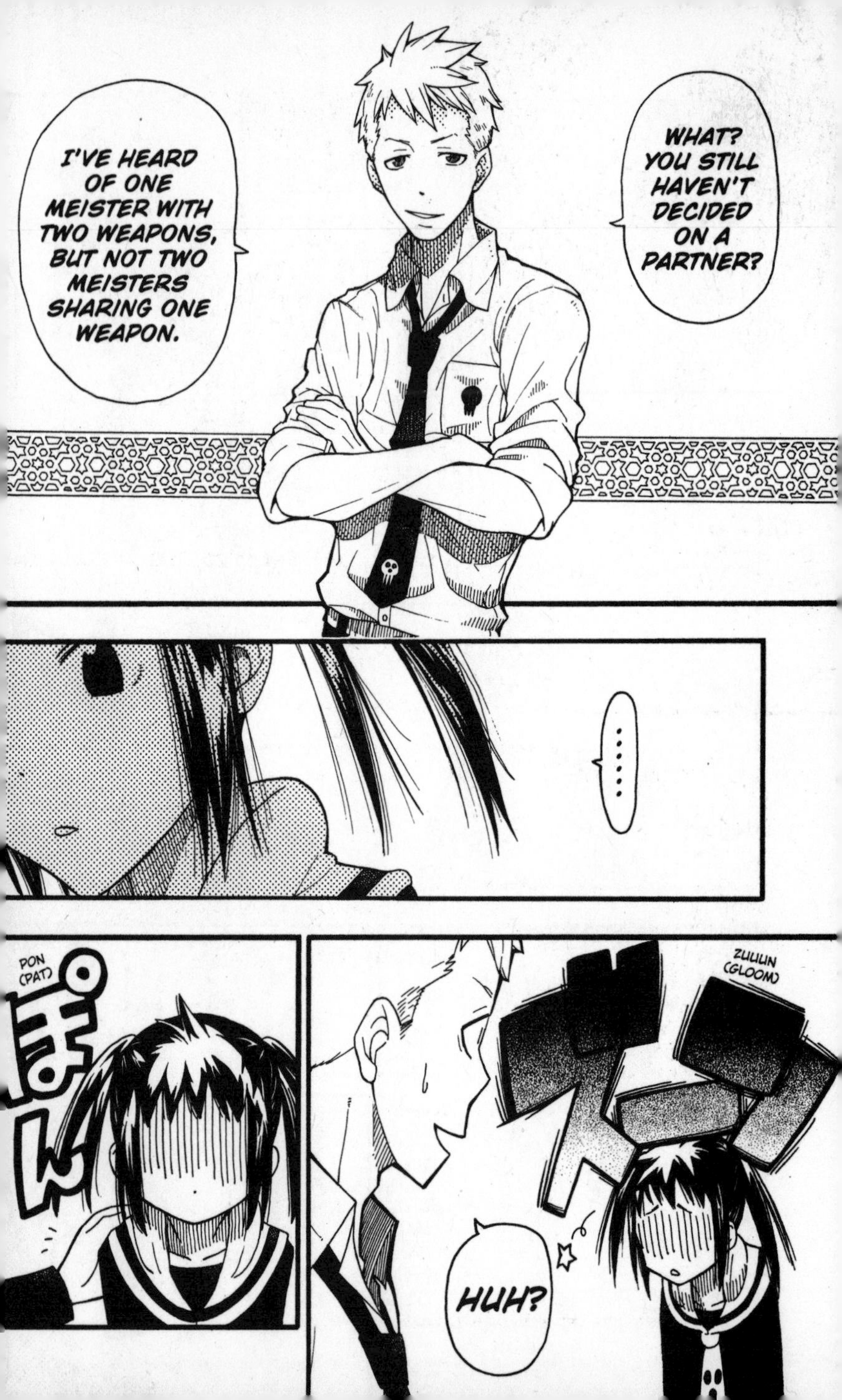
WHAT? YOU STILL HAVEN'T DECIDED ON A PARTNER?
I'VE HEARD OF ONE MEISTER WITH TWO WEAPONS, BUT NOT TWO MEISTERS SHARING ONE WEAPON.
……
ZUUUN (GLOOM)
HUH?
PON (PAT)
ぽん

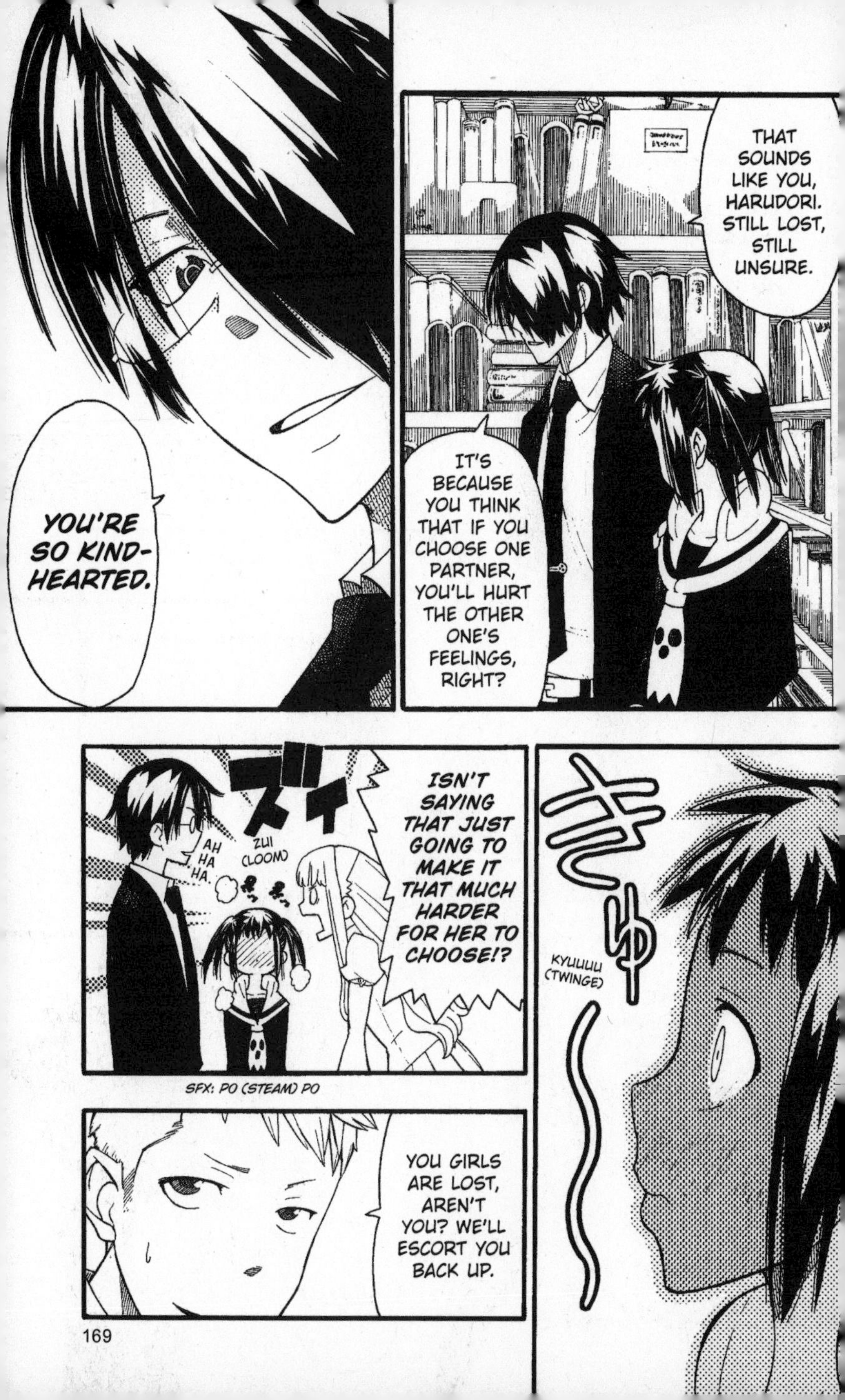
THAT SOUNDS LIKE YOU, HARUDORI. STILL LOST, STILL UNSURE.
IT'S BECAUSE YOU THINK THAT IF YOU CHOOSE ONE PARTNER, YOU'LL HURT THE OTHER ONE'S FEELINGS, RIGHT?
YOU'RE SO KIND-HEARTED.
KYUUUU (TWINGE)
ZUI (LOOM)
AH HA HA.
ISN'T SAYING THAT JUST GOING TO MAKE IT THAT MUCH HARDER FOR HER TO CHOOSE!?
SFX: PO (STEAM) PO
YOU GIRLS ARE LOST, AREN'T YOU? WE'LL ESCORT YOU BACK UP.

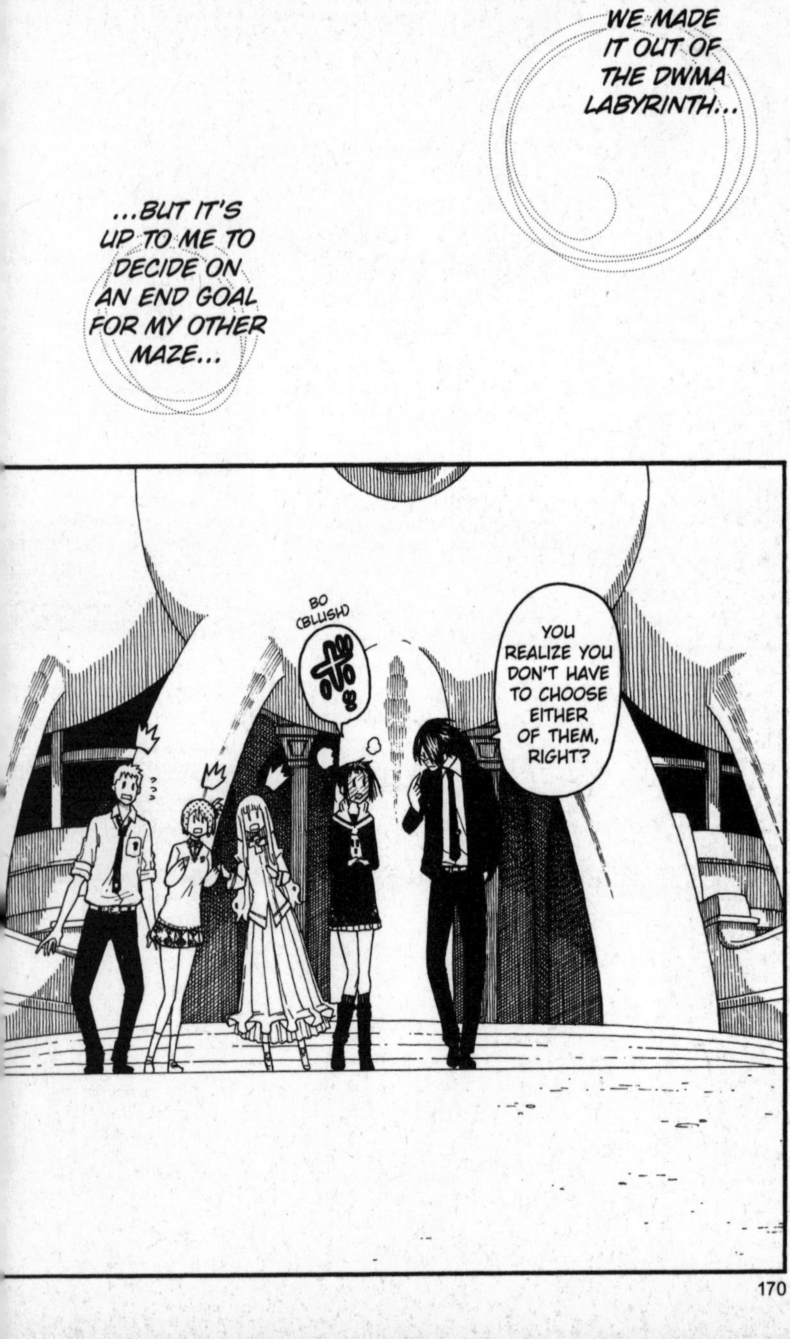
WE MADE IT OUT OF THE DWMA LABYRINTH...
...BUT IT'S UP TO ME TO DECIDE ON AN END GOAL FOR MY OTHER MAZE...
YOU REALIZE YOU DON'T HAVE TO CHOOSE EITHER OF THEM, RIGHT?
BO (BLUSH)

SOUL EATER NOT!

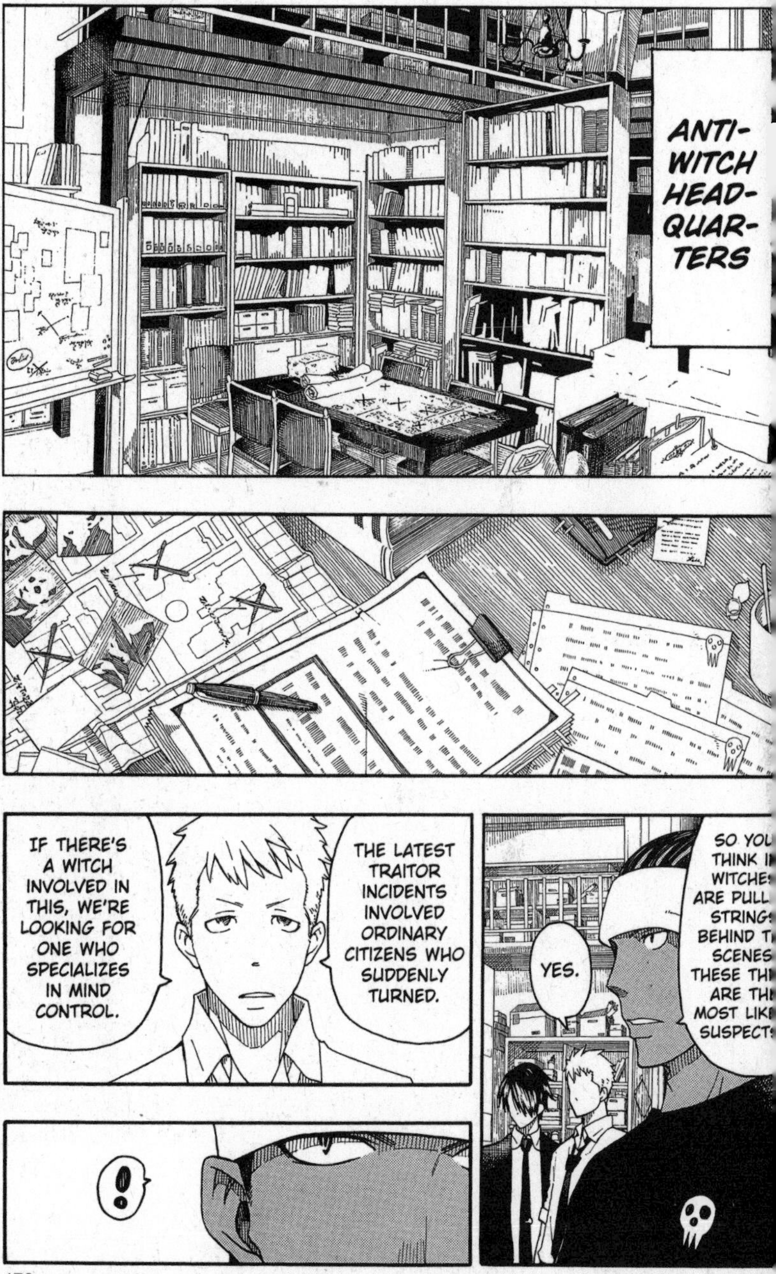
ANTI-WITCH HEAD-QUARTERS
SO YOU THINK I WITCHES ARE PULL STRINGS BEHIND T SCENES THESE TH ARE TH MOST LIK SUSPECTS
YES.
THE LATEST TRAITOR INCIDENTS INVOLVED ORDINARY CITIZENS WHO SUDDENLY TURNED.
IF THERE'S A WITCH INVOLVED IN THIS, WE'RE LOOKING FOR ONE WHO SPECIALIZES IN MIND CONTROL.
!

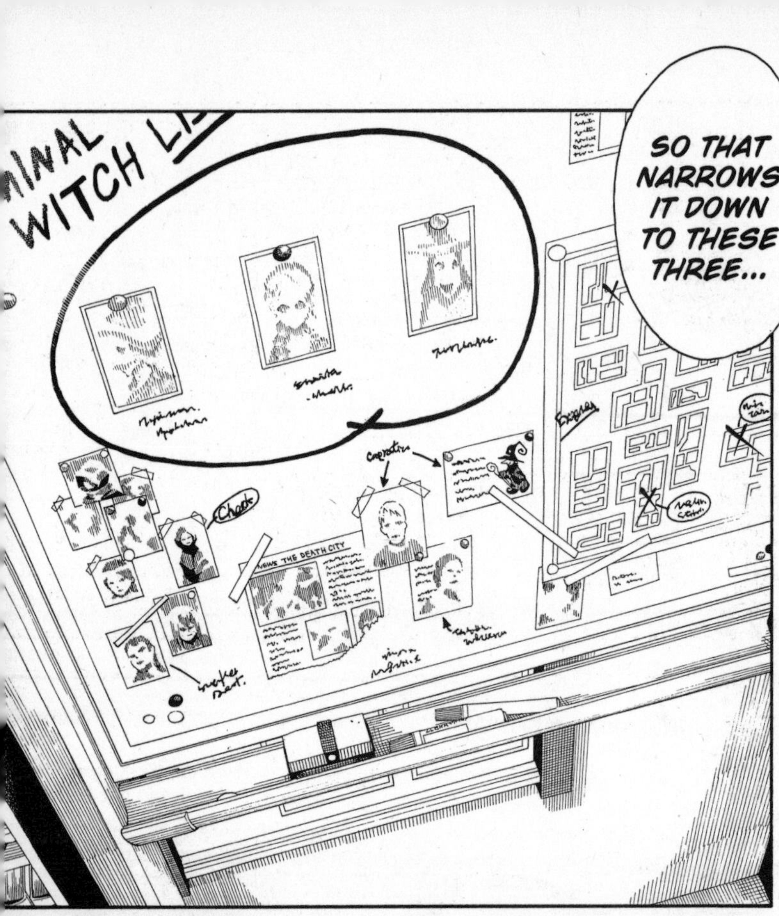
SO THAT NARROWS IT DOWN TO THESE THREE...

SOUL EATER NOT!

CHAPTER 14: SCORPION!

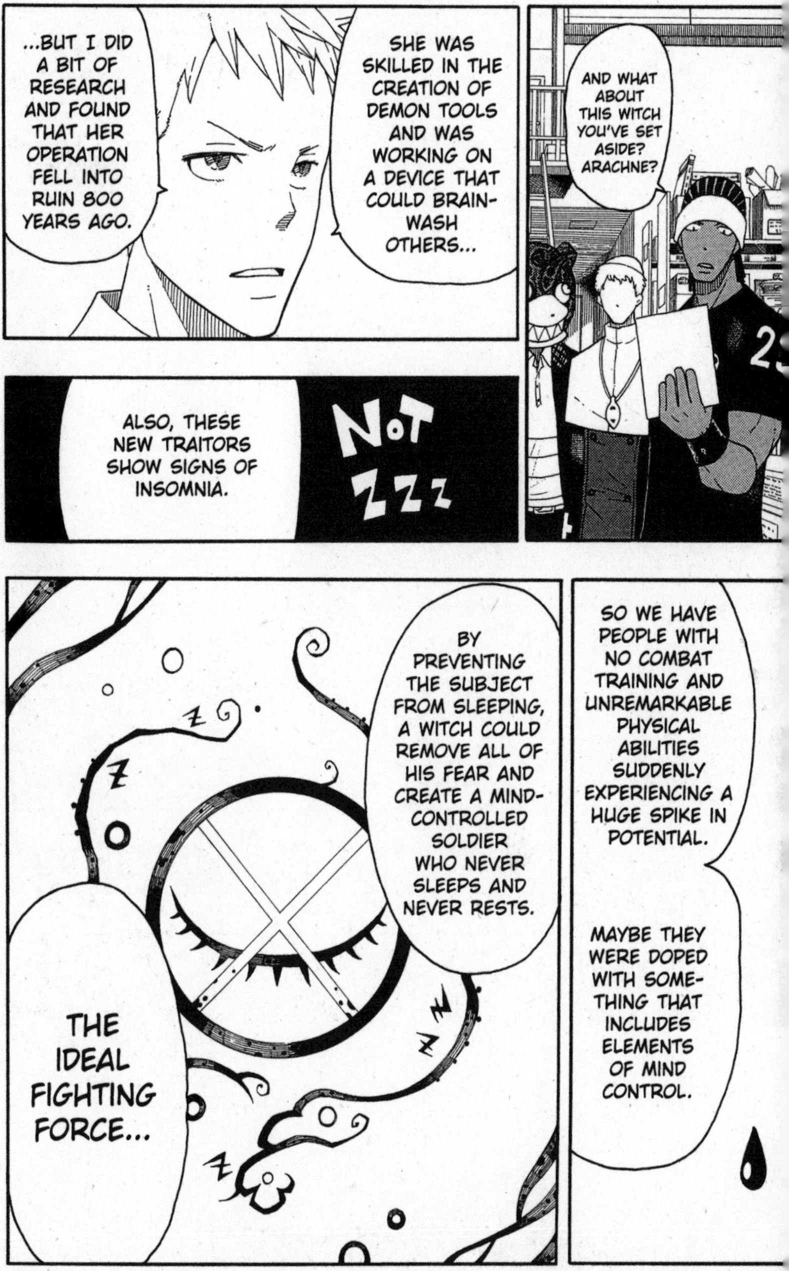
AND WHAT ABOUT THIS WITCH YOU'VE SET ASIDE? ARACHNE?
SHE WAS SKILLED IN THE CREATION OF DEMON TOOLS AND WAS WORKING ON A DEVICE THAT COULD BRAIN-WASH OTHERS...
...BUT I DID A BIT OF RESEARCH AND FOUND THAT HER OPERATION FELL INTO RUIN 800 YEARS AGO.
ALSO, THESE NEW TRAITORS SHOW SIGNS OF INSOMNIA.
NoT ZZZ
SO WE HAVE PEOPLE WITH NO COMBAT TRAINING AND UNREMARKABLE PHYSICAL ABILITIES SUDDENLY EXPERIENCING A HUGE SPIKE IN POTENTIAL.
MAYBE THEY WERE DOPED WITH SOME-THING THAT INCLUDES ELEMENTS OF MIND CONTROL.
BY PREVENTING THE SUBJECT FROM SLEEPING, A WITCH COULD REMOVE ALL OF HIS FEAR AND CREATE A MIND-CONTROLLED SOLDIER WHO NEVER SLEEPS AND NEVER RESTS.
THE IDEAL FIGHTING FORCE...

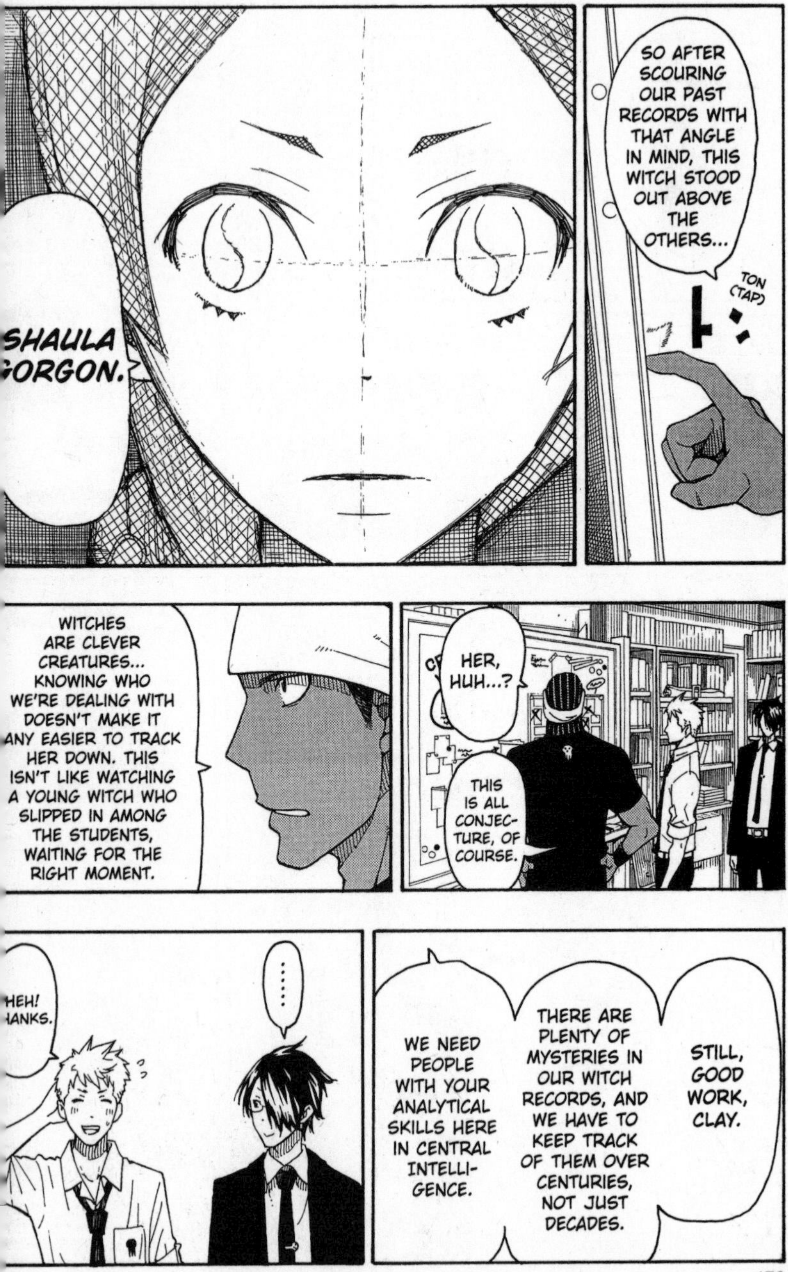

SO AFTER SCOURING OUR PAST RECORDS WITH THAT ANGLE IN MIND, THIS WITCH STOOD OUT ABOVE THE OTHERS...
TON (TAP)
SHAULA GORGON.
HER, HUH...?
THIS IS ALL CONJECTURE, OF COURSE.
WITCHES ARE CLEVER CREATURES... KNOWING WHO WE'RE DEALING WITH DOESN'T MAKE IT ANY EASIER TO TRACK HER DOWN. THIS ISN'T LIKE WATCHING A YOUNG WITCH WHO SLIPPED IN AMONG THE STUDENTS, WAITING FOR THE RIGHT MOMENT.
STILL, GOOD WORK, CLAY.
THERE ARE PLENTY OF MYSTERIES IN OUR WITCH RECORDS, AND WE HAVE TO KEEP TRACK OF THEM OVER CENTURIES, NOT JUST DECADES.
WE NEED PEOPLE WITH YOUR ANALYTICAL SKILLS HERE IN CENTRAL INTELLIGENCE.
......
HEH! HANKS.

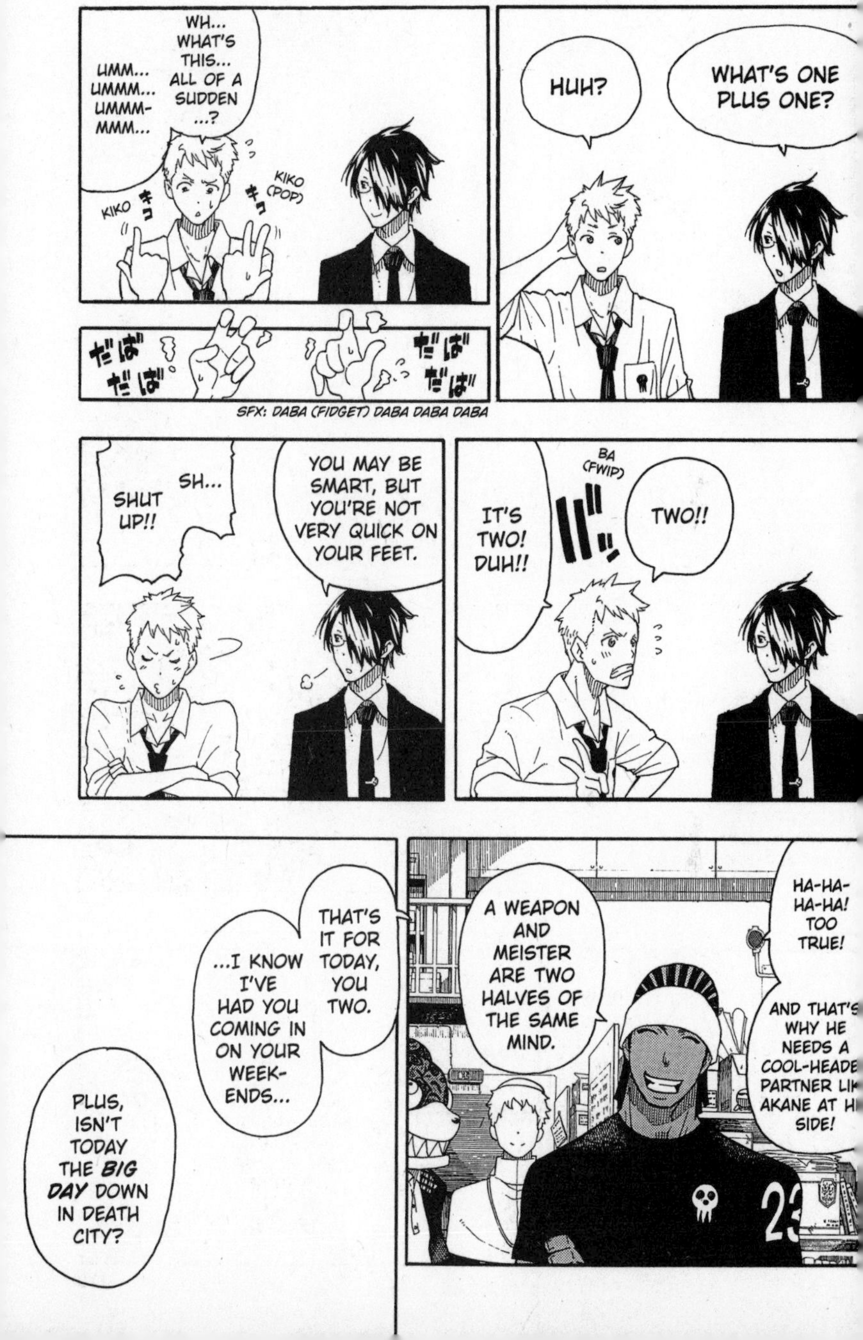
WHAT'S ONE PLUS ONE?
HUH?
WH... WHAT'S THIS... ALL OF A SUDDEN ...?
UMM... UMMM... UMMM-MMM...
KIKO (POP) キコ
KIKO キコ
だば だば
だば だば
SFX: DABA (FIDGET) DABA DABA DABA
TWO!!
BA (FWIP)
IT'S TWO! DUH!!
YOU MAY BE SMART, BUT YOU'RE NOT VERY QUICK ON YOUR FEET.
SH... SHUT UP!!
HA-HA-HA-HA! TOO TRUE!
AND THAT'S WHY HE NEEDS A COOL-HEADE PARTNER LIK AKANE AT H SIDE!
A WEAPON AND MEISTER ARE TWO HALVES OF THE SAME MIND.
THAT'S IT FOR TODAY, YOU TWO.
...I KNOW I'VE HAD YOU COMING IN ON YOUR WEEK-ENDS...
PLUS, ISN'T TODAY THE ***BIG DAY*** DOWN IN DEATH CITY?
23

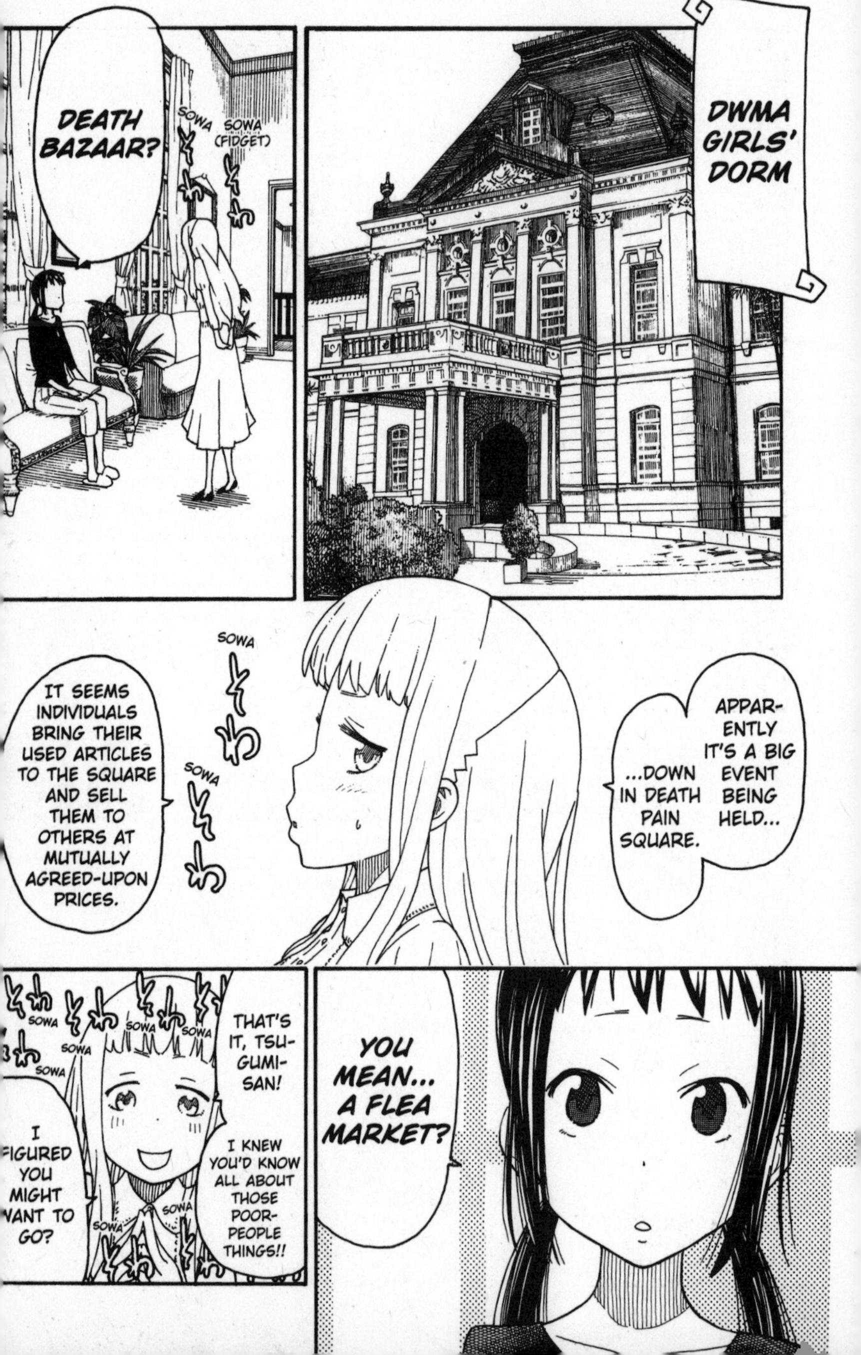
DWMA GIRLS' DORM
DEATH BAZAAR?
SOWA
SOWA (FIDGET)
APPARENTLY IT'S A BIG EVENT BEING HELD...
...DOWN IN DEATH PAIN SQUARE.
SOWA
SOWA
IT SEEMS INDIVIDUALS BRING THEIR USED ARTICLES TO THE SQUARE AND SELL THEM TO OTHERS AT MUTUALLY AGREED-UPON PRICES.
YOU MEAN... A FLEA MARKET?
SOWA SOWA SOWA SOWA SOWA
THAT'S IT, TSUGUMI-SAN!
I KNEW YOU'D KNOW ALL ABOUT THOSE POOR-PEOPLE THINGS!!
I FIGURED YOU MIGHT WANT TO GO?
SOWA SOWA

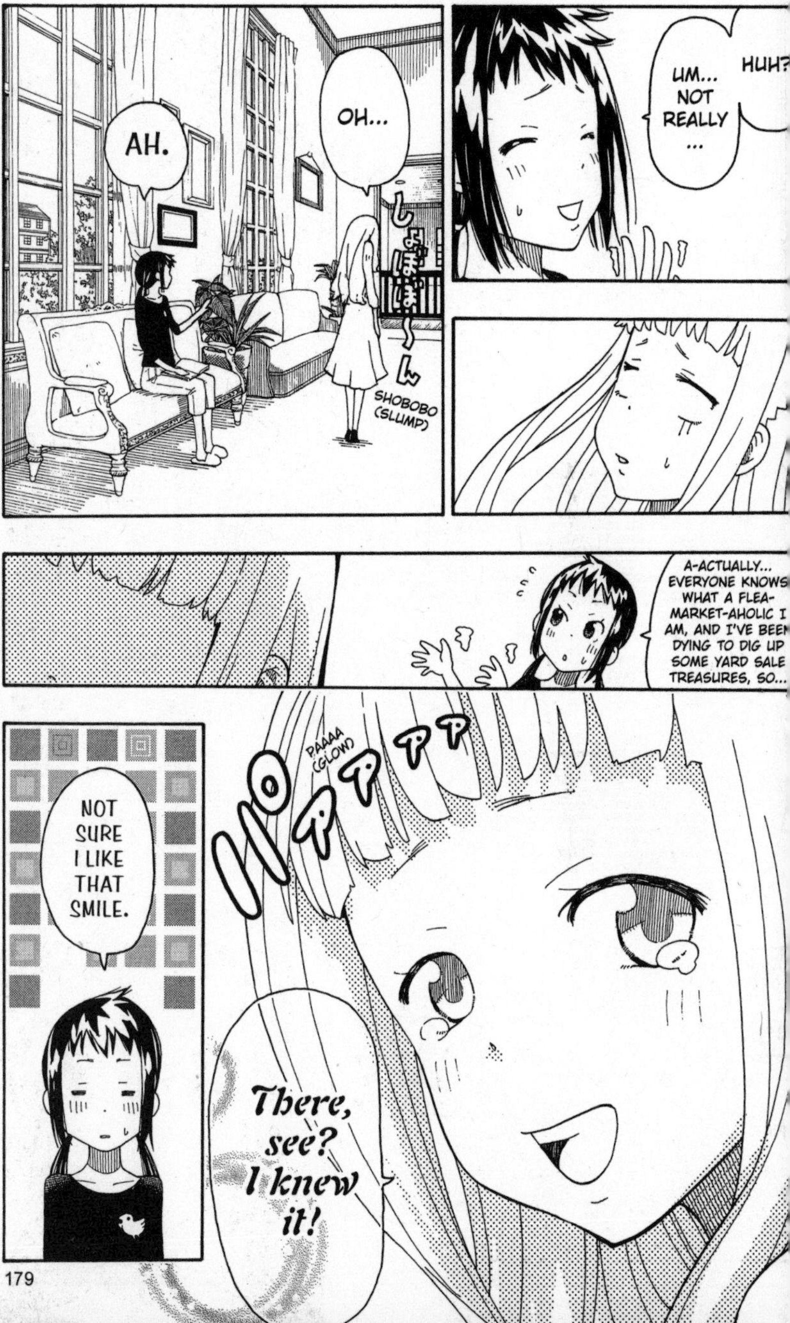
HUH?
UM... NOT REALLY...
OH...
AH.
しょぼぼ～ん
SHOBOBO (SLUMP)
A-ACTUALLY... EVERYONE KNOWS WHAT A FLEA-MARKET-AHOLIC I AM, AND I'VE BEEN DYING TO DIG UP SOME YARD SALE TREASURES, SO...
PAAAA (GLOW)
There, see? I knew it!
NOT SURE I LIKE THAT SMILE.

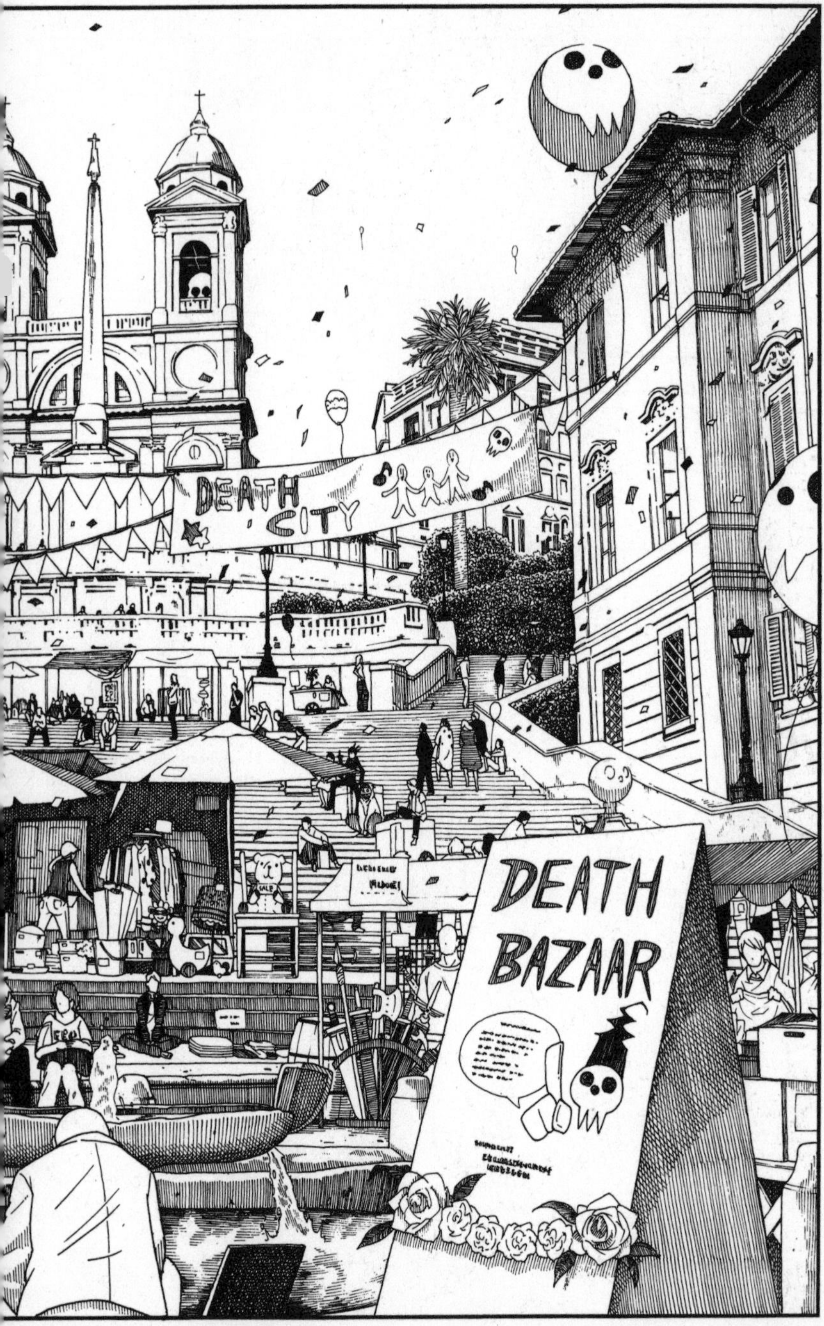
DEATH CITY
DEATH BAZAAR

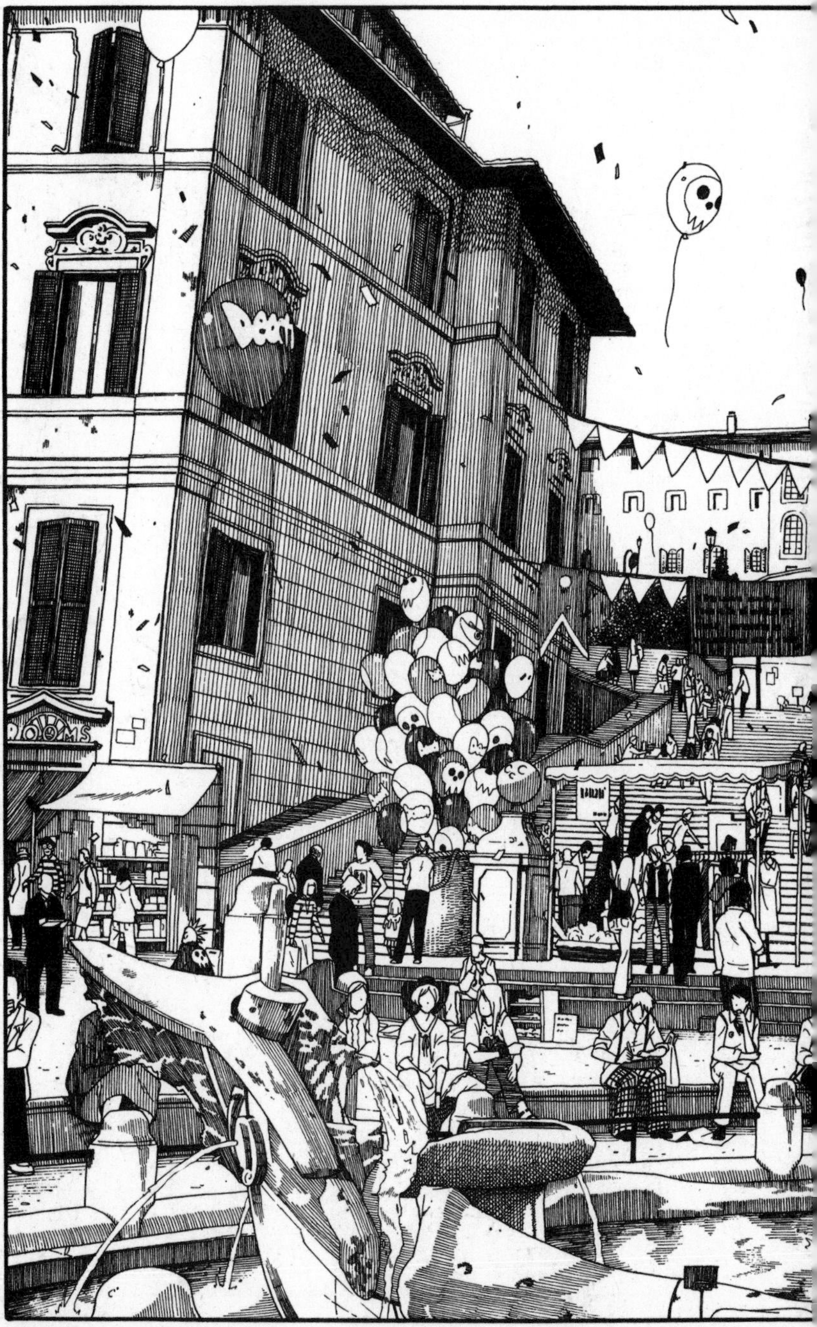
Death
ROOMS

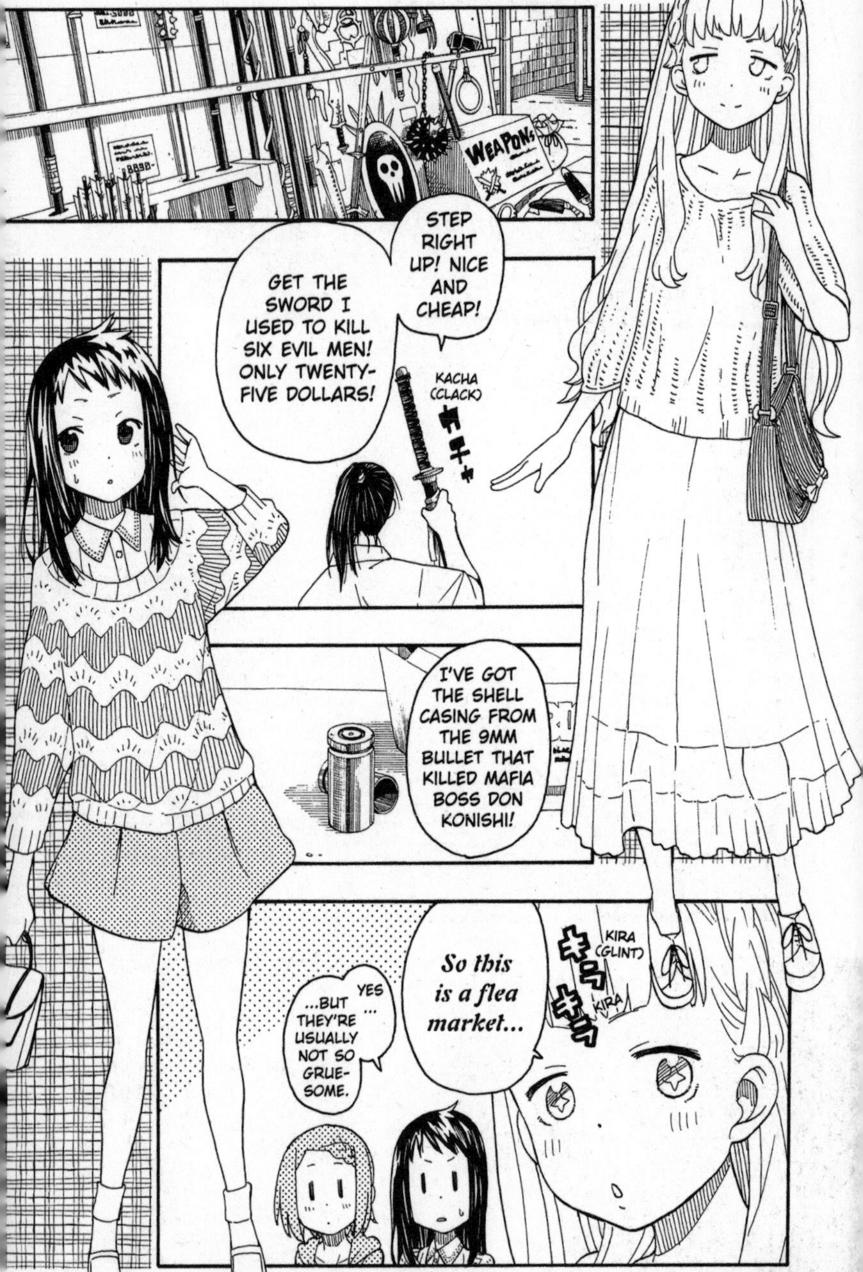
WEAPONS
STEP RIGHT UP! NICE AND CHEAP!
GET THE SWORD I USED TO KILL SIX EVIL MEN! ONLY TWENTY-FIVE DOLLARS!
KACHA (CLACK)
I'VE GOT THE SHELL CASING FROM THE 9MM BULLET THAT KILLED MAFIA BOSS DON KONISHI!
KIRA (GLINT)
KIRA
So this is a flea market...
YES ...
...BUT THEY'RE USUALLY NOT SO GRUE-SOME.

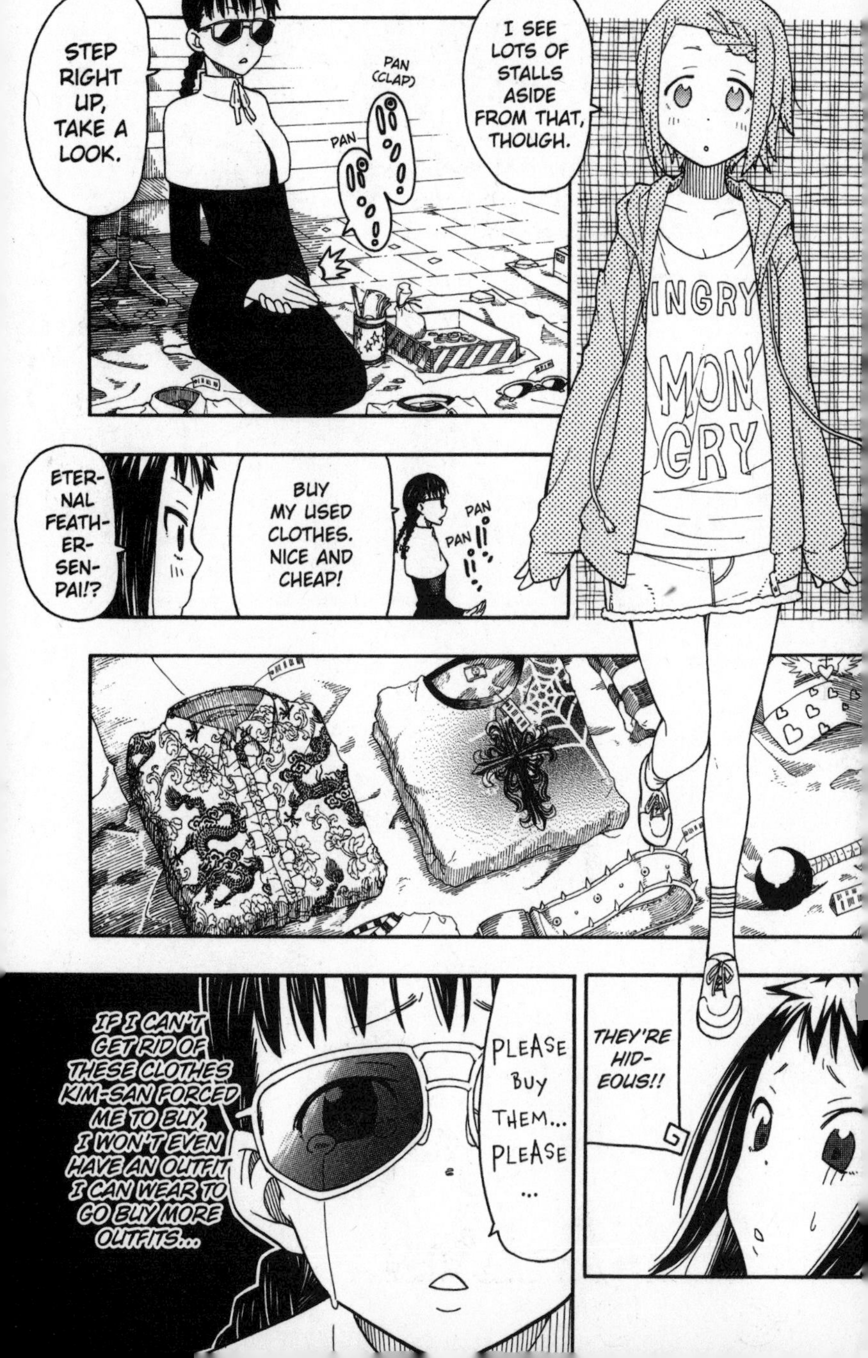
I SEE LOTS OF STALLS ASIDE FROM THAT, THOUGH.
STEP RIGHT UP, TAKE A LOOK.
PAN (CLAP)
PAN
BUY MY USED CLOTHES. NICE AND CHEAP!
PAN
PAN
ETERNAL FEATHER-SENPAI!?
THEY'RE HIDEOUS!!
PLEASE BUY THEM... PLEASE ...
IF I CAN'T GET RID OF THESE CLOTHES KIM-SAN FORCED ME TO BUY, I WON'T EVEN HAVE AN OUTFIT I CAN WEAR TO GO BUY MORE OUTFITS...
INGRY MON GRY

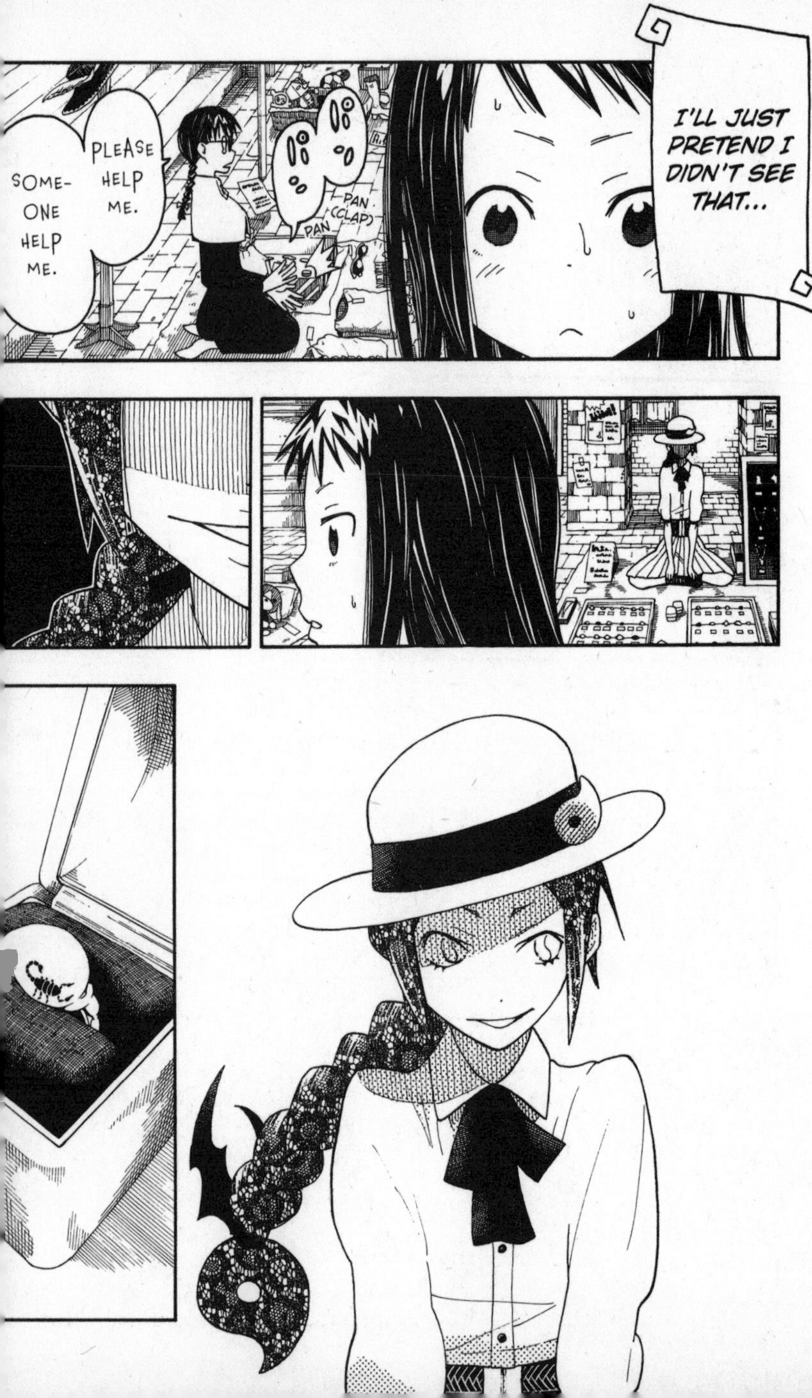
I'LL JUST PRETEND I DIDN'T SEE THAT...
PAN (CLAP) PAN
PLEASE HELP ME.
SOME-ONE HELP ME.

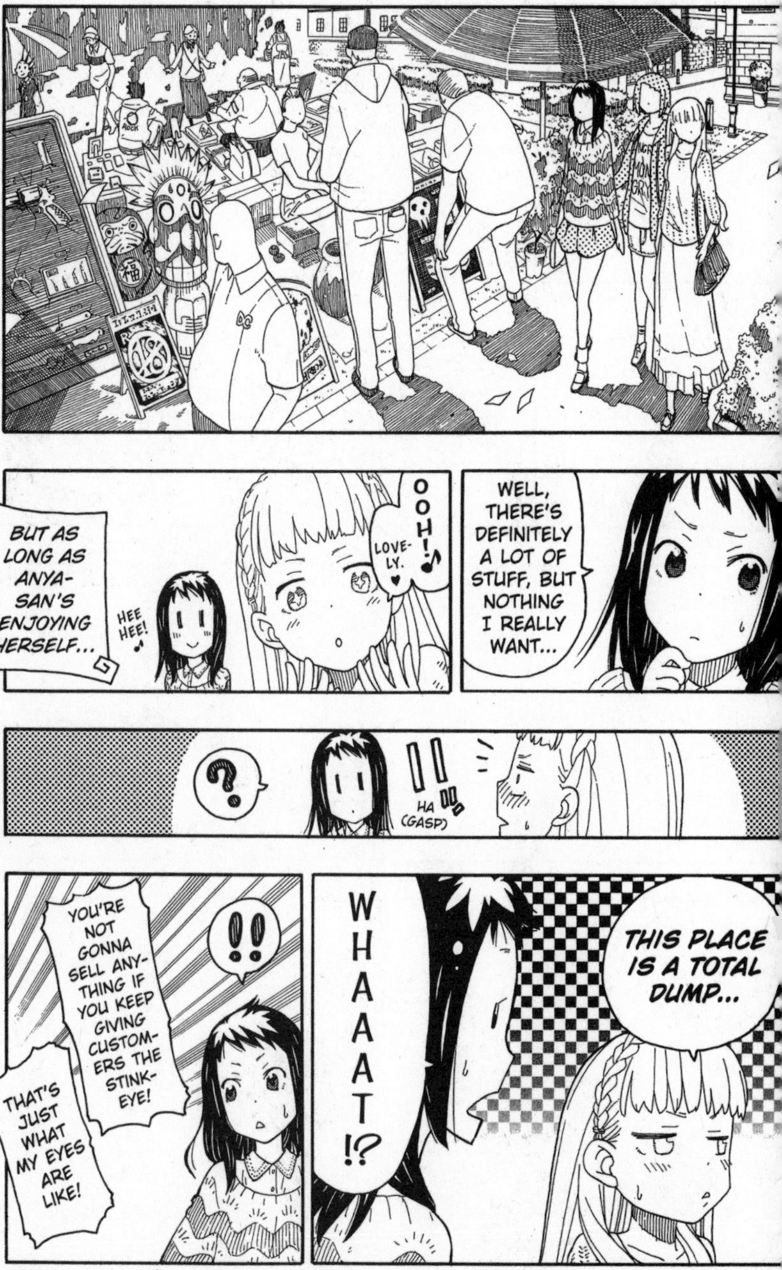

WELL, THERE'S DEFINITELY A LOT OF STUFF, BUT NOTHING I REALLY WANT...
OOH!♪
LOVE-LY. ♥
BUT AS LONG AS ANYA-SAN'S ENJOYING HERSELF...
HEE HEE! ♪
!!
HA (GASP)
!!
?
THIS PLACE IS A TOTAL DUMP...
WHAAAT!?
!!
YOU'RE NOT GONNA SELL ANY-THING IF YOU KEEP GIVING CUSTOM-ERS THE STINK-EYE!
THAT'S JUST WHAT MY EYES ARE LIKE!

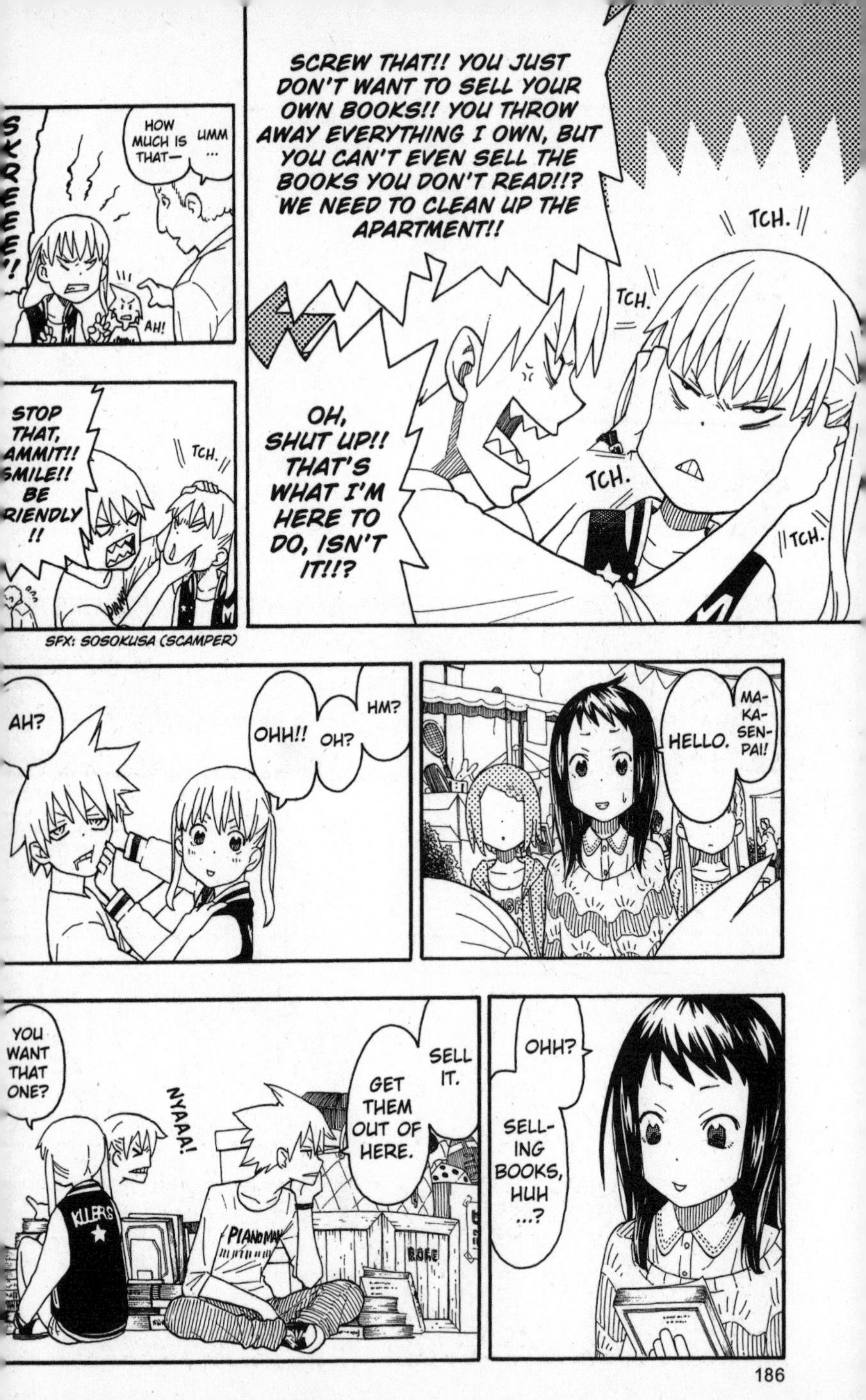
SCREW THAT!! YOU JUST DON'T WANT TO SELL YOUR OWN BOOKS!! YOU THROW AWAY EVERYTHING I OWN, BUT YOU CAN'T EVEN SELL THE BOOKS YOU DON'T READ!!? WE NEED TO CLEAN UP THE APARTMENT!!
TCH.
TCH.
TCH.
TCH.
OH, SHUT UP!! THAT'S WHAT I'M HERE TO DO, ISN'T IT!!?
UMM ...
HOW MUCH IS THAT—
SKREEEE!!
AH!
STOP THAT, AMMIT!! SMILE!! BE RIENDLY !!
TCH.
SFX: SOSOKUSA (SCAMPER)
MA-KA-SEN-PAI!
HELLO.
HM?
OH?
OHH!!
AH?
OHH?
SELL-ING BOOKS, HUH ...?
SELL IT.
GET THEM OUT OF HERE.
NYAAA!
YOU WANT THAT ONE?

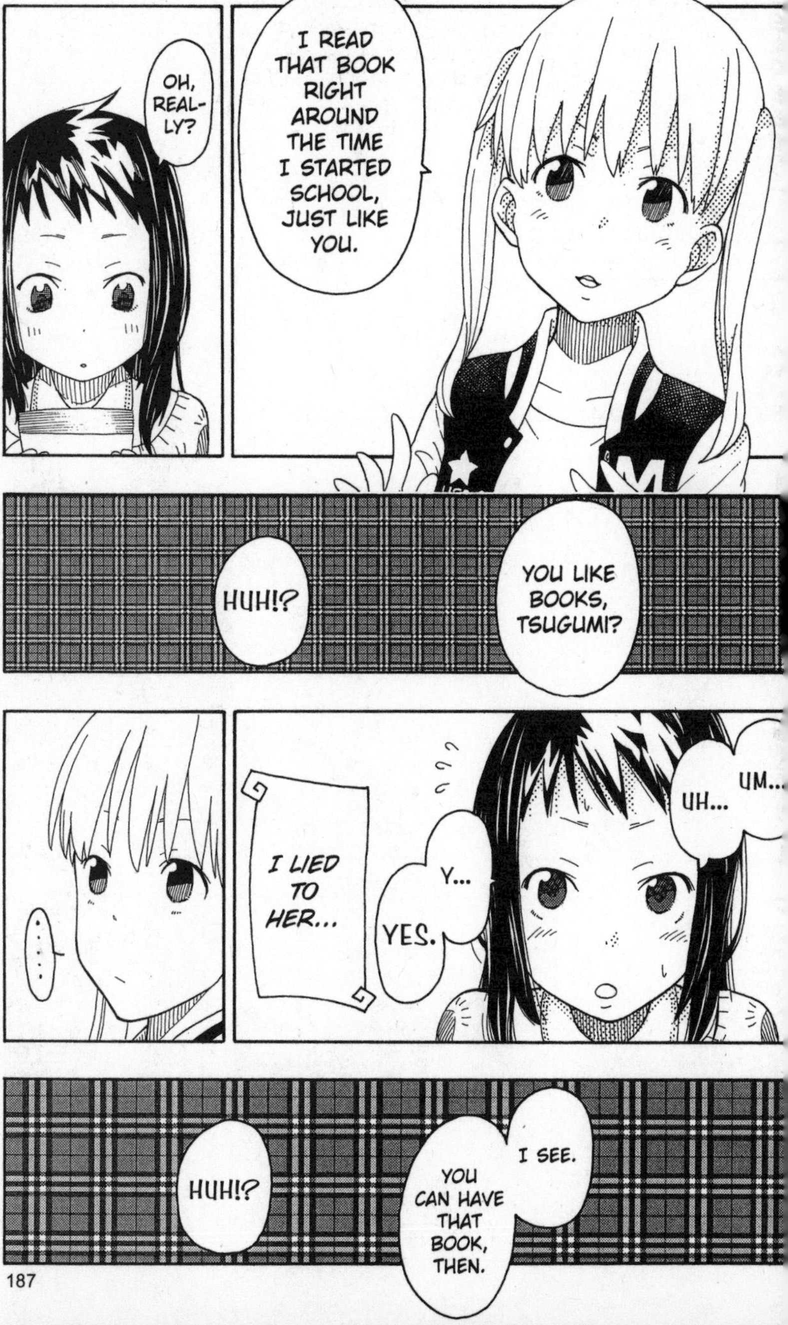
I READ THAT BOOK RIGHT AROUND THE TIME I STARTED SCHOOL, JUST LIKE YOU.
OH, REALLY?
YOU LIKE BOOKS, TSUGUMI?
HUH!?
UM...
UH...
Y...
YES.
I LIED TO HER...
......
I SEE.
YOU CAN HAVE THAT BOOK, THEN.
HUH!?

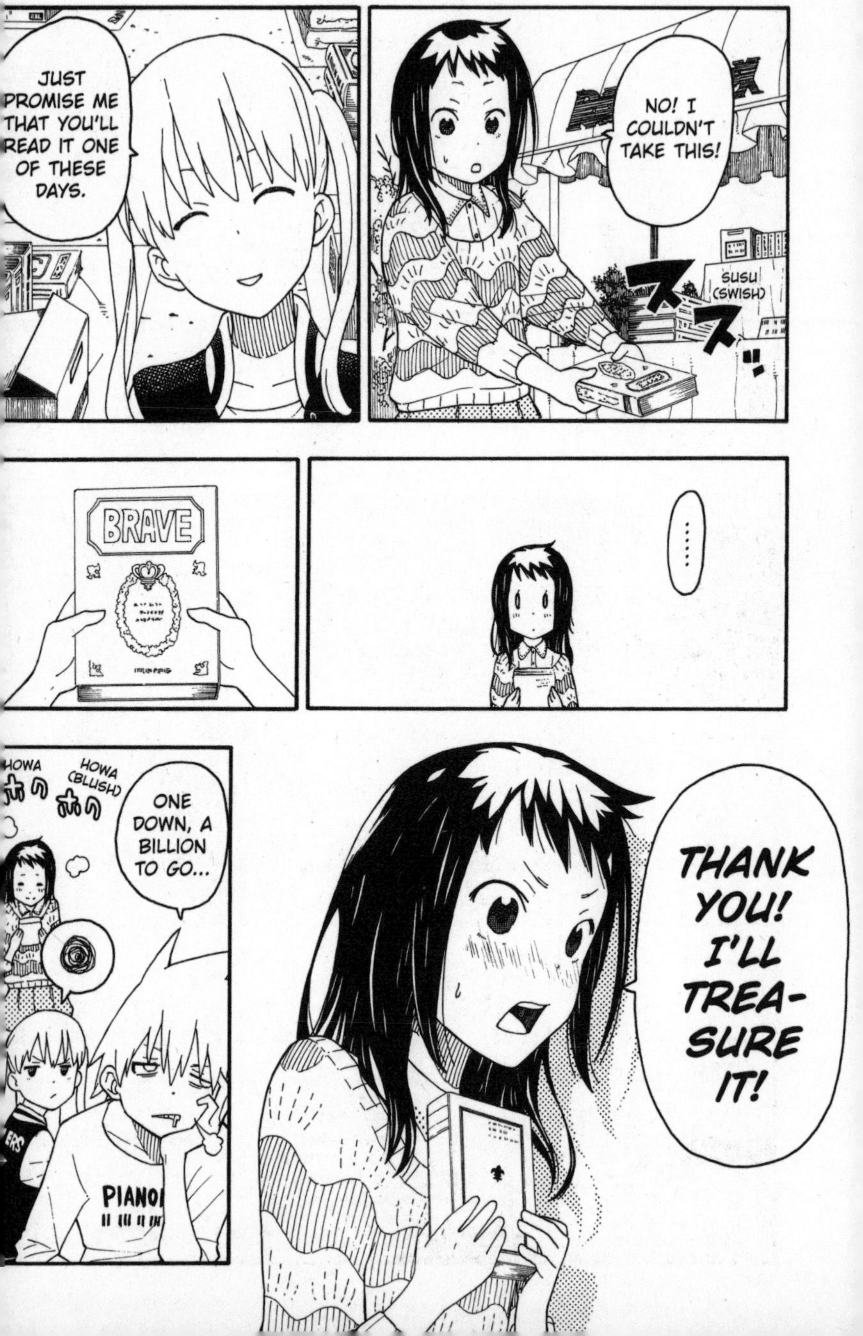
NO! I COULDN'T TAKE THIS!
SUSU (SWISH)
JUST PROMISE ME THAT YOU'LL READ IT ONE OF THESE DAYS.
......
BRAVE
THANK YOU! I'LL TREASURE IT!
HOWA
HOWA (BLUSH)
ONE DOWN, A BILLION TO GO...
PIANO

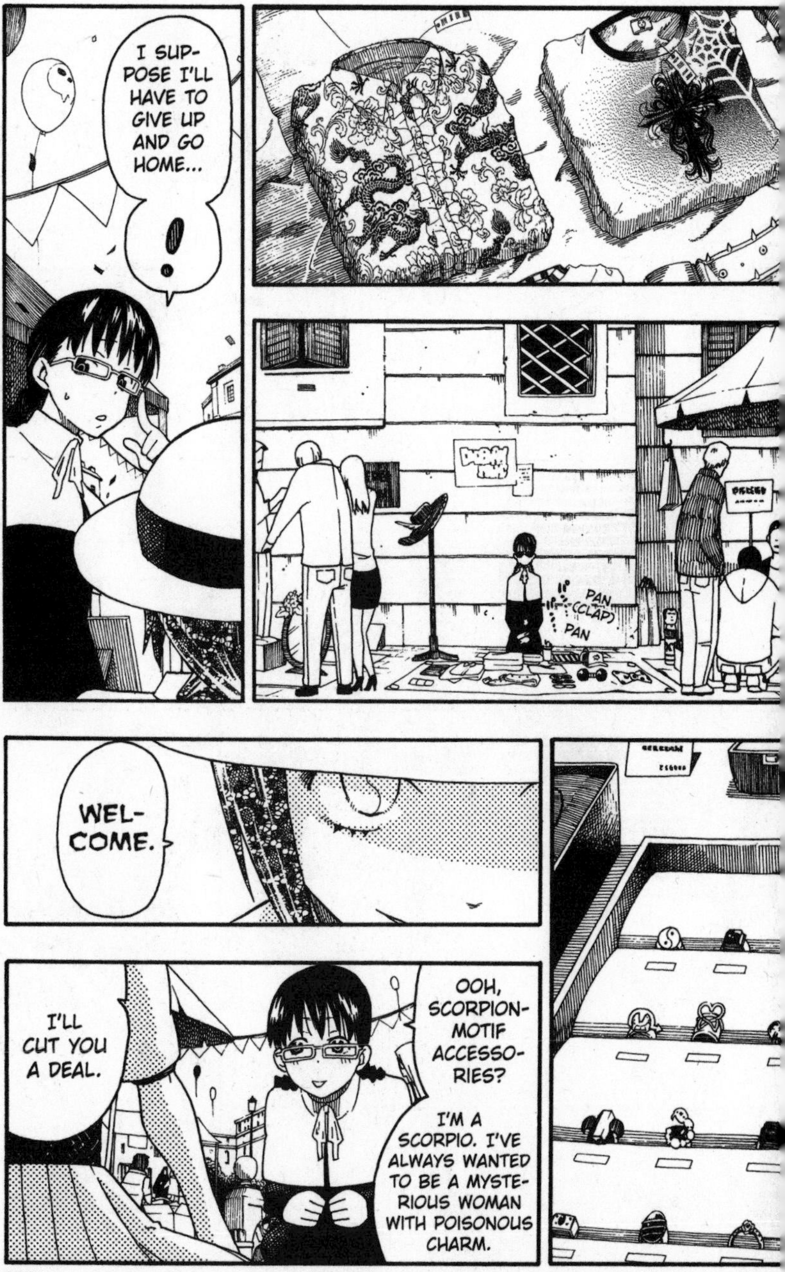
PAN (CLAP) PAN
I SUPPOSE I'LL HAVE TO GIVE UP AND GO HOME...
!
WELCOME.
OOH, SCORPION-MOTIF ACCESSORIES?
I'M A SCORPIO. I'VE ALWAYS WANTED TO BE A MYSTERIOUS WOMAN WITH POISONOUS CHARM.
I'LL CUT YOU A DEAL.

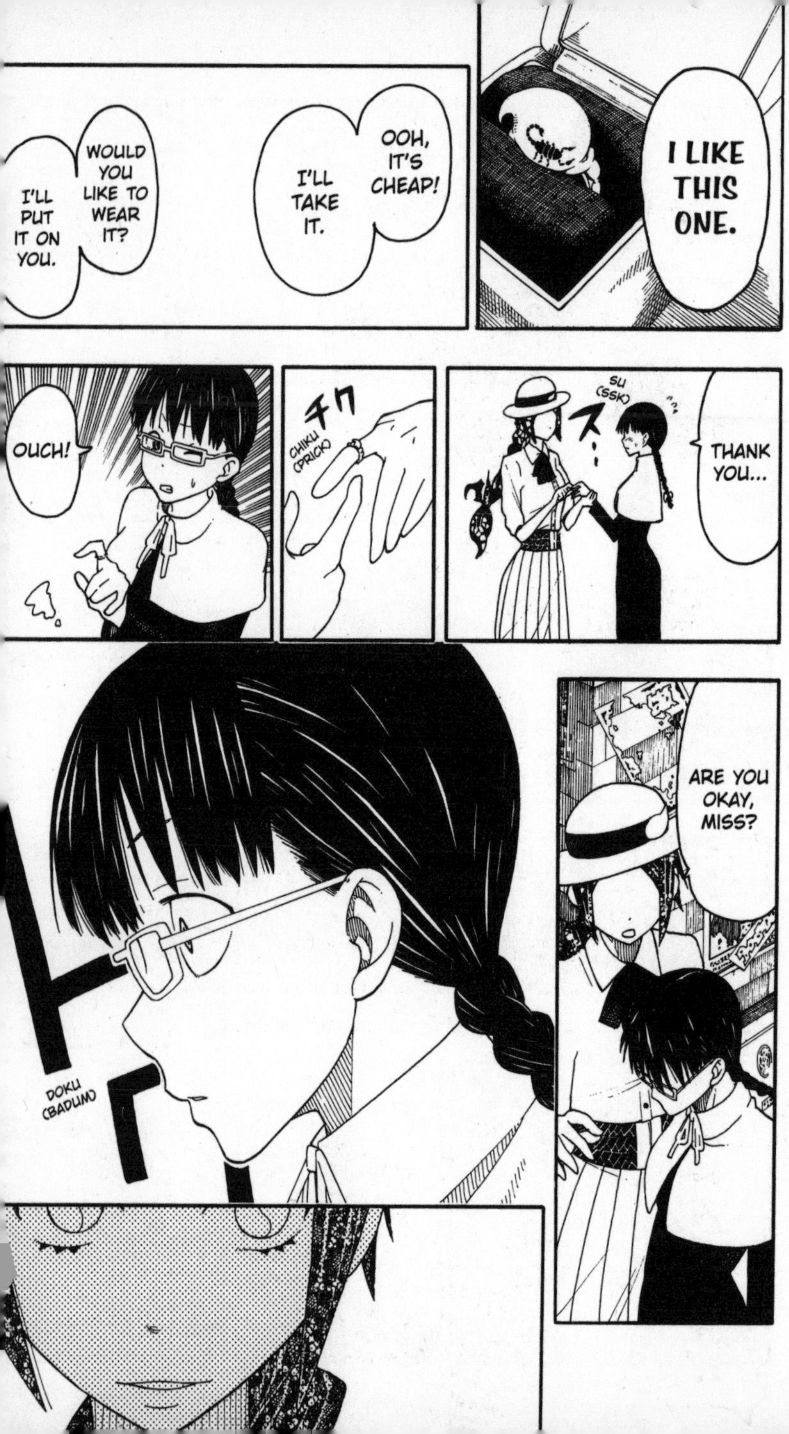
I LIKE THIS ONE.
OOH, IT'S CHEAP!
I'LL TAKE IT.
WOULD YOU LIKE TO WEAR IT?
I'LL PUT IT ON YOU.
THANK YOU...
ス
SU (SSK)
チク
CHIKU (PRICK)
OUCH!
ARE YOU OKAY, MISS?
DOKU (BADUM)

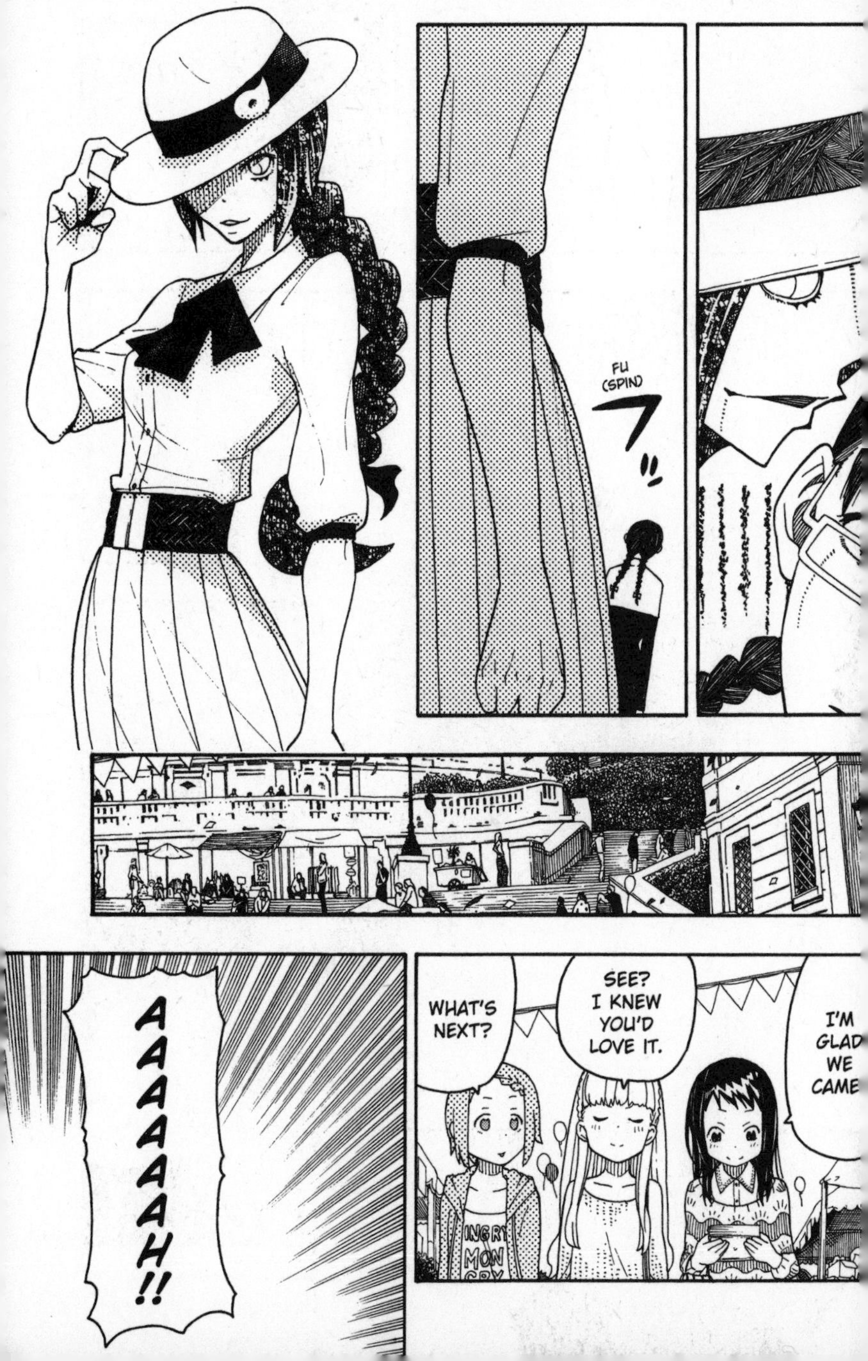
FU (SPIN)
I'M GLAD WE CAME
SEE? I KNEW YOU'D LOVE IT.
WHAT'S NEXT?
AAAAAAAH!!

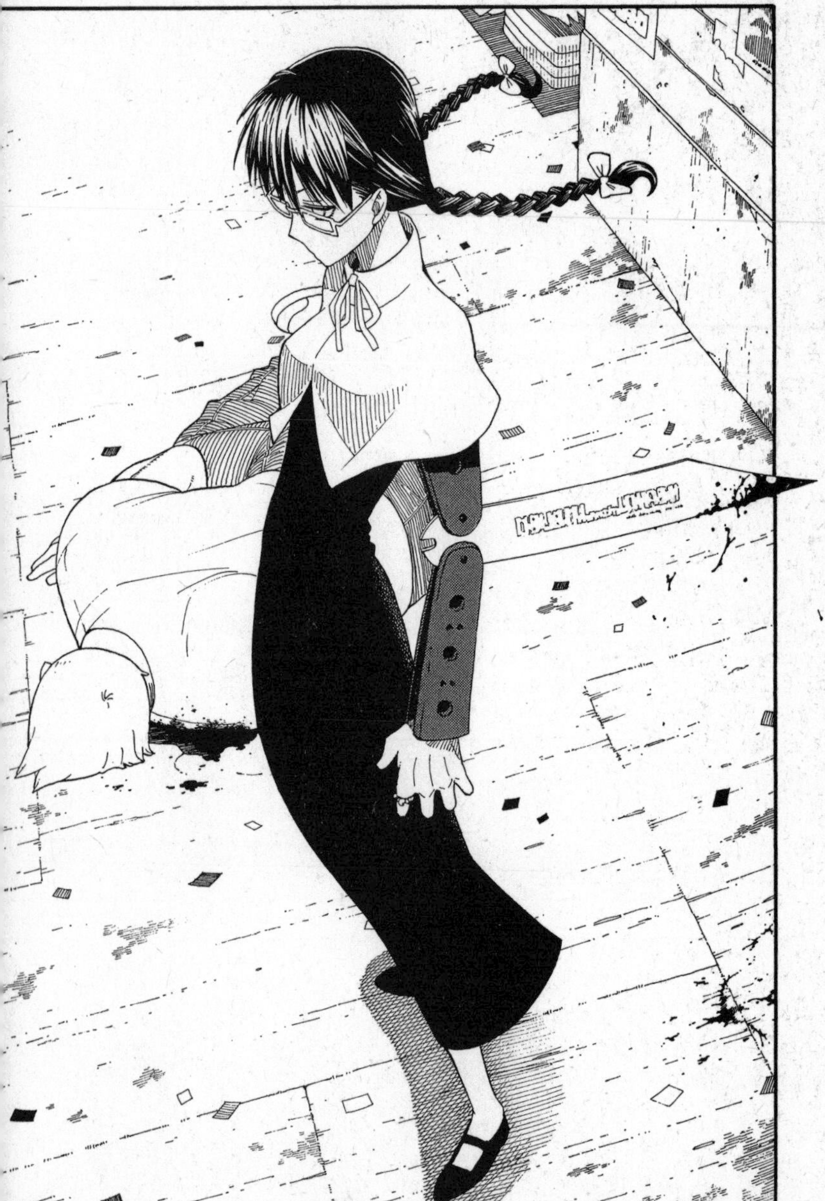

SOUL EATER NOT!

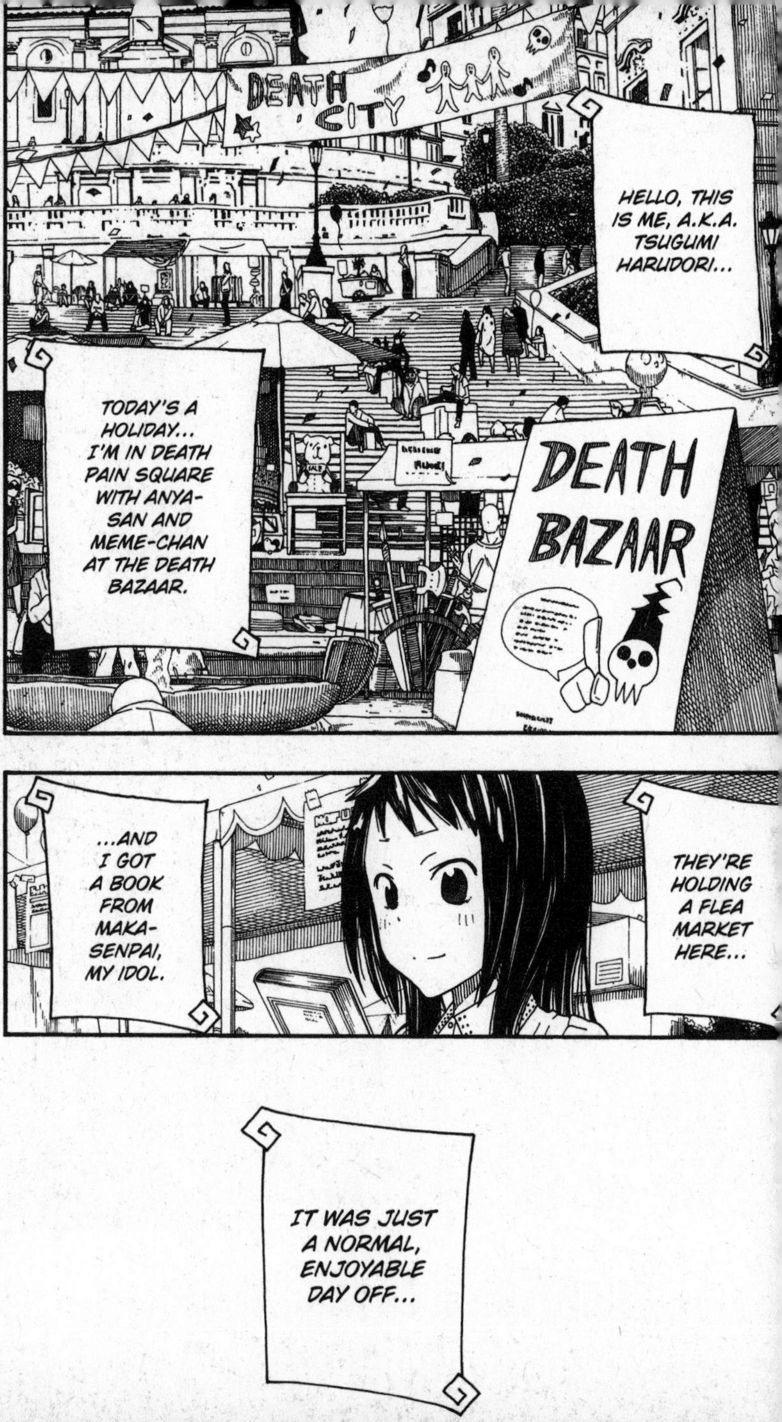
DEATH CITY
HELLO, THIS IS ME, A.K.A. TSUGUMI HARUDORI...
TODAY'S A HOLIDAY... I'M IN DEATH PAIN SQUARE WITH ANYA-SAN AND MEME-CHAN AT THE DEATH BAZAAR.
DEATH BAZAAR
THEY'RE HOLDING A FLEA MARKET HERE...
...AND I GOT A BOOK FROM MAKA-SENPAI, MY IDOL.
IT WAS JUST A NORMAL, ENJOYABLE DAY OFF...

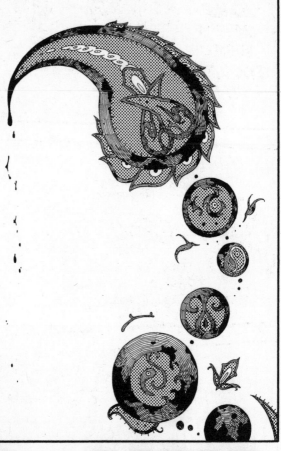

SOUL EATER NOT!

CHAPTER 15: BRAINWASHED!

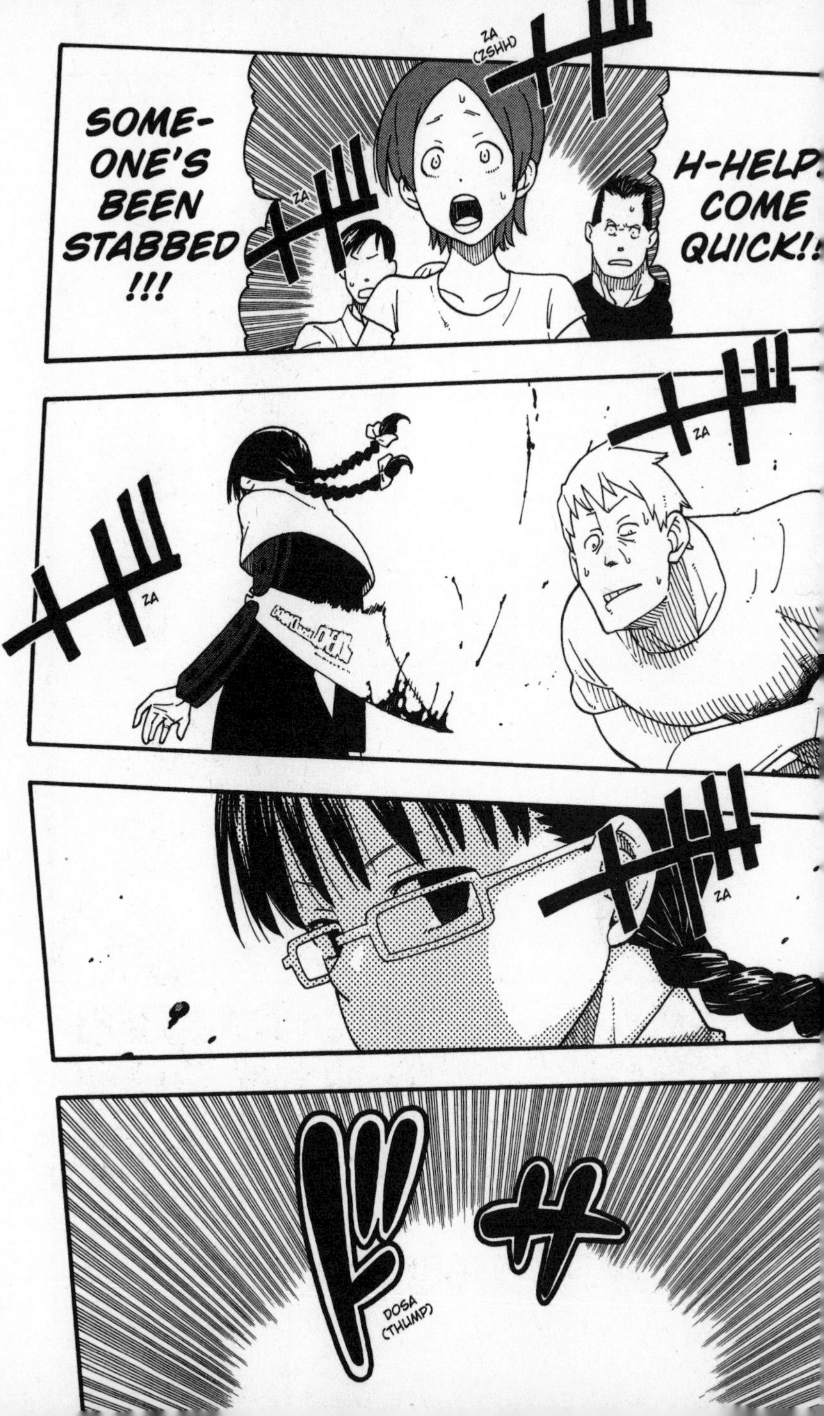
ZA (ZSHH)
H-HELP! COME QUICK!!
SOME-ONE'S BEEN STABBED !!!
ZA
ZA
ZA
ZA
DOSA (THUMP)

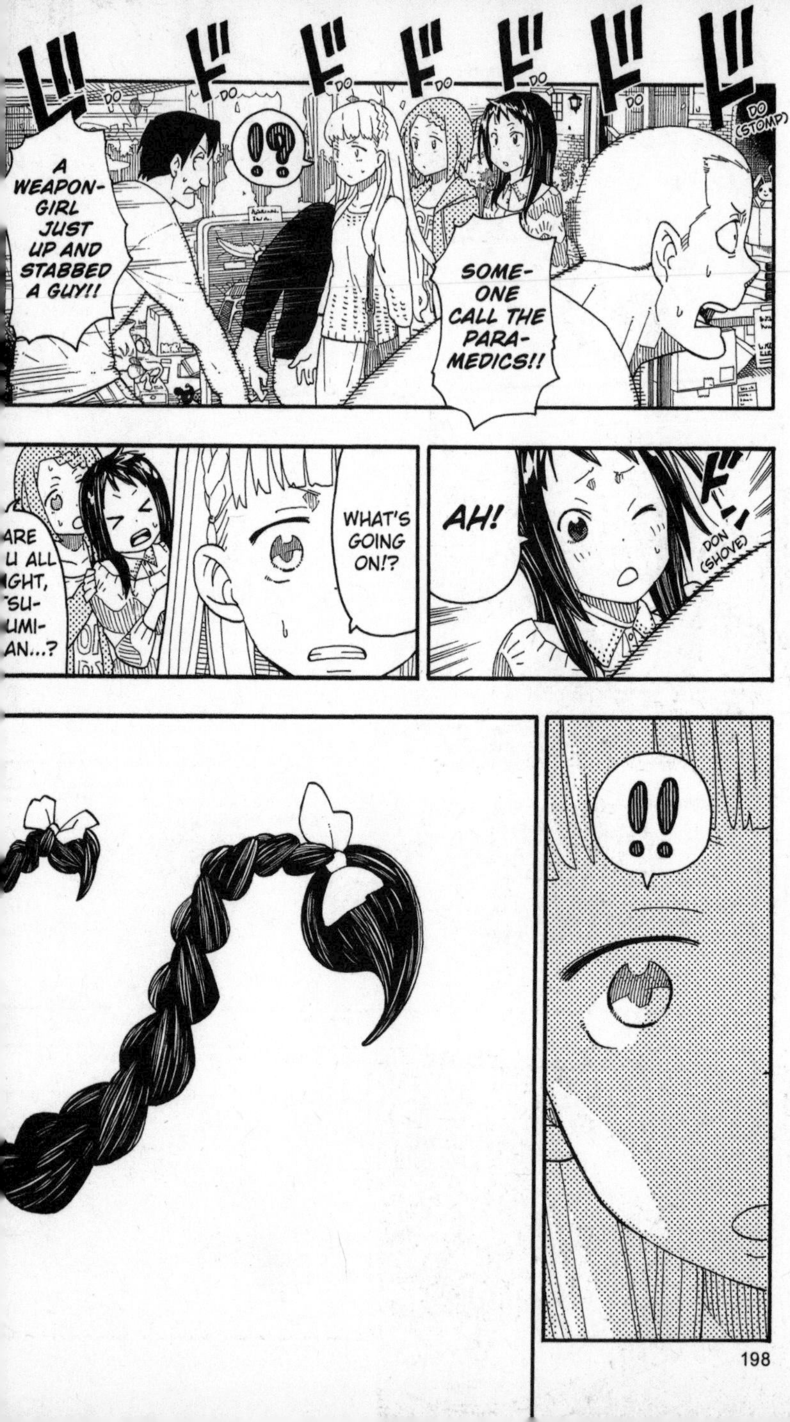

DO (STOMP)
DO
DO
DO
DO
DO
SOME-ONE CALL THE PARA-MEDICS!!
!?
A WEAPON-GIRL JUST UP AND STABBED A GUY!!
DON (SHOVE)
AH!
WHAT'S GOING ON!?
ARE U ALL IGHT, TSU-UMI-AN...?
!!

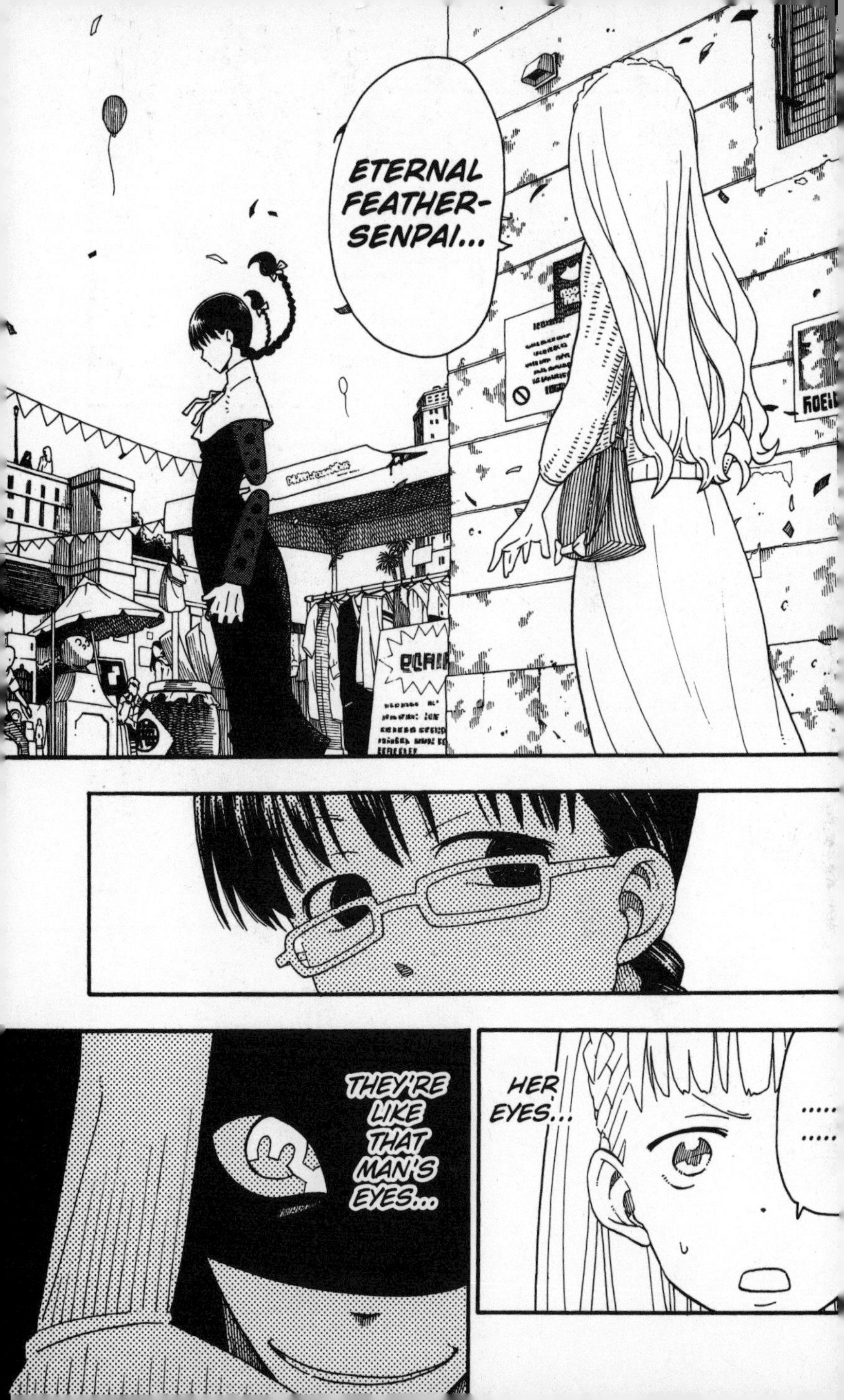
ETERNAL FEATHER-SENPAI...
HER EYES...
......
......
THEY'RE LIKE THAT MAN'S EYES...

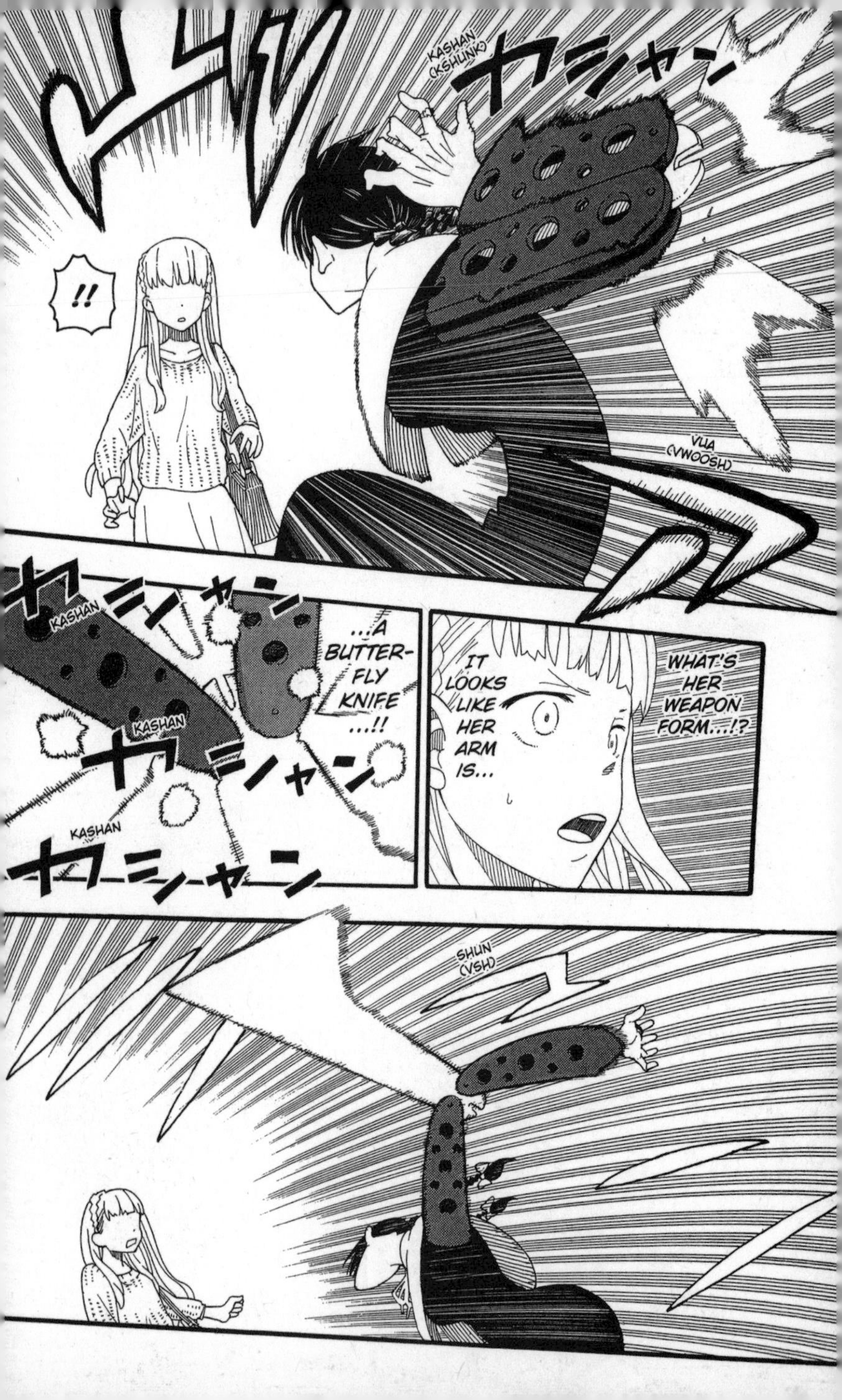
KASHAN (KSHUNK)
!!
VUA (VWOOSH)
WHAT'S HER WEAPON FORM...!?
IT LOOKS LIKE HER ARM IS...
KASHAN
...A BUTTERFLY KNIFE...!!
KASHAN
KASHAN
SHUN (VSH)

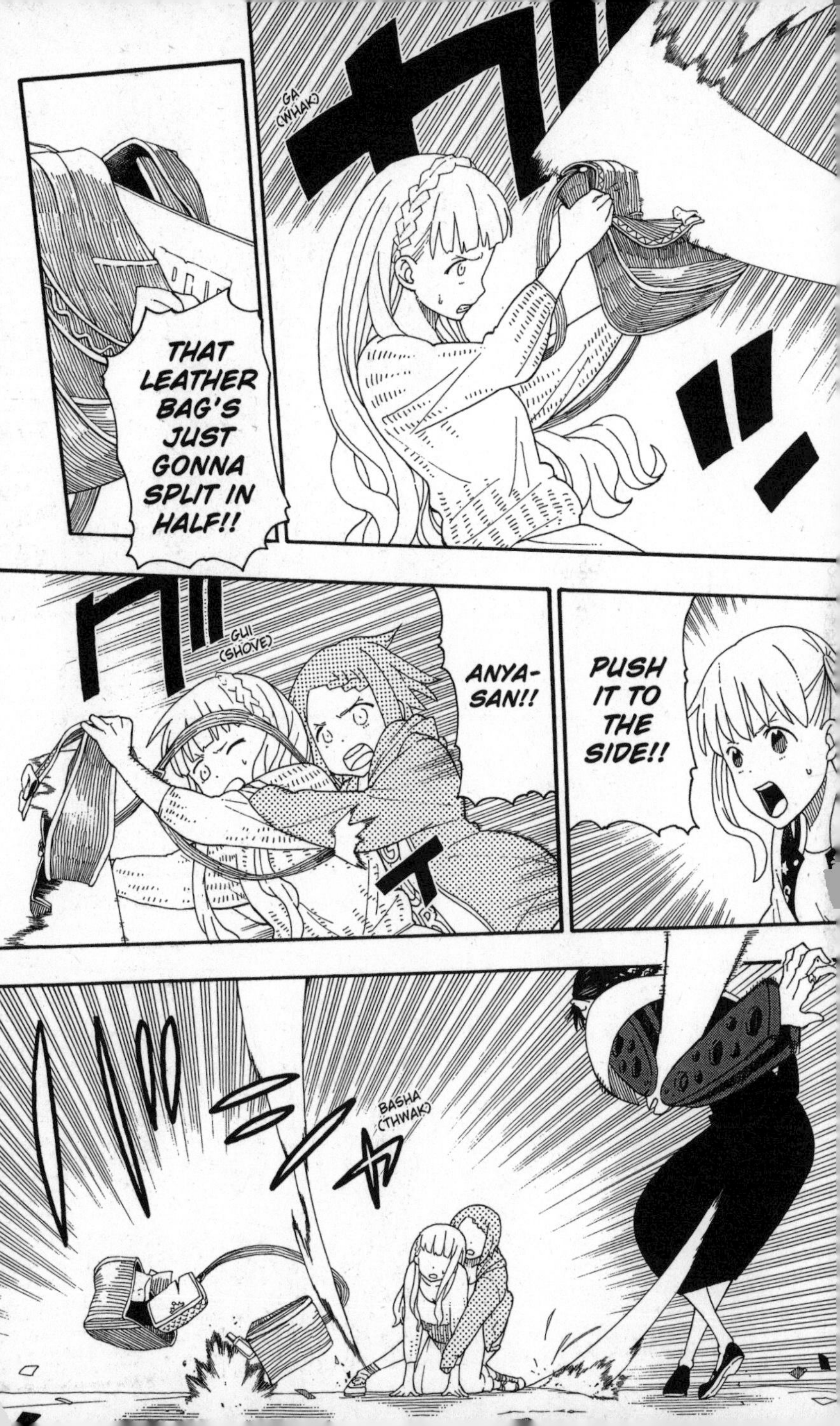
GA
(WHAK)
THAT LEATHER BAG'S JUST GONNA SPLIT IN HALF!!
PUSH IT TO THE SIDE!!
ANYA-SAN!!
GUI
(SHOVE)
BASHA
(THWAK)

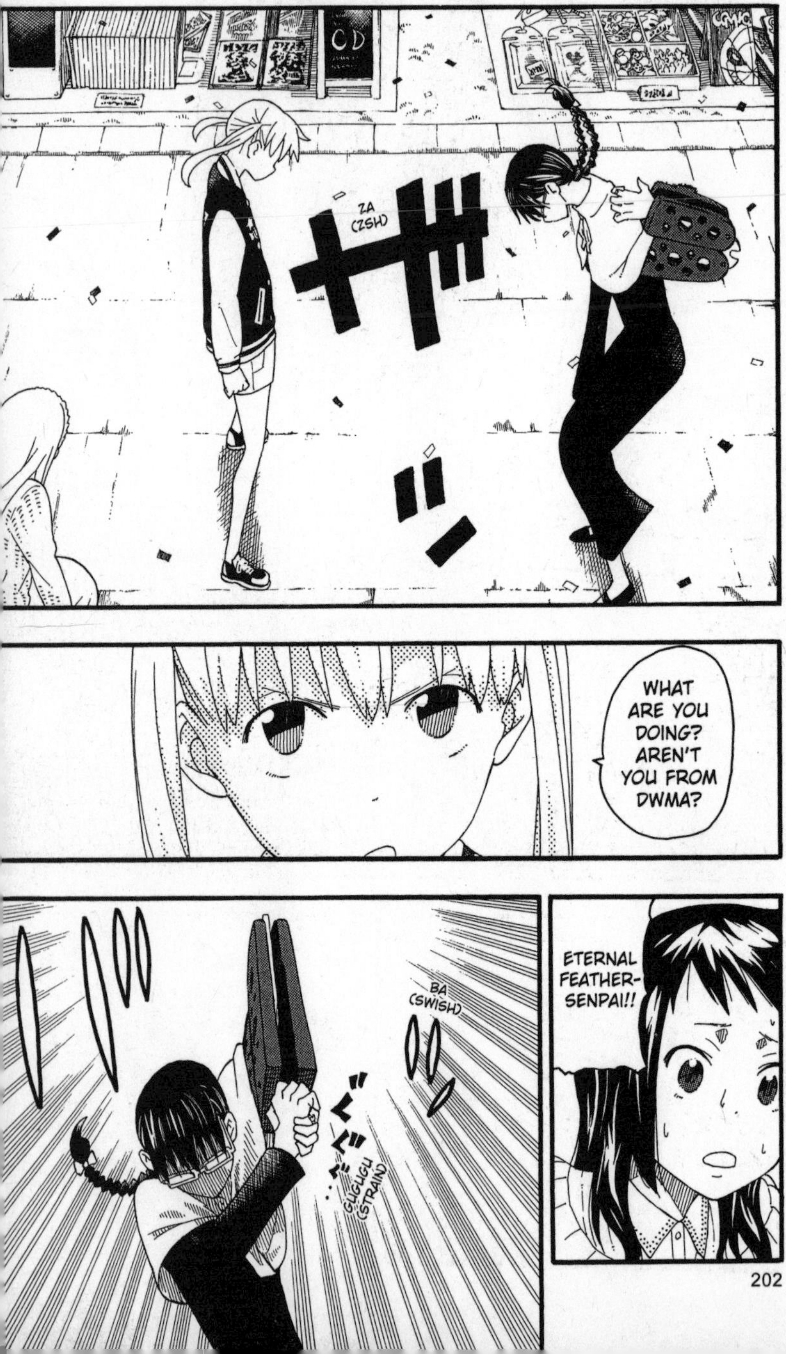
ZA (ZSH)
WHAT ARE YOU DOING? AREN'T YOU FROM DWMA?
ETERNAL FEATHER-SENPAI!!
BA (SWISH)
GUGUGU (STRAIN)

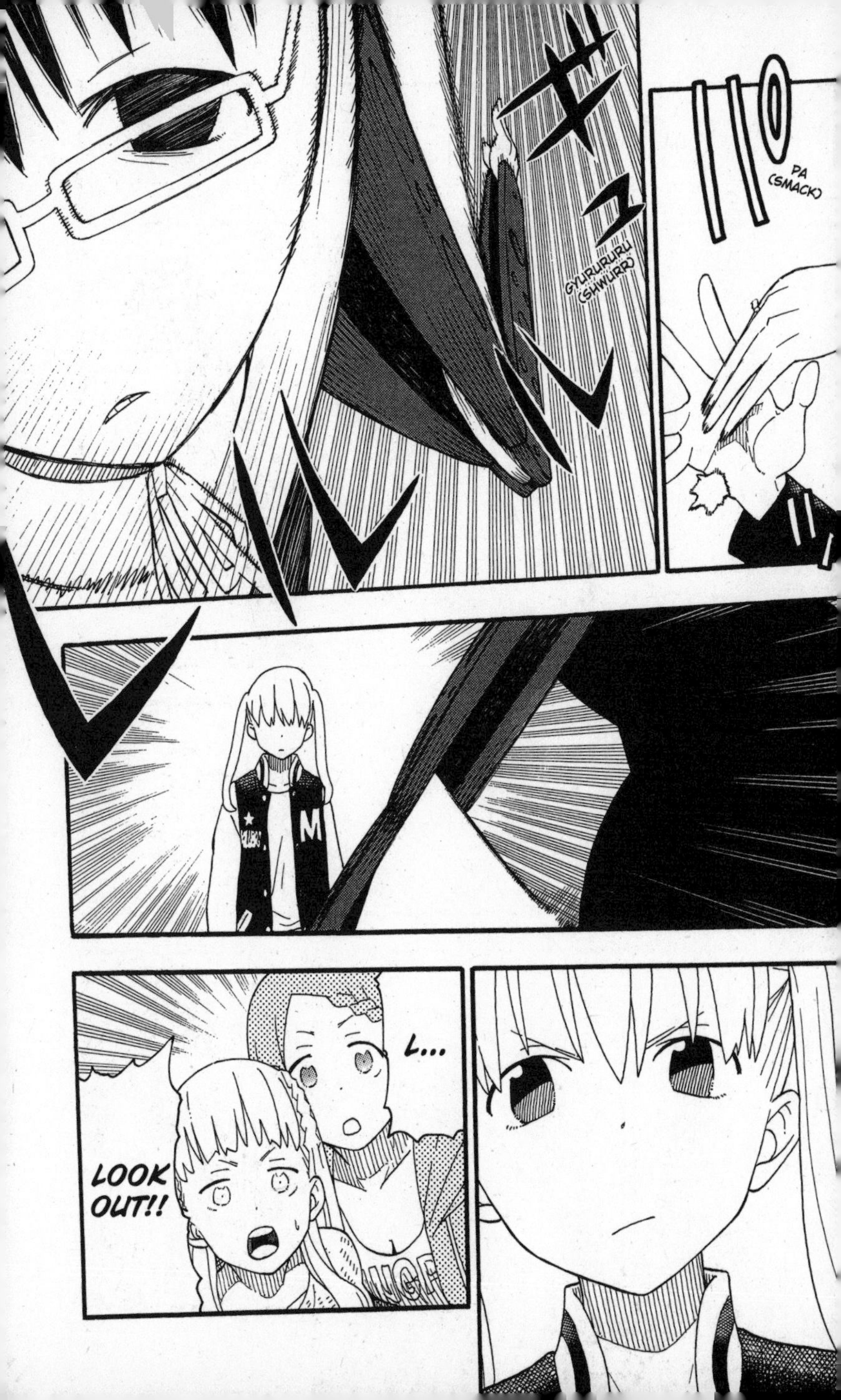
PA (SMACK)
GYURURURU (SHWURR)
L...
LOOK OUT!!

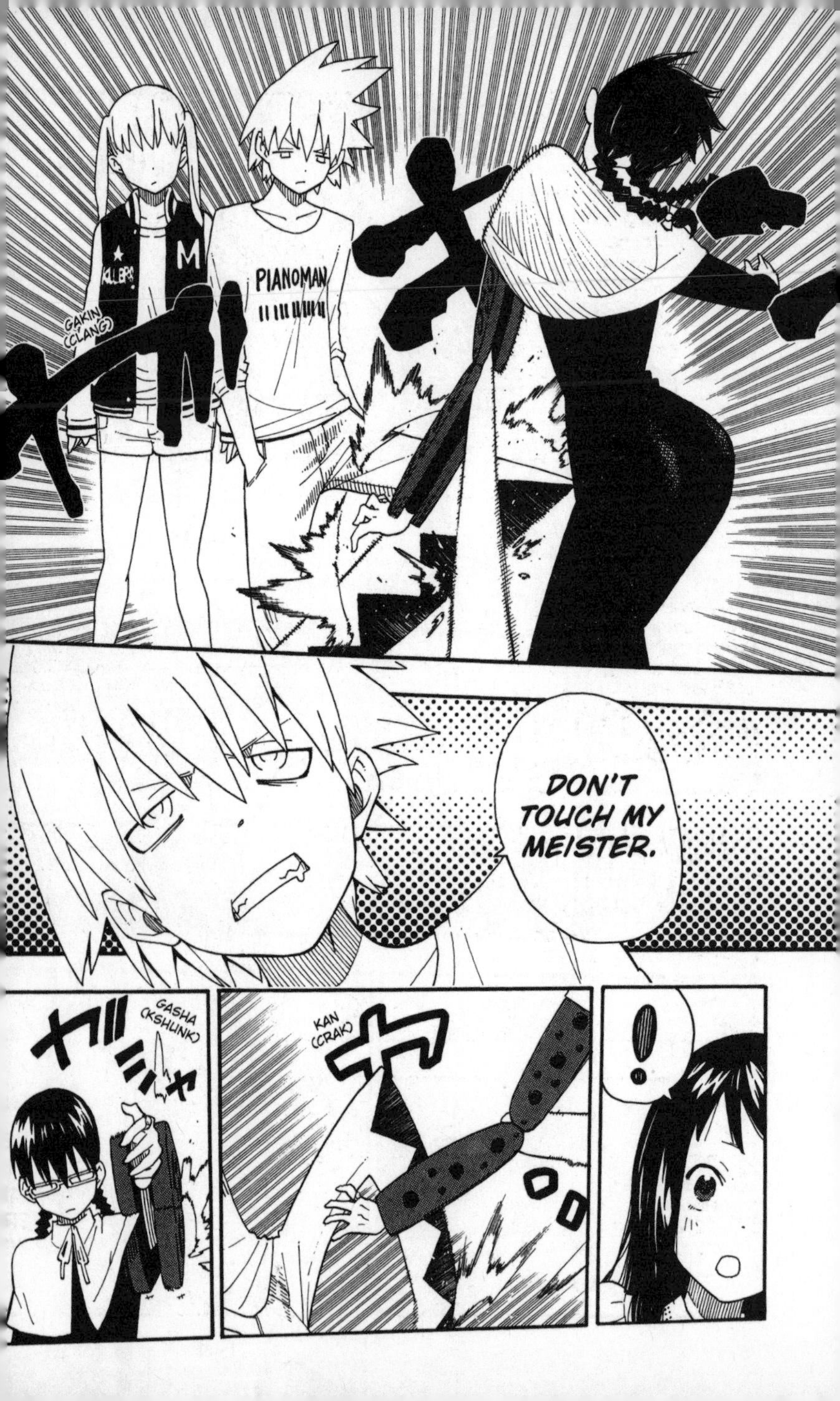
GAKIN (CLANG)
DON'T TOUCH MY MEISTER.
!
KAN (CRAK)
GASHA (KSHUNK)

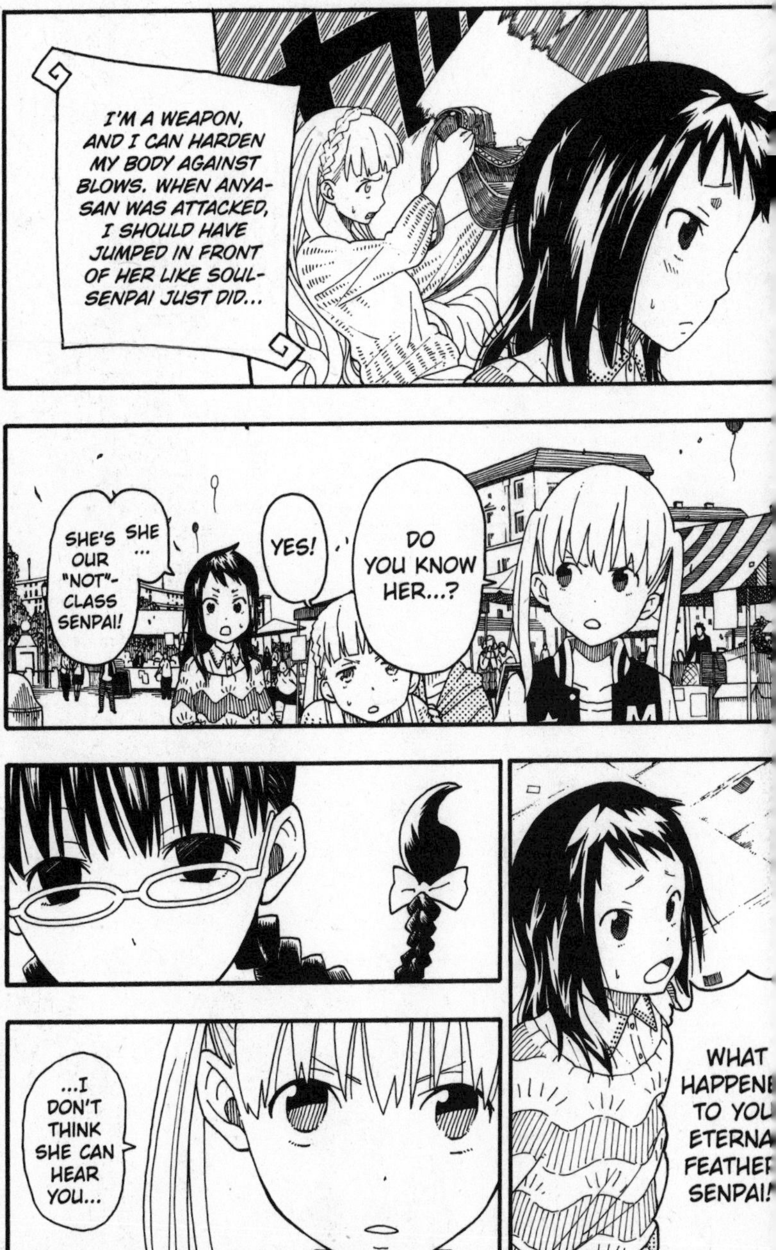
I'M A WEAPON, AND I CAN HARDEN MY BODY AGAINST BLOWS. WHEN ANYA-SAN WAS ATTACKED, I SHOULD HAVE JUMPED IN FRONT OF HER LIKE SOUL-SENPAI JUST DID...
DO YOU KNOW HER...?
YES!
SHE ...
SHE'S OUR "NOT"-CLASS SENPAI!
WHAT HAPPENE TO YOU ETERNA FEATHE SENPAI!
...I DON'T THINK SHE CAN HEAR YOU...

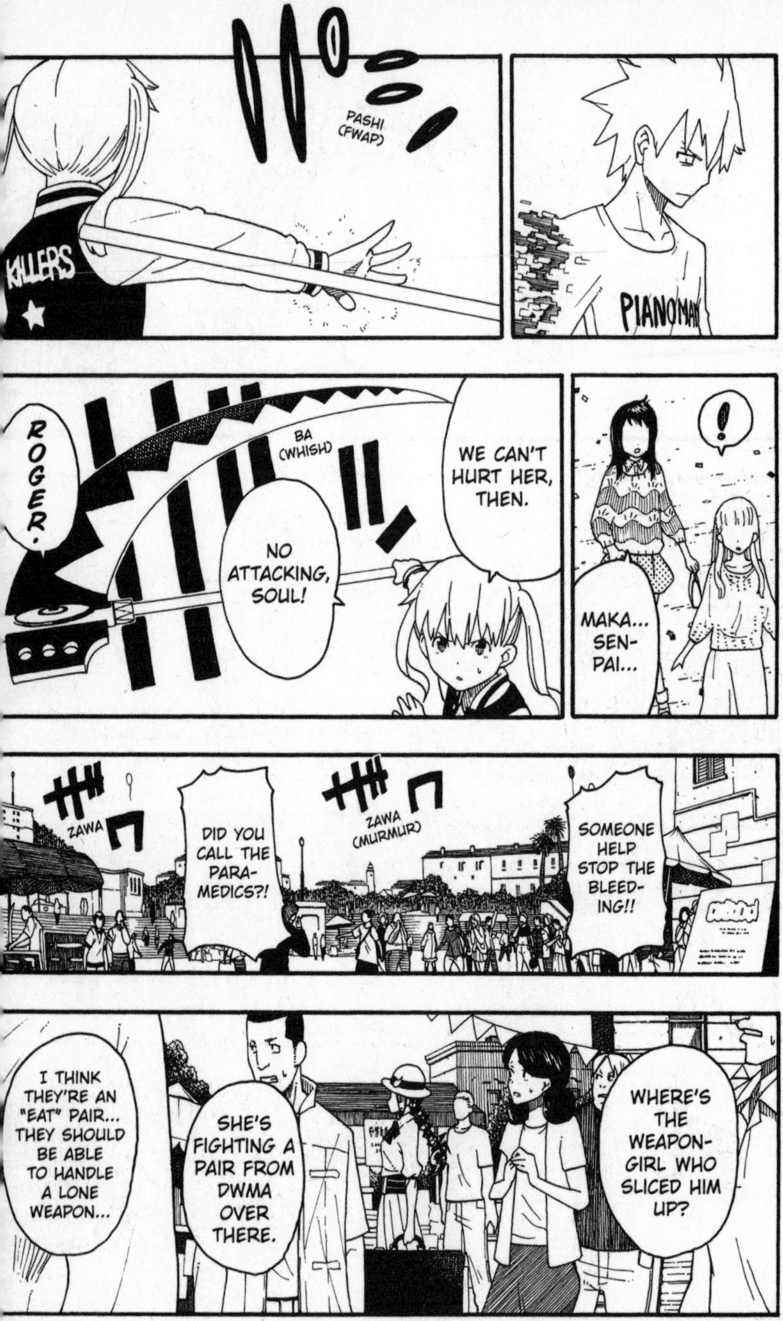
PIANOMAN
PASHI (FWAP)
KILLERS
!
MAKA... SEN-PAI...
WE CAN'T HURT HER, THEN.
BA (WHISH)
NO ATTACKING, SOUL!
ROGER.
SOMEONE HELP STOP THE BLEED-ING!!
ZAWA (MURMUR)
DID YOU CALL THE PARA-MEDICS?!
ZAWA
WHERE'S THE WEAPON-GIRL WHO SLICED HIM UP?
SHE'S FIGHTING A PAIR FROM DWMA OVER THERE.
I THINK THEY'RE AN "EAT" PAIR... THEY SHOULD BE ABLE TO HANDLE A LONE WEAPON...

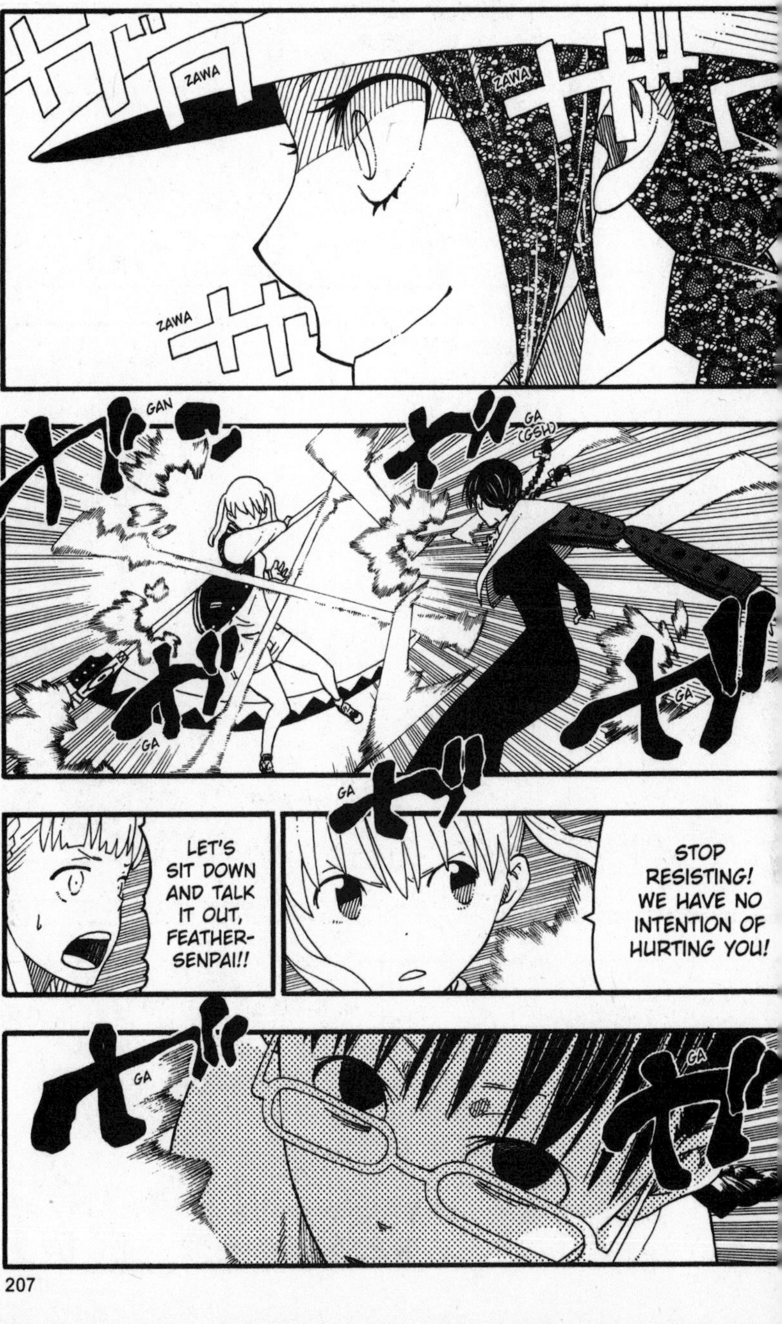
ZAWA
ZAWA
ZAWA
GA (GSH)
GAN
GA
GA
GA
STOP RESISTING! WE HAVE NO INTENTION OF HURTING YOU!
LET'S SIT DOWN AND TALK IT OUT, FEATHER-SENPAI!!
GA
GA

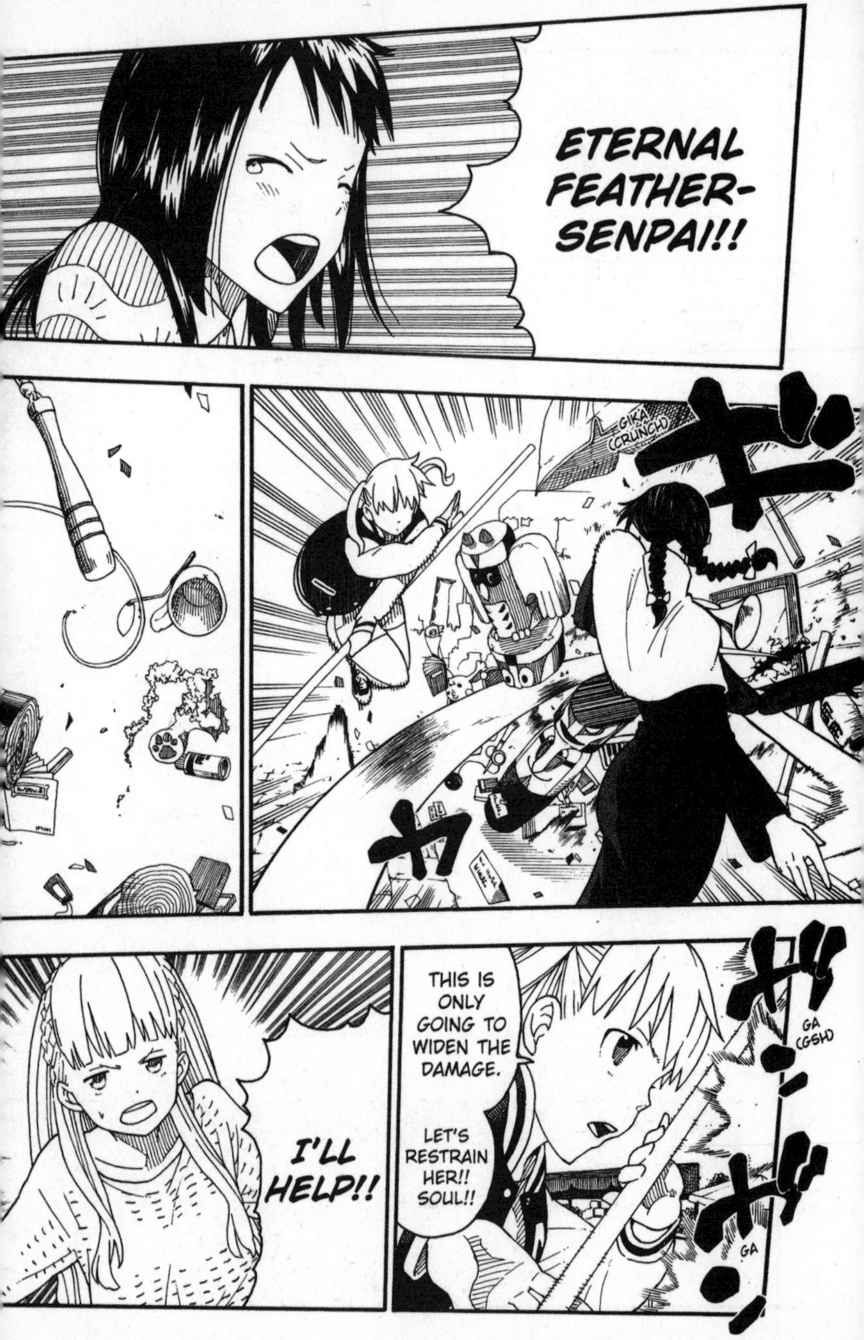
ETERNAL FEATHER-SENPAI!!
GIKA (CRUNCH)
THIS IS ONLY GOING TO WIDEN THE DAMAGE.
LET'S RESTRAIN HER!! SOUL!!
GA (GSH)
GA
I'LL HELP!!

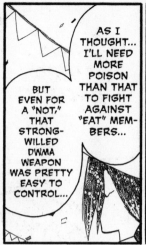

AS I THOUGHT... I'LL NEED MORE POISON THAN THAT TO FIGHT AGAINST "EAT" MEMBERS...

BUT EVEN FOR A "NOT," THAT STRONG-WILLED DWMA WEAPON WAS PRETTY EASY TO CONTROL...

CAN'T HAVE THEM SUBDUE MY **TEST SUBJECT** AND EXAMINE HER.

ALL RIGHT...

LET'S WRAP UP THIS EXPERIMENT BY TESTING THE EXTENT OF THE BRAIN-WASHING.

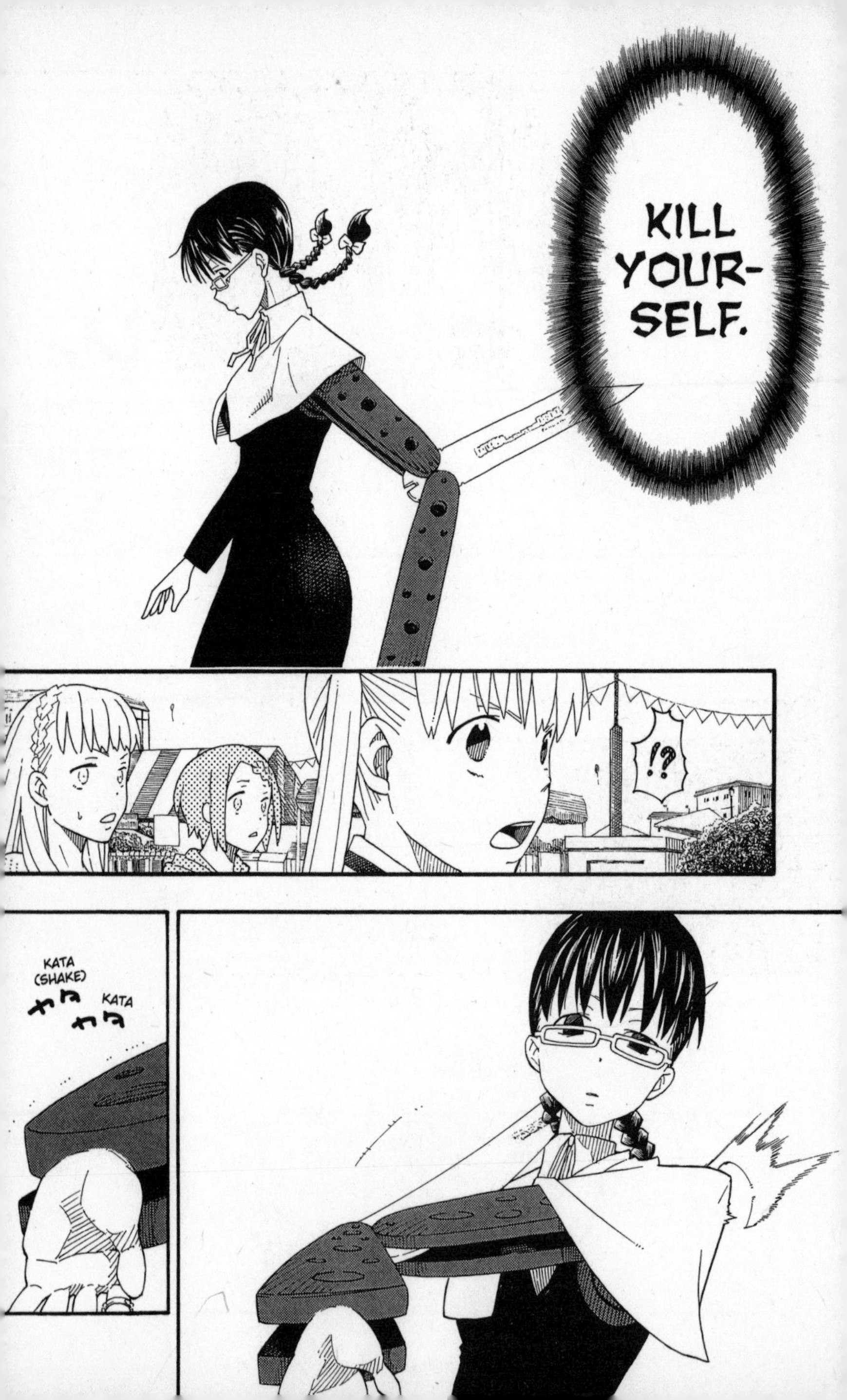
KILL YOUR-SELF.
!?
KATA (SHAKE)
KATA

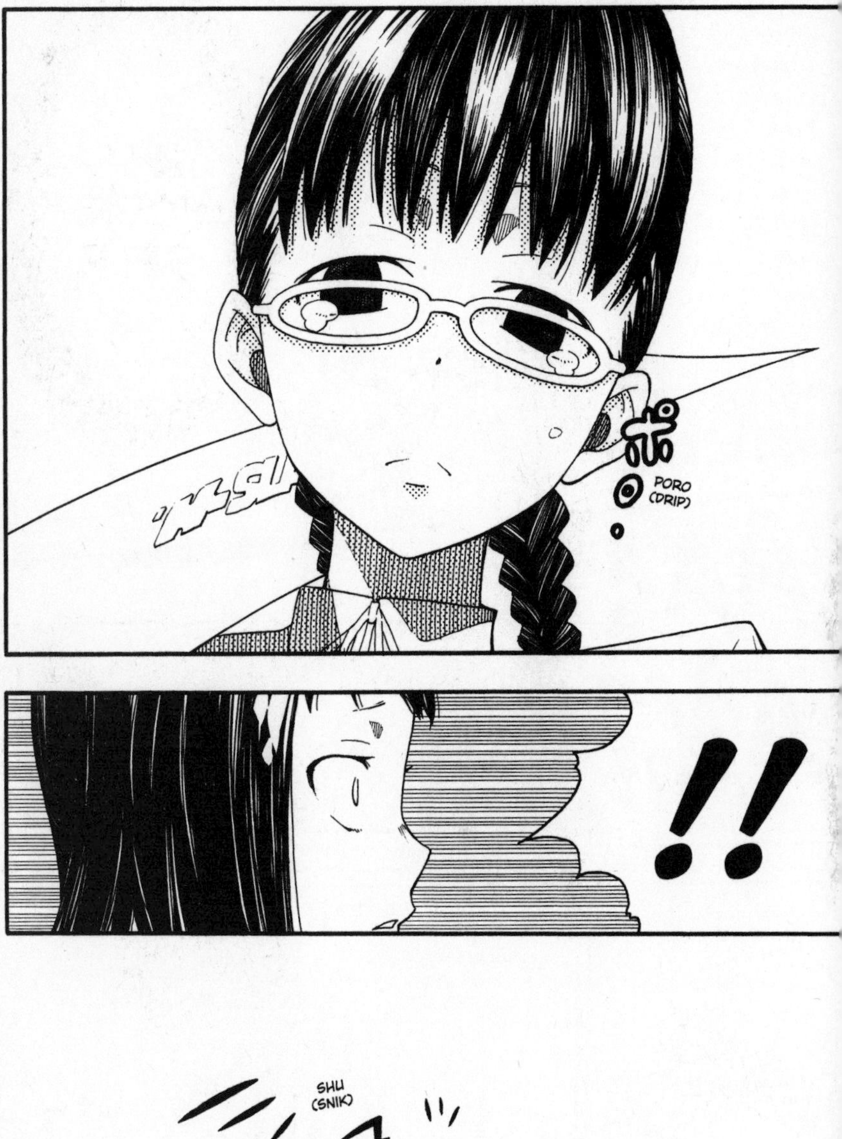
PORO
(DRIP)
!!
SHU
(SNIK)

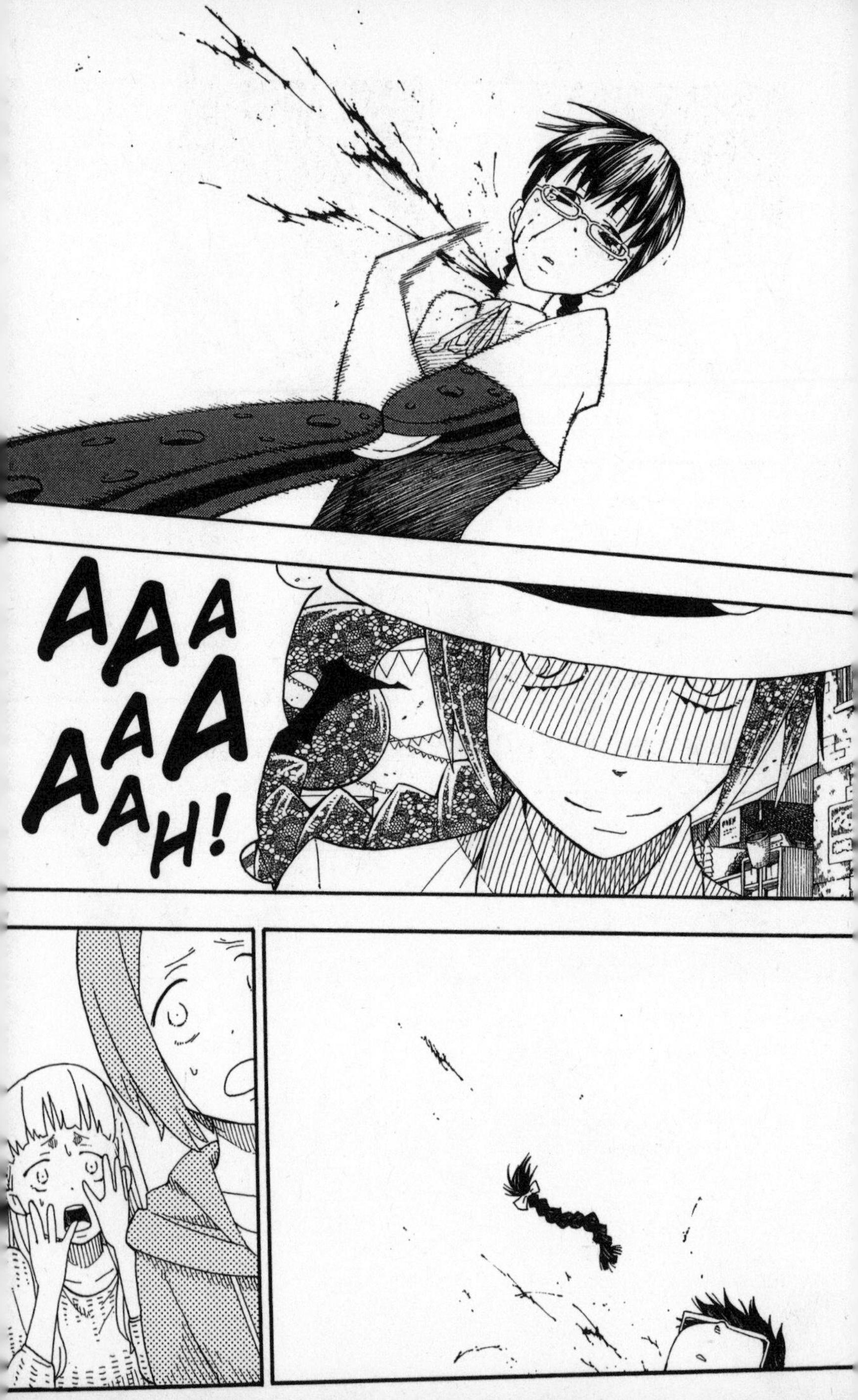
AAAAAAAH!

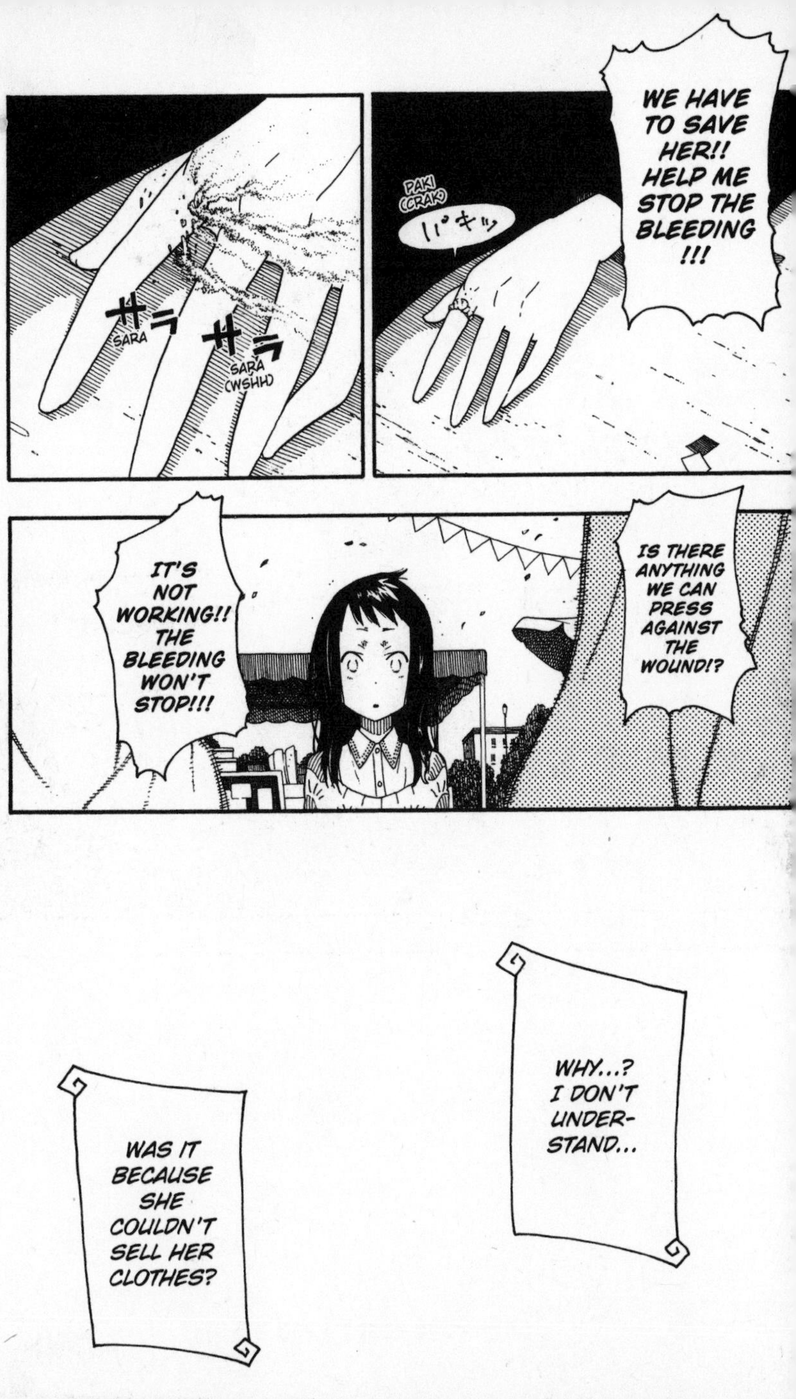
WE HAVE TO SAVE HER!! HELP ME STOP THE BLEEDING!!!
パキッ
PAKI (CRAK)
サラ
SARA
サラ
SARA (WSHH)
IS THERE ANYTHING WE CAN PRESS AGAINST THE WOUND!?
IT'S NOT WORKING!! THE BLEEDING WON'T STOP!!!
WHY...? I DON'T UNDER-STAND...
WAS IT BECAUSE SHE COULDN'T SELL HER CLOTHES?

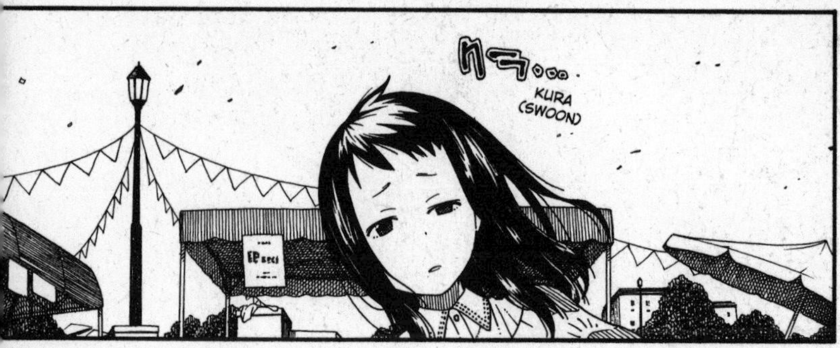
KURA
(SWOON)

WHY
DID THIS
HAPPEN
......?

SOUL EATER NOT! 2 END

SOUL EATER NOT!

後書きマンガ あつし屋 ノット支店

AFTERWORD MANGA
ATSUSHIYA
NOT! LOCATION

Title designed by:
Me (Left Hand)

IT'S A PLEASURE TO SEE YOU ALL AGAIN! THANK YOU!
PA (SWISH)
AS USUAL, I'VE BEEN LEADING A SUPER-FUN LIFE...
NYO (POKE)
I DUNNO, WASN'T THE END OF THE VOLUME KINDA... SAVAGE?
HUH!? BUT FOR A "SAVAGE BUT SUPER-FUN LIFE," IT SEEMED TO ME LIKE WE WERE KIND OF LACKING IN THE VIOLENCE DEPARTMENT...
YOU MEAN THAT'S THE REASON THIS HAPPENED TO ME...?
GAGANTOSU (GAGONG)
AAAAH! GHOST!!

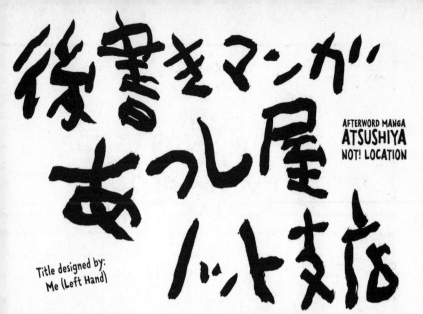

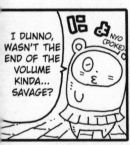

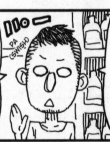

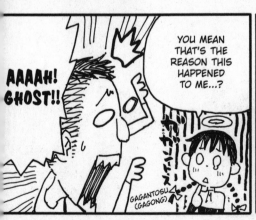

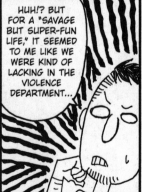

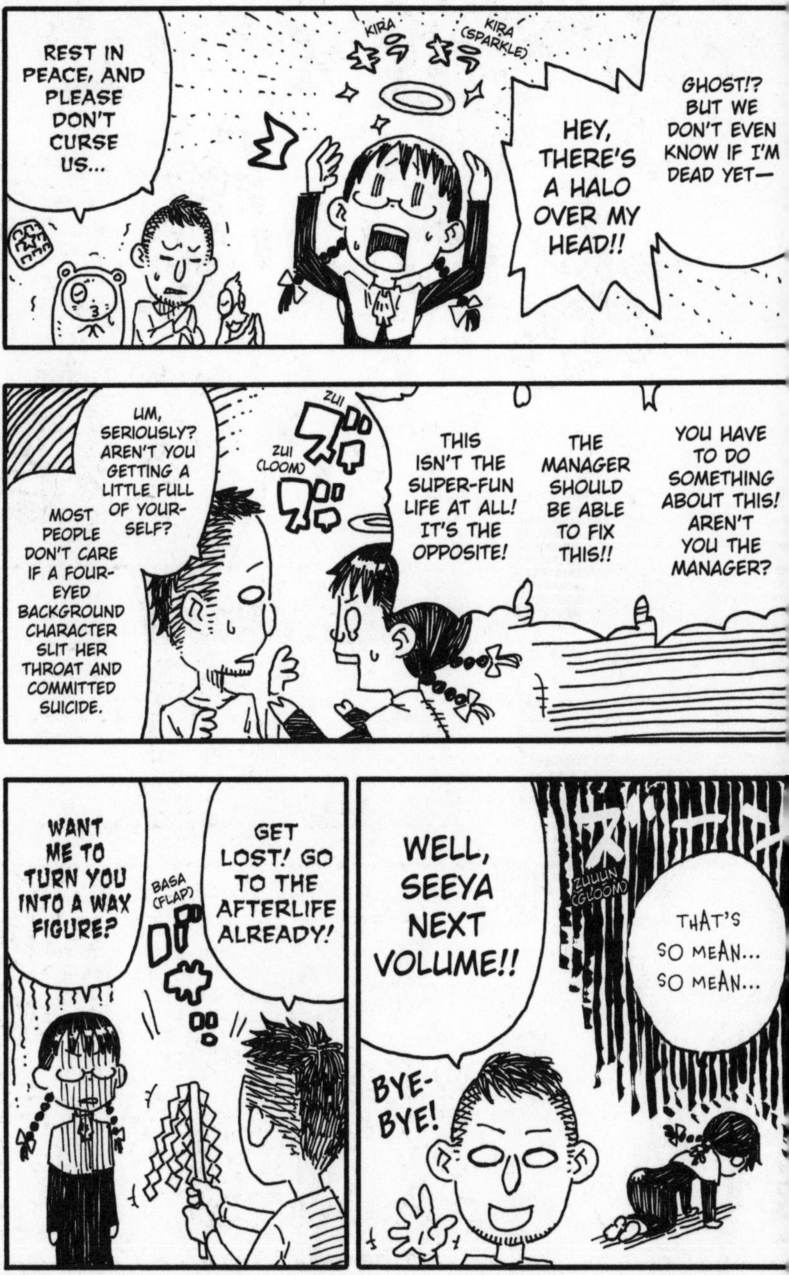
GHOST!? BUT WE DON'T EVEN KNOW IF I'M DEAD YET—
HEY, THERE'S A HALO OVER MY HEAD!!
KIRA (SPARKLE)
KIRA
REST IN PEACE, AND PLEASE DON'T CURSE US...
YOU HAVE TO DO SOMETHING ABOUT THIS! AREN'T YOU THE MANAGER?
THE MANAGER SHOULD BE ABLE TO FIX THIS!!
THIS ISN'T THE SUPER-FUN LIFE AT ALL! IT'S THE OPPOSITE!
ZUI
ZUI (LOOM)
UM, SERIOUSLY? AREN'T YOU GETTING A LITTLE FULL OF YOURSELF?
MOST PEOPLE DON'T CARE IF A FOUR-EYED BACKGROUND CHARACTER SLIT HER THROAT AND COMMITTED SUICIDE.
THAT'S SO MEAN... SO MEAN...
ZUUUN (GLOOM)
WELL, SEEYA NEXT VOLUME!!
BYE-BYE!
GET LOST! GO TO THE AFTERLIFE ALREADY!
BASA (FLAP)
WANT ME TO TURN YOU INTO A WAX FIGURE?

PREVIEW

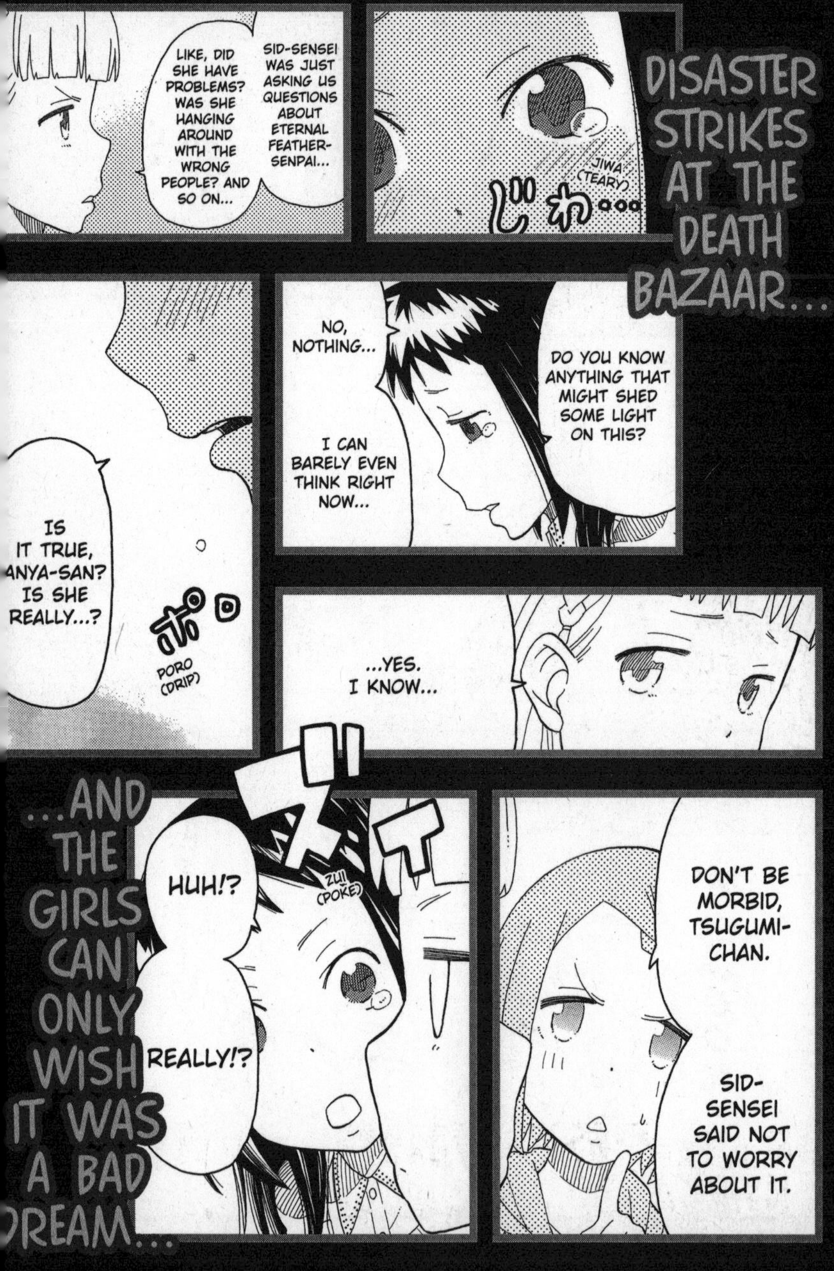
DISASTER STRIKES AT THE DEATH BAZAAR...
JIWA (TEARY)
SID-SENSEI WAS JUST ASKING US QUESTIONS ABOUT ETERNAL FEATHER-SENPAI...
LIKE, DID SHE HAVE PROBLEMS? WAS SHE HANGING AROUND WITH THE WRONG PEOPLE? AND SO ON...
DO YOU KNOW ANYTHING THAT MIGHT SHED SOME LIGHT ON THIS?
NO, NOTHING...
I CAN BARELY EVEN THINK RIGHT NOW...
...YES. I KNOW...
IS IT TRUE, ANYA-SAN? IS SHE REALLY...?
PORO (DRIP)
DON'T BE MORBID, TSUGUMI-CHAN.
SID-SENSEI SAID NOT TO WORRY ABOUT IT.
ZUI (POKE)
HUH!?
REALLY!?
...AND THE GIRLS CAN ONLY WISH IT WAS A BAD DREAM...

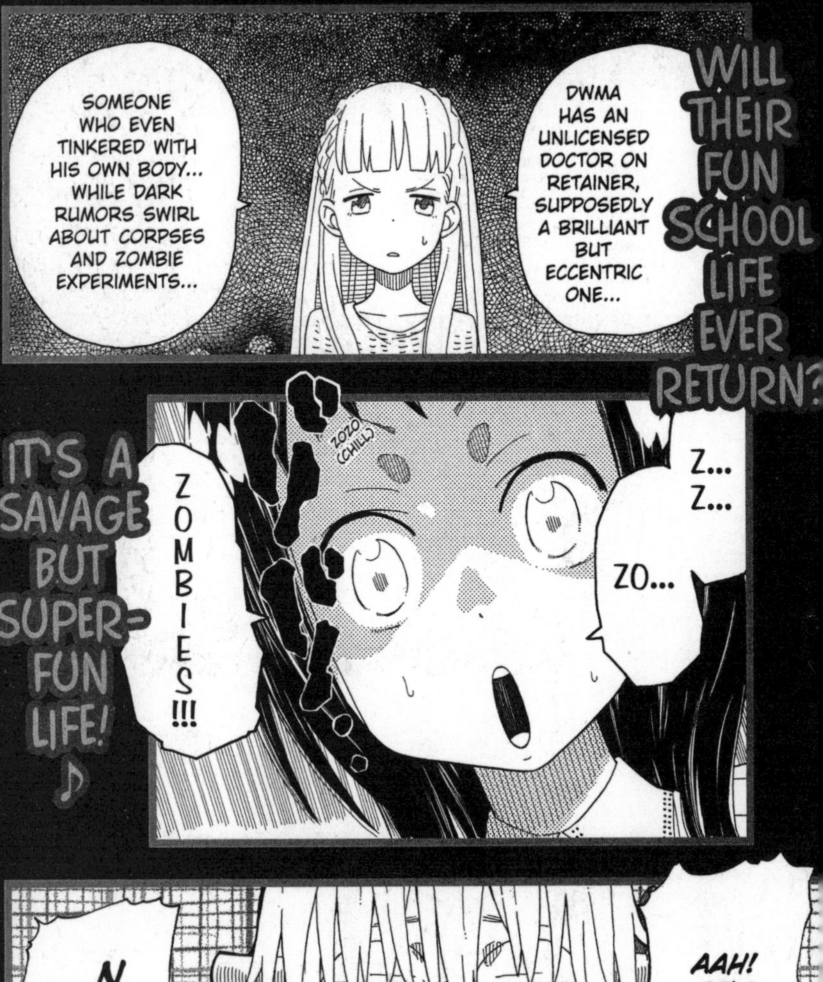
DWMA HAS AN UNLICENSED DOCTOR ON RETAINER, SUPPOSEDLY A BRILLIANT BUT ECCENTRIC ONE...
SOMEONE WHO EVEN TINKERED WITH HIS OWN BODY... WHILE DARK RUMORS SWIRL ABOUT CORPSES AND ZOMBIE EXPERIMENTS...
WILL THEIR FUN SCHOOL LIFE EVER RETURN?
Z... Z... ZO...
ZOZO (CHILL)
ZOMBIES!!!
IT'S A SAVAGE BUT SUPER-FUN LIFE! ♪
AAH! IT'S COMING THIS WAY!!
HERA HERA (SMIRK)
NOOOOO!!

SOUL EATER NOT! CONTINUES IN VOLUME 3!

To be continued

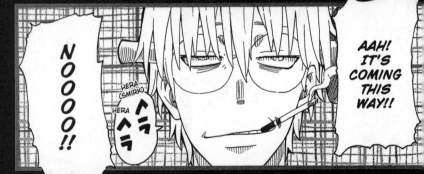

Translation Notes

Common Honorifics

no honorific: Indicates familiarity or closeness; if used without permission or reason, addressing someone in this manner would constitute an insult.

-san: The Japanese equivalent of Mr./Mrs./Miss. If a situation calls for politeness, this is the fail-safe honorific.

-sama: Conveys great respect; may also indicate that the social status of the speaker is lower than that of the addressee.

-kun: Used most often when referring to boys, this indicates affection or familiarity. Occasionally used by older men among their peers, but it may also be used by anyone referring to a person of lower standing.

-chan: An affectionate honorific indicating familiarity used mostly in reference to girls; also used in reference to cute persons or animals of either gender.

-senpai: A suffix used to address upperclassmen or more experienced coworkers.

-sensei: A respectful term for teachers, artists, or high-level professionals.

Page 62
"Riverbank pumpkin": The term "*dote-kabocha*," which refers to wild pumpkins growing on embankments built around rivers, is considered a goofy, old-fashioned insult in Japan. Because such pumpkins were once left to grow for the sake of the poor and hungry, any that weren't harvested would become cracked and rotten. Therefore, to call someone a "*dote-kabocha*" implies that he or she is common/unwanted/ugly.

Page 65
***Tamagoyaki*:** Literally meaning "grilled/cooked egg," this Japanese take on the omelette consists of many layers of cooked eggs rolled up and sliced.

Page 62
***Sukeban*:** A Japanese slang word referring to the boss of a girl gang. While the concept is outdated now, in the late 1970s and '80s, girl gangs were a fairly common sight (alongside their male counterparts) and were involved in drug use, vandalism, and street fights.

Page 182
Don Konishi: A flamboyant and outspoken fashion designer who made news when he famously criticized the out-of-touch fashion of former Prime Minister Yukio Hatayama. The use of his name here plays on the mafia "Don" title.

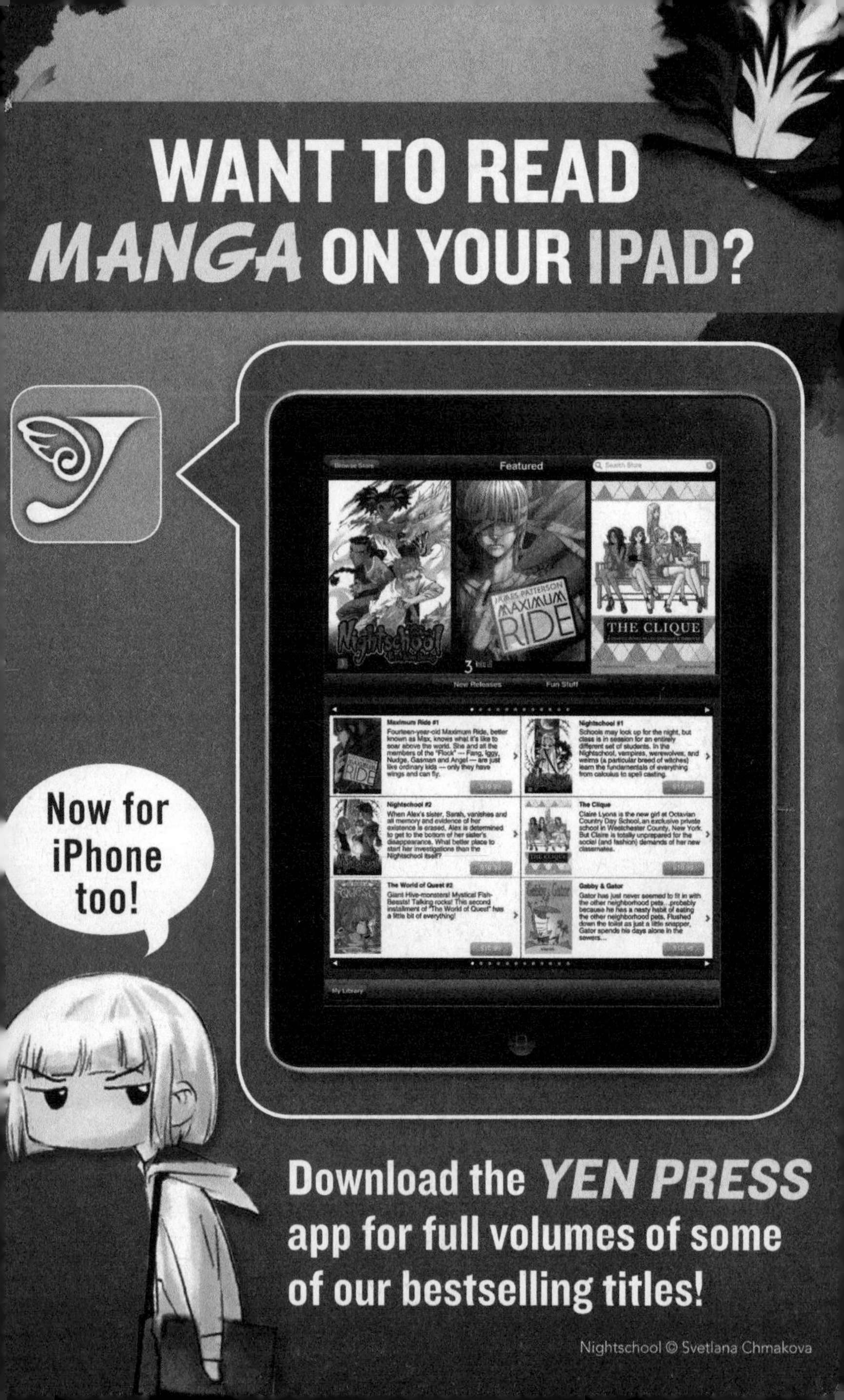
WANT TO READ
MANGA ON YOUR IPAD?
Now for iPhone too!
Download the YEN PRESS app for full volumes of some of our bestselling titles!
Nightschool © Svetlana Chmakova

To become the ultimate weapon, one boy must eat the souls of 99 humans...

...and one witch.

Maka is a scythe meister, working to perfect her demon scythe until it is good enough to become Death's Weapon—the weapon used by Shinigami-sama, the spirit of Death himself. And if that isn't strange enough, her scythe also has the power to change form—into a human-looking boy!

SOUL EAT

Translation: Stephen Paul

Lettering: Abigail Blackman

SOUL EATER NOT! Vol. 2 © 2012 Atsushi Ohkubo / SQUARE ENIX. All rights reserved. First published in Japan in 2012 by SQUARE ENIX CO., LTD. English translation rights arranged with SQUARE ENIX CO., LTD. and Yen Press, LLC through Tuttle-Mori Agency, Inc.

English translation © 2012 by SQUARE ENIX CO., LTD.

Yen Press
1290 Avenue of the Americas
New York, NY 10104

www.YenPress.com

Yen Press is an imprint of Yen Press, LLC. The Yen Press name and logo are trademarks of Yen Press, LLC.

First Yen Press Edition: October 2012

ISBN: 978-0-316-22106-1

10 9

BVG

Printed in the United States of America